ISAIAH 1-39
A Commentary in the Wesleyan Tradition

*New Beacon Bible Commentary

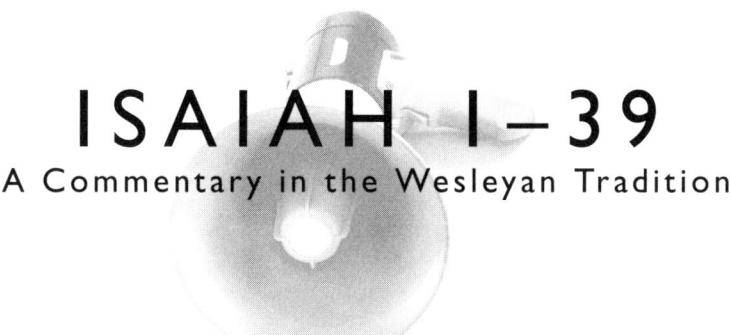

ISAIAH 1–39
A Commentary in the Wesleyan Tradition

Barry L. Ross

BEACON HILL PRESS
OF KANSAS CITY

Copyright 2016 by Beacon Hill Press of Kansas City

Beacon Hill Press of Kansas City
PO Box 419527
Kansas City, MO 64141
www.BeaconHillBooks.com

ISBN 978-0-8341-3546-8

Printed in the United States of America

All rights reserved. No part of this publication may be reproduced, stored in a retrieval system, or transmitted in any form or by any means—for example, electronic, photocopy, recording—without the prior written permission of the publisher. The only exception is brief quotations in printed reviews.

Cover Design: J.R. Caines
Interior Design: Sharon Page

Unless otherwise indicated all Scripture quotations are from the *Holy Bible, New International Version*® (NIV®). Copyright © 1973, 1978, 1984, 2011 by Biblica, Inc.™ Used by permission. All rights reserved worldwide. Emphasis indicated by underlining in boldface quotations and italic in lightface quotations.

The following versions of Scripture are in the public domain:
The American Standard Version (ASV).
The King James Version of the Bible (KJV).

The following copyrighted versions of Scripture are used by permission:
The Holy Bible, English Standard Version (ESV), copyright © 2001 by Crossway Bibles, a division of Good News Publishers. All rights reserved.

The *New American Standard Bible*® (NASB®), © copyright The Lockman Foundation 1960, 1962, 1963, 1968, 1971, 1972, 1973, 1975, 1977, 1995.

The *New Jerusalem Bible* (NJB), copyright © 1985 by Darton, Longman & Todd, Ltd., and Doubleday, a division of Bantam Doubleday Dell Publishing Group, Inc. Reprinted by permission.

JPS Hebrew-English Tanakh: The New JPS Translation according to the Traditional Hebrew Text (NJPS), © 2000 by The Jewish Publication Society. All rights reserved.

The *New King James Version* (NKJV). Copyright © 1979, 1980, 1982 Thomas Nelson, Inc.

The *New Revised Standard Version* (NRSV) of the Bible, copyright 1989 by the Division of Christian Education of the National Council of the Churches of Christ in the USA. All rights reserved.

The *Revised Standard Version* (RSV) of the Bible, copyright 1946, 1952, 1971 by the Division of Christian Education of the National Council of the Churches of Christ in the USA. All rights reserved.

Library of Congress Cataloging-in-Publication Data
Names: Ross, Barry Lowell, 1938- author.
Title: Isaiah 1-39 / Barry L. Ross.
Description: Kansas City, MO : Beacon Hill Press of Kansas City, 2016. |
  Series: New Beacon Bible commentary | Includes bibliographical references.
Identifiers: LCCN 2016017365 | ISBN 9780834135468 (pbk.)
Subjects: LCSH: Bible. Isaiah, I-XXXIX—Commentaries.
Classification: LCC BS1515.53 .R67 2016 | DDC 224/.107—dc23 LC record available at https://lccn.loc.gov/2016017365

The Internet addresses, email addresses, and phone numbers in this book are accurate at the time of publication. They are provided as a resource. Beacon Hill Press of Kansas City does not endorse them or vouch for their content or permanence.

DEDICATION

To my beloved wife of fifty-four years, Margaret
with deep gratitude for her love, support,
and continuing encouragement

COMMENTARY EDITORS

General Editors

Alex Varughese
    Ph.D., Drew University
    Professor of Biblical Literature
    Mount Vernon Nazarene University
    Mount Vernon, Ohio

Roger Hahn
    Ph.D., Duke University
    Dean of the Faculty
    Professor of New Testament
    Nazarene Theological Seminary
    Kansas City, Missouri

George Lyons
    Ph.D., Emory University
    Professor of New Testament
    Northwest Nazarene University
    Nampa, Idaho

Section Editors

Robert Branson
    Ph.D., Boston University
    Professor of Biblical Literature
        Emeritus
    Olivet Nazarene University
    Bourbonnais, Illinois

Alex Varughese
    Ph.D., Drew University
    Professor of Biblical Literature
    Mount Vernon Nazarene University
    Mount Vernon, Ohio

Jim Edlin
    Ph.D., Southern Baptist Theological
        Seminary
    Professor of Biblical Literature and
        Languages
    Chair, Division of Religion and
        Philosophy
    MidAmerica Nazarene University
    Olathe, Kansas

Kent Brower
    Ph.D., The University of Manchester
    Vice Principal
    Senior Lecturer in Biblical Studies
    Nazarene Theological College
    Manchester, England

George Lyons
    Ph.D., Emory University
    Professor of New Testament
    Northwest Nazarene University
    Nampa, Idaho

CONTENTS

General Editors' Preface	11
Acknowledgments	13
Abbreviations	15
Bibliography	19
Table of Sidebars	25
INTRODUCTION	27
A. The Importance of the Book of Isaiah	27
B. Isaiah the Person	28
C. The Canonical Book of Isaiah	29
D. The Texts and Language of the Book of Isaiah	31
E. Theological Themes in Chapters 1—39	32
1. Yahweh as the Holy One of Israel	32
2. Yahweh as Savior, the One Who Saves, Who Brings Salvation	33
3. Yahweh as Sovereign	34
4. Yahweh and the Nations	35
F. The Structure of Chapters 1—39	36
COMMENTARY	39
I. JUDAH'S SICKNESS AND ITS CAUSES; THE SYRIAN-ISRAELITE THREAT (1:1—12:6)	39
A. A People in Rebellion (1:1-31)	40
1. Superscription (1:1)	40
2. No Justice in Zion (1:2-31)	41
B. A People Cleansed (2:1—4:6)	49
1. Superscription (2:1)	50
2. The Mountain of Yahweh (2:2-5)	50
3. The Day of Yahweh (2:6-22)	52
4. Jerusalem Staggers, Judah Is Falling (3:1-15)	58
5. Sackcloth for Fine Clothing (3:16—4:1)	63
6. The Branch of Yahweh (4:2-6)	65
C. The Vineyard of the Yahweh Sebaoth (5:1-30)	67
1. A Vineyard on a Fertile Hillside (5:1-7)	68
2. The Law of Yahweh Sebaoth Rejected (5:8-25)	70
3. The Light Is Gone, the Land Is Darkened (5:26-30)	75

- D. Isaiah in the Divine Council (6:1-13) — 77
- E. King Ahaz: Trust God or Assyria? (7:1-25) — 85
  1. Hearts Shaken but Do Not Lose Heart! (7:1-9) — 86
  2. The Sign of Immanuel (7:10-17) — 90
  3. In that Day: Only Briars and Thorns (7:18-25) — 93
- F. The Flood Waters of Assyria (8:1-22) — 94
  1. Quick to the Plunder, Swift to the Spoil (8:1-4) — 95
  2. Immanuel! (God Is with Us!) (8:5-8) — 96
  3. With Us Is God! (Immanuel!) (8:9-10) — 97
  4. Fear Yahweh! (8:11-15) — 97
  5. Bind Up the Testimony (8:16-22) — 98
- G. Unto Us a Child Is Born (9:1-7 [8:23—9:6 HB]) — 100
- H. Yahweh's Upraised Hand (9:8 [7 HB]—10:4) — 104
- I. The True Sovereign and the Arrogant Assyrian (10:5-34) — 109
  1. Arrogant Assyria, a Tool in God's Hand (10:5-19) — 109
  2. A Remnant Will Return (10:20-27) — 112
  3. Assyria Felled (10:28-34) — 114
- J. The Branch from Jesse (11:1-16) — 115
- K. A Song to the Holy One of Israel (12:1-6) — 120

II. YAHWEH, SOVEREIGN OF ALL NATIONS (13:1—27:13) — 125
- A. A Prophecy Concerning Babylon and Assyria (13:1—14:27) — 127
  1. Yahweh Gathers His Worldwide Army (13:1-5) — 128
  2. Yahweh's Day of Burning Anger (13:6-16) — 129
  3. Babylon Overthrown (13:17-22) — 130
  4. Yahweh's Compassion on Jacob (14:1-2) — 131
  5. A Taunt against Babylon's King (14:3-21) — 132
  6. Babylon's Name Wiped Out (14:22-23) — 135
  7. Yahweh Will Break Assyria (14:24-27) — 136
- B. A Prophecy Concerning Philistia (14:28-32) — 137
- C. A Prophecy Concerning Moab (15:1—16:14) — 142
  1. The Attack on Moab and Its Effects (15:1-9) — 142
  2. Asylum Requested (16:1-5) — 143
  3. Loss of Raisin Cakes Bewailed (16:6-7) — 144
  4. Isaiah/Yahweh Laments for Moab (16:8-12) — 145
  5. The Fulfillment of the Prophecy (16:13-14) — 145
- D. Prophecies Concerning Damascus and Cush (17:1—18:7) — 147
  1. The Demise of Damascus and Ephraim (17:1-6) — 148
  2. The Holy One of Israel: Maker, Savior, Rock (17:7-11) — 149
  3. Chaff Driven before the Wind (17:12-14) — 150
  4. Yahweh's Message to the People of the World (18:1-7) — 150
- E. A Prophecy Concerning Egypt (19:1—20:6) — 153
  1. Consulting Idols and Mediums Results in Confusion (19:1-4) — 154
  2. The Nile Will No Longer Support National Life (19:5-10) — 154
  3. The Stupidity of Pharaoh's Political Advisers (19:11-15) — 156

		4. Yahweh Makes Himself Known to the Egyptians (19:16-25)	157
		5. Isaiah's Shocking Behavior (20:1-6)	159
	F.	Prophecies Concerning Babylon, Dumah, and Arabia (21:1-17)	161
		1. A Prophecy Concerning the Wilderness of the Sea (21:1-10)	162
		2. A Prophecy Concerning Dumah (21:11-12)	166
		3. A Prophecy in/within Arabia (21:13-17)	166
	G.	Two Cases of Divine Grace Flaunted (22:1-25)	168
		1. A Prophecy Concerning the Valley of Vision (22:1-14)	169
		2. Yahweh's Word Concerning Shebna and Eliakim (22:15-25)	174
	H.	A Prophecy Concerning Tyre (23:1-18)	176
		1. Devastation of Southern Phoenicia (23:1-14)	178
		2. Tyre's Future Restoration (23:15-18)	181
	I.	Two Cities and Yahweh Triumphant (24:1—27:13)	182
		1. The Earth Laid Waste (24:1-23)	183
		a. The Earth Is Devastated (24:1-6)	183
		b. Joy Is Banished from the Earth (24:7-12)	184
		c. Glorify Yahweh! (24:13-16a)	185
		d. Terror All Around (24:16b-18a)	186
		e. Earth Is Violently Shaken (24:18b-20)	186
		f. Yahweh Sebaoth Will Reign (24:21-23)	186
		2. Yahweh Sebaoth's Banquet (25:1-12)	188
		a. Yahweh, a Refuge for the Poor and Needy (25:1-5)	189
		b. Yahweh Sebaoth Prepares a Banquet (25:6-8)	190
		c. Rejoicing in Yahweh's Salvation (25:9-12)	190
		3. In that Day (26:1—27:1)	192
		a. A City Whose Gates Are Open (26:1-6)	193
		b. A Level Path; Rejected Grace (26:7-15)	194
		c. Failure in Witness, but New Life from the Dust (26:16-19)	196
		d. God's People vs. the People of the Earth (26:20—27:1)	197
		4. God's Vineyard Revisited; A Fortified City Desolated; A Great Trumpet Blown (27:2-13)	197
		a. God's Vineyard Revisited (27:2-6)	197
		b. The Fortified City Desolated (27:7-11)	198
		c. A Great Trumpet Is Blown (27:12-13)	199
III.	A RIGHTEOUS KING WILL REIGN (28:1—39:8)		201
	A.	Will Judah Trust Egypt or Yahweh? (28:1—33:24)	203
		1. Drunken Rulers of Ephraim, Scoffing Rulers of Judah (28:1-29)	203
		a. Woe to Ephraim's Drunken Leaders (28:1-13)	203
		b. Yahweh's Work in Zion: Strange and Alien (28:14-22)	205
		c. The Parable of the Wise Farmer (28:23-29)	207
		2. God's City Ariel, and the House of Jacob (29:1-24)	209
		a. Ariel, Ariel (29:1-14)	210
		b. The Potter and the Clay (29:15-16)	213
		c. The Deaf Will Hear, the Blind Will See (29:17-21)	213
		d. Jacob Will Accept Instruction (29:22-24)	214

	3. Woe to Those Who Form an Alliance with Egypt (30:1—31:9)		215
		a. Egypt: Rahab the Sitting One (30:1-7)	216
		b. Isaiah's Message Rejected (30:8-14)	218
		c. Yahweh Will Show Compassion (30:15-18)	219
		d. Yahweh Will Grace His People (30:19-26)	220
		e. The Name of Yahweh Will Shatter Assyria (30:27-33)	221
		f. Satire: Egypt Is Merely Human; Assyria Will Fall by a Nonhuman Sword (31:1-9)	222
	4. Behold! A King Will Reign According to Righteousness (32:1-20)		226
		a. Princes Will Rule According to Justice (32:1-8)	226
		b. Harvest Taken, Cities Deserted (32:9-14)	228
		c. The Spirit Poured Out; Fertile Fields (32:15-20)	230
	5. Yahweh, the King, Forgives Zion (33:1-24)		231
		a. Zion, Filled with Yahweh's Justice and Righteousness (33:1-6)	232
		b. Zion Betrayed, Treaties Broken (33:7-12)	233
		c. Zion, a Dread for Sinners, a Refuge for the Righteous (33:13-16)	234
		d. Zion, an Undisturbed Grazing Place (33:17-24)	236
B. Judgment's Desert, Redemption's Garden (34:1—35:10)			239
	1. The Earth Is Turned into a Desert (34:1-17)		239
		a. Yahweh Judges the Nations (34:1-4)	240
		b. Yahweh's Sword Falls upon Edom (34:5-8)	241
		c. Edom, a Habitation for Desert Creatures (34:9-17)	242
	2. Judah Is Turned into a Garden (35:1-10)		244
C. Hezekiah and the Assyrian Threat; Hezekiah and Babylon (36:1—39:8)			247
	1. Hezekiah and the Assyrian Threat (36:1—37:38)		248
		a. Sennacherib's First Surrender Demand: Verbal (36:1-20)	249
		b. Isaiah's Counsel: Do Not Fear! (36:21—37:7)	253
		c. Sennacherib's Second Demand: Written (37:8-13)	255
		d. Hezekiah's Response: A Prayer to Yahweh (37:14-20)	256
		e. Yahweh's Response to Hezekiah's Prayer (37:21-35)	258
		f. Yahweh's Mysterious Intervention (37:36-37)	260
		g. Sennacherib's Assassination (37:38)	260
	2. Hezekiah's Sickness and Babylon (38:1—39:8)		262
		a. Sickness and Mortality (38:1-22)	263
		(1) Hezekiah's Sickness and Promised Recovery (38:1-8)		263
		(2) The Writing on Mortality (38:9-22)		264
		b. Hezekiah and the Babylonian Envoys (39:1-8)	266

GENERAL EDITORS' PREFACE

The purpose of the New Beacon Bible Commentary is to make available to pastors and students in the twenty-first century a biblical commentary that reflects the best scholarship in the Wesleyan theological tradition. The commentary project aims to make this scholarship accessible to a wider audience to assist them in their understanding and proclamation of Scripture as God's Word.

Writers of the volumes in this series not only are scholars within the Wesleyan theological tradition and experts in their field but also have special interest in the books assigned to them. Their task is to communicate clearly the critical consensus and the full range of other credible voices who have commented on the Scriptures. Though scholarship and scholarly contribution to the understanding of the Scriptures are key concerns of this series, it is not intended as an academic dialogue within the scholarly community. Commentators of this series constantly aim to demonstrate in their work the significance of the Bible as the church's book and the contemporary relevance and application of the biblical message. The project's overall goal is to make available to the church and for her service the fruits of the labors of scholars who are committed to their Christian faith.

The *New International Version* (NIV) is the reference version of the Bible used in this series; however, the focus of exegetical study and comments is the biblical text in its original language. When the commentary uses the NIV, it is printed in bold. The text printed in bold italics is the translation of the author. Commentators also refer to other translations where the text may be difficult or ambiguous.

The structure and organization of the commentaries in this series seeks to facilitate the study of the biblical text in a systematic and methodical way. Study of each biblical book begins with an ***Introduction*** section that gives an overview of authorship, date, provenance, audience, occasion, purpose, sociological/cultural issues, textual history, literary features, hermeneutical issues, and theological themes necessary to understand the book. This section also includes a brief outline of the book and a list of general works and standard commentaries.

The commentary section for each biblical book follows the outline of the book presented in the introduction. In some volumes, readers will find section ***overviews*** of large portions of scripture with general comments on their overall literary structure and other literary features. A consistent feature of the commentary is the paragraph-by-paragraph study of biblical texts. This section has three parts: ***Behind the Text***, ***In the Text***, and ***From the Text***.

The goal of the ***Behind the Text*** section is to provide the reader with all the relevant information necessary to understand the text. This includes specific historical situations reflected in the text, the literary context of the text, sociological and cultural issues, and literary features of the text.

In the Text explores what the text says, following its verse-by-verse structure. This section includes a discussion of grammatical details, word studies, and the connectedness of the text to other biblical books/passages or other parts of the book being studied (the canonical relationship). This section provides transliterations of key words in Hebrew and Greek and their literal meanings. The goal here is to explain what the author would have meant and/or what the audience would have understood as the meaning of the text. This is the largest section of the commentary.

The ***From the Text*** section examines the text in relation to the following areas: theological significance, intertextuality, the history of interpretation, use of the Old Testament scriptures in the New Testament, interpretation in later church history, actualization, and application.

The commentary provides ***sidebars*** on topics of interest that are important but not necessarily part of an explanation of the biblical text. These topics are informational items and may cover archaeological, historical, literary, cultural, and theological matters that have relevance to the biblical text. Occasionally, longer detailed discussions of special topics are included as ***excursuses***.

We offer this series with our hope and prayer that readers will find it a valuable resource for their understanding of God's Word and an indispensable tool for their critical engagement with the biblical texts.

Roger Hahn, Centennial Initiative General Editor
Alex Varughese, General Editor (Old Testament)
George Lyons, General Editor (New Testament)

ACKNOWLEDGMENTS

I began my preparation for writing a commentary on the book of Isaiah, not in Isaiah itself, of course, but in the world of the language and historical context of the OT. I cannot name all the teachers in my academic journey who gave input in these areas, but I must acknowledge some key ones. In the early stages of my journey, some half century ago, Haiim B. Rosén introduced me to the delights of (Israeli) Hebrew, and Yohanan Aharoni opened my senses to the value of knowing the geography of the biblical lands and of gathering up all that archaeology might offer to enhance one's understanding of the biblical texts. Both professors shared their teaching time at the Hebrew University, Tel Aviv, with us young students at the Institute of Holy Land Studies, Jerusalem.

Dennis Kinlaw, at Asbury Theological Seminary, continued guidance of my studies in biblical Hebrew. Later, at the University of Michigan, Louis Orlin broadened my grasp of the vast history of the Mesopotamian world and its empires, and their impact on what the OT writers viewed as their "world." At the same institution George Cameron introduced me to the wonders of reading Akkadian texts, with Herbert B. Huffmon later building on that foundation at Drew University through reading of additional Akkadian texts. The reading of these texts further opened the Mesopotamian world's context, which later I would find indispensable in writing a commentary on Isaiah, a prophet who lived with that world always in his "backyard" or on his "doorstep."

I thank my adjunct OT teaching colleague Robert (Bob) Branson at Anderson University School of Theology, who suggested in 2010 that I should consider accepting this assignment to write the two volumes on Isaiah for the New Beacon Bible Commentary series. I am also thankful to Alex Varughese, a fellow PhD student at Drew University in the 1970s, who edited this volume; I have enjoyed working with Alex and appreciate his insightful suggestions for making my comments more readable.

This assignment has been far more than a mere academic exercise in the study of an ancient text. I have sensed God's Spirit at work in and through the text and most of all in my own spirit as his Word continues to deepen its roots in my inner being.

ABBREVIATIONS

With a few exceptions, these abbreviations follow those in *The SBL Handbook of Style* (Alexander 1999).

General

→	see the commentary at
AD	anno Domini (precedes date)
Akk.	Akkadian language
BC	before Christ (follows date)
ca.	circa
cent.	century
ch(s)	chapter(s)
diss.	dissertation
ed.	edited by; editor; edition
e.g.	for example
emph.	emphatic
esp.	especially
et al.	*et alii*, and others
etc.	*et cetera*, and the rest
f(f).	and the following one(s)
fem.	feminine
fl.	flourished (exact dates of birth and death are unknown)
HB	Hebrew Bible
Heb.	Hebrew
ibid.	*ibidem*, in the same place
i.e.	*id est*, that is
impv.	imperative
lit.	literally
LXX	Septuagint (the Greek translation of the OT)
masc.	masculine
MT	Masoretic Text (the Hebrew text of the OT)
n(n).	note(s)
n.d.	no date
no(s).	number(s)
n.p.	no page; no place; no publisher
NT	New Testament
OT	Old Testament
p(p).	page(s)
pass.	passive
pbk.	paperback
pl.	plural
pres.	present
pron.	pronoun
ptc.	participle
repr.	reprinted
rev.	revised
sec.	section
sg.	singular
SP	Syriac Peshitta
Syr.	Syriac
Tg(s).	Targum(s); Targumic
v(v)	verse(s)
Vg.	Vulgate (Latin translation of both OT and NT)
vol(s).	volume(s)
vs.	versus

Modern English Versions

ASV	American Standard Version
ESV	English Standard Version
KJV	King James Version

NASB	New American Standard Bible	
NIV	New International Version	
NJB	New Jerusalem Bible	
NJPS	Tanakh: The Holy Scriptures: The New JPS Translation according to the Traditional Hebrew Text	
NKJV	New King James Version	
NRSV	New Revised Standard Version	
RSV	Revised Standard Version	

Print Conventions for Translations

Bold font	NIV (bold without quotation marks in the text under study; elsewhere in the regular font, with quotation marks and no further identification)
Bold italic font	Author's translation (without quotation marks)
Behind the Text:	Literary or historical background information average readers might not know from reading the biblical text alone
In the Text:	Comments on the biblical text, words, phrases, grammar, and so forth
From the Text:	The use of the text by later interpreters, contemporary relevance, theological and ethical implications of the text, with particular emphasis on Wesleyan concerns

Old Testament

Gen	Genesis	Dan	Daniel	**New Testament**		
Exod	Exodus	Hos	Hosea	Matt	Matthew	
Lev	Leviticus	Joel	Joel	Mark	Mark	
Num	Numbers	Amos	Amos	Luke	Luke	
Deut	Deuteronomy	Obad	Obadiah	John	John	
Josh	Joshua	Jonah	Jonah	Acts	Acts	
Judg	Judges	Mic	Micah	Rom	Romans	
Ruth	Ruth	Nah	Nahum	1—2 Cor	1—2 Corinthians	
1—2 Sam	1—2 Samuel	Hab	Habakkuk			
1—2 Kgs	1—2 Kings	Zeph	Zephaniah	Gal	Galatians	
1—2 Chr	1—2 Chronicles	Hag	Haggai	Eph	Ephesians	
Ezra	Ezra	Zech	Zechariah	Phil	Philippians	
Neh	Nehemiah	Mal	Malachi	Col	Colossians	
Esth	Esther		(Note: Chapter and verse numbering in the MT and LXX often differ compared to those in English Bibles. To avoid confusion, all biblical references follow the chapter and verse numbering in English translations, even when the text in the MT and LXX is under discussion.)	1—2 Thess	1—2 Thessalonians	
Job	Job			1—2 Tim	1—2 Timothy	
Ps/Pss	Psalm/Psalms			Titus	Titus	
Prov	Proverbs			Phlm	Philemon	
Eccl	Ecclesiastes			Heb	Hebrews	
Song	Song of Songs/ Song of Solomon			Jas	James	
				1—2 Pet	1—2 Peter	
Isa	Isaiah			1—2—3 John	1—2—3 John	
Jer	Jeremiah			Jude	Jude	
Lam	Lamentations			Rev	Revelation	
Ezek	Ezekiel					

Apocrypha

Bar	Baruch
Add Dan	Additions to Daniel
Pr Azar	Prayer of Azariah
Bel	Bel and the Dragon
Sg Three	Song of the Three Young Men
Sus	Susanna
1—2 Esd	1—2 Esdras
Add Esth	Additions to Esther
Ep Jer	Epistle of Jeremiah
Jdt	Judith
1—2 Macc	1—2 Maccabees
3—4 Macc	3—4 Maccabees
Pr Man	Prayer of Manasseh
Ps 151	Psalm 151
Sir	Sirach/Ecclesiasticus

Tob	Tobit	
Wis	Wisdom of Solomon	

Pseudepigrapha
- Ascen. Isa. — *Ascension of Isaiah*
- 1 En. — *1 Enoch*

Dead Sea Scrolls
- 1QIsaᵃ — Isaiahᵃ
- 1QS — *Serek Hayakad* or *Rule of the Community*
- 1QSa — *Rule of the Congregation* (Appendix a to 1QS)

Josephus
- Ant. — *Jewish Antiquities*

Secondary Sources: Journals, Periodicals, Major Reference Works, and Series

BDB	*Gesenius Hebrew and English Lexicon of the Old Testament*
CAD	*The Assyrian Dictionary of the Oriental Institute of the University of Chicago.* Chicago, 1956-.
EDB	*Eerdmans Dictionary of the Bible*
HALOT	*Hebrew and Aramaic Lexicon of the Old Testament*
ISBE	*International Standard Bible Encyclopedia.* Edited by G. W. Bromiley. 4 vols. Grand Rapids, 1979-1988.
KAI	*Kanaanäische und aramäische Inschriften*
NICOT	*New International Commentary on the Old Testament*
NIDB	*New International Dictionary of the Bible*
TDOT	*Theological Dictionary of the Old Testament*

Greek Transliteration

Greek	Letter	English
α	alpha	a
β	bēta	b
γ	gamma	g
γ	gamma nasal	n (before γ, κ, ξ, χ)
δ	delta	d
ε	epsilon	e
ζ	zēta	z
η	ēta	ē
θ	thēta	th
ι	iōta	i
κ	kappa	k
λ	lambda	l
μ	mu	m
ν	nu	n
ξ	xi	x
ο	omicron	o
π	pi	p
ρ	rhō	r
ρ	initial rhō	rh
σ/ς	sigma	s
τ	tau	t
υ	upsilon	y
υ	upsilon	u (in diphthongs: au, eu, ēu, ou, ui)
φ	phi	ph
χ	chi	ch
ψ	psi	ps
ω	ōmega	ō
ʽ	rough breathing	h (before initial vowels or diphthongs)

Hebrew Consonant Transliteration

Hebrew/Aramaic	Letter	English
א	alef	ʼ
ב	bet	b
ג	gimel	g
ד	dalet	d
ה	he	h
ו	vav	v or w
ז	zayin	z
ח	khet	ḥ
ט	tet	ṭ
י	yod	y
כ/ך	kaf	k
ל	lamed	l
מ/ם	mem	m
נ/ן	nun	n
ס	samek	s
ע	ayin	ʽ
פ/ף	pe	p; f (spirant)
צ/ץ	tsade	ṣ
ק	qof	q
ר	resh	r
שׂ	sin	ś
שׁ	shin	š
ת	tav	t; th (spirant)

BIBLIOGRAPHY

Abegg, Martin, Jr., Peter Flint, and Eugene Ulrich. 1999. *The Dead Sea Scrolls Bible: The Oldest Known Bible Translated for the First Time into English.* New York: HarperSanFrancisco.
Achtemeir, Paul J. 1985. *Harper's Bible Dictionary.* New York: HarperSanFrancisco.
Aharoni, Yohanan. 1966. The Use of Hieratic Numerals in Hebrew Ostraca and the Shekel Weights. *Bulletin of the American Oriental Society* 184:13-19.
Aharoni, Yohanan, Michael Avi-Yonah, Anson F. Rainey, and Ze'ev Safrai. 1993. *The Macmillan Bible Atlas.* Rev. 3rd ed. Jerusalem: Carta.
Albright, W. F., tr. 1969. The Moabite Stone. In *Ancient Near Eastern Texts Relating to the Old Testament.* 3rd ed. Edited by James Pritchard. Princeton: Princeton University. Pp. 320-21.
Andersen, Francis I. 1976. *Job: An Introduction and Commentary.* Tyndale Old Testament Commentaries. Downers Grove, IL: InterVarsity.
Anderson, Francis I., and David Noel Freedman. 1989. *Amos: A New Translation with Introduction and Commentary.* Anchor Bible 24A. Edited by W. F. Albright and D. N. Freedman. New York: Doubleday.
Archer, Gleason L., and Gregory Chirichigno. 1983. *Old Testament Quotations in the New Testament.* Chicago: Moody.
Artzi, Pinhas. 2008. The Mesopotamian Background of the Term *'hryt hymym* in the World-Peace Vision of Isaiah 2:2a. Edited by Chaim Cohen, et al. In *Birkat Shalom: Studies in the Bible, Ancient Near Eastern Literature and Postbiblical Judaism Presented to Shalom M. Paul on the Occasion of His Seventieth Birthday.* Vol. 1. Winona Lake, IN: Eisenbrauns. Pp. 427-31.
Aster, Shawn Zelig. 2007. The Image of Assyria in Isaiah 2:5-22: The Campaign Motif Reversed. *Journal of the American Oriental Society* 127:249-78.
Baldwin, Joyce C. 1964. ṢEMAḤ as a Technical Term in the Prophets. *Vetus Testamentum* 14:93-97.
Barré, Michael L. 2004. "Tarshish Has Perished": The Crux of Isaiah 23,10. *Biblica* 85:115-19.
Beale, G. K. 1991. Isaiah VI 9-13: A Retributive Taunt against Idolatry. *Vetus Testamentum* 41:257-78.
Bence, Clarence. 1996. *Romans: A Bible Commentary in the Wesleyan Tradition.* Indianapolis: Wesleyan Publishing House.
Berlin, Adele, and Marc Zvi Brettler, eds. 2004. *The Jewish Study Bible.* New York: Oxford University Press.
Biblia Hebraica. 1937. Edited by Rudolf Kittel. 3rd. ed. Württemberg: Deutsche Bibelgesellschaft.
Biblia Hebraica Quinta. 2004—. Edited by various scholars. Stuttgart: Deutsche Bibelgesellschaft.
Biblia Hebraica Stuttgartensia. 1977. Edited by Paul Kahle. Stuttgart: Deutsche Bibelgesellschaft.
Blenkinsopp, Joseph. 2000. *Isaiah 1-39.* Anchor Bible 19. New York: Doubleday.
Blomberg, Craig L. 1992. *Matthew.* New American Commentary 22. Nashville: Broadman & Holman. Logos Bible Software 4.
Bright, John. 2000. *A History of Israel.* 4th ed. Louisville, KY: Westminster John Knox.
Brinkman, J. A. 1964. Merodach-Baladan II. In *Studies Presented to A. Leo Oppenheim, June 7, 1964.* Edited by Robert D. Biggs and A. Leo Oppenheim. Chicago: Oriental Institute. Pp. 6-53.
———. 1965. Elamite Military Aid to Merodach-Baladan. *Journal of Near Eastern Studies* 24:161-66.
Brueggemann, Walter. 1997. *Theology of the Old Testament: Testimony, Dispute, Advocacy.* Minneapolis: Fortress.
Burrows, Millar. 1958. The Conduit of the Upper Pool. *Zeitschrift für die alttestamentliche Wissenschaft* 70:221-27.
Calvin, John. 1850. *Commentary on the Book of the Prophet Isaiah: Volume First.* Translated by William Pringle. Grand Rapids: Christian Classics Ethereal Library (http://www.ccel.org).
Charles, R. H. 1900. *The Ascension of Isaiah: Translated from the Ethiopic Version.* London: Adam and Charles Black.
Childs, Brevard S. 1974. *The Book of Exodus: A Critical, Theological Commentary.* Old Testament Library. Philadelphia: Westminster.
———. 1979. *Introduction to the Old Testament as Scripture.* Philadelphia: Fortress.
———. 2001. *Isaiah.* Old Testament Library. Louisville, KY: Westminster John Knox.

Chisholm, Robert B., Jr. 2002. *Handbook on the Prophets*. Grand Rapids: Baker Academic.
Clements, R. E. 1980 (repr. 1982). *Isaiah 1-39*. New Century Bible Commentary. Grand Rapids: Eerdmans.
Cooley, Robert E. 1983. Gathered to His People: A Study of a Dothan Family Tomb. In *The Living and Active Word of God: Studies in Honor of Samuel J. Schultz*. Edited by Morris Inch and Ronald Youngblood. Winona Lake, IN: Eisenbrauns. Pp. 47-58.
Curtis, Adrian, ed. 2009. *Oxford Bible Atlas*. 4th ed. Oxford: Oxford University.
De Backer, Fabrice Y. 2009. Evolution of War Chariot Tactics in the Ancient Near East. *Ugarit-Forschungen* 41:29-47.
———. 2012. Les archers de siège néo-assyriens. In *Organization, Representation, and Symbols of Power in the Ancient Near East: Proceedings of the 54th Rencontre Assyriologique Internationale at Würzburg 20-25 July 2008*. Winona Lake, IN: Eisenbrauns. Pp. 429-48.
de Vaux, Roland. 1971. *The Bible and the Ancient Near East*. New York: Doubleday.
Dotan, Aron, ed. 2001. *Biblia Hebraica Leningradensia: Prepared according to the Vocalization, Accents, and Masora of Aaron ben Moses ben Asher in the Leningrad Codex*. Peabody, MA: Hendrickson.
Dothan, Trude, and Moshe Dothan. 1992. *People of the Sea: The Search for the Philistines*. New York: Macmillan.
Driver, G. R. 1937. Linguistic and Textual Problems: Isaiah I-XXXIX. *Journal of Theological Studies* 38:36-50.
Durham, John I. 1987. *Exodus*. Word Biblical Commentary 3. Waco, TX: Word.
Eiselen, Frederick Carl. 1907. *Sidon: A Study in Oriental History*. New York: Columbia University. Google e-book.
Eph'al, Israel. 1982. *The Ancient Arabs: Nomads on the Borders of the Fertile Crescent, 9th—5th Centuries B.C*. Jerusalem: Magnes Press.
Finklestein, J. J. 1952. The Middle Assyrian *Šulmānu*-Texts. *Journal of the American Oriental Society* 72:77-80.
Firth, David G., and H. G. M. Williamson. 2009. *Interpreting Isaiah*. Downers Grove, IL: IVP Academic.
Fleming, George. 1869. *Horse-shoes and Horse-shoeing: Their Origin, History, Uses, and Abuses*. London: Chapman and Hall. Google e-book.
Fretheim, Terence E. 1984. *The Suffering of God: An Old Testament Perspective*. Overtures to Biblical Theology 14. Philadelphia: Fortress.
Gardiner, A. H. 1944. Horus the Behdetite. *Journal of Egyptian Archaeology* 30:23-60.
Gesenius, W., E. Kautzsch, and A. E. Cowley. 1910. *Gesenius Hebrew Grammar*. Oxford: Clarendon.
Gibson, John C. L. 1971. *Hebrew and Moabite Inscriptions*. Vol. 1 of *Textbook of Syrian Semitic Inscriptions*. Oxford: Clarendon.
Ginsberg, H. L. 1968. Reflexes of Sargon in Isaiah after 715 B.C.E. *Journal of the American Oriental Society* 88:47-53.
Goldingay, John. 2001. *Isaiah*. New International Biblical Commentary on the Old Testament. Peabody, MA: Hendrickson.
Gonen, Rivka. 1975. *Weapons of the Ancient World*. London: Cassell.
Grayson, Albert K. 1991. *Assyrian Rulers of the Early First Millennium BC I (1114-959 BC)*. The Royal Inscriptions of Mesopotamia, Assyrian Periods, Vol. 2. Toronto: University of Toronto.
Hamilton, Victor P. 1990. *The Book of Genesis, Chapters 1-17*. New International Commentary on the Old Testament. Grand Rapids: Eerdmans.
Hartley, John. 1982. The Use of Typology Illustrated in a Study of Isaiah 9:1-7. *God's Word for Today: An Inquiry into Hermeneutics from a Biblical Theological Perspective*. In Wesleyan Theological Perspectives, Vol. 2. Anderson, IN: Warner. Pp. 195-220.
Jenni, Ernst, and Claus Westermann. 1997. *Theological Lexicon of the Old Testament*. 3 vols. Translated by Mark E. Biddle. Peabody, MA: Hendrickson.
Kaiser, Otto. 1972. *Isaiah 1-12: A Commentary*. Old Testament Library. Translated by R. A Wilson. Philadelphia: Westminster.
———. 1974. *Isaiah 13-39: A Commentary*. Old Testament Library. Translated by R. A. Wilson. Philadelphia: Westminster.
King, Phillip J., and Lawrence E. Stager. 2001. *Life in Biblical Israel*. Louisville, KY: Westminster John Knox.
Kitchen, K. A. 1973. *The Third Intermediate Period in Egypt (1100-650 B.C.)*. Warminster: Aris & Philips.

Koehler, Ludwig, and Walter Baumgartner. 1995—2000. *Hebrew and Aramaic Lexicon of the Old Testament: The New Koehler-Baumgartner in English.* Leiden: E. J. Brill. Accordance Bible Software.

Korpel, Margo C. A. 1996. Structural Analysis as a Tool for Redaction Criticism: The Example of Isaiah 5 and 10:1-6. *Journal for the Study of the Old Testament* 69:53-71.

Lessing, Reed. 2003. Satire in Isaiah's Tyre Oracle. *Journal for the Study of the Old Testament* 28:89-112.

Lim, Timothy H. 2002. *Pesharim.* London: Sheffield Academic.

Lubetski, Meir. 2000. Beetlemania of Bygone Times. *Journal for the Study of the Old Testament* 91:3-26.

———. 2008. The Land Named for an Insect. In *Thinking Towards New Horizons: Collected Communications to the XIXth Congress of the International Organization for the Study of the Old Testament, Ljubljana 2007.* Ed. Matthias Augustin and Hermann Michael Niemann. Frankfurt: Peter Lang. Pp. 103-12.

Luckenbill, Daniel D. 1924. *The Annals of Sennacherib.* University of Chicago Oriental Institute Publications, Vol. 2. Edited by James Henry Breasted. Chicago: University of Chicago.

———. 1925. The Black Stone of Esarhaddon. *American Journal of Semitic Languages and Literature* 41:165-73.

———. [1926] 1968. *Ancient Records of Assyria and Babylonia.* Vol. 1: *Historical Records of Assyria from the Earliest Times to Sargon.* Vol. 2: *Historical Records of Assyria from Sargon to the End.* Edited by James Henry Breasted. New York: Greenwood.

Macintosh, A. A. 1980. *Isaiah XXI: A Palimpsest.* Cambridge: Cambridge University.

Markoe, Glenn E. 2000. *Peoples of the Past: Phoenicians.* Berkeley, CA: University of California.

Mawby, L. 1999. "Why Grapes Grow Here." N.p. Cited June 20, 2012. Online: http://www.lmawby.com/index.php?route=/enjoy/writings/why-grapes-grow-here.

McKay, J. W. 1970. Helel and the Dawn-Goddess: A Re-examination of the Myth in Isaiah XIV 12-15. *Vetus Testamentum* 20:451-64.

McKinion, Steven A. ed. 2004. *Isaiah 1—39.* Ancient Christian Commentary on Scripture: Old Testament. Vol. 10. Downers Grove, IL: InterVarsity.

Meissner, Bruno. 1920. *Babylonien und Assyrien I.* Heidelberg: Carl Winter.

Meyers, Eric M. 1970. Secondary Burials in Palestine. *Biblical Archaeologist* 33:2-29.

Miles, Johnny. 2006. Re-reading the Power of Satire: Isaiah's "Daughters of Zion," Pope's "Belinda," and the Rhetoric of Rape. *Journal for the Study of the Old Testament* 31:193-219.

Millard, A. R. 1985. Sennacherib's Attack on Hezekiah. *Tyndale Bulletin* 36:61-77.

Motyer, J. Alec. 1993. *The Prophecy of Isaiah: An Introduction and Commentary.* Downers Grove, IL: InterVarsity.

Mounce, Robert H. 1977. *The Book of Revelation.* New International Commentary on the New Testament 17. Grand Rapids: Eerdmans.

Murray, John. 1965. *The Epistle to the Romans.* Vol. 2: *Chapters 9 to 16.* New International Commentary on the New Testament. Grand Rapids: Eerdmans.

Niehaus, Jeffrey. 1992. Amos. In *Hosea, Joel, and Amos.* Vol. 1 of The Minor Prophets: An Exegetical and Expository Commentary. Edited by Edward McComiskey. Grand Rapids: Baker. Pp. 315-494.

Oswalt, John N. 1986. *The Book of Isaiah, Chapters 1-39.* New International Commentary on the Old Testament. Grand Rapids: Eerdmans.

———. 1998. *The Book of Isaiah, Chapters 40-66.* New International Commentary on the Old Testament. Grand Rapids: Eerdmans.

Pritchard, James B., ed. 1958. *The Ancient Near East: An Anthology of Texts and Pictures.* Princeton: Princeton University.

———, ed. 1969. *Ancient Near Eastern Texts Relating to the Old Testament.* 3rd ed. CD-ROM. Logos Bible Software. Print ed.: Princeton: Princeton University.

Pulikottil, Paulson. 2001. *Transmission of Biblical Texts in Qumran: The Case of the Large Isaiah Scroll 1QIsa^a.* Journal for the Study of the Pseudepigrapha Supplement Series 34. Edited by Lester L. Grabbe and James H. Charlesworth. Sheffield: Sheffield Academic.

Rignell, L. G. 1957. Isaiah Chapter I. Some exegetical remarks with special reference to the relationship between the text and the book of Deuteronomy. *Studia theologica* 11:140-58.

Ross, Barry L. 1979. The Individual in the Community: Personal Identification in Ancient Israel. PhD diss., Drew University.

Seitz, Christopher R. 1993. *Isaiah 1-39: A Bible Commentary for Teaching and Preaching.* Louisville, KY: John Knox.

Shipp, R. Mark. 2002. *Of Dead Kings and Dirges: Myth and Meaning in Isaiah 14:4b-21.* Academia Biblica, No. 11. Atlanta: Society of Biblical Literature.

Smith, Gary V. 2007. *Isaiah 1-39.* New American Commentary 15A. Nashville: B&H Publishing. Amazon Kindle.

Smith, George. 1878. *History of Sennacherib, Translated from the Cuneiform Inscriptions.* Edited by A. H. Sayce. Edinburgh: Williams and Norgate. Google e-book.

Speiser, E. A. 1958. Census and Expiation in Mari and Israel. *Bulletin of the American Schools of Oriental Research* 149:17-25.

Stinespring, W. F. 1965. No Daughter of Zion: A Study of the Appositional Genitive in Hebrew Grammar. *Encounter* 26:133-41.

Strassler, Robert B., ed. 2007. *The Landmark Herodotus: The Histories.* Book 2. Translated by Andrea L. Purvis. New York: Pantheon Books. Random House Digital (2009).

Stuart, Douglas. 1976. The Sovereign's Day of Conquest. *Bulletin of the American Schools of Oriental Research* 221:159-64.

———. 1987. Amos. In *Hosea-Jonah.* Word Biblical Commentary 31. Waco, TX: Word. Pp. 274-400.

Sweeney, Marvin A. 1996. *Isaiah 1-39 with an Introduction to Prophetic Literature.* Forms of the Old Testament Literature 16. Edited by Rolf P. Knierim and Gene M. Tucker. Grand Rapids: Eerdmans.

Tadmor, Hayim. 1958. The Campaigns of Sargon II of Assur. *Journal of Cuneiform Studies* 12:22-40, 77-100.

———. 1994. *The Inscriptions of Tiglath-Pileser III King of Assyria.* Jerusalem: Israel Academy of Sciences and Humanities.

Taylor, Joan E. 1995. The Asherah, the Menorah, and the Sacred Tree. *Journal for the Study of the Old Testament* 66:29-54.

Thiele, Edwin R. 1965. *The Mysterious Numbers of the Hebrew Kings: A Reconstruction of the Chronology of the Kingdoms of Israel and Judah.* Grand Rapids: Eerdmans.

Ussishkin, David. 1982. *The Conquest of Lachish by Sennacherib.* Tel Aviv: Tel Aviv University.

———. 2004. *The Renewed Archaeological Excavations at Lachish (1973-1994).* Publication of the Institute of Archaeology 22. Tel Aviv: Tel Aviv University.

———. 2006. Sennacherib's Campaign to Philistia and Judah: Ekron, Lachish, and Jerusalem. In *Essays on Ancient Israel in Its Near Eastern Context: A Tribute to Nadav Na'aman.* Edited by Yaira Amit and Nadav Na'aman. Winona Lake, IN: Eisenbrauns. Pp. 339-57.

VanGemeren, Willem A., ed. 1997. *New International Dictionary of Old Testament Theology and Exegesis.* 4 vols. Grand Rapids: Zondervan.

von Rad, Gerhard. 1959. The Origin of the Concept of the Day of Yahweh. *Journal of Semitic Studies* 4:97-108.

———. 1962. *Old Testament Theology.* Vol. 1: *The Theology of Israel's Historical Traditions.* Translated by D. M. G. Stalker. New York: Harper & Row.

Waltke, Bruce K., and M. O'Connor. 1990. *An Introduction to Biblical Hebrew Syntax.* Winona Lake, IN: Eisenbrauns. Accordance Bible Software.

Watts, John D. W. 2000. *Isaiah 34-66.* Word Biblical Commentary 25. Rev. ed. Nashville: Thomas Nelson.

———. 2005. *Isaiah 1-33.* Word Biblical Commentary 24. Rev. ed. Nashville: Thomas Nelson.

Wesley, John. Reprint, n.d. *Wesley's Notes on the Whole Bible.* Christian Classics Ethereal Library. pdf download.

Westermann, Claus. 1967. *Basis Forms of Prophetic Speech.* Translated by Hugh Clayton White. London: Lutterworth.

White, Lynn Townsend. 1962. *Medieval Technology and Social Change.* London: Oxford University. ACLS Humanities E-book.

Wildberger, Hans. 1991. *Isaiah 1-12: A Commentary.* A Continental Commentary. Translated by Thomas H. Trapp. Minneapolis: Fortress.

———. 1997. *Isaiah 13-27: A Commentary.* A Continental Commentary. Translated by Thomas H. Trapp. Minneapolis: Fortress.

———. 2002. *Isaiah 28-39: A Continental Commentary.* Translated by Thomas H. Trapp. Minneapolis: Fortress.

Williamson, H. G. M. 2007 repr. *A Critical and Exegetical Commentary on Isaiah 1-27 in Three Volumes.* Vol. 1: *Commentary on Isaiah 1-5.* London: Clark.

Wise, Michael, Martin Abegg Jr., and Edward Cook. 1996 (pbk. ed. 1999). *The Dead Sea Scrolls: A New Translation*. New York: HarperSanFrancisco.

Wiseman, D. J. 1955. Assyrian Writing-Boards. *Iraq* 17:3-13.

Witherington, Ben, III. 2003. *Revelation*. New Cambridge Bible Commentary. Cambridge: Cambridge University.

Wong, Gordon. 2008. Make Their Ears Dull: Irony in Isaiah 6:9-10. *Trinity Theological College Journal* 16:24-34.

Young, Edward J. 1965. *The Book of Isaiah*. Vol. 1: *Chapters 1 to 18*. New International Commentary on the Old Testament. Grand Rapids: Eerdmans.

TABLE OF SIDEBARS

Title	Location
The Holy One of Israel	1:4
Yahweh Sebaoth/The Lord Almighty	1:9
The Boasts of the Assyrian Kings	2:2
Divination	2:6
The ANE Battle Horse and Chariot	2:7
Idols	2:8
Lebanon, Bashan, and Ships of Tarshish	2:12-17
Assyrian Population Deportations	5:13
Sheol in the OT	5:14
King Uzziah	Behind the Text for 6:1-13
Who Was Tiglath-Pileser III?	7:1
Samaria	9:9
Cities of the Assyrian King's Boast in Isa 10:8-9	10:8-11
The Demise of the Assyrian Empire	10:16-19
Midian and the Rock of Oreb	10:24-27
Excursus: A Theological Basis for Yahweh's Sovereignty over the Nations	Overview for Part 2
Babylon	Behind the Text for 13:1—14:27
The Trees of Lebanon and the Assyrian Kings	14:4b-8
Moab in the OT	16:13-14
Damascus	Behind the Text for 17:1—18:7
Asherahs	17:7-8
The Nile River	19:5-10
Flax and Linen	19:5-10
Sargon II and the Ashdod Rebellion	20:1-6
War Crime in the Ancient World	21:10
The Assyrian War Chariot, Archers, and Shield Bearers	22:8-11
Apocalypse of Isaiah	24:1—27:13
The Timbrel and the Harp	24:10-12
Alcoholic Beverages in the OT	28:7-8
The Plumb Line	28:16-19
Siege Ramps, Battering Rams, and Towers	29:2-3
Rahab, the Sea Monster	30:6-7
Lions in Ancient Palestine	31:4
Mourning in the OT	32:10-14
Tents, Stakes, and Ropes	33:20
Assyrian Descriptions of Corpses on the Battlefield	34:3-4
Assyria's Attacks on Samaria, Hamath, Sepharvaim, and Arpad	36:18-20
The Cherubim	37:16
The Angel of the Lord	37:38
Eunuchs	39:5-7

INTRODUCTION

A. The Importance of the Book of Isaiah

The contents and great length of the book of Isaiah has given it great prominence in both Judaism and Christianity, alongside the other lengthy prophetical books of Jeremiah and Ezekiel.

In Judaism, Isaiah takes first place for citations from the prophetical books in rabbinic literature. Additionally, of the "haftarot" (prophetic readings chanted in synagogue on Sabbaths, holidays and fast days), nineteen are from Isaiah (compared to nine from Jeremiah and ten from Ezekiel) (Berlin and Brettler 2004, 780).

In Christianity, the NT writers quote from Isaiah at least sixty-two times (Archer and Chirichigno 1983, 92-134). Many quotations from and allusions to the book of Isaiah are found in the writings of the patristic preachers/interpreters of the early centuries of the church. The first-century patristic interpreters (and the NT writers) usually read Isaiah in the Greek LXX, which, from a Jewish viewpoint, came to be considered a Christian book. By the fifth century, however, the Latin-speaking fathers most commonly read Isaiah from Jerome's Latin Vulgate, a translation of the OT made from the Hebrew (McKinion 2004, xvii-xviii). There are only a few commentaries on Isaiah from the pens of the early church interpreters: three passage-by-passage commentaries were by Eusebius of Caesarea (ca. 260/263-340), Jerome (ca. 347-420), and Cyril of Alexandria (ca. 375-444; fl. 412-444) (ibid., xviii). These interpreters, and others, viewed Isaiah as primarily announcing the coming of Jesus the Messiah. With this, he was warning Israel of their loss of God's blessing for their rejection of Messiah Jesus, and the extension of that blessing to the Gentiles, a fulfillment of God's promise to Abraham to bless all nations (ibid., xxi).

B. Isaiah the Person

What we know of the prophet Isaiah as a person is found within Isaiah 1—39 (and from 2 Kgs 18—20, which is a parallel of Isa 36—39). His name, "Isaiah" (*yěša'yāhû* [1:1], from *yš'*), means "Yahweh saves/has saved." Thus his very name points to the concept of salvation, an essential characteristic of God, and a theme that recurs throughout this whole book (see 25:9; 33:22; 35:4; 37:20; 37:35; 38:20; 43:12; 45:17, 22; 49:25; 51:5; 59:1; 61:10; 62:1; 63:1). Isaiah had a wife whom he calls "the prophetess" (8:3), and two sons named "Shear-Jashub" (7:3) and "Maher-Shalal-Hash-Baz" (8:3).

It is traditionally assumed that Isaiah lived and ministered primarily in and around the city of Jerusalem. Two of his personal appearances in the book place him in Jerusalem, as counselor to two Judean kings, first to Ahaz the father, then to Hezekiah his son.

In Isaiah's first appearance as royal counselor he met King "Ahaz at the end of the aqueduct of the Upper Pool, on the road to the Launderer's Field" (7:3); this was most likely somewhere in the lower Kidron Valley, south of Jerusalem (Burrows 1958, 227; Wildberger 1991, 295). In this meeting, Isaiah urged Ahaz not to seek assistance from Assyria against the threatening alliance of Israel and Syria (734 BC); rather, he urged him to place his trust fully in Yahweh for protection and deliverance. However, Ahaz rejected Isaiah's counsel.

Isaiah's second appearance as royal counselor took place during the reign of Hezekiah son of Ahaz; he had both verbal (through messengers) and face-to-face correspondence with Hezekiah. These encounters took place within the city of Jerusalem. The counsel given through messengers was that Hezekiah should not seek Egyptian assistance against the impending threat of Assyrian invasion (701 BC). Rather, similar to the counsel given to his father Ahaz, he urged Hezekiah to trust fully in Yahweh for the protection and deliverance of Jerusalem (37:1-7, 21-35; 38:4-7, 21). Unlike his father Ahaz, Hezekiah did heed Isaiah's advice.

An additional appearance, a kind of postscript, is one in which Isaiah initiated a visit to Hezekiah following a visit to Jerusalem by some Babylonian messengers after Hezekiah had recovered from a near-death illness (39:3-7). In this visit with Hezekiah, Isaiah (re)introduced Babylon and the effect this power broker will have upon Judah in the distant future, leading to Judah's exile.

We see Isaiah in one other event, recorded in ch 6. On a certain day, dated vaguely as post-King Uzziah's death (739 BC), while perhaps in the setting of worship in the Jerusalem temple, Isaiah encountered the majesty of Yahweh's holiness that changed him deep within his spiritual being (ch 6). In this encounter with **the Sovereign One** (*'ădônāy* [v 1]), **the King, Yahweh Sebaoth** (*hammelek yhwh ṣĕbā'ôt* [v 5]), Isaiah acknowledged that he was "a man of unclean lips" (*'îš ṭĕmē' śĕpātayim* [v 5]); Yahweh in response told him through "one of the seraphim": "your guilt [*'ăwôneḵā*] is taken away" and **your sin** [*ḥaṭṭā'tĕḵā*] **is forgiven** (v 7). Yahweh then gave him a commission to persistently continue to preach to Judean ears, eyes, and hearts that will, in response, persistently continue to reject his and Yahweh's word.

We do not find in the book of Isaiah a record of Isaiah's call to serve as a prophet of Yahweh. His experience in the temple (ch 6) has often been interpreted as such, but, in fact, does not constitute a prophetic call. Already, in 5:1 Isaiah "emerges as spokesman for Yahweh" (Seitz 1993, 52). There, in a song about Yahweh's vineyard, Isaiah says, "I will sing for the one I love." Also, in 5:9 we hear Isaiah saying, **In my ears! Yahweh Sebaoth**. Isaiah is declaring in 5:9 that Yahweh has spoken and his prophet has heard! Thus he already viewed himself as a privileged participant in the deliberations of the divine council (Clements 1980, 63; compare Amos 3:7), even prior to his temple experience of ch 6.

The pseudepigraphal *Ascension of Isaiah* (possibly dating to ca. AD 88-100) contains a tradition ascribing to Isaiah martyrdom during the reign of Hezekiah's son Manassseh by being sawn in two (*Ascen. Isa.* 5:1-16) (Charles 1900, lxxi, 40-42). The writer of the NT book of Hebrews speaks of some OT faithful who were "sawed in two" (11:37), apparently reflecting this tradition.

C. The Canonical Book of Isaiah

The traditional assumption has been that the whole of the contents of canonical Isaiah, which the NIV simply entitles "Isaiah," is to be credited directly to the prophet "Isaiah son of Amoz" (1:1). The opening verse of the scroll speaks of ***the vision of Isaiah son of Amoz, which he envisioned concerning Judah and Jerusalem during the days of the kings of Judah: Uzziah, Jotham, Ahaz, and Hezekiah*** (1:1). The intention of this verse does appear to be that the reader should understand that, in some way, the contents of the entire scroll do relate to the prophet Isaiah of Jerusalem and to his spoken messages. This verse, however, functions as a superscription, an editorial title, and need not imply that the eighth-century BC prophet Isaiah of Jerusalem authored the whole of the book's contents (chs 1—66) (Goldingay 2001, 2). Scholars have suggested, and continue to suggest varying schemas for the formation of the canonical book of Isaiah as we know it. The stark fact is, however, that we have insufficient information on which to form any definitive conclusion as to the ancient process of the gathering together and formation of this canonical scroll.

A close study of the contents of the entire scroll leads many to the conclusion that the book of Isaiah is what Goldingay calls "a many-voiced book, throughout which the voice of Yahweh comes to us" (ibid., 3). Scholars commonly divide the book into two units, chs 1—39 and chs 40—66, calling them, for convenience sake, First Isaiah and Second Isaiah.

In First Isaiah (in this commentary, "Book 1"), the "voices" that we hear are those of Isaiah himself and the narrator/editor who speaks about Isaiah in the third person. These "voices" speak in the years 739 to 700 BC when Assyria is dominant on the world's scene.

In Second Isaiah (in this commentary, "Book 2"), we hear the "voices" of prophets and preachers, who, under the guidance of God's Spirit, preach Yahweh's message to God's people in later historical settings, often reusing/repreaching Isaiah's messages and thoughts, with new applications for new situations. These historical settings, apparently during the dominance of Babylonian and Persian powers, however, have sometimes been pushed into the background, so that they are nearly unidentifiable, or not identifiable at all.

The final edited canonical text of the Isaiah scroll is what Childs describes as "a coherent witness in its final received form to the ways of God with Israel" (2001, 4). Thus the "message [of Second Isaiah is not] a specific commentary on the needs of exiled Israel, but its message relates to the redemptive plan of God for all of history" (Childs 1979, 326).

This commentary will deal with the book of Isaiah in its received canonical form, believing this to be the most productive approach. Historical contexts and background will be addressed within the context of commentary on the text as appropriate.

D. The Texts and Language of the Book of Isaiah

The book of Isaiah is written in Hebrew. From the eleventh century AD onward, many rabbinic and academic scholars made reference to the "ben Asher" Hebrew manuscript(s) of the Tanakh/OT. This manuscript, so it was said, had been copied in the early eleventh century or earlier by Aaron ben Moses ben Asher, of the ben Asher family of scribes living and working in Tiberius. They were called Masoretes; thus their copies/preservation of the consonantal text of the Hebrew Scriptures became known as the Masoretic Text, or MT. The ben Asher Masoretes developed a system of "points," representing vowels and accents, which they added to the consonantal Hebrew text to preserve how they believed the words were to be correctly pronounced. This system became known as the Tiberian pointing (as opposed to the Babylonian pointing, developed among the Jews remaining in the Babylonian Diaspora). Scholars through the past several centuries, however, had not (and still have not) seen any of the original ben Asher texts (Dotan 2001, ix). Since the late 1800s, however, a Hebrew manuscript of the whole OT, now preserved in the National Library of Russia in Leningrad and referred to as the Leningrad Codex (a codex is in handwritten book form rather than on a scroll), has become identified as (apparently) closely connected with the ben Asher manuscripts. As noted in its colophon, a scribe named Samuel ben Jacob wrote this codex in Cairo in 1008 or 1009. Jacob claims to have copied both the consonants and vowel pointing from the manuscripts of "the master Aaron ben Moses ben Asher . . . very accurately" (ibid.). Included in this complete eleventh-century AD Hebrew copy of the OT, of course, is the book of Isaiah. The Leningrad Codex was the primary textual basis for the third edition of *Biblia Hebraica* (*BHK*, 1937), for *Biblia Hebraica Stuttgartensia* (*BHS*, 1977), and for the presently ongoing *Biblia Hebraica Quinta* (*BHQ*).

Thus until the mid-twentieth century AD the Leningrad Codex was the earliest complete Hebrew copy of the book of Isaiah available to scholars and translators. In 1947, however, a complete scroll manuscript copy of Isaiah (1QIsa^a) was discovered in a cave at Qumran, determined to date from about 125 BC. Parts of an additional twenty manuscript copies of Isaiah were eventually discovered in other caves along the Dead Sea, written over the course of nearly two centuries (125 BC to AD 60). Other (nonbiblical) Dead Sea scrolls show Isaiah to be one of the most quoted biblical books; this, along with the discovery of fragments of five pesharim on Isaiah, highlights the high popularity and influential position of the book of Isaiah among those at Qumran (Abegg, Flint, and Ulrich 1999, 267-70). Pesharim (sg. pesher) are commentaries on the OT prophetical books and Psalms that view the prophecies contained in them as applying to or being fulfilled in the time of the commentator, that of the Roman Empire. The five Isaiah pesharim date from 100 BC to AD 70 and are numbered 4Q162-165 (Lim 2002, 27).

There are, of course, numerous variants in the Qumran Isaiah scrolls when compared with the MT; many modern-day scholars consider these variants to be "errors." Pulikottil, however, in a recent in-depth study of the complete Qumran Isaiah scroll 1QIsa^a, based on the American Schools of Oriental Research published photos, concludes that the Qumran scribes should be viewed as scholars working with the texts within the standards of their own times. As such, while indeed being copyists, they were also editors working with a biblical text that had not yet been standardized. Their omissions, additions, and changes were not due to sloppy, careless inattention to the text from which they were copying; rather, they were concerned with producing a *better* text through "harmonization," "explication," "modernization," and "contextual changes." They thus felt a freedom "to express their reading of the text in a way they thought appropriate" (2001, 202-3, 214).

Other early textual resources available to today's translators of the book of Isaiah are themselves translations: Greek Septuagint (LXX), Aramaic Targum Jonathan on the Prophets (Tg.), the Syriac Peshitta (SP), and the Latin Vulgate (Vg.).

E. Theological Themes in Chapters 1—39

1. Yahweh as the Holy One of Israel

According to Isaiah's personal report in ch 6 ("I saw," "I cried," "I heard," "I said" [vv 1, 5, 8, 11]), while one day routinely worshipping in the Jerusalem temple, during an unexpected visionary experience of God's overwhelming presence, seraphim were calling out, "Holy, holy, holy is the LORD Almighty" (or **Yahweh Sebaoth** [v 3]). From that experience, Isaiah came to a new and profound understanding of the holiness of Yahweh. Goldingay suggests that "the whole book [of Isaiah] works out the implications of that vision" in the "awareness that Yahweh is the Holy One of Israel" (2001, 7-8).

At both the opening and closing of the canonical Isaianic message, there is a play on the term "know" (from *yd'*) in association with Yahweh's title "the Holy One of Israel" (*qĕdôš yiśrā'ēl*). The message opens with God's people having "forsaken the LORD" and having "spurned the Holy One of Israel" (1:4; 5:24), and thus they no longer "know" him (1:3; 5:19). "Zion" (= Jerusalem), representing the people of God, is left isolated, sick and helpless in the middle of a desolated and devastated kingdom of Judah (1:7-8). In the conclusion of the canonical Isaianic message, however, we see a repentant "Zion"/"Jacob," to which "Redeemer" (*gô'ēl*; there is no article in the Hebrew) comes (59:20), and, as "the Holy One of Israel," endows it "with splendor" (or **beauty**) (60:9). To (re)splendored "Zion," "nations," "kings," "foreigners," and "oppressors"

(60:3, 10, 14), all representing past enemies of God's people, now are coming **because of the reputation of Yahweh** (*lĕšēm yhwh*, lit. *for the name of Yahweh*). And, they come bringing the "children" of God's people born in exile throughout the Diaspora (60:9). This great migration to Zion will be the work of Yahweh! As they see this, no longer will God's people reject him (as they were doing in ch 1), but, says God, "you will know that I, the LORD, am your Savior, your Redeemer, the Mighty One of Jacob" (60:16). Here, we hear an echo of Yahweh's long ago words to Moses and the Israelites at the time of his promise to bring them out of Egypt and into the land of Canaan: "I will redeem you with an outstretched arm . . . Then you will know that I am the LORD your God" (Exod 6:6-7).

Of the twenty-seven occurrences of the title "the Holy One of Israel" throughout the canonical book of Isaiah, thirteen occur in Isa 1—39. Those in 1:4; 5:19, 24 are noted above. In 10:17, we find a variation: "The Light of Israel . . . their Holy One," as a "fire," burns up the Assyrian army "in a single day." In 10:20, when "the remnant of Israel" (the northern kingdom) emerges from its 722 BC Assyrian devastation, it "will truly rely on the LORD, the Holy One of Israel." In 12:6, Yahweh's greatness as "the Holy One of Israel" is cause for the "people of Zion" to "shout aloud and sing for joy." In 17:7, **humanity** (*hā'ādām*) recognizes "the Holy One of Israel" as "their Maker," turning away from the worship of "the work of their hands" (17:8). In 29:19-20, "the humble" and "the needy" "rejoice in the Holy One of Israel," who vanquishes "the ruthless" and "the mockers." In 30:10-13, because Judah's "seers" and "prophets" reject "the Holy One of Israel," their judgment comes "suddenly, in an instant." In 31:1, a "Woe" is pronounced against Judah's leaders, who do not seek the help of "the Holy One of Israel," but "go down to Egypt for help" against the Assyrians. Lastly, Assyrian Sennacherib, having "ridiculed and blasphemed . . . the Holy One of Israel" (37:23), is led away with Yahweh's "hook" in his "nose" and "bit" in his "mouth," like a work animal or a slave fully subject to the wishes of a master (37:29).

2. Yahweh as Savior, the One Who Saves, Who Brings Salvation

The first occurrence of Yahweh as "Savior" (*môšîa'*) occurs in relation to "the Egyptians" (19:16-25). While it is not clear whether it is Yahweh himself or one whom he sends who is "savior," "defender," and the one who "will rescue them" (v 20), it is through this act of saving that a reciprocal knowing results: "The LORD will make himself known [from *yd'*] to the Egyptians, and in that day they will acknowledge [from *yd'*] the LORD" (v 21). Here is an echo of Yahweh's earlier promise that the Egyptians and/or Pharaoh "will know" him through his act of saving Israel (Exod 7:5, 17; 8:10, 22; 9:14; 14:4, 18).

In Isa 25:8-9, in conjunction with God's promise that he "will swallow up death forever" (v 8), Israel declares its trust "in him" because "he saved us," and invites the whole community to "rejoice and be glad in his salvation" (v 9). The inhabitants of "Zion"/"Jerusalem" (33:20) look to Yahweh as their "judge," "lawgiver" and "king," and the one "who will save us" (v 22). The promise of God's salvation strengthens "those with fearful hearts" (35:4). In the face of Assyrian Sennacherib's threat against Jerusalem, King Hezekiah prays, "LORD our God, deliver us [*hôšî'ēnû*, **save us**, from *yš'*] from his hand, so that all the kingdoms of the earth may know that you, LORD, are the only God" (37:20). Thus, in chs 1—39 both Israelites and non-Israelites come to "know" Yahweh through his gracious acts of salvation.

3. Yahweh as Sovereign

God's sovereignty over nations, peoples, and individuals is recognized in the many occurrences of the title "Adonai" (*'ădōnāy*) throughout chs 1—39 in statements both about him and in direct address to him. This title is translated by the NIV most commonly as "Lord" (as opposed to "LORD" for Yahweh), but four times in chs 1—39 as "Sovereign" (fourteen times in chs 40—66). "Sovereign" implies authority over something or someone. *'Ădōnāy*, "Sovereign," often occurs alone, and sometimes in the fuller title *'ădōnāy yhwh ṣĕbā'ôt*, **Sovereign Yahweh of Armies/Hosts**.

In the account of his transforming encounter with God in the Jerusalem temple (ch 6), Isaiah speaks of God only one time as **the King, Yahweh Sebaoth** (*hammelek yhwh ṣĕbā'ôt* [v 5]), once **about** and twice **to** God as **the Sovereign One** (*'ădōnāy*): I saw the **Sovereign One** (v 1); I heard the voice of the **Sovereign One** (v 8); then I said, "For how long, **O Sovereign One**?" (v 11). In this title, Isaiah acknowledges God's absolute authority, not only over human history and nations, but also over himself, individually, as God's servant. And no matter how small or great an influence a servant may have in the larger scheme of history, that servant must obey and speak only for his or her **Sovereign**.

The following texts illustrate some examples of God's acts of sovereignty in chs 1—39:

In 7:7 Isaiah demonstrates Yahweh's sovereignty over the outcome of the course of human events. The prophet says that the Israelite-Syrian alliance intended to overthrow and replace Judah's reigning king (Ahaz) with one (Tabeel) favorable to joining their rebellion against Assyria's encroachment (of 735-733 BC) is not to be feared: "Sovereign LORD says, 'It [i.e., the alliance] will not **stand**, it [i.e., the overthrow] will not happen.'"

In 7:14 and 7:20, during the Israelite-Syrian threat of 734 BC, it is "Sovereign" who gives King Ahaz the "sign" of "Immanuel" as encouragement to trust him, but it is also "Sovereign" who warns Ahaz that if he fails to trust, then the "king of Assyria" will soon fall upon him like a **hired razor**.

In 25:6-8, Isaiah affirms Yahweh's sovereignty over "death," which all humans face. One of the gifts offered humankind at the great "feast" that **Yahweh Sebaoth** prepares at the end of time is the abolishment of death: ***Sovereign Yahweh will swallow up death forever, and he will wipe away tears from all faces***.

In 38:14 and 16, Hezekiah, in the distress of his illness, cries out to **Sovereign**: "**O Sovereign**, come to my aid," and then, "**O Sovereign**, . . . You restored me to health and let me live." Here, Hezekiah affirms Israel's understanding that Yahweh's sovereignty extends over the realm of human illness, even to the point of delaying death.

4. Yahweh and the Nations

In his prayer to "LORD Almighty, the God of Israel," requesting deliverance from Sennacherib's planned attack against Jerusalem (37:14-20), King Hezekiah theologically links Yahweh's lordship "over all the kingdoms of the earth" with his creatorship of "heaven and earth" (v 16). This theological connection is rooted in Gen 1—11. Thus all nations (*gôyim*) and peoples (*'ammîm*) of the earth are Yahweh's subjects. The nations, however, have historically rejected their status as Yahweh's subjects.

Throughout the book of Isaiah, Yahweh is involved with the nations and peoples of the earth: he judges them and uses them as his agents to judge Israel and Judah; ultimately, however, he receives them back to himself. Bookending the whole of canonical Isaiah are the "nations." In 2:2-3, pointing to the distant future ("in the last days"), the "nations" and "peoples" are not in rebellion, but of their own volition are streaming "up to the mountain of the LORD." There, they seek to learn Yahweh's "ways" (*děrākîm*), "law" (*tôrâ*), and "word" (*dābār*). In 66:18-20, the "nations and languages" are gathered to Yahweh's "holy mountain in Jerusalem," there to both see Yahweh's "glory" and to make it known "among the nations."

Throughout chs 1—39 the nations are dealt with a number of times. In 10:5-34, ***the Sovereign Yahweh Sebaoth*** (*hē'ādôn yhwh ṣěbā'ôt*) shows himself sovereign over arrogant Assyria. In 11:10-16, the "nations" no longer are allowed to retain possession of "the exiles of Israel"/"the scattered people of Judah," as Yahweh brings them home on a specially constructed "highway." In 12:4-5, that which Yahweh "has done" for his people will be made "known among the nations." In 13:1—14:27, Yahweh gathers his worldwide army to overthrow both Assyria and Babylon. In 19:23-25, a metaphorical "highway" will connect the two nations of "Egypt" and "Assyria," facilitating these historical enemies as they together worship Israel's God. And, what is most shocking is that **Yahweh Sebaoth**, in forgiveness and acceptance, endows these two arrogant mockers of Israel's God with the loving titles "my people" and "my handiwork," titles that one expects to be applied only to Israel: "Egypt my people, Assyria my handiwork."

F. The Structure of Chapters 1—39

This commentary divides chs 1—39 into three parts:
1. JUDAH'S SICKNESS AND ITS CAUSES; THE SYRIAN-ISRAELITE THREAT (chs 1—12). *Chapters 1—12* are divided into two units: chs 1—5 and 7—12.
   a. *The focus of chs 1—5* is on Zion/Jerusalem and Judah, in which Jerusalem is depicted as a city of injustice and unrighteousness, upon which Yahweh is about to bring judgment (chs 1—2). Yet there is hope for future restoration and salvation (chs 3—5).
   b. *The focus of chs 6—12* is upon Isaiah's prophetic ministry during the latter part of the eighth century BC. This unit begins with Isaiah in the Jerusalem temple, with his spiritual eyes open to perceive, encountering the holiness of God in a way he had never before experienced. The unit further highlights Isaiah's prophetic activity in this period as adviser to King Ahaz during a Syrian-Israelite threat against Judah/Jerusalem. He urges the king to fully trust Yahweh for protection, rather than calling upon Assyria for assistance. Alas! King Ahaz did not heed Isaiah's advice. In this unit, one of Isaiah's primary prophetic viewpoints is that Yahweh will have the last word against arrogant Assyria, and, eventually he will bring about its total destruction.
2. YAHWEH, SOVEREIGN OF ALL NATIONS (chs 13—27). *Chapters 13—27* are divided into two units: chs 13—23 and 24—27.
   a. *The focus of chs 13—23* is upon Yahweh's sovereignty over the nations of the world. The unit names prophetic oracles specifically concerning Babylon, Assyria, Philistia, Moab, Damascus, Cush, Egypt, and Tyre. The essence of Isaiah's prophetic word to Judah/Jerusalem is that the kingdoms/nations of this world are transient and cannot be trusted; Judah's only sure trust is in Yahweh, who is the Creator of all kingdoms, peoples, and nations.
   b. *The focus of chs 24-27* is upon Yahweh Sebaoth's ultimate triumph over the whole earth, and his future "eschatological" reign on/from Mount Zion. There, Yahweh prepares a great banquet; to this banquet Yahweh invites all peoples of the earth, including his own scattered people, which he gathers from all areas of their diaspora. One of the prime benefits offered to humankind at this banquet will be the abolishment of death.

3. A RIGHTEOUS KING WILL REIGN (chs 28—39). *Chapters 28—39 are divided into four units:* ch 28—33, 34—35, 36—37, and 38—39.
   a. *The focus of chs 28—33* is upon the crucial question that Yahweh's prophet Isaiah asks of Judah's leaders and of King Hezekiah: In whom will you place your trust for Jerusalem's deliverance from Assyrian king Sennacherib's 701 BC threat of siege and attack? Will your trust be in Yahweh or in the vagaries of possible Egyptian military help? Hezekiah's answer will be revealed in chs 36—37.
   b. *The focus of chs 34—35* is upon a contrastive eschatological imagery: Edom, representing the earth's nations, is transformed into a wasteland with no human inhabitant, while Judah's wilderness is transformed into a highly productive garden.
   c. *The focus of chs 36—37* is upon Assyrian king Sennacherib's 701 BC threat of attack against Jerusalem. It is in this unit that one learns of King Hezekiah's decision to heed Prophet Isaiah's earlier counsel: he chooses to fully trust in Yahweh. It is here also that one learns of Yahweh's response to Hezekiah's trust in miraculously delivering the city in one night.
   d. *The focus of chs 38—39* is upon a near-death sickness of King Hezekiah and his recovery as a gift from Yahweh in response to his trust. A "postscript" follow-up visit to Hezekiah by a group of messengers sent from the king of Babylon (who had heard of Hezekiah's illness) is the final piece in this first "book." Isaiah personally appears here for the last time, giving King Hezekiah a prediction concerning the future of some of his offspring who will be taken to Babylon to serve as eunuchs (39:7). This prediction carries hints of Judah's future exile to Babylon (Nebuchadnezzar's deportations of 597 and 587 BC). The reader is thus prepared for the 160 or so year jump into the future to ca. 539/538 BC, the timeline with which ch 40 opens with its word of comfort and hope: that God/Sovereign Yahweh is about to come to Jerusalem bringing his exiled people home from their Babylonian exile (40:1, 10).

COMMENTARY

I. JUDAH'S SICKNESS AND ITS CAUSES; THE SYRIAN-ISRAELITE THREAT: 1:1—12:6

Overview

Historical references are lacking in chs 1—5. Only Zion, Judah, and Israel are mentioned by name (1:4, 8; 2:1, 3; 3:1, 8, 16, 17, 26; 4:3, 4, 5; 5:3, 7, 19, 24). At the very outset, Isaiah presents Judah as morally sick nearly unto death, with God's people in a state of spiritual rebellion, as children against a parent. Jerusalem has become a city of injustice and unrighteousness (chs 1—2). Yahweh is presented as poised to bring judgment upon his beloved city and people, while speaking of the "day *of* the Branch of **Yahweh**" (4:2) as a hope for future restoration and salvation (chs 3—5).

Chapters 6—12 give significantly more historical data. Chapter 6 opens with Isaiah's spiritually transforming experience with an encounter with the holiness of Yahweh in the temple. Chapters 7—12 present Isaiah's prophetic activity during the Syrian-Israelite threat against Judah during the latter third of the eighth century BC. Also included are Isaiah's prophecies concerning Yahweh's coming judgment upon and future destruction of Assyria, the imperial power broker of Isaiah's world.

A. A People in Rebellion (1:1-31)

BEHIND THE TEXT

Chapter 1 is a composite of units (v 1, vv 2-9, 10-17, 18-20, 21-26 and 27-31), each possibly spoken or written independently and at differing times. Verses 2-31, however, now together function as an introduction to the whole of the book of Isaiah.

The focus of vv 2-31 is upon "our God" (*ĕlohēnû* [v 10]). Other names/titles, however, occur: "the LORD" (*yhwh* [vv 2, 4, 9, 11, 18, 20, 28]), "the Lord" (*hā'ādôn* [v 24]), "the Holy One of Israel" (*qĕdôš yiśrā'ē* [v 4]), "the LORD Almighty" (*yhwh ṣĕbā'ôt* [vv 9, 24]), and "the Mighty One of Israel" (*'ăbîr yiśrā'ēl* [v 24]). It is against God that his "children . . . have rebelled" (v 2), whose sins have brought isolation and desolation upon Zion (v 8). It is God who calls his children to "stop doing wrong" (v 16) so that he might make their "sins [though] like scarlet, . . . white as snow" (v 18). It is God who invites his children through repentance into a salvation that enables God to restore Zion to faithfulness, filled with "justice" and "righteousness" (v 27).

IN THE TEXT

1. Superscription (1:1)

■ 1 **The vision concerning Judah and Jerusalem that Isaiah son of Amoz saw** serves as a superscription to what follows. It appears to intend that the reader understand that the contents of the entire scroll in some way relate to **the vision . . . that Isaiah son of Amoz** envisioned in the days of the **kings of Judah**.

Vision (*ḥăzôn*, from *ḥāzâ*) commonly describes seeing with the physical eyes but also denotes insight perceived within one's inner being. Thus it suggests that prophets see, with God-opened eyes, what others do not see. Here, it encompasses the literary materials in the entire sixty-six chapters, which find their roots in and are developed from the vision of **Isaiah** of Jerusalem for **Judah and Jerusalem** (Watts 2005, 7; Childs 2001, 11). The prophet's name, **Isaiah** (*yĕša'yāhû*), means "Yahweh saves/has saved") and thus points to an essential characteristic of God, and to a central theme of this whole book (compare 25:9; 33:22; 35:4; 37:20, 35; 38:20; 43:12; 45:17, 22; 49:25; 51:5; 59:1; 61:10; 62:11; 63:1).

We know nothing of Isaiah outside of this book (and 2 Kgs 18—20, a parallel of Isa 36—39). Hebrews 11:37 speaks of some of the OT faithful being "sawed in two," most likely reflecting a tradition appearing in the apocryphal *Ascension of Isaiah* (possibly dating to AD 88-100), that Isaiah was martyred in this manner under King Manasseh (Charles 1900, lxxi, 40-42).

Concerning Judah and Jerusalem indicates the subject of this book. Before the Assyrian capture of Samaria (722 BC), Isaiah also spoke a prophetic warning to the northern kingdom. See, e.g., 9:8-21 [7-20 HB], where they are addressed variously as Ephraim, Samaria, and Israel. **Judah and Jerusalem**, as a word pair, serve as a generic designation for the sacred community, yet are also physical, geographical locations, toward which the prophecy of this book is directed. Both Yahweh's people and Yahweh's land/city will be the recipients of his salvation.

2. No Justice in Zion (1:2-31)

■ **2-3** Isaiah's prophecy opens with what appears to be a simulated court scene. Yahweh is both accuser and judge, his rebellious people are the defendants, "heavens" and "earth" are the witnesses.

Moses had summoned **heavens** and **earth** (v 2) to witness Yahweh's covenant agreement with Israel (Deut 4:26; 30:19; 31:28; 32:1). Isaiah now calls them to witness the violation of that covenant: the **children** have **rebelled** against the parent. **My people** (*'ammî* [Isa 1:3]) recalls Yahweh's covenant declaration at Sinai: they would "know" him because he had delivered them from Egyptian bondage (Exod 6:7). **Rebelled** (*pāša'*) is to willfully turn away from all familial ties; it is as if Israel is saying to God that we are no longer your children; we disavow your parenthood (compare Isa 30:9). Moreover, **Israel does not know** (*lo' yāda'* [1:3], a willful rejection of Yahweh's deliverance and continuing care. In contrast, the **ox** and the **donkey**, domestic work animals, each **knows** (*yāda'*), and thus obeys, its **master** (compare Jer 8:7).

■ **4** *Alas* [*hôy*] **sinful nation** accentuates the grief-stricken sense of loss expressed in this verse (Oswalt 1986, 87; compare KJV, NKJV, NASB). Yahweh addresses Israel as **nation** (*gôy*), **people** (*'am*), and **children** (*bānîm*). **Children** signals that those in rebellion against Yahweh (Isa 1:2) are still the object of accusation. The pairing of **nation** and **people** implies that both the larger national corporate entity, with its leaders ("rulers" [vv 10, 23]; "leaders" and "rulers" [v 26]), and the citizens of Israel individually, are equally guilty (Williamson 2007, 41) of the sin of having **forsaken Yahweh** and having **spurned the Holy One of Israel**.

Four terms describe the loss of relationship between Yahweh the parent and Israel.

Sinful (*ḥōṭē'*, from *ḥāṭā'*): "to miss (a mark), fall short, err." God's people are a **sinful** [lit. "sinning"] **nation**, habitually failing to do what is right. The OT contexts of the use of this term indicate that the "error" is not against specific laws but against failure to act within the norms of justice, resulting in injuries to relationships within the community, both to persons and to God (Wildberger 1991, 22; Jenni and Westermann 1997, 1:409).

Guilt (*'āwōn*, from *'āwâ*): "to be perverted, bend, grow crooked, turn aside, twist." It points to one's defective inner character, often describing the state/standing of a person before the authority against whom one has sinned (Ps 90:7-8). God's **people** have twisted God's way to their own way: their **guilt is great**.

Evildoers (*mere'îm*) are those who perpetrate unacceptable actions that bring harm to the life of one's community (VanGemeren 1997, 3:1154). Such an evil action, once perpetrated, becomes a concrete reality (Jenni and Westermann 1997, 3:1252), taking on a life of its own, continuing its harmful effects throughout the community.

Yahweh's **children** are **given to corruption** (*mašḥîṭîm*, from *šāḥat* means "to become corrupt, spoil, ruin, break"); corruption indicates a continual breaking of and from the ways of the parent. Moses had likewise accused the Israelites of being "corrupt" (*šiḥēt*) toward Yahweh, and of being "not his children" (Deut 32:5).

Isaiah now defines the sin that has wrought such disruption in the whole community of Yahweh's people: they have **forsaken** [*'āzab*] **Yahweh** and **spurned** [*nā'aṣ*] **the Holy One of Israel**. Though *'āzab* occasionally is used for divorce (e.g., Isa 54:6; 60:15), its majority occurrences are theological, in the context of the covenant tradition (Jenni and Westermann 1997, 2:868) (compare Deut 29:25 [24 HB]; 31:16-18; Jer 1:16; 2:13, 17, 19; 5:7). *Nā'aṣ* implies a turning away from someone or something, so that one's back is toward that someone or something. Thus his beloved children have utterly rejected their God, the **Holy One of Israel**.

The Holy One of Israel

The title "the Holy One of Israel" occurs twenty-seven times in the book of Isaiah. It speaks of a God who, in his character, is morally and ethically pure. As Creator he is the absolute contrast of his created humanity whose character begets lying, stealing, and murder (Oswalt 1986, 33). Concretely, God's holiness is expressed in his past actions on behalf of his people when he listened to their cry and redeemed them out of their Egyptian bondage (Exod 2:23-25; 14:30-31). His active holiness is reflected/echoed in the title of Lev 19, "Be holy because I, the LORD your God, am holy" (v 2). This title/command is followed by a sample listing of how his people are to live out holiness in everyday life as a reflection of his holiness. Fourteen times the rationale given for God's people to act in holiness as God acts in holiness is, "I am the LORD/I am the LORD your God," and the fifteenth time, "I am the LORD your God, who brought you out of Egypt" (v 36). So, God's holiness is seen in his act of redemption. It is this "living God" (Isa 37:4, 17) and his holiness that his people have rejected, turning their backs, now to face "gods [of] . . . wood and stone, fashioned by human hands" (v 19), gods that do not "answer [and] cannot save them from their troubles" (46:7).

■ **5-6** Yahweh's children have persisted in **rebellion** (*sārâ* [v 5], from *sûr*, meaning "to turn aside, defect," and, theologically, "to apostatize"). It is the technical term for enticing someone to defect from the way of life commanded by Yahweh, who had redeemed them from Egyptian slavery (Deut 13:5 [6 HB]). Such apostasy has resulted in suffering the consequence of metaphorical bodily illness, resulting from being repeatedly **beaten** from **foot** (Isa 1:6) to **head**. The wounds are unattended, **open**, no soothing **olive oil** administered, not **bandaged** (compare Deut 27—30 for the consequences of turning away from Yahweh's commandments).

■ **7-8** The imagery now changes to depict a **desolate** (*šmmh* [v 7]) land: **cities burned, . . . fields . . . stripped by foreigners**, a kingdom **laid waste . . . by strangers**, consequences of rebellion/apostasy. Isaiah's description finds correspondence in the context of Yahweh's promises of blessings and threats of curses in the covenant tradition: if they obey/worship Yahweh, then he will drive out the inhabitants of the land, though not all at once, lest the land become "desolate" (*šmmh* [Exod 23:29]), but if they do not listen to Yahweh, then their land will be "laid waste" (*šmmh* [Lev 26:33]). The threat of **foreigners** and **strangers** stripping their fields and depriving them of eating the produce of their seed crops and vineyards is also rooted in the covenant tradition (Lev 26:16; Deut 28:30-33).

Daughter Zion (*bat ṣiyôn* [v 8]) is Jerusalem, representing Yahweh's beloved but rebellious children. Jerusalem now stands unprotected, like a watchman's **shelter** or **hut** in the middle of a **vineyard** or **cucumber field**, highlighting its isolation.

The imagery of vv 7-8 surely does figuratively depict Judah's spiritual condition (Oswalt 1986, 90-91), but there is also historical reality underlying this description when viewed in the context of Sennacherib's 701 BC invasion. In his account of this campaign into Palestine, Sennacherib states that he sieged and conquered forty-six of Hezekiah's walled cities and numerous villages. From them he deported 200,150 inhabitants (Pritchard 1969, 288). Thus Jerusalem (**Zion**) alone remained, **like a city under siege**.

■ **9** Isaiah draws on the historical memory of **Sodom** and **Gomorrah**, which, though not overthrown in war, were cities upon which the judgment of ***Yahweh Sebaoth*** fell (compare Gen 19). In comparison, Yahweh's present judgment has allowed Zion more **survivors**.

Yahweh Sebaoth/The Lord Almighty

Yahweh Sebaoth (*yhwh ṣĕbā'ôt*) occurs 267 times in the OT (62 times in Isaiah; only in Jeremiah is the title used more often), and a longer form (*yhwh 'ĕlōhê ṣĕbā'ôt*, **Yahweh God Sebaoth**) 18 times (e.g., Amos 3:13). Prophet Micaiah sees the "multitudes of heaven" assembled around Yahweh's heavenly throne (1 Kgs 22:19); Joshua came face-to-face with the "commander of the army [*ṣĕbā'*] of **Yahweh**" (Josh 5:14); the psalmist addresses Yahweh's "heavenly hosts, you his servants who do his will" (Ps 103:21), who are in parallel with "you his angels, you mighty ones who do his bidding" (v 20). This title, then, ascribed to Yahweh authority over all heavenly beings. Yet his authority extended also to Israel's armies, for David came against Goliath "in the name of **Yahweh Sebaoth**, the God of the armies of Israel" (1 Sam 17:45).

■ **10** In Isa 1:2 "hear"/"listen" was an invitation to heaven and earth to participate as witnesses to Yahweh's charge against his children; now, **hear/listen** constitute a command that Jerusalem's **rulers** and **people** pay attention: they are about to be confronted with the **word** [*dābar*] **of Yahweh** and the **instruction** [*tôrâ*] **of our God**. The metaphorical reference to **Sodom** and **Gomorrah** makes clear that, though the sin of Yahweh's children may not be the same as that of those ancient cities, the destructive judgment that fell on those cities is just as likely to fall upon them in their own time.

The gravity of their sin is the rejection of Yahweh's **instruction** (*tôrâ*), his divine revelation through wisdom instruction, priestly teaching, and prophetic word. If heeded, this Torah would give his children knowledge for life lived to the full under the blessings of the Father. The covenant encompasses all of Torah, and at the center of Torah is justice extended downward from the rulers to the people, and among the people outwardly to one's neighbors. And this is precisely the point of this chapter: Jerusalem/Zion, once the "faithful city . . . once . . . full of justice" (v 21), is now filled with all manner of injustice, both in attitude and action. Both rulers and people live in self-delusion, believing that multiple sacrifices and festivals will hide these acts of injustice from God.

■ **11-15** Not so! Your multiple **sacrifices, burnt offerings, fattened animals** (v 11), **meaningless offerings, incense** that is **detestable** (v 13), **appointed festivals** (v 14)—all these, declares Yahweh, give me **no pleasure** (v 11); yes, **I hate them**, the sheer multiplicity of them are **a burden to me** (v 14). I cannot even look at **your hands** (v 15), extended outward, palms turned upward, expectantly ready to receive my blessings. No, **I hide my eyes from you** [because] **your hands are full of blood**. Blood is *dāmîm* (pl.), the usual form in the context of violently shed blood (e.g., Gen 4:10; Exod 22:2), in contrast to *dām* (sg.), the blood of sacrifice.

Isaiah is associating these prayers with the actions of sacrifice that are taking place in the temple (Isa 1:11). Thus the **blood** on the **hands** (v 15) may be the actual blood of the just-sacrificed offering, reminding him of the figurative blood (guilt) on the hands of "murderers" now filling the once "faithful city" (v 21). In Israel's tradition, only one "who has clean hands and a pure heart" was to be allowed into Yahweh's "holy place" (Ps 24:3-4; Williamson 2007, 98).

■ **16-17** How, then, does one qualify to bring the mandatory sacrifices into the temple precincts, so that both offering and offerer are acceptable before the Lord? **Wash and make yourselves clean** (v 16), or "Wash, to be clean!" (Oswalt 1986, 98). This is not a cultic, ritualistic washing with water, but an ethical renewal, a repenting, a change of heart (compare David's request, Ps 51:2, 7, 10).

While it is God's grace that extends this washing, to receive God's grace the people must act. Note these three commands: **take your evil deeds out of my sight; stop doing wrong** (Isa 1:16); **learn to do right** (v 17). The causative verbal forms of the latter two indicate habitual practice: *stop practicing evil*; *learn to practice good*. In a deliberate act of the will, one must replace habitual ways of behaving in evil ways with habitual ways of doing good, which is critical to community life.

Habitually *seeking* justice (*diršû mišpāṭ*) must replace habitually practicing evil (v 17). The OT occurrences of the verbal root *šāpaṭ* that underlies the noun **justice** describe a wide range of actions, by both God (40 percent) and persons in authority (60 percent), so that order, or "justice," is preserved in society (VanGemeren 1997, 4:214). Isaiah gives a concrete example of habitual injustice that must be corrected: right is not on the side of the **fatherless** and the **widow** in the courts. Those who should be judging righteously, the "rulers," are taking "bribes" and "gifts" (v 23) to issue rulings against those who have no male to defend them. But God cares deeply for the fatherless and the widow, and he expects his people to mirror his character in their actions (Deut 10:17-19; 24:17-22). Job, highly placed in his community, is one who mirrored God's character in this area of justice (Job 29:12-14; 31:16-18, 21).

■ **18** The invitation, **Come now, let us settle the matter**, speaks of a God who does not stand aloof from his beloved (though rebellious) children, with words of condemnation only. No, he now graciously holds out the offer of forgiveness. **Sins** of **scarlet/red/crimson** (the color of blood-guilt, possibly an allusion to the bloody hands of Isa 1:15) imply that this very color has stained his children in their innermost beings. **Scarlet/crimson** was not a natural color, being made from a dye extracted from the eggs of the kermes worm (*coccus ilicis*). **Snow** and **wool**, however, are naturally **white** and represent what the inner nature of Yahweh's children will be after he has removed their sins and the stains of those sins (VanGemeren 1997, 4:300; Motyer 1993, 48). **Let us settle the matter** refers to the alternatives given in vv 19 and 20.

■ **19-20** Alternative one: if his children are **willing and obedient**, . . . **the land will continue to sustain them** in abundance (v 19). Alternative two: if they **resist and rebel**, extinction **by the sword** will be their lot (v 20). The choice is theirs. This choice must come from the heart, where "willingness" is born. Both attitude and act are in the choice: attitude determines the act. These two alternatives are rooted in the covenant tradition (compare Lev 26:3-26, esp. vv 3-5, 10: if "careful to obey," they will eat of the abundance of the land, and vv 23-25: if "hostile," the "sword" will "avenge the breaking of the covenant").

■ **21** Isaiah's deep sorrow and pathos concerning the breakdown of societal **justice** and **righteousness** in Yahweh's beloved city Zion (v 27) is signaled by the opening exclamation of this section: *'êkâ*, **Oh!** or **Alas!** Elsewhere, *'êkâ* occurs in the context of a lament over the death of a person, city, or kingdom (e.g., 2 Sam 1:19-27; Jer 9:19; 48:17; Lam 1:1; 2:1; 4:1-2). Here, Zion is not yet destroyed physically, but she is spiritually and morally dead, likened to a **prostitute**, one who has turned away from being **faithful** to her rightful husband. Earlier in this chapter, the people's turning to other deities/idols has been the focus of their rebellion against Yahweh. This turning away of Zion, which **once was full of justice**, this replacing of Yahweh with other deities has led to a gross absence of justice. Zion, the unfaithful city, no longer reflects the character of the God, whose daughter she claims to be. In fact, Isaiah characterizes those who perpetrate such unfaithfulness, such injustice, as **murderers** (from *rāṣaḥ*) or "assassins" (Watts 2005, 38). Here we see a violation of both halves of the Ten Commandments: spiritual harlotry ("You shall have no other gods before me" [Exod 20:3]) has led to gross violation of human rights within society ("You shall not murder [*rāṣaḥ*]" [Exod 20:13]). Although *rāṣaḥ* at times is used to describe the act of unpremeditated killing (e.g., Num 35; Deut 4:42; Josh 20), when used by the prophets and wisdom teachers, the concept of intentional, violent killing is in view (e.g., Job 24:14; Ps 94:6; Prov 22:13; Hos 6:9). Thus the term here in Isa 1:21 describes actions resulting from personal hatred and malice (Childs 1974, 420-21).

■ **22-23** The imagery of moral degeneration continues with the highlighting of the unexpected: **silver**, once pure, now is impure with the very **dross** from which it was purified; the **choice wine**, once processed and purified, has been **diluted with water** (v 22). These are imageries of the **rulers**, persons expected to dispense justice to all, especially to the **fatherless** and **widow**, those among the most defenseless in Israelite society (v 23). But, no, these rulers have become **rebels**, spurning the Lord's command to do justice (Exod 23:6, 8; Deut 16:19). The **rulers**, blinded by **bribes** and **gifts**, no longer know righteousness from unrighteousness, justice from injustice. The irony is that the unexpected (injustice) has become the expected; one cannot get justice in Jerusalem's legal system.

■ **24-28** Isaiah composites three divine titles for the supreme King who announces both judgment and restoration in Isa 1:24-28: ***the Sovereign One*** (*hā'ādôn*), **Yahweh Sebaoth** (*yhwh ṣĕbā'ôt*), and **the Mighty One of Israel** (*'ăbîr yiśrā'ēl* [v 24]). These three titles sum up who the Lord is: sovereign in status, omnipotent in power, and absolute ruler (Motyer 1993, 49).

The city's **leaders** (*šōpĕtîm*, ***judges***) and **rulers** (*yō'ĕṣîm*, ***counselors***) (v 26) were the king's appointees, the first to administer justice, the second to give political services; both have become the Lord's **foes/enemies** (v 24) through their immoral and unethical practices. As one who has absolute power, Yahweh may choose how he will respond to such blatant disregard for his Torah requirements (→ 1:10) of justice and righteousness (v 21). **I will turn my hand against** (v 25) indicates Yahweh's change from support to chastisement. But he chooses a twofold response: **I will . . . avenge** (v 24) and **I will restore** (v 26), an unexpected coupling, yet two sides of the same coin. Vengeance includes a renewed process of refining: to **purge away your dross** and **remove all your impurities** (v 25) draws us back to the imagery of v 22. Thus restoration of the moral and ethical life of Jerusalem **as in days of old** (v 26) is perhaps an allusion to an idealistic view of life under the rule of David (Williamson 2007, 145; Wildberger 1991, 70). This entails the removal of the rebellious "rulers" (v 23), replacing them with ***judges*** and ***counselors*** who will act within Yahweh's will.

God's process of vengeance and restoration will result in **Zion** becoming known as **the City of Righteousness, the Faithful City** (v 26). This will include both the preservation of the city's **penitent ones** (v 27) and the removal of those who persist in their sinning and do not repent (v 28). Note the Hebrew word order of v 28: **But a crushing** [*wěšeber*, Qal ptc.] **[*for*] rebels** [*pš'*] **and sinners** [*ḥṭ'*] **together, and those who forsake** [*'zb*] **Yahweh, they will perish** (*klh*, "to bring to a complete end," = the ultimate fate of the wicked). **Sinners** is a participle (*ḥaṭṭā'îm*, "continual sinning" [Gesenius 1910, 84be]), indicating their persistence in sinning. These three terms—**rebels, sinners,** and **forsake**—are an "echo" from 1:2-4, occurring in the same order, forming an inclusio to ch 1.

■ **29-30** These verses graphically illustrate the demise of those who persist in their sinning and thus have no part in the future of a redeemed Zion (Childs 2001, 23).

Isaiah mentions **sacred oaks in which** the people **have delighted** (v 29). Such "sacred" trees elsewhere are associated with illicit cult practice, often with sexual connotations (e.g., Isa 57:5; Jer 2:20; 3:13; Hos 4:12-13). These "sacred" trees may well have been various types of the "Asherah," living trees (not a "pole" as usually translated), representations of fertility goddesses, as seen in depictions from Egypt, Babylon, Mari, Canaan, and Phoenicia (Taylor 1995, 40-44). Making offerings to idols was also a part of what took place "under every spreading tree and every leafy oak" (Ezek 6:13). The prophets continuously condemned such in Israelite worship. Isaiah makes a play here on the word **chosen**: long before, Moses had reminded the people on the way to Canaan that Yahweh God has *chosen* them to be his treasured people (Deut 7:6); later, Joshua, upon the verge of settling the land, had challenged them to *choose* the

God whom they would serve (Josh 24:15), and they had sworn allegiance to Yahweh. Now, however, says Isaiah, it is **gardens that you have chosen** (Isa 1:29), gardens in which you offer sacrifices and burn incense (65:3). If these sacred trees and gardens are associated with the fertility cult of the Canaanite deities Baal and Ashtoreth, the participants in the rituals would have expected the blessing of increased fertility in children, livestock, and crops. But Isaiah's promise is that the result would be just the opposite: they would be **ashamed** and **disgraced**. Wildberger observes that, "one is put to shame when one is deceived by that in which one has trusted" (1991, 77). So, to trust in, to delight in the gods represented by the sacred trees and gardens, is to be deceived and to deceive oneself, and thus to dry up **like an oak with fading leaves, like a garden without water** (1:30). But note the contrast in Ps 1:3.

■ **31** A by-product of the deceit noted above is that the worshipper of the idols at the sacred trees and gardens believes himself to be a **mighty man**, when, in fact, he is nothing but **tinder**, or "lint," the chaff or outer covering of the flax fibers (the technical English term is "tow"), weak and unfit for spinning, but highly flammable. Thus both the idol worshipper and **his work** (word, wealth, and worship practices) become the **spark** "which sets ablaze the whole rotten system" (Williamson 2007, 162), and there will be **no one to quench the fire** of Yahweh's anger.

FROM THE TEXT

The court scene in this chapter conveys the message that breaking the covenant with God is a serious offense, an act that would compel God to take action against those who are engaged in covenant breaking activities. The text indicates that our rejection of God's love, his parental love for his children, is a clear display of our rebellious attitude toward his authority and our decision to break off any relationship with him. Our rebellion against God affects all areas of life, society, and even future generations. The text also reminds us that if the people of God do not deal with sin in their personal and corporate life, it can become a habitual way of life. God's judgment on sinners is a reality in the text; the text, however, also makes clear that the tension between God's judgment and his will is to show grace to the sinner. The hope for Judah's future in the text and for our sinful world is in God's commitment to be a gracious God (v 9). Even in judgment, he shows mercy. In this text as well as in the rest of the narrative of Scripture, judgment is not God's last word. Paul makes it clear when he states, "But God demonstrates his own love for us in this: While we were still sinners, Christ died for us" (Rom 5:8).

The central focus of Isa 1:2-31 is whether or not those in positions of political and judicial power in Judah generally, and in Jerusalem in particular (rulers/judges/counselors), can be held accountable for gross breach of the covenant with God, especially injustice toward the defenseless widow and orphan. And, can they successfully hide this breach behind blatant and overzealous acts of sacrifice, offerings and worship?

The prophetic response is that, on the one hand, yes, under the terms of the covenant between Yahweh and his children, they can and are held responsible and are roundly condemned for receiving bribes and gifts from those who accuse the poor in court. In so doing, in the sentiments of Prophet Amos' earlier condemnation, they are selling out the righteous innocent for the mere price of "a pair of sandals" (Amos 2:6) and thus are depriving the poor of receiving "justice in the courts" (5:12).

The prophetic response, on the other hand, is that, no, they cannot hide behind the appearance of their religiosity. The outward shell is of no value without a solid inner core of God's grace and love of justice that values all persons in society as full members of God's family, each entitled to just and righteous treatment. Isaiah here is also one with his predecessor Amos, through whose mouth Yahweh expressed his hatred for their religious feasts and assemblies, his nonacceptance of their burnt, grain, and fellowship offerings, and his refusal to any longer listen to their singing and harp playing. In the place of all this empty show of piety Yahweh demanded that, "justice roll on like a river, righteousness like a never-failing stream" (5:21-24).

So, what can be done? There can be no remedy except a radical intervention: Yahweh, himself, "the Mighty One of Israel" (Isa 1:24), will remove the unjust officials, replacing them with judges and counselors who know and do justice. And thus Jerusalem will be redeemed (v 27).

But, how can such a turnaround be effected? Does such justice and righteousness come only from within repentant hearts? Or does it come only from God? Oswalt suggests that, from the broad context of Isaiah, it is both: it is as God, who "is the source of all righteousness and justice," acts, and as human beings choose "to do what God makes possible," that such a restoration can be made possible (1986, 110; compare Isa 1:25-26; 33:5; 51:4-5; 53:11; 56:1).

B. A People Cleansed (2:1—4:6)

A superscription introduces chs 2—4: "what Isaiah . . . saw concerning Judah and Jerusalem" (2:1; compare 1:1). The text moves immediately to a depiction of the temple in a distant future, established on "the mountain of **Yahweh**" (2:2-4), from which Yahweh is the supreme judge for all peoples. It moves then to a radical cleansing of the city of Jerusalem and its inhabitants (chs 3—4). The unit concludes with an appeal to the wilderness tradition: the "cloud of smoke," the "flaming fire," and "the glory" (of Yahweh) now reside on "Mount Zion," to provide "shelter and shade," a "refuge and hiding place"

(4:5-6), presumably for those who gather at the temple to which "all nations will stream" (2:2).

IN THE TEXT

1. Superscription (2:1)

■ 1 *The word/message* [*haddābār*], **which** Isaiah son of Amoz saw is for Judah and Jerusalem, from the same prophet of the previous chapter, who speaks from insights gained through God-opened eyes.

2. The Mountain of Yahweh (2:2-5)

■ 2 Verses 2-5 are nearly word for word identical with Mic 4:1-3. Most likely each prophet drew independently from a source held commonly by both priestly and prophetic communities (Oswalt 1986, 115). *The message* is both about a future and the now: there will come a time, in the distant future, when the Lord will bring peace among the nations, abolishing war; in the now his people are to live in light of that expectation.

Recent scholarship has suggested the eighth century BC rise of the Assyrian Empire as a possible background of Isaiah's declaration that it is Yahweh whom all nations will eventually recognize as universally sovereign. The Assyrian ideological propaganda was that their deity Ashur's universal sovereignty gave Assyria power unlimited by geographic boundaries, and that the Assyrian Empire would last forever (Aster 2007, 253). The Assyrian kings, in their records, claim kingship of the whole world, ascribing their invincible power to the Assyrian deities, especially to Ashur.

Isaiah would be the first of the OT prophets to contend with the "phenomenon of 'one empire'" and also was knowledgeable of the coming transfer of that imperial power to Assyria's "destroyer and successor, Babylon" (compare Isa 39:5-7; Artzi 2008, 430). Nearly two centuries later, during the rule of the Persian Empire, Babylon's successor, Zechariah would prophesy that in a distant future Yahweh will be the supreme and only king over the entire earth, and it will be his name only, Yahweh, which will be recognized (14:9). And in defiance of the Persian rulers, who also declared themselves to be "great kings," Malachi will speak as Yahweh's mouthpiece, "'I am a great king,' says the LORD Almighty, 'and my name is to be feared among the nations'" (1:14).

The Boasts of the Assyrian Kings

Some examples of the Assyrian kings' boasts are: "Adad-nirari [reigned 810-783 BC], great king, legitimate king, king of the world, king of Assyria . . . whom Ashur . . . had chosen . . . whose throne they established firmly; . . . who has made submit to his feet the princes within the four rims of the earth" (Pritchard 1969, 281); "Sennacherib [reigned 704-681 BC], king of the world, king of Assyria" (ibid., 288); "Esarhaddon [reigned 680-669 BC], great king, legitimate king,

king of the world, king of Assyria . . . king of the four rims (of the earth)" (ibid., 289). Note also that, in the 701 BC Assyrian invasion of Judea and subsequent siege of Jerusalem, the Assyrian field commander referred to Sennacherib as "the great king, the king of Assyria" (Isa 36:4, 13) and mockingly declared that in view of the inability of any conquered nation's god to deliver its land from "the hand of the king of Assyria," Yahweh, too, would be unable to "deliver Jerusalem from [his] hand" (36:18-20).

In the political reality of Isaiah's time, **all nations** were subjected to the imperial power of Assyria and its deity Ashur, centered in Nineveh. Isaiah is aware that this power will be passed to another imperial power, centered in Babylon. And though Isaiah makes no mention of the imperial powers beyond Babylon, the book of Daniel expresses the biblical awareness that imperial powers would continue to follow each other. Yet, **in the last days** (*bĕ'aḥărit hayyāmîm*), that is, at some time in the distant future, when Assyria and all empires that follow have disappeared, the **nations** will realize the sham of the claims of these "world" powers and turn to the only remaining **established power, the mountain of *Yahweh's* temple**; it is from here that Yahweh will make himself known to the nations of the world.

■ **3 Many peoples** encourage one another to embark upon pilgrimage, saying, **Let us go up to the mountain of *Yahweh*, to the temple of the God of Jacob.** Go up (*'ālâ*) is the usual term for pilgrimage to the sanctuary (e.g., Ps 122:4). There is purpose in this pilgrimage: to receive instruction in **his ways**, and having received instruction, to **walk in his paths**. Why? Because it is **from Zion** that Yahweh's **word** (*dābār*) and **law** [*tôrâ*] **will go out**. This is Yahweh's "word" and "law" that his beloved "children" rejected in the previous chapter (Isa 1:4, 10), now embraced by "the nations" (v 4).

■ **4** True world peace is the focus of this verse. How ironic that it is **the nations** (*haggôyim*), from which Yahweh had chosen Israel to be a people (*'am*) to know him and walk in his ways, that are now called **peoples** (*'ammîm*); they are the ones who acknowledge that it is Yahweh, the universal Ruler, who will **judge** and **settle** international **disputes**. In this distant future, when all human imperial powers have fallen, the implements of war, symbolized by **swords** and **spears**, will be taken to the metal smiths, who **will beat** them into agricultural tools. Motyer suggests this peaceful, agricultural environment to be "symbolic of the return to Eden" (1993, 54). Thus nations will give up **war** as the means by which to settle international disputes.

■ **5 Let us** signals Isaiah's identification with his, and Yahweh's, people, the **descendants of Jacob**: just as the Gentiles, in that future day, will choose to walk in Yahweh's ways, so **let us** now, in that expectation, choose to **walk in the light of *Yahweh*.**

FROM THE TEXT

The theme of light and darkness appears throughout the book of Isaiah. Light is associated with worship of Yahweh and following his teachings, while darkness is associated with worship of idols. In 5:20, however, some persons have reversed their moral thinking: they now call darkness/evil light, and light/good they call evil. In 5:30, war has obscured the light, so that one sees only darkness. In 13:10, the heavenly bodies, stars, sun, and moon, do not "show their light" as punishment for evil throughout the world. In 9:2 [1 HB], Isaiah speaks of the sudden dawning of "a great light," God himself, upon his people, dispelling darkness and the shadow of death. In 30:26, both moon and sun brighten to "the light of seven full days," signaling Yahweh's healing grace. In 42:6 and 49:6 Yahweh's messiah Servant is to be "a light for the Gentiles." Yahweh is the Creator of both light and darkness in 45:7. Yahweh sends Babylon into darkness in 47:5. In 51:4, Yahweh's justice becomes "a light to the nations." Light, healing, God's presence and guidance are associated with sharing food with the hungry, and attending the needs of the oppressed in 58:1-11. But, in 59:9-11, when justice and righteousness are not practiced, there is no light; rather, one gropes in the darkness like a blind person, while in 60:1-3, Yahweh, himself, is the light that rises like the dawn upon his people, dispelling the darkness, and to the brightness of that light, the nations and kings of the earth come.

In the New Testament John records Jesus' witness that he himself is "the light of the world" and that those who follow after him "will never walk in darkness, but will have the light of life" (John 8:12). John further talks of those who "live as Jesus did" (1 John 2:6), as equivalent to "liv[ing] in the light," which produces love for one's brother or sister. But "walk[ing] around in the darkness" produces the opposite (vv 9-11). John insists that it is by obeying Jesus' "word" that "love for God is truly made complete in" us (v 5). Isaiah says it is God's word that the nations will stream to Zion to seek. It is God's word that will bring about cessation of hate and war between nations, between peoples, within families, and between siblings (Isa 2:3-4).

3. The Day of Yahweh (2:6-22)

BEHIND THE TEXT

The focus of these verses is on the contrast between God and humankind. God is exalted in his elevated temple in Zion, to which many nations will stream. He will humble the house of Jacob, which, in arrogance and pride (vv 9, 11, 17), has turned away from the Lord to worship "idols . . . the work of their hands" (v 8); rather than trust in God, Jacob trusts in "silver and gold," "horses," and "chariots" (v 7). In this section, God is given the title **Yahweh Sebaoth**, who "has a day" (v 12; see also vv 11, 17, 20) in which "he rises to shake the earth" (vv 19, 21).

In 13:6 Isaiah speaks of "the day of the Lord." Other prophets speak of such a "day" (e.g., Joel 1:15; 2:1, 11, 31 [3:3 HB]; Amos 5:18, 20; Zeph 1:7, 14; Zech 14:1; Mal 4:5 [3:23 HB]). Scholars have noted that most of these references are in association with military conquest (e.g., von Rad 1959, 103). That is, Yahweh is the great conquering King who comes vanquishing the forces of darkness and evil. Stuart points out that in the background of this prophetic concept of the Day of Yahweh, at least partially, may be the ancient Near Eastern tradition that a truly great king would possess sufficient power and authority to finish off his enemies in a single day of military campaign (1976, 159-64; he cites thirteen Sumerian, Hittite, Egyptian, Assyrian, Phoenician, Syrian, and Moabite documents).

Building upon this concept, Isaiah here would be challenging this boast of human kings: there is only one great King with the universal power and authority sufficient to carry out such a single-day overthrow of all idols (Isa 2:18, 20) and the deities they represent, and the very real forces of evil that hold humankind imprisoned in darkness; that great King is **Yahweh Sebaoth** (v 12) (von Rad 1959, 104).

IN THE TEXT

■ **6** Here begins a lament, accusing Yahweh of having **abandoned** his **people**. The **descendants of Jacob** is applied here to the southern kingdom (Judah) but may also include the northern kingdom (Israel). The historical context for the indictment that follows may be Ahaz's construction of an Assyrian altar in the Jerusalem temple (2 Kgs 16:10-20); at this time Judah was enjoying economic prosperity, and Israel was still an independent kingdom. **Abandoned** (*nāṭaš*) does not imply rejected, in the sense of no longer being Yahweh's people, but rather to be allowed to "experience the consequences of their faithlessness" (Wildberger 1991, 105). They remain "my people" (Isa 3:12, 15). Note the stark contrast of 2:3 with v 6: those who are not God's people, the *gôyyim*, now come to God's city to learn the ways (v 3) that God's people, his *'am*, have rejected (v 6). God's people are **full of superstitions from the East**, most likely Assyria and Babylonia; **they practice divination like the Philistines**, who live to the west. God's people have taken unto themselves the **pagan** worship practices of neighbors on both sides, practices the pagans apparently have rejected!

Divination

Divination is the practice of determining the future or the unknown through observing patterns and movements in nature or human life. Two that

Israel practiced were dreams (Num 12:6) and the casting of lots (Josh 7:14-15). Also, the king of Babylon cast lots with arrows, consulted idols, and examined the liver of a sacrificial animal (Ezek 21:21 [26 HB]). Astrology, the observation of the movements of heavenly bodies, widely practiced in Babylonia and Egypt, was condemned in the OT (Deut 4:19). The "pagans" (Isa 2:6) used divination and magic to attempt to manipulate the gods and their own destinies. Oswalt observes that "God called the Hebrews to commit their security to him in trust . . . [but] they have listened to the nations" (1986, 123).

■ 7 The **silver and gold**, representing material wealth, would have been primarily in the coffers of the ruling class as they had the power to require high taxation, and in the hands of business owners as international trade prospered during the reigns of Jeroboam II (783-741 BC) in Israel and Uzziah (783-742 BC) in Judah. During the reigns of these two kings, peace between the two kingdoms enabled them to expand their borders (2 Kgs 14:25; 2 Chr 26:6-8) till their territories together nearly equaled that at the height of Solomon's earlier reign.

Horses and **chariots**, representing military might, most usable in battle in the northern kingdom with its more open plains, were also usable in the southern areas of Judah, as shown from the excavations at the city of Lachish (Ussishkin 1982, 105; 2004, 81, 87; 2006, 344). Though the Chronicler does not list horses and chariots in Uzziah's war readiness, he does say that Uzziah had "a well-trained army . . . of 307,500 men," providing them with "shields, spears, helmets, coats of armor, bows and slingstones" (2 Chr 26:11, 13, 14).

The accumulation of gold, silver, horses, and chariots, however, was in violation of God's prohibition against the king acquiring them (Deut 17:16-17). Moses had warned that the accumulation of such would lead to proud hearts and a forgetting of "the LORD your God" (Deut 8:10-18). In Ps 20:7 [8 HB] reliance on horses and chariots is soundly rejected (compare Mic 5:10 [9 HB]; Hag 2:22; Zech 9:10).

The ANE Battle Horse and Chariot

Some skilled archers rode into battle on horses in the ancient Near East. Primarily, however, horses were used to pull war chariots, usually two horses to a chariot. From tomb wall paintings and carvings, the Egyptian regular battle chariot contained a crew of three (a driver, an archer, and a shield bearer) while the Assyrian battle chariot contained a crew of four (a driver, an archer, and two shield bearers) (Gonen 1975, 90, 92).

■ 8 The mention of **idols** appears incongruent with the accumulation of wealth and buildup of military armaments. Wealth and military armaments, however, become objects of a nation's trust, rather than the protection and strength of Yahweh. Just so, idols (**the work of their hands**) shaped in the image of humans are a blatant substitution for the worship of Yahweh. Israel has put its trust in the deities that the idols represent, rather than in the Creator God, who **shaped humankind from the clay of the earth** (Gen 2:7) "in the image of God" (1:27).

Idols

The term "idols" as *'ĕlîlîm* ("nothing," "null") occurs ten times in Isaiah (2:8, 18, 20 [2x]; 10:10, 11; 19:1, 3; 31:7 [2x]), and six times elsewhere (Lev 19:4; 26:1; Pss 96:5 [= 1 Chr 16:26]; 97:7; Ezek 30:13; Hab 2:18). Its adjective form in Job 13:4 describes physicians as "worthless." Isaiah, then, is saying that idols are worthless, nothing, or "no-gods" (Oswalt 1986, 123).

■ **9** Pride has enticed the human heart to seek to set itself above God. The wisdom teacher declared, "Pride brings a person low" (Prov 29:23). Just so, Isaiah, seemingly quoting from a wisdom saying, declares that not only the house of Jacob (v 6) but generally **people** [*'ādām*] **will be brought low and everyone** [*'îš*] **humbled**. Wildberger suggests that "one bows down before the idols and then, in a very different sense, has to bow down in submission [to God] as a consequence of the first act" (1991, 110).

The final phrase of this verse seems abrupt and somewhat harsh: **do not forgive them**. Does Isaiah have no compassion? Does he truly wish no forgiveness for humanity? This commentator does not think so. Yet Israel's sin is so deep and arrogantly defiant that God cannot act "as if the sin had not been committed"; ultimately, it "cannot simply be forgotten, it must be punished" (Oswalt 1986, 124-25).

■ **10-11** At the appearance of **Yahweh**, when seen clearly in the light of **the splendor of his majesty** (v 10), **human pride** (v 11) drives **the arrogant** to seek escape in **the rocks** (v 10) or in holes **in the ground**. Amos, however, declares that there is no place of escape when Yahweh appears, not in the depths of Sheol, the heights of the heavens, nor in the depths of the sea (9:2-3).

The splendor of his majesty is language reminiscent of the Assyrian kings' boast concerning their own terrifying appearance as conquering kings. Sennacherib, for example, writes, "Luli, king of Sidon, whom the terror-inspiring glamor of my lordship had overwhelmed," and, "Hezekiah himself, whom the terror-inspiring splendor of my lordship had overwhelmed" (Pritchard 1969, 287-88). No, insists Isaiah, **in that day** no supposed splendor of any earthly king will inspire the dread of judgment as the **fearful presence** (v 10) and **splendor of Yahweh's majesty**. No earthly king, no arrogant human will stand; **Yahweh** alone will be exalted (v 11).

■ **12-17** This passage, too, focuses on the **arrogance** and **pride** of humankind (v 17), which, in **a day** when **Yahweh Sebaoth** (v 12) sweeps through the land, **will be brought low** (v 17) and **humbled** (vv 12, 17). Prideful humanity is said to be **lofty** (*rām*) and **exalted** (*niśśā'*) (v 12); both terms are also applied to the **towering** [*rām*] **mountains** and **high** [*niśśā'*] **hills** (v 14). Perhaps here the prophet anticipates the application of these two terms to Yahweh, the only one truly worthy of such majesty: "I saw **Yahweh**, high [*rām*] and exalted [*niśśā'*], seated on a throne" (6:1).

Yahweh's sweep through the land appears to begin from the north, metaphorically uprooting the **cedars of Lebanon** and the **oaks of Bashan** (2:13); continuing southward, he moves the **mountains** of Israel/Judah (v 14), passing through their towns, bringing down **lofty tower** and **fortified wall** (v 15). Yahweh's sweep ends with the mention of **every *ship of Tarshish*** and **every stately vessel** (v 16), bringing to mind Judah's southernmost port of Ezion Geber on the northern tip of the Gulf of Aqaba; from there these ships carried out lucrative international commerce. All these (mountains, walled cities, ships) metaphorically represent **human pride** (v 17); all **will be brought low**. As in v 11, no arrogant human will stand; **Yahweh** alone will be exalted (v 17).

Lebanon, Bashan, and Ships of Tarshish

Lebanon, located north of both the ancient kingdom and modern state of Israel, on the eastern end of the Mediterranean Sea, is known in the OT primarily for the famed "cedars of Lebanon," which were used in the construction of Solomon's Jerusalem temple (1 Kgs 5:6-12 [20-26 HB]). The psalmists mention them poetically in Pss 29:5; 92:12 [13 HB]; and 104:16.

Bashan, located east of the Jordan and Sea of Galilee, stretched from the Jabbok River northward to Mount Hermon. The name means "smooth/flat land." It included a forest region, known for its "oaks of Bashan" (Isa 2:13; Ezek 27:6), and pasture land that nourished fine cattle (Ps 22:12 [13 HB]; Amos 4:1).

Tarshish and ships of Tarshish are mentioned in 1 Kgs 22:48 [49 HB]; Ps 48:7 [8 HB]; Isa 2:16; 23:1, 14; 60:9; Ezek 27:25). Tarshish was a city of commerce, possibly established by the Phoenicians, as Isaiah speaks of Tarshish in his prophecy against Tyre (Isa 23:1, 6, 10), and Ezekiel mentions Tarshish exchanging "silver, iron, tin and lead" with Tyre (Ezek 27:12). The exact location of Tarshish, however, has never been determined. The most likely option appears to be toward the western reaches of the Mediterranean Sea, perhaps Tartessos in southern Spain. The "ships of Tarshish" traveled to and from ports other than Tarshish, so the term became a set expression for large commercial ships, probably Phoenician related.

■ **18** As in v 8, Isaiah again mentions the **idols** (*'ĕlîlîm*), which, in Yahweh's sweep of the land, **will totally disappear**, or ***vanish***, a term used elsewhere to describe those things of very temporary nature: grass ("sweep . . . away" [Ps 90:5]) or days ("fly away" [Job 9:25]). "In other words," suggests Williamson, "the idols are things of no lasting worth or substance" (2007, 227).

■ **19-21** The focus here is on the response to the **splendor of [Yahweh's] majesty** (Isa 2:19, 21). **People will flee** (v 19) is (lit.) *they will enter*; *they* is ambiguous: does it refer to the idols of v 18 that hide in **caves in the rocks** and **holes in the ground**, or to "everyone humbled" of v 9, who are commanded in v 10, "Go into the rocks, hide in the ground"? In any case, it is ***humankind/ people*** (*hā'ādām*) who **will throw [*idols*] away** (v 20), when they realize the worthlessness of their self-made **idols of silver and idols of gold**, and when they realize their idols' inability to give them any protection when Yahweh **rises to shake the earth** (vv 19, 21). It is to the dwelling places of **moles and bats** (v 20), the unclean, that humbled humanity consigns these once highly valued objects (plated with silver and gold!). Moreover, when viewed against the **splendor of [*Yahweh's*] majesty** (v 21), these idols, **made to worship** (v 20), are seen for what they truly are: nothing but junk!

■ **22** This verse at first appears to focus on the nothingness of **humans** (*hā'ādām*) when compared to God. **Stop trusting** in that which is nothing! But, the **breath** [*nĕšāmâ*] **in their nostrils** (*bĕ'appô*), along with "humans" and "nostrils," echoes the creation of humankind by the Creator (Gen 2:7). Thus Isaiah is saying that the existence of humankind, the creature, points toward the Creator. Why, then, should one place trust in untrustworthy, created humans that are no different from oneself? How foolish! Look to the Creator. Trust the one who put **breath** in the **nostrils** of all humankind. Wesley asks, "What excellency is in him [humankind], considered in himself, and without dependence on God?" (Wesley n.d., 3755-56).

FROM THE TEXT

This passage declares that **Yahweh Sebaoth** ultimately will allow nothing to receive the honor and worship that is due him as the Creator of all creation (v 12). No human will be allowed to continue to elevate himself or herself above the Creator, nor to place above him the creations of human hands, as though humankind, the creature, were the Creator. Later in Isaiah, in a parody on idol making, the prophet speaks of the one who "makes a god, his idol; he bows down to it and worships. He prays to it and says, 'Save me! You are my god!'" (44:17). "Such a person," declares the prophet, "feeds on ashes . . . deluded" by his own heart (v 20). Isaiah clearly links idolatry to human pride and arrogance, which often takes the form of worship of the self. Israel's wisdom tradition warns about God's opposition to "the proud" but reminds of his "favor to the humble" (Prov 3:34; compare 1 Pet 5:5*b*). The antidote to idolatry is submission and humility before God; following Israel's wisdom tradition, James reminds his readers that the Lord will lift up those who humble themselves before him (Jas 4:10).

It is in the midst of this self-deluded bondage that both those of the **house of Jacob** (Isa 2:6), God's chosen ones, and **humankind** (v 9) generally, will realize their great folly when the full light of the "splendor of [**God's**] majesty" (vv 10, 19, 21) shines upon them. The only human response to such a revealing is to hide. Isaiah says that it is from "the fearful presence of **Yahweh**" (v 19) that humans will flee, but like Adam and Eve, it is likewise the guilty conscience that drives us to become fugitives from God (Mounce 1977, 162-63). The Apostle John's graphic portrayal of kings, princes, generals, rich, mighty, slaves, and free who "hid in caves and among the rocks of the mountains," attempting to hide "from the face of him who sits on the throne and from the wrath of the Lamb," from "the great day of their wrath" (Rev 6:15-17), reflects Isaiah's "day" of **Yahweh Sebaoth** (Isa 2:12). But, for the person whose worship is directed toward nothing or no one other than the Creator, there is no reason for fear or guilt at the Lord's appearance. In fact, his appearance can be anticipated with great joy.

4. Jerusalem Staggers, Judah Is Falling (3:1-15)

BEHIND THE TEXT

This passage opens with **For behold** (*kî hinnēh* [v 1]), signaling a link with 2:6-22 and its theme of the pride of humankind. What follows (3:1-15) is God's response to Jerusalem and Judah: the ruling classes—the military, the judicial, the religious, the "offices that give civil community stability and direction" (Childs 2001, 33)—will be removed. Yahweh will replace those with experience in leadership with "youths" and "children" (v 4), derisive terms for those, no doubt adults, who have not yet experienced any form of significant leadership responsibility. These may be the weak Judean leaders who followed one after another early in Isaiah's ministry, "as the nation seemed bent upon devouring itself before Assyria could reach it" (Oswalt 1986, 131).

Into this vacuum of capable leadership is depicted general anarchy: a "neighbor" will "oppress" a "neighbor," "the young will rise up against the old," and the **worthless**/"nobody" will insult "the honored" (v 5). This passage concludes with a brief court scene, with Yahweh passing judgment on the "elders and leaders" for taking "plunder from the poor" (v 14) and for "crushing my people" (v 15). Here, Isaiah shares much with Amos and Micah in their eighth-century condemnation of the ruling classes' injustice to the poor and oppressed (see Amos 2:7; 5:10-13; 8:5-6; Mic 2:1-2; 3:1-3, 9-11).

IN THE TEXT

■ **I** *The Sovereign* [*hā'ādôn*] **Yahweh Sebaoth** (compare 1:24) signals God as Judge, about to take action against **Jerusalem and Judah**. This action will be **to** take away **supply and support**. How God will do this is not indicated: perhaps through inept decisions of corrupt leadership or through the attack of enemies. Two such attacks occurred during Isaiah's ministry. The first, precipitated by King Ahaz's wickedness, resulted in a joint Israelite—Syrian attack, with further attacks from Edom, Philistia, and Assyria (7:1; 2 Chr 28:5-21). The second was an Assyrian attack against Hezekiah (2 Kgs 18:17—19:36; Isa 36—37).

The result of God's action is that **supply** (*maš'ēn* [masc.]) and **support** (*maš'ĕnâ* [fem.]), something like the English "bag and baggage" (Oswalt 1986, 132), that upon which **Jerusalem and Judah** depend for stability in daily life, will be in great want. Even ***bread*/food** [*ehem*] and . . . **water**, essentials provided by the leaders of the city and state, will be unavailable. Note the plea of having no food in v 7. Amos, when preaching at Samaria to those "who oppress the poor and crush the needy" (Amos 4:1), notes the response of "Sovereign **Yahweh**" (v 5): a withholding of bread and water (vv 6-8).

Isaiah 3:2-7 clarifies that it is the leadership that, in fact, is the focus of the coming removal; thus, Oswalt suggests that ***bread*** and **water** may be figurative for the leaders upon whom the citizens of Jerusalem and Judah have come to rely, rather than relying upon Yahweh (1986, 132).

■ **2-3** Of those in leadership mentioned for removal, the king and the priest are absent. The king possibly is omitted, as Williamson suggests (2007, 244), because he was one of a kind, while all others are part of a class. Or the list is intended to apply locally rather than at the level of state leadership. Oswalt surmises (1986, 133, citing Delitzsch), that real power no longer was in the hands of the king but had passed into "the hands of nobles and great men." The text of Jeremiah indicates this to be so in the early sixth century BC when Jeremiah was prophesying during King Zedekiah's reign (Jer 38:4-6, 25-27). But, why is the priest not mentioned (when in Isa 28:7 he is listed along with the prophet)? Williamson suggests that perhaps the list is intended to be representative rather than comprehensive (2007, 243).

Hero (*gibbôr* [v 2]) is a man in any class who has become famous or infamous through some "heroic" exploit, not necessarily military, though often so (see, e.g., the list of David's thirty-seven "mighty men" (*gibbôrîm*) and some of their exploits in 2 Sam 23:8-39).

Warrior (*'îš milḥāmâ*) designates both soldiers conscripted at time of war and members of a standing army (Num 31:28; Deut 2:14-16; Judg 20:17).

Judge (*šôpēṭ*) refers to members of society who have proven themselves to be wise in leadership and are concerned with the administration of justice. They thus would be looked to for decisions of societal importance, including matters of legal dispute.

The **prophet** (*nābî'*) was certainly recognized as one who claimed to receive a divine word from God. But that word, from the perspective of others, could be either accepted or rejected. Whether or not the prophet was the holder of an official office is not clear.

The **diviner** (*qôsēm*) is one who attempts to determine the future or discover hidden knowledge through various signs or omens or magical powers. It is condemned as a practice in many instances in the OT. (Compare Deut 18:9-13; Isa 44:25; Jer 14:14-16; Ezek 22:26-29; Mic 3:1-2, 7, 9; Zech 10:2.)

The **elder** (*zāqēn*) belongs to a class of persons recognized by the community, because of their age. The wisdom that comes with age and experience qualifies them to arbitrate disputes and legal matters on behalf of others (compare Ruth 4:1-12; Josh 20:3-4). Whether the community elects/appoints the **elder** to such an office is not clarified. It may be that they are gathered ad hoc as needed.

A **captain of fifty** was a rank in the army (Isa 3:3). Williamson suggests that the **captain of fifty** belonged to the "largest single group of military officers," and thus was representative of all military officers (2007, 246). For other ranks, see 1 Sam 17:18, 55; Exod 18:21.

The MT of **man of rank** is *one whose face is lifted up* (*nĕśû' pānîm*); elsewhere it is translated "dignitaries" (Isa 9:15 [14 HB]), "highly regarded" (2 Kgs 5:1), and "an honored man" (Job 22:8). Thus the expression is applied to persons in different roles or positions, whom their peers hold in high regard.

The **counselor** (*yô'ēṣ*), or *adviser*, is at times applied to an individual official close to the king, whom the king consults for advice (2 Sam 15:12; 16:23; 1 Chr 27:33). At other times, this role resides in a group of "elders" whom the king consults for counsel or advice (1 Kgs 12:6; 2 Chr 10:6).

In the phrase **skilled craftsman** (*ḥăkam ḥărāšîm*), *ḥăkam* means "wise," but when describing one's ability in a given occupation, it has the sense of skilled. *Ḥărāšîm* occurs only here in the OT; thus its meaning is unclear. The phrase, however, is here closely paired with **clever enchanter** (*nĕbôn lāḥaš*). *Nĕbôn* is from the root *byn*, "to understand," and means something like "expert in"; *lāḥaš* is from a root meaning "to whisper" (Koehler and Baumgartner 1995-2000, 527) and means "enchantment" or "incantation." Thus **skilled craftsman** (*ḥăkam ḥărāšîm*) might be something like "skilled in magic arts."

■ 4 The loss of all capable, experienced leadership in Jerusalem, and in the towns of Judah, has created a leadership vacuum. Into this vacuum are thrust **mere youths** (*nĕ'ārîm*)—not in age but in experience—persons still dependent upon someone superior, such as an adult son still in his father's household or an adult family servant (see Judg 8:20; 1 Sam 17:33; 1 Kgs 3:7; Jer 1:6-7). These inexperienced leaders are also called **children** (*ta'ălûlîm*, from a root with the most probable meaning here, "capricious/mischievous"), thus, *mischievous ones*. These become the **officials** (*śārîm*, those normally appointed by the king, charged with legal, military, and administrative duties), who **will**

rule over. Thus into this leadership vacuum will be those incapable, by experience, wisdom, or social standing to govern: incompetents!

■ **5** This vacuum of competent governing leadership is filled with general anarchy: the breakdown of both political and societal moral norms. In the political realm is oppression from within, **man against man, neighbor against neighbor**. In the realm of societal moral norms, the **young** generation will **rise up against**, repudiating the wisdom and counsel of the **old** generation. **Young** is paralleled with **nobody,** from the root *qhl* II, "be of low esteem," "treat with contempt," "dishonor," "detest" (VanGemeren 1997, 3:924). The form here is a passive participle, "one who is of low esteem" or "has been treated with contempt" (compare Prov 12:9). **Old** is paralleled with **honored**, from the root *qbd*, "be heavy," "be honored," "to honor" (ibid., 2:577). The form here also is a passive participle, "one who is honored" or "has been given honor." Thus the implication is that the present cadre of leadership has treated the younger generation with contempt, as "nobodies." In response, they now **rise up against** their elders with the same contemptible disdain with which they, themselves, have been treated (compare Mic 7:5-6).

■ **6** Although **father's house** (*bêt 'āb*) can refer to the physical house in which a family dwells (e.g., Gen 24:23), most often in the OT it is a technical term for "the extended family" (Ross 1979, 62). Given the overall deterioration of societal norms depicted in the previous verses, this is the most apparent meaning here. In the apparent economic collapse that has ensued in this era of incompetent leadership, is there at least one among the ***male relatives*** within the extended family who still owns a **cloak**? A simple cloak will give such a person status to assume the position no one else wants: the family's **leader**. But this is no enviable position, for it is to assume responsibility for **this heap of ruins** (*hammakšēlâ hazzo't*; compare v 8), a metaphor for the disastrous condition of the extended family.

■ **7** But **in that day** the one found with a cloak forcefully declines, **I have no remedy** (lit. ***I will not be a binder***, that is, one who binds up wounds, a healer). With **no food or clothing** to satiate others' hunger, or covering for either modesty or cold, the cloak owner declines to accept healing leadership.

■ **8** **Jerusalem staggers** (*kāšělâ yěrûšālaim*; *kāšělâ* echoes *makšēlâ*, "heap of ruins" of v 6) because Jerusalem, like the families that make up her inhabitants, has become a metaphorical "heap of ruins." **Judah is falling** conveys the same idea; the nation as a whole and the capital city are without proper leadership and support form Yahweh. This has happened because the beloved city and the nation are in revolt, ***because*** their ***tongue*** and deeds are against ***Yahweh,*** defying ***the eyes of his glory*** (*kābôd*). A person received "standing" in the community from his or her *kābôd*, such as children, wealth, or age/wisdom; "usually this is understood as something that can be perceived or expressed" (von Rad 1962, 1:239). God's **glory** is displayed in the heavens (Ps 19:1 [2 HB]); Isaiah declares that the entire earth is filled with his "glory" (Isa 6:3). Yet, in the **presence** (lit. *eyes*) of such obvious *glory*, the people of Jerusalem and Judah persist in doing their own thing!

■ **9** God's people make no attempt to *hide their Sodom-like sin*; in fact, **they parade** it before the world. *Sodom-like sin* may imply simply their manner of arrogant public display, or it may indicate the practice of homosexuality as in Gen 19:1-11. As in Isa 1:4, **alas** (*'ôy*) best expresses Isaiah's anguish and despair: *Alas for their own selves, for they have rewarded themselves evil.*

■ **10-11** Here we hear echoes of wisdom teaching, which contrasts the rewards of a life of righteousness with those of a life of evil (compare Prov 11:19; 12:14; 31:30-31). Thus, amid the warning of disaster to come, Isaiah offers a word of hope: *For* the **righteous, good** (Isa 3:10), but *for* the **wicked***:* **Woe!** (v 11).

■ **12** It appears to be Yahweh who twice laments, **my people! Youths** (compare v 4), here called **women**, now oppressively **rule over them**. On the one hand, these youthful leaders may be characterized as **women** because they are derisively viewed as not yet having reached the age of full manhood. On the other hand, they may be derisively "women-like," as, for instance, when Isaiah derisively describes the Egyptians becoming *like women* ("weaklings" [NIV]) when *Yahweh Sebaoth* "raises [his hand] against them" (19:16). Likewise, Nahum (3:13) mocks the defenders of Nineveh, "Look at your troops—they are all *women*" ("weaklings" [NIV]).

Israel's **guides** (*'šr*, meaning "walk straight," "lead on," "reprove"), are *leading* God's people **astray,** *turning* them **from the path**. According to wisdom teaching, Judah's leaders should be teaching the people to "walk [*'šr*] in the *path of understanding*" (Prov 9:6).

■ **13-15** Such inept leadership brings divine intervention. In a metaphorical **court**, Yahweh **rises** from his judge's seat to pronounce a **judgment against the elders and leaders**, those who have been given the responsibility of keeping God's **vineyard** and ensuring justice for **the poor**. But, no, they have **ruined**, or *burned, consumed*, the **vineyard**, a metaphorical reference for God's people (compare Isa 5:7). They have ruined God's vineyard by finding legal ways to rob **the poor**, those who have no voice in the legal system. And, the ill-gotten **plunder**, exhibit A introduced as evidence, is right there **in your houses** for all to see, says Isaiah. Isaiah is not alone among the eighth-century prophets to bring this accusation against the upper level of society enriching themselves at the expense of the poor (see Amos 2:6-8; 3:9-11; 6:4-7; Mic 2:1-3; 3:1-4, 9-12; compare Prov 22:22-23).

FROM THE TEXT

This passage declares at the very beginning that the societal breakdown to be detailed following is an act of judgment by **Yahweh Sebaoth** (Isa 3:1). The removal of the present leadership is not the result of an uprising of the general population against a corrupt cadre of heroes and warriors, judges and prophets, and clever enchanters; rather, it is Yahweh who is removing the powerful from their positions of power. They have used their positions to enrich themselves at the expense of the poor. In doing so, they have not only themselves turned away from the worship of Yahweh but have caused the people entrusted to them also to turn from right paths of living. Yahweh's tolerance of such actions has come to an end. The old order, however, cannot simply be cleaned up or injected with "new blood"; it must be removed, even if, for a time, the replacement is incapable of competent leadership. During this period of judgment and cleansing, the people will indeed suffer. But God has a long-range view: a future "day" when, under the leadership of "the Branch of **Yahweh**," his people again "will be called holy" (4:2-3).

5. Sackcloth for Fine Clothing (3:16—4:1)

BEHIND THE TEXT

Though this section pictures the women of Jerusalem in somewhat graphic detail, it is Yahweh, mentioned four times, who is the focus. He speaks: "**Yahweh** says" (3:16); he acts in judgment: "**Yahweh** will make their scalps bald" (v 17), "**Yahweh** will snatch away their finery" (v 18); he acts in redemption: "**Yahweh** will wash away the filth of the women of Zion" (4:4). The women are both actual and metaphorical for the general population of the city; they illustrate the "silly behavior of the wealthy, who will shortly suffer humiliation and shame" (Childs 2001, 34). "In that day," mentioned three times (3:18; 4:1, 2), provides a link with the preceding text (2:11-12).

IN THE TEXT

■ **16-17** The description of **the women of Zion** best fits women of the upper level of Jerusalem's society. The turning of elegant **necks**, the **flirting with their eyes**, the **swaying hips** (v 16)—all are calling out, "Look at my beauty! This is who I am! Worship me!" They do not know that, "Charm is deceptive, and beauty is fleeting," that it is the "woman who fears the LORD" who "is to be praised." They do not know that it is a woman's "works" that "bring her praise," works such as providing well for her family or sharing her wealth with the poor (Prov 31:30-31).

In their obsession with their own beauty, the Jerusalem women suddenly will find themselves to be women of shame, for at the instigation of ***the Sovereign*** (*'ădonāy* [Isa 3:17*a*]), their **heads** will be disfigured with **sores**, and, **Yahweh** (*yhwh* [v 17*b*]) **will make their scalps** [*pāt*] **bald** (*'rh*, a root meaning "to make bare, expose, strip naked" [VanGemeren 1997, 3:527]). Miles proposes that *pāt* should be read "as a connotation for the female genitalia," and thus translates, "And Yhwh shall expose their genitalia" (2006, 202, 197).

■ **18-23** Again, it is ***the Sovereign*** (*'ădonāy*) who **will snatch away** from his people all **finery** (v 18), a term that covers the whole list of items to follow. These items represent those things that a person could put on one's body to further one's natural beauty and attractiveness, not in themselves necessarily wrong, except when they become the cause of pride. Many of these items of women's **finery** occur only in this passage and are, thus, difficult to translate with confidence.

■ **24** Isaiah may have in view here Judah's future exile. The terms **stench**, **rope**, **baldness**, and **sackcloth** are descriptive of exile, the reality following the snatching away of all props of human pride. A word seems to be missing in the last line of this verse in the MT Hebrew, which reads, "for instead of beauty [blank]." The NIV (and others) supply **branding**. The Great Isaiah Scroll from Qumran (1QIsaᵃ), however, reads, "for instead of beauty shame" (*bšt*). Indeed, when all prideful props have been removed, and nothing remains but our naked selves, even **sackcloth** cannot hide our shame.

■ **25-26** Zion now is pictured as widowed wife ***emptied*** because of the lack of **men** (*mětîm*, "husbands"), paralleled with **warriors**. The description is of a city emptied of her male population by **sword** and **battle** (v 25). It is the **gates** (*pětāḥîm*, lit. "entrances" [v 26]) of the personified city that **lament and mourn**, for all activity that normally transpires at the city gates (trade, business dealings, legal hearings and decisions, foot traffic in and out) has ceased.

■ **4:1** The emptying of the city's male population is made even more poignant by the ratio of **seven women** to **one man**. A woman's identity in ancient Israelite culture received validation by association with a male. Ross has shown in a study of the ninety-seven females identified by name in the OT literature (excluding genealogies), the primary identification of ninety of them (93 percent) is with reference to some immediate male family member, mainly as "wife of," "daughter of," or a combination of both (1979, 34, 87). Thus we hear the desperate cry of Zion's unmarried women to acquire a man's **name** that their **disgrace** be removed (widows still retained their identity as "wife of" their deceased husbands). To be called "wife of" so-and-so only would be sufficient. No support of **food** or **clothes** would be expected.

FROM THE TEXT

The desire to appear important, to be more than we really are, is universal, and thus not far from any one of us. Though Isaiah depicts the women of Jerusalem as the haughty ones, they are merely representative of all, female or male, who attempt to live "so wrapped up in human affairs that there is no time to bow down before God" (Wildberger 1991, 156). With the writer of Ps 8, in the awareness of the absolute majesty of the "name" of the Lord and his "glory" revealed in the heavens, our only appropriate response is to bow before him and cry out, "What is mankind [*ĕnôš*, 'frail, mortal man'] that you are mindful of them, human beings [*ben 'ādām*] that you care for them?" (Ps 8:4 [5 HB]).

6. The Branch of Yahweh (4:2-6)

BEHIND THE TEXT

"In that day" begins this passage, linking it with what has come before (compare Isa 2:11-12, 17, 20; 3:7, 18; 4:1). Previous occurrences have signaled God's judgments and destruction in an indefinite future time. Here, however (4:2), Yahweh's "day" is positive, bringing restoration and cleansing to "Zion"/"Jerusalem." The city now becomes a place in which a remnant of people "called holy" (v 3) resides, in contrast to a city filled with corrupt leaders taking bribes, dispensing injustice, and oppressing the defenseless. Jerusalem becomes a place of "shelter and . . . refuge" (v 6).

IN THE TEXT

■ **2** The interpretation of **the Branch of Yahweh** (*ṣĕmaḥ yhwh*) divides most contemporary commentators from those of earlier generations (two exceptions are Oswalt 1986 and Motyer 1993). The Targum translated the phrase as "the messiah of Yahweh" (*mšyḥ' dyhwh*) while the Septuagint translated it as "thereupon God shined" (*epilampsei ho theos*), which may indicate a different Hebrew source text or "is simply the result of a rather free translation of the text" (Wildberger 1991, 165).

The difference in translation for modern commentators hangs on the understanding of the meaning of *ṣĕmaḥ* in this Isaiah context. The deciding factor seems to be whether or not the commentator views the entire passage as messianic. If yes, then *ṣĕmaḥ* will be interpreted as referring to a future messianic figure and translated as "Branch" or "Shoot"; if no, the term will be interpreted as, for example, "a reference to what God will make grow in the natural realm" (Williamson 2007, 307). Those who do not view the term here as having messianic connotations also generally do not view the occurrences of this term and the figure it represents—in Jer 23:3-5, 14-26; Zech 3:8; and 6:9-15—as having messianic connotations. This, of course, in a circular type of reasoning, has bearing on how one interprets the meaning of the term in Isa 4:2.

Baldwin, however, in a careful exegesis of these Jeremiah and Zechariah passages, has convincingly shown that the term *ṣĕmaḥ* in those passages does speak of a future messianic figure and that "the Shoot is someone still to come, one whom Yahweh will cause to rise from obscurity to become a temple-builder, a king and a priest" (1964, 97). He further demonstrates that our Isaiah passage is messianic, and the occurrence of the term *ṣĕmaḥ* in this passage is the beginning of its use in a messianic sense (→ 4:3-4 below, on the priestly washing and cleansing of Zion's sins). Childs, too, views this passage as speaking of "God's time of eschatological judgment and salvation," in which the **branch** is the "messianic bringer of salvation," and the words **beautiful and glorious, and the fruit of the land** is "playing on the eschatological theme of a return to paradise" (2001, 36).

After the judgment that has fallen upon Judah and Jerusalem, it is said that there are some **survivors in Israel**. Some commentators view this passage as a postexilic addition, and thus here is reference to those surviving the Assyrian and Babylonian deportations of both the northern and southern kingdoms (701 and 587 BC). Could it not be, however, in view of the Exodus and wilderness language in vv 5-6, that Isaiah is using **Israel** here in the general sense of God's people, as they were known when they came out of Egypt long before? The following verse identifies the **survivors**.

4:3-4

■ **3-4** The "survivors" of v 2 are those **who are left** [*hanniš'ār*] **in Zion, who remain** [*hannôtār*] **in Jerusalem** (v 3). They are the ones whose **filth** and **bloodstains** Yahweh **will wash away** (*rāḥaṣ*) **and cleanse** (*yādîaḥ*, from *dwḥ*) through **a spirit of judgment and a spirit of fire** (v 4). Elsewhere, *dwḥ* occurs only in 2 Chr 4:6 and Ezek 40:12 for priestly ceremonial washing, and *rḥṣ*, though a general term for washing, is applied in Exod 40:12 in the same sense. Baldwin suggests that Isaiah's use of these terms indicates a "sacrificial washing," thereby enabling the survivors to be designated **holy** (*qādôš* [v 3]) or "set apart" (1964, 93).

Those who have survived the calamity of judgment, therefore, have come out on the other side having experienced an inner spiritual transformation. Oswalt points out that "the purpose of the Exodus and the giving of the law" was to help God's people to "be holy as he is holy" (see Lev 19:2; 22:31-33; 1986, 147). This resonates with the Exodus language in Isa 4:5-6.

All who are recorded among the living, or *everyone written for/unto life*, on the one hand, could be simply a reference to a written registry of citizens of **Jerusalem**. On the other hand, in the eschatological, messianic context of this passage, it must refer to a higher registry of those who, recognizing the evil of their ways, have repented and turned unto God's ways (compare Ps 69:28; Dan 12:1-2; Mal 3:16).

■ **5-6 Create** (*bārā'*), used only of God's activity, signals a new beginning for **Mount Zion** and for **those who assemble** there (v 5). God, in an act of new creation, had brought out of Egypt a people intended to be holy/set apart (*qādôš*) unto himself (note the words "were . . . fruitful," "multiplied greatly," "the land was filled" in Exod 1:7, terms that appear at the accounts of creation [Gen 1:28] and re-creation following the flood [Gen 9:7]). So now, God is newly creating a place of **shelter** and **refuge** for *its* [i.e., Mount Zion's] **assemblies** (Isa 4:6). The presence of the **cloud of smoke by day** (v 5) and the **flaming fire by night**, along with the **glory** (of Yahweh), indicates Isaiah's intended parallel with the Exodus and wilderness event. But, whereas these were confined to the tabernacle in the earlier event (Exod 40:34), now, in this new creation, all of **Mount Zion** comes under the protection of the **canopy** (consisting of the **cloud** and **fire**). The **glory** represents the dwelling presence of God himself, and **those who assemble there** must be "holy" (v 3) to dwell in the presence of a holy God. Who are those who assemble there? Surely the prophet intends Jerusalem's citizens who have repented and turned back to God. Additionally, he many have in mind those who "in the last days" from "all nations will stream . . . to the mountain of the LORD" to learn "his ways" and "walk in his paths" (2:2-3). Isaiah, then, envisions a newly created people of God gathered from all the nations of the earth.

FROM THE TEXT

At the heart of this passage is the concept of a people "called holy" (4:3), living in the presence of a holy God. As noted above, God's intention for his people, when he brought them out of Egypt, was for them to become a holy people (Exod 19:6), living in holiness before him and in the midst of their neighbors. God's requirement of them, and of us, is to "be holy because I, the LORD your God, am holy" (Lev 19:2). Peter, with this OT requirement in view, commands that we are no longer to be conformed to the "evil desires" by which we previously lived (1 Pet 1:14), but now, in our "behavior," we are to be holy "like the Holy One" who has called us (v 15 NASB). We can live in such a way only as we, like those in Zion who are said to be washed and cleansed by the Spirit, have been "born again" (v 23) through the blood of Messiah Jesus.

C. The Vineyard of the Yahweh Sebaoth (5:1-30)

BEHIND THE TEXT

At first glance this chapter appears to begin a new section of the book of Isaiah. Yet, in actuality, the vineyard metaphor thematically links it with the previous chapters. In 1:8, "Daughter Zion" represents a remnant left in the Lord's vineyard following an unidentified invasion that has left a desolate countryside, burned cities, and stripped fields (1:7). In 3:14, it is noted that the elders and leaders had "ruined [God's] vineyard"; this brought the Lord to pass judgment on behalf of his people. In this present chapter, the Lord will "make [his vineyard] a wasteland" (5:6), with no promise of survivors.

Chapter 5 consists of three segments. The first (vv 1-7) is a song presented in parable genre about a vineyard (vv 1, 3, 4, 5), which, as the song progresses, is revealed as belonging to Yahweh. There are two singers. The first is the poet/prophet singing in the first person (vv 1-2) on behalf of Yahweh, "the one I love" (v 1), to an unnamed audience. The second, also singing in the first person, is Yahweh (vv 3-7) singing to the "dwellers in Jerusalem and people of Judah" (v 3) about the same vineyard as the first singer. The vineyard is revealed (v 7) to be the combined "nation of Israel" and "people of Judah." This segment sets the stage for the next segment of judgment oracles.

The second segment (vv 8-25) consists of two "woe" judgment oracles (vv 8-10, 11-12) followed by two "therefore" consequence oracles (vv 13, 14-17), then four additional "woe" judgment oracles (vv 18-19, 20, 21, 22-23), followed by two "therefore" consequence oracles (vv 24, 25).

The third segment (vv 26-30) consists of a summons from the Lord for "the distant **nation**" (v 26) (most likely the prophet has in mind the Assyrian Empire) as an instrument in his hands to bring about his judgment upon his people. This judgment is said to come "in that day" (v 30), but "that day" is not an eschatological day as in chs 2 and 4 but is an event of destructive war in real time. Isaiah, however, metaphorically describes this destructive time in terms of primeval chaos: "the roaring of the sea," the "land" covered by "darkness," and *the light*, such as should remain, "darkened by clouds" (5:30).

IN THE TEXT

1. A Vineyard on a Fertile Hillside (5:1-7)

■ 1 Isaiah, the first singer, sings, **I will sing *on behalf of* [*Yahweh*] the one I love *concerning* his vineyard**. Thus Yahweh is the owner of the vineyard.

■ 2 As Yahweh is elsewhere depicted engaged in what are usually seen as human activities (e.g., a potter forming humankind [Gen 2:7], a planter/husbandman of a garden [vv 8-9], a tailor of garments [3:21], a shepherd [Ezek 34]), he is here depicted as an owner/farmer. The farmer chose "a fertile hillside" (Isa 5:1), a testimony to his knowledge of viticulture, for grapevines are best planted on hillsides and slopes, where they will receive a greater strength of the sun's rays falling at an angle perpendicular to the hillside (Mawby 1999, n.p.). The farmer has **dug** the soil and **cleared** away the many **stones**. These two actions would have been done simultaneously, or at least the surface stones first removed. The digging would have produced more stones, which would have been removed before making the soil ready for the planting of **choicest vines**. Some of the stones no doubt were later used to construct a **watchtower**, which could serve as storage for tools, a resting or temporary dwelling place for workers, and for guarding the vineyard during the fruit ripening and harvesttime. No doubt some stones were also used to construct a "wall" (v 5). And, to be fully prepared for producing the wine that would be the logical end product of his labors, the farmer **cut out a winepress**, normally a two-level vat in solid rock, where workers would tread out the juice from the grapes.

Yahweh *waited expectantly for* [$qāwâ$] **grapes** (the MT does not have **good**). But when three to six years later (the time it takes from the initial planting to first harvest) he sent his workers among the vines for the first harvest, these vines had produced only *rotting* fruit ($bĕ'ušêm$, from $b'š$). Williamson suggests that, from the meaning of $b'š$, to "have a bad smell, stink," the vines have produced "diseased" or "rotting" grapes, a disease that "develops late in the growing season" (2007, 320, 338). This disease has affected/infected the entire crop of grapes, and, as the song will reveal, there is nothing to do but destroy the whole mess (v 5).

■ **3-4** The owner/farmer (v 7 reveals him to be **Yahweh Sebaoth**) now sings to his audience, the **dwellers in Jerusalem and people of Judah** (v 3). They are his **vineyard** (this, too, will be revealed in v 7). With his question, **What more could have been done for my vineyard?** (v 4), the owner/singer subtly draws his audience in as unwitting jury to pass judgment upon themselves. The implied audience's reply would be a sympathetic agreement that the owner had certainly been a faithful husbandman and that the **vineyard**, contrary to expectation, was certainly to be faulted for having produced only *rotting fruit*.

■ **5-6** The owner's implied reply is that it is so. And, still conspiring with his unsuspecting audience, he shares his plan: he will return his **vineyard** (v 5) to the uncultivated and wild state it was before he ever set hoe in the soil: **hedge . . . destroyed**, **wall** broken and **trampled**, vines no longer **pruned** nor **hoed** (v 6); choking out the untended vines, the ground would produce only **briers and thorns**. The end result would be that this once beautiful vineyard would become **a wasteland**. The owner will **command** and **the clouds** will withhold **rain**. The withholding of rain was one of the curses promised for disobeying Yahweh's "commands" (Deut 28:15, 23-24). Perhaps some in the owner's audience are beginning to wonder, Is this fellow singing about us?

■ **7** The song reverts to Isaiah, the first singer. Identities are now revealed: the owner is **Yahweh Sebaoth** (compare Isa 1:9, 24; 2:12; 3:1, 15); his **vineyard** is **the nation of Israel** and **the people of Judah**, further identified as **the *planting*** [$nēṭā'$] **he delighted in**. Elsewhere, God "will plant"/"planted" ($nṭ'$) his people in the land (Exod 15:17; 2 Sam 7:10; Pss 44:2 [3 HB]; 80:8, 15 [9, 16 HB]). And this planting was the object of the Lord's **delight**, the same term that metaphorically describes God's parental "delight" in his son Ephraim (Jer 31:20).

A wordplay follows **he *hoped* for** or ***waited expectantly* for** [*kwh*] **justice** (*mišpāṭ*): ***Behold!*** **bloodshed** (*mišpāḥ*). **Righteousness** (*sĕdāqâ*): ***Behold!*** **cries of distress** (*sĕ'āqâ*). In Isa 1:21, Zion is already depicted as no longer a city of justice and righteousness, but a city of murderers. We now hear the **cries** of the oppressed widows and fatherless of 1:17, and the poor of 3:14, whose houses have been plundered by their elders and leaders, those who have ruined the Yahweh's vineyard.

2. The Law of Yahweh Sebaoth Rejected (5:8-25)

■ **8** Though it is not clear to which class of society Isaiah speaks this **woe** (*hôy*) oracle, the essential message is clear: there are those in Judah who, through their covetous desire, are expanding their holdings by ***adding*** **house to house** and ***joining*** **field to field**. On the one hand, they are possibly doing this through "legal" means, so that they cannot be brought to book in the courts. But "legal" does not necessarily mean right or just.

On the other hand, Micah, who prophesies in the same time period as Isaiah, speaks a "woe" oracle against those of both the northern and southern kingdoms who have "power to do it," the "it" being that they "covet fields and seize them, and houses, and take them," defrauding the powerless of "their homes" and "inheritance" (2:1-2).

Isaiah adds that such actions, if allowed to continue unabated, will create a situation in which **no space is left** for others to live. This blatant exploitation of the poor by the rich shows the callous disregard for the theological premise that the land and its use was a gift from God and that each portion of land was to remain within the family to whom it was originally allocated (Lev 25:23-28; Ezek 46:16-18; Num 27:1-11; Ruth 4:1-4).

A further consequence of this practice is that the rich landowners will eventually **live alone in the land**. The verb is a causative passive here, ***you are/will be made to dwell***. Williamson observes that this "may reflect an appreciation of the fact that ultimately the land was God's gift to his people and that no one 'dwelt' there except by his grace" (2007, 354).

■ **9-10** Isaiah begins v 9 with, ***In my ears! Yahweh Sebaoth*** (v 9). Yahweh has spoken! His prophet has heard! He has heard Yahweh's word against those who garner wealth (**great houses . . . a . . . vineyard** [vv 9-10]) at the misfortune of others: they may dwell in them for a while, but something or someone, as yet unnamed, will drive these **occupants** (v 9) from their **houses**, leaving the houses **desolate** in the middle of the fields. Not only desolation but also the elements of nature, controlled by God, will work against the new landowners. Crop produce will be far below expectations: **a bath of wine** (v 10) equals about eight gallons, apparently far less than **a ten-acre vineyard** would be expected to produce; **an**

ephah of grain equals about a half bushel, only one-twelfth of the six-bushel **homer of seed** in the original planting. Kaiser observes, "There is no blessing upon ownership which is not morally justified" (1972, 67).

■ **11-12** Isaiah's second **woe** (*hôy*) oracle in this chapter is no doubt directed at the same level of society as the previous one (v 8). It is those with wealth who can afford **wine** from **early in the morning** (*babbōqer*) until **late at night** (*nešep*, **twilight**), until **they are inflamed with** it (v 11). And, as at most **banquets**, those skilled in the playing of **harps** (*kinôr*), **lyres** (*nebel*), **pipes** (*tōp*), and **timbrels** (*ḥālîl*) are present (v 12). Isaiah's point is that the banqueting and consuming of alcohol has so absorbed the lives of these revelers that **they have no regard for the deeds** [*pō'al*] **of Yahweh, no respect for the work of his hands** (*ma'ăśê yādîw*).

Korpel has noted the contrast between this passage and Ps 92:1-4 [2-5 HB] (1996, 58). There we find the psalmist praising, making music, and "proclaiming [Yahweh's] love in the morning" (*babbōqer*), and his "faithfulness at night" (*ballêlôt*). The psalmist mentions the "lyre" (*nebel*) and the "harp" (*kinôr*), instruments used to accompany his praise singing, two of the four instruments accompanying the drunken feasts in Isaiah's condemnation. Moreover, it is "your deeds [*pō'al*], **Yahweh**" and "what your hands have done" (*ma'ăśê yādêkā*) about which the psalmist is absorbed throughout his day. The contrast is stark: for the psalmist, it is God at work both in the world at large and in his own private world that gives him hope on down into "old age," where he will continue to "flourish" and "bear fruit" (vv 13-14). Those whom Isaiah says revel in alcoholic drinking, however, "no longer have any interest in or ability to recognize how God is at work in the world" (Oswalt 1986, 160). This insensitivity leads directly to the consequence in the next verse.

■ **13 Therefore**, declares Yahweh, my only recourse now is to remove **my people** (*'ammî*) from the land to which I brought them long ago. Indeed, they were not a strange people, but the descendants of those of whom long ago in Egypt Yahweh had declared, **I will take you** *to me* [*lî*] *for a* **people** [*lĕ'ām*], **and I will be** *to you* **God,** *and because of this* **you will know** [*wîda'tem*, from *yd'*] that I, **Yahweh,** am . . . **your God** (Exod 6:7).

The NIV's **will go into exile** is perfect tense (*gala*, from *glh*), **have gone into exile**. This is the "prophetic perfect," an action or event that the prophet envisions as already having been completed, though yet in the future. While Isaiah may not have in view the ultimate Judean exile to Babylon (587 BC), the Assyrian practice of exile of large numbers of the population of conquered kingdoms was certainly known by Isaiah's time. This removal of God's **people,** says Isaiah, is because of a **lack of *knowledge*** (*dā'at*, from *yd'*).

From the time of God's choosing them and bringing them out of Egypt and into Canaan, his **people** were to come to know what his requirements were for a just and righteous society. In this they had utterly failed. The scene depicted in v 13, of **those of high rank** and **the common people**, without regard for status, is that of prisoners being forced-marched into exile: many will **die of hunger** and **thirst**. Williamson observes that this "punishment is a reversal of the feasting and drinking" of vv 11-12 (2007, 373).

Assyrian Population Deportations

The Assyrians initiated the practice of deporting large numbers of the populations of conquered kingdoms, resettling them in other parts of their empire. These deportations would especially include the higher ranking, ruling persons of towns and cities. Often, an exchange of populations would be made, for the longer ranging purpose of breaking down the ethnic makeup of a people, to lessen the potential for future rebellion against empirical rule. See Pritchard (1969, 278, 283) for descriptions of Shalmaneser III and Tiglath-Pileser III deportations.

■ **14** Without regard for class, **nobles**, **masses**, **brawlers and revelers** are among the exiles. These are the ones who, in the previous verses, indulged from morning to night in drinking parties with the music makers, in total disregard for Yahweh and his work in the world. It is these who, succumbing to the rigors of the long march into exile, **descend** into *Sheol, who widens its throat and opens its mouth without measure*.

Sheol in the OT

Sheol in the OT has a range of meanings. It can mean simply "death," the condition when breath or life leaves the body, or "grave," the place where the lifeless body is placed. This seems to be what Jacob meant when he said to his sons, "You will bring my gray hair down to Sheol in sorrow" (Gen 42:38 NASB). In contrast to the heights of "heaven," Sheol is sometimes thought of as a place of great depth, as in the psalmist's affirmation, "If I make my bed in Sheol, behold, You are there" (Ps 139:8 NASB). Job, in the midst of his suffering, asked of God, ***Who will put me in Sheol, hiding me, concealing me until your nose*** [*'appekā*] ***has turned back?*** (Job 14:13). The metaphorical meaning of *'ap* is usually "anger," but in view of Job's reference to God's creation of him in v 15, the literal meaning may best express that Job expects God to breathe life into him once more, when he calls him out of Sheol (Andersen 1976, 173). Generally, however, Sheol in the OT is viewed as a shadowy place where all the dead, good and bad, go. What lies beyond Sheol is not made clear in the OT. It was not until the death and resurrection of Jesus that we gain more clarity on what lies beyond this present life.

■ **15-16** We have seen the content of these two verses previously in 2:9, 11, and 17. Oswalt views the repetition as the author "adapting an earlier thought to a new setting" or the expansion of "the implication of an earlier thought into a fuller treatment" (1986, 161).

In comparing chs 2 and 5 we note the following: in ch 2 humanity is "humbled" (vv 9, 11) because of its idolatry (v 8). In ch 5 humanity is **humbled** (v 15) because of its blatant disregard for the "deeds of **Yahweh**" (v 12), through its drunken debauchery (v 11). The two are not unrelated, in that idolatry treats Yahweh as totally nonessential in how one conducts one's private life; drunkenness renders one incapable of discerning how one is supposed to regard others in the public sphere: treating them with the **justice** and **righteous acts** that **Yahweh Sebaoth** demands (v 16). Thus, in 2:11 and 17, Isaiah states that "**Yahweh** alone will be exalted." In 5:7, he adds that there is found neither "justice" nor "righteousness" in the "vineyard of **Yahweh Sebaoth**." Thus it is now **Yahweh Sebaoth, the holy God**, who is **exalted by his justice** and shows himself **holy by his righteous acts** (v 16). It is in these acts of judgment that God is seen to be the **holy** [$q\bar{a}d\hat{o}š$] **God**, the one set apart from all other supposed deities. His very nature demands **justice** and **righteous acts**, which includes judgment.

■ **17** God's judgment brings the **ruins of the rich**, indicating Jerusalem's condition after exile (v 13). The once busy, lively city has reverted to **pasture** in which **sheep will graze**. This is not some "idyllic pastoral scene," however, but a complete and irrevocable judgment similar to the return of the vineyard to its precultivated state in vv 5-6 and its interpretation in 7:23-25 (Williamson 2007, 376).

The MT of the second line of 5:17 reads **strangers** will feed. The NIV follows the LXX, **lambs will feed**, which is a logical parallel with **sheep** in the previous line. While **strangers** does not appear to be a logical parallel, Motyer suggests that "strangers" are "temporary stayers," just as the **sheep** who **graze**. He thus sees this as a "subtlety of the MT" (1993, 72).

■ **18-19** Isaiah pronounces **woe** (*hôy*) against those who mock both his word of coming judgment and **the Holy One of Israel** (v 19), who is to bring that judgment. The charge is serious, the scene depicted comical. A loaded **cart** usually is pulled along by a beast of burden. But here, like beasts of burden, the mockers are hitched with **cords/ropes** to a **cart** loaded down with their own **sin** and **wickedness**, dragging it everywhere they go (v 18). Believing themselves free of Yahweh's demands, they are burdened with their own evil ways.

At the heart of their evil ways is disbelief, evidenced in the mocking challenge for God to **hurry** and bring **his work/plan** to pass. When is this going to happen, Isaiah? When will this "exile" (v 13) take place? When will this so-called "vineyard" (v 5) be destroyed? When will sheep graze among the ruins of our beloved Jerusalem (v 17)? Only when we **see it**, and thus **know it**, will we believe.

■ **20-21** Isaiah's **woe** (*hôy*) against those who mock God points out that their sin is a total turning on its head of all expected standards of goodness in Israelite society. That which God demands as the right and just way to live, Isaiah characterizes as **good, light,** and **sweet** (v 20). These mockers now say that their own **evil, darkness,** and **bitter** ways are what are right and just. Here is a connection with Isaiah's plea in 1:16-17: "Stop doing wrong. Learn to do right." Indeed, to reverse their evil ways, these mockers must undergo a process of (re)learning: to be **wise in their own eyes and clever in their own sight** (v 21) speaks of convinced heart attitudes from which spring the habitual **evil, darkness,** and **bitter** actions of daily life (v 20). Proverbs informs us that to "fear **Yahweh**" we cannot "be wise in [our] own eyes" (3:7). Thus we learn to do right by learning to "fear **Yahweh**."

■ **22-23** Isaiah links **drinking wine** (v 22) with the taking of a **bribe** (v 23) and *denying* justice. **Heroes** (*gibbôrîm* [v 22]) and **champions** (*'anšê ḥayil*) are military terms, but these are not men famous for military prowess. They are famous for their drinking from morning to night (v 11) and are the judges of the land **who acquit the guilty for a bribe, but deny justice to the innocent** (v 23). They have turned their God-appointed responsibility on its head (compare Deut 16:18-19; Amos 2:8; 4:1; 6:6).

■ **24 Therefore** points to a description of the judgment still to come, with metaphors of the coming destruction. Isaiah's previous "woe" accusations (Isa 5:8-23) are summarized in terms of God's people having **rejected the law of Yahweh Sebaoth** and **spurned the word of the Holy One of Israel.** The judgment metaphors (v 24) are comparative: just as such-and-such . . . , so is such-and-such. Both metaphors are agricultural: just as **straw** and **dry grass** *are eaten/devoured* (*'kl*, NIV's **lick up**) by **fire**, so the **roots** and **flowers** (a merism = two contrasting parts expressing the whole) of a plant or tree **decay** and **blow away** when all life support is removed. The implied plant or tree metaphor is the rulers of Judah.

■ **25** Again, **therefore** points to a following consequence. The tenses of v 25 point to that which has already happened. The metaphor of this verse involves two of Yahweh's anthropomorphic body parts: **Yahweh's nose burned** [*ḥārâ 'ap yhwh*, a metaphor for anger] *and he stretched out his hand* (*wayyiṭ* [from *nṭh*] *yādô*). This, too, is a merism expressing the totality, the intensity of Yahweh's response to **his people: he *struck* them down.** Thus the judgment has already begun with some act of Yahweh, which has already been experienced. **The mountains *shook*** may refer to the earthquake that occurred during Uzziah's reign (Amos 1:1; Zech 14:5). The resulting scene is appalling: **dead bodies are like *dung* in the streets.** This may be reference to the visual senses: one cannot walk the streets of a city in an animal-dependent culture without seeing the ever-present piles of animal (often, donkey and oxen) dung; or it may be a reference to the olfactory senses: just as the smell of the animal dung assaults the nostrils, just so does the stinking odor of decaying corpses.

3. The Light Is Gone, the Land Is Darkened (5:26-30)

■ **26** Verses 26-30 describe the fuller judgment that is still to come. Verse 26 expresses the sovereignty of God (**Yahweh Sebaoth**, "the Holy One of Israel" [v 24]) over the **nations**. Although **the distant nations** (*gôyim marāḥôq*) is plural, the pronouns following are singular: **he whistles for** *it*, **here** *it comes*. Thus a single *nation* is in view, for which Yahweh **lifts up a banner** and **whistles**. In 7:18 Isaiah warns Judah's king Ahaz that, "In that day *Yahweh* will whistle for flies from the Nile delta in Egypt and for bees from the land of Assyria," yet continues the warning with only the imminent Assyrian threat. Likewise, in 5:26 it is most likely Assyria that is in view, since the Assyrian army will invade Judah in Isaiah's lifetime (in 701 BC), destroying most of its towns and attempting to besiege Jerusalem. The characterization of the one coming **swiftly and speedily** also aptly fits the Assyrian army. Wildberger notes the examples of Tiglath-Pileser I's boast of marching from Suhi-land to Carchemish in a single day, and Ashurbanipal's conquering of Elam in merely a month (1991, 240 [citing B. Meissner 1920, 109]).

■ **27-29** This description portrays a seemingly nearly superhuman army: **not one** soldier **grows tired or stumbles**, . . . **slumbers or sleeps** (v 27); every soldier's equipment (**belt, sandal strap, arrows, bows** [vv 27-28]) is in tiptop shape; trained war **horses** have **hooves** that **seem like flint** (v 28). Even the **chariot wheels**, with their spinning spokes, are reminders of a **whirlwind**, perhaps a reminder that Yahweh's "way is in the whirlwind and the storm, and clouds are the dust of his feet" (Nah 1:3), and that war is like "violent winds on a stormy day" (Amos 1:14). The rumble of the advancing army with their numerous chariots is a **roar . . . like that of the lion** (v 29).

But surely soldiers must sleep, sandal thongs do break, and unshod warhorses' hooves do wear down, forcing abandonment of lame horses. We find no evidence that horses were shod as early as Assyrian times (White 1962, 57-59). The earliest written reference to a type of iron shoe being nailed to horses' hooves appears to be that done by the ancient Gauls and Celts around AD 500-600 (Fleming 1869, 369-70).

Though Isaiah presents a hyperbolic picture of the power and invincibility of the army that is to come against Judah, he does so to point out that when Yahweh moves in judgment against his people, he will use earthly powers to do so, whether or not those powers recognize him or his will. And, in that time of judgment, when the **lions** [symbolizing the invading army] . . . **seize their prey**, there will be **no one to rescue**.

■ **30 In that day** of God's judgment, the sound of the Assyrian army on the march is now metaphorically **like the roaring of the sea**, out of its bounds, like a tsunami, pouring over the land. And if one were to try to escape, how can one even see where to run? ***Behold! Darkness! Distress! And the light, it is***

darkened by the clouds! But it is more than **clouds** stirred up by battle that cover the land of Judah. Evil has darkened the spiritual sensitivity of the hearts of God's people, a sensitivity that can be restored only through a heart cleansing such as Isaiah will experience in ch 6.

FROM THE TEXT

In the book Isaiah personally appears for the first time in 5:1 ("I will sing for the one I love"). It is here that Isaiah "emerges as spokesman for Yahweh" (Seitz 1993, 52). It is here, then, that we should begin Isaiah's "call." It has been noted that v 9 (***In my ears! Yahweh Sebaoth***) also is indication that Isaiah, at this point, views himself privy to the divine council (Clements 1980, 63), a privilege Yahweh has granted only to "his servants the prophets" (Amos 3:7). Thus Isaiah's "call" to be Yahweh's spokesperson does not begin later in Isa 6, as is often assumed, though it is certainly fleshed out there. In that encounter, in a very special session of the divine council, into which Isaiah is invited, he experiences a cleansing that sets him apart for a special assignment.

The focus of ch 5 is on the pride of God's people, both of the northern kingdom ("the nation of Israel") and of the southern kingdom ("the people of Judah") (v 7). At the time of Isaiah's word of judgment, both kingdoms still stand. Assyria will be called to bring judgment upon Israel, which will disappear as an independent kingdom in 722 BC. Later, in 701 BC, Assyria's armies will devastate Judah's towns, leaving Jerusalem, though not captured or destroyed, isolated like an abandoned "hut" (1:8) in the middle of a field.

The early church theologians made many applications of this chapter in their preaching and teaching, some of which still speak to us today. Jerome (ca. 347-420) saw a parallel between Isaiah's song about the vineyard in 5:1-7 (indeed, held these verses to have been a prophecy about Christ, "the loved one") and Christ's weeping over Jerusalem and her coming destruction by Rome (Matt 23:37-38; Luke 19:41-44). The abandonment of Jerusalem after the Roman destruction was similar to God's abandonment of the vineyard (*Commentary on Isaiah* 2.5.1, cited in McKinion 2004, 38-39). The Venerable Bede (ca. 672-735), in commenting on "those who draw sin along with cords" (Isa 5:18), says, "The person who heaps sins upon sins, . . . is like one lengthening the cords with which he can be bound and scourged adding to them little by little" (*Homilies on the Gospels* 2.1, cited in ibid., 43). Caesarius of Arles (ca. 470-543), concerning "those who call evil good" (v 20), admonishes those who have responsibility for hearing cases, that to accept "earthly gifts" and thus decide unjustly, they will lose eternity. He urges them, "Observe justice in every case with all your strength, and think more carefully of the salvation of your soul" (*Sermon* 55.3, cited in ibid., 44).

D. Isaiah in the Divine Council (6:1-13)

BEHIND THE TEXT

Scholars are divided on the question as to whether or not ch 6 records Isaiah's inaugural call; that is, was this "an experience with God that resulted in his becoming a prophet" of Yahweh? (Childs 2001, 32). This commentary takes the position that Isaiah's experience within the divine council does not constitute his initial call, as he was already functioning as the spokesperson of Yahweh in the previous chapters (note the first-person references in 5:1 and 9, and → From the Text for ch 5, above). The book of Isaiah does not anywhere give us an account of Isaiah's initial call to serve as a prophet of Yahweh.

Rather than view the chapter from the standpoint of Isaiah's experience (though he did, indeed, experience the reality of a vision of God), we should focus on God. God chooses this moment in the life of Isaiah to reveal himself in a radically new way, so that his prophet is changed in a way previously inconceivable. This personal change prepares Isaiah for a prophetic assignment that is linked to God's past decision and declaration of judgment upon both Israel and Judah in chs 1—5. It is also linked to the future, the carrying out of that judgment, but with an offer of hope and salvation, in chs 7—12. The immediate future will include Judah's king Ahaz's refusal to accept Isaiah's invitation to trust Yahweh rather than Assyria (see chs 7—9).

Thus in ch 5 God's vineyard will be destroyed. In ch 6, God reveals his holiness, his very essence, as the basis out of which he has the sovereign right to bring about this near total destruction of his "vineyard" (5:1), until "the land is utterly forsaken" (6:12). Yet, still in ch 6, amid this total destruction, Yahweh still speaks of "stumps" that are "holy seed" (v 13), "a testimony to the emergence of a faithful remnant, which springs from the ashes of Israel's destruction, a new creation of God and his Messiah" (Childs 2001, 59).

King Uzziah

Uzziah was king over Judah from 792/91-740/39 BC (Thiele 1965, 205), for a total of fifty-two years. He was co-regent, however, for a number of years with both his father, Amaziah, at the beginning of his reign and with his son, Jotham, at the end of his reign, so he was king alone for probably only about seventeen years. It was while his father, Amaziah, was being held captive in Samaria (2 Kgs 14:8-14; 2 Chr 25:17-24) that Uzziah was made king. Amaziah was released and returned to Jerusalem, but in 768/67 BC he fled to Lachish, where he was assassinated (2 Kgs 14:19; 2 Chr 25:27). Uzziah then became sole king.

Uzziah revitalized Judah economically: he dug cisterns and built towers in the desert, expanded livestock in the foothills and plains, and had people working in the vineyards in the hills; he organized and equipped a well-trained army (2 Chr 26:10-15); he expanded Judah's control eastward, westward, and southward, and thus became powerful and famous. But in 750 BC, "his pride led to his downfall," when, acting as priest, he burned incense in the temple (2 Chr 26:16). The Lord struck him with leprosy for his pride and angry defiance of the reprimand of Azariah the priest. Banned from the temple, he lived out the rest of his years until his death in a separate house, with his son Jotham governing the kingdom (2 Chr 26:16-21).

IN THE TEXT

■ 1 It was **in the year *of the death of* King** Uzziah (740/739 BC) that Isaiah declares, **I saw the *Sovereign*** (*'ădōnāy*). Isaiah does not say if this experience occurred before or after King Uzziah's death. That is not his point. The point is that it was in *that* year of Uzziah's death that the ***Sovereign*** chose to break in upon Isaiah and radically change his life. (Uzziah would be replaced in about four years by his evil grandson Ahaz, who would seek Assyrian help rather than trust Yahweh for protection against the threat of a Syrian-Israelite coalition.) ***Sovereign*** predominates as Isaiah's choice of titles to describe God in this account (vv 1, 8, and 11), in direct address, **O *Sovereign*.** (***Yahweh Sebaoth*** is the seraphims' title [v 3], and Isaiah's title in apposition with "the King" [v 5].) Why ***Sovereign*?** In this title, Isaiah recognizes in some new way God's absolute lordship over, not only history, nations, and peoples, but also over himself as God's servant. Out of this experience, Isaiah becomes the sent one (→ v 8). And a servant must obey and speak only for his ***sovereign***.

The focus point of Isaiah's vision is the ***Sovereign* . . . seated on a throne**. Only kings sit upon thrones, and usually they do so when about to pronounce a judgment. So, in this initial instance, God, by his very position upon **a throne**, signals to his servant who he is, and what Isaiah will soon acknowledge, that he is "the King" (v 5). Moreover, he, the ***Sovereign***, is **high and exalted**. Here is connection with the theme of 2:11 and 17, where all attempts of humans to exalt themselves are brought to naught, and "***Yahweh*** alone will be exalted."

Did this vision experience take place in the earthly Jerusalem **temple**, or was Isaiah transported into the heavenly realm of God's abode and there have a glimpse into God's heavenly throne room, similar to what the Apostle John experienced when on the island of Patmos (Rev 4:1-8)? Most commentators opt for the Jerusalem **temple** as the venue, most likely on an occasion when Isaiah had routinely come to worship. And what he **saw** was God's presence so immense that the **temple** itself could contain only the **hem of his robe**. **Temple** is *hêkāl*, a loanword from Sumerian *e-gal* ("big house," "palace"), via Akkadian *ēkallu* (*HALOT* 245). In Babylonian and Assyrian texts, the word is used of the palace where both the deity, who is the true king, and the human king, the deity's earthly representative, dwell. It is used, for example, for the Babylonian king's "palace" in 2 Kgs 20:18. "So here the temple is God's palace. He is king, not Uzziah or Jotham or Ahaz" (Oswalt 1986, 178).

■ **2** Attending the ***Sovereign*** was an unspecified number of **seraphim** (*seraph* [sg.], *-im* [Heb. masc. pl.]), heavenly beings, whose function appears to be to serve God as he wills (as in Isa 6:6) and to be constantly chanting God's praises. The minimum number was certainly two, but Wildberger, who equates the function of the **seraphim** with the "***host*** of heaven" (1 Kgs 22:19), suggests them to be "*a great number* [emphasis original] of praising and serving beings" (1991, 264). The Hebrew noun *šĕrap* may be related to the verb *śārap*, "to burn." Thus these heavenly beings may be the ***burning/fiery ones***. Oswalt observes that fire is associated often in the OT with God's holiness, and thus "it would be entirely appropriate for those who declare that holiness" (1986, 179).

Because Isaiah describes the **seraphim** with **faces**, **feet**, and hands (Isa 6:2, 6), some commentators view them as having humanlike bodies. The truth is, however, we have no factual idea what these heavenly creatures actually looked like. Isaiah further describes them as **each *having*** six wings (that is, three pairs). With one pair **they *were covering*** their **faces**, with a second pair **they *were covering*** their **feet**, and with a third pair **they were flying**. There is general agreement that the covering of their **faces** is so that they may not inadvertently look upon the face of the holy Creator, just as the human Moses was forbidden (Exod 33:20; compare Judg 13:22).

Why, however, were they covering their **feet**? There is much speculation, mostly focusing on a widely held, supposed OT euphemistic use of "feet" for the human male genitalia. There is, however, no textual support for this assumption, though sometimes Ruth 3:4-8 (Oswalt 1986, 179) or Exod 4:25 (Wildberger 1991, 265) are cited. When Ruth approached Boaz and "uncovered his feet," this act may have been nothing more than a symbolic act of grasping another's feet in supplication, much as the Shunammite woman did to Elisha (2 Kgs 4:27). Moreover, the text describing Zipporah's circumcision of her son (Exod 4:25) is ambiguous as to whose "feet" she touched with the cut-off foreskin: the MT text has "his feet" (NIV's insertion of "Moses'" is interpretive and not supported in the manuscripts), which may well have been the son's feet (Childs 1974, 103). Nothing in the text indicates that "feet" is a euphemism for Moses' genitals (contra Durham 1987, 58). Motyer observes that to interpret the **feet** of the **seraphim** euphemistically as sexual parts would inappropriately attribute sexuality to these heavenly beings. He suggests, rather, that in ***covering*** their **feet**, they were indicating a choice to carry out only the Lord's commands (1993, 76).

Another possibility is that the act of ***covering*** their **feet** was a symbolic expression of the seraphim's impurity in relation to the holiness of God (compare Exod 3:5 [Moses]; Josh 5:15 [Joshua]: "Take off your sandals, for the place where you are standing is holy"). The third pair of wings, with which the seraphim **were flying**, also may be a symbolic expression of the seraphim's readiness to be dispatched with a mission from God. Isaiah's experience of recognizing his own spiritual condition ("I am a man of unclean lips") in the presence of the holiness of "the King, the LORD Almighty" (Isa 6:5), and his response to the commission of **the Sovereign** ("Here am I. Send me!") (v 8), seem to correlate with the responses of the seraphim.

■ **3** It is **Yahweh Sebaoth** that the seraphim declare is **holy, holy, holy**. In parallel with this is **his glory**, which is *the fullness of* **the whole earth**. But, what does it mean that God is **holy**? This has been defined in a number of ways: his divine perfection, his inner moral character, his separateness from all that is sinful, and his ethical behavior. It is all of these. But it is the last, his ethical behavior, that is what is visible and seen and thus defined by the seraphim's parallel term **glory** (*kābôd*), whose root meaning is "to be heavy." From this are derived various extended meanings, such as: "dignity," "honor," "wealth," "respect" (VanGemeren 1997, 2:577-87).

In a very real sense, God's holiness is explainable only from that which is observable and visible (→ 1:4). One psalmist sings: "The heavens declare the glory of God; . . . the work of his hands" (Ps 19:1). Another sings: "The heavens proclaim his righteousness, and all peoples see his glory" (97:6). It is, then, all of creation, including the heavens and the earth and all created beings and things upon the earth, that make up God's **glory**. All this, the seraphim (and Isaiah) are declaring, belong to **Yahweh Sebaoth** alone. This sets him apart from all other so-called gods. The exiled Jews in Babylonia will later be challenged: "'To whom will you compare me? Or who is my equal?' says the Holy One. Lift up your eyes and look to the heavens: Who created all these? . . . **Yahweh** is the everlasting God, the Creator of the ends of the earth" (Isa 40:25, 28*b*).

■ **4** As the seraphim chanted, so thunderous was **the sound of their voices** that the *foundations of the* **thresholds shook**. Isaiah, while lying prostrate at the very entrance to the temple, describes what he senses at that level. By implication the whole building must have been shaking. With eyes uplifted to view the Sovereign on his throne, **the temple** (*habbayit*, "the house," the outer sanctuary, not the inner throne room) **was** *filling* **with smoke**. Possibly this was from the altar of incense. The smoke may have been to block Isaiah's view of God, since in the rest of the vision Isaiah speaks no more of seeing, but only of hearing the voice of the Sovereign (v 8) and conversing with that voice (vv 9, 11).

■ **5** So overwhelmed is Isaiah he can only exclaim, **Woe to me!** Scholars are divided as to what Isaiah next said. The Hebrew is *nidmêtî*, but the verb form here could be from one of three roots: *dmh*, *dmm*, or *dwm*. These roots and the terms derived from them occur in various situations, among which are announcements of catastrophes still to come, accounts of reactions to these announcements, and in accounts of misfortunes already experienced. These reactions are translated variously, according to the context: silent/speechless, unable to move, mortally afraid, or ruined/destroyed/undone (*TDOT* 3:263).

Some contexts, however, give no criteria by which to determine which of these meanings is intended. Isaiah's temple vision experience is such a context. For example, English versions have chosen: "I am undone" (ASV, KJV, NKJV), "I am lost" (ESV, NJPS, NRSV, RSV), **I am ruined** (NASB, NIV). Commentators, too, differ: "I am destroyed" (Oswalt 1986, 171), "I am undone" (Young 1965, 231), "I was silent" (Watts 2005, 101). Wildberger argues for "I must be silent" on the basis of context: "Isaiah spoke about the uncleanness of his *lips* [emphasis original]" (1991, 250). Oswalt argues that "destroyed" more adequately expresses Isaiah's "conviction that he cannot continue to exist having seen what he has" (1986, 171).

What has Isaiah seen? The Hebrew word order is significant: **the King, Yahweh Sebaoth, my eyes have seen**. In the year that good King Uzziah died, and the nation is without a capable, God-serving leader, Isaiah's **eyes** are opened with new insight: he now has seen **the King** of the whole universe, the one who commands all the armies of both heaven and earth. It is no doubt this insight that later (701 BC) gave Isaiah his prophetic word to King Hezekiah to hold steady and trust God when the Assyrian field commander bragged that "the great king, the king of Assyria" would destroy Jerusalem (Isa 36—37, esp. 36:4).

But Isaiah sees more: he sees himself as **a man of unclean lips, *dwelling among a people of unclean lips***. The **lips** symbolize Isaiah's inner being, from which come his attitudes, will, decisions, and actions. It is in the inner being, symbolized often in the OT as the heart, where "sin" and *iniquity* (v 7) reside.

In some way unexplained, it was *because* (*kî*, not the NIV's *and*) Isaiah saw **the King** that he recognized his own **unclean** (*ṭāmē'*) condition. Isaiah now sees himself in the brilliant light of the holy God, whose character is always for his creation. In stark reality, Isaiah, who identifies himself with his people, understands that his character (and theirs) is in no sense a mirror of God's character. In the light of such a revelation, perhaps both aspects of *nidmêtî* are appropriate: Isaiah is struck with the realization that without some transforming work of God in his innermost being, he is indeed "undone"/"lost"/**ruined**, and in that realization is stunned into "silence."

■ **6-7** In a profound divine response of grace to Isaiah's new understanding of his deeply flawed character, **one of the seraphim flew . . . from the altar** to Isaiah **with a live coal in his hand** (v 6) and **touched** his **mouth** (v 7). Since Isaiah is looking toward the interior of the temple, the **altar** (v 6) would most likely have been the altar of incense located in the holy place, not the altar of sacrifice located behind him in the courtyard. The action, of course, is visionary, but with deep significance. This is no mere ceremonial ritual, for, accompanying the symbolic action of touching Isaiah's **mouth** is the seraph's words to him in v 7: **taken away** [sār] *is* **your guilt** ['ăwôneka] *and* **your sin** [ḥaṭṭā'tĕkā] *is forgiven* (tĕkupār).

Of what **sin** is Isaiah guilty, for which he must be *forgiven*? The clue is in the fact that he identifies with his "people of unclean lips" (v 5). Oswalt points out that the uncleanness of which Isaiah has been accusing his people to be guilty, is "arrogant self-sufficiency" (1986, 185). Now, in the brilliant, all-revealing light of the presence of the holy God, Isaiah discovers himself to be guilty of the same **sin**. What, then, does God require of Isaiah? Is it an act of atonement, usually requiring an animal sacrifice and an official priestly ritual? No. Only confession! And this Isaiah has done (v 5). In response, of his own initiative, God grants the penitent sinner forgiveness.

■ **8** Having heard the voices of the seraphim calling in praise (v 3), and he himself having cried out in fear (v 5), Isaiah now hears *the Sovereign* inquire, **Whom shall I send? And who will go for us?** God does not address his question directly to Isaiah but to unidentified offstage beings, perhaps a host of attendants surrounding him, as in Micaiah's vision (1 Kgs 22:19-23; compare Job 1—2; Ps 89:6-7; Zech 1:8-17; 3:1-10). Isaiah, having been forgiven and given new life from what he thought was sure death, is now given the opportunity to freely volunteer to serve his **Sovereign**. So, in joyous and thankful abandon, Isaiah responds, **Behold me!** (hinnē + objective nî, something like, "Look at me/check me out!"). **Send me!**

■ **9-10** These verses are called by many the "hardening" commission, with the following core concept: God commissioned Isaiah to preach to the people in such a way as to ensure that they will not receive God's word of salvation, and thus not repent; hence they would not return to God for healing. If they were to do so, then God could not bring his already predetermined judgment upon them. That is, God does not want them to repent.

The overall tenor of the book of Isaiah (and of the whole of the OT), however, is that God is always open to the repentance of any person or group of persons. So, we must not interpret Isaiah's commission in the way outlined above. The possible either-way effect of the preaching of the OT prophets upon their hearers must not be overlooked. The prophets did not speak on their own initiative, or out of their own imagination. They insisted that the message they spoke was not their own but was received from God and thus was God's word (e.g., Jer 1:4, 9; 2:1; 3:6; et al.). That word, when spoken, always elicited a response: either acceptance or rejection. Acceptance resulted in God's forgiveness, healing, and restoration; rejection resulted in increasing hardness of heart and ultimately God's judgment.

The view taken in this commentary of God's commission to Isaiah is that he is faithfully to continue to preach, as he has already been doing, but with a renewed fervor and intensity, knowing now that the only antidote to his people's uncleanness is the same as was for his own: confession that they are, indeed, unclean and in need of receiving God's forgiveness and removal of their iniquity. At the same time, Isaiah will know that his preaching will be met with resistance and rejection, much as Jeremiah (a century later) was told (whose mouth was also God-touched at his commissioning): "the kings of Judah, its officials, its priests and the people . . . will fight against you" (Jer 1:18-19).

The Sovereign does not make Isaiah wait. The reply is immediate: **Go and *say to* this people** (Isa 6:9). **This people**, on the one hand, may mean simply the people of Judah, with no pejorative connotation. On the other hand, one is reminded of the dialogue between God and Moses in Exod 32, where God, who is angry with the people for their sin with the golden calf, refers to them as "***this*** people" in parallel with "stiff-necked people" (Exod 32:9), and Moses reminds God twice that they are "your people" (vv 11, 12).

The phrases **be ever hearing** and **be ever seeing** both represent a Hebrew construction that indicates the continuation of the activity (Isa 6:9). Thus: ***Hear, hearing! See, seeing!*** But, the continual **hearing** results in **never understanding** (*byn*), and the continual **seeing** results in **never perceiving** (*yd'*, ***knowing***).

Is it indeed Isaiah's assignment to produce ***hearts*** that become **calloused**, **ears** that become **dull**, and **eyes** that become ***closed*** (v 10)? The Hebrew has three imperatives: ***make fat the hearts of this people, its ears make heavy, its eyes make blind!*** On the face of it, it does appear that this is what Isaiah is to do. But if we understand that prophetic preaching, if resisted and rejected, will have this exact effect, then this is the effect Isaiah's preaching will indeed have (see comment above).

But how is the second half of the verse to be interpreted? **Lest they might see . . . hear . . . understand . . . and turn and be healed**. Gordon Wong argues convincingly for a rhetorical use of persuasive irony in vv 9-10. "Divine judgment is not an idle threat. . . . [yet] Isaiah's commission was to urge repentance, not prevent it." The irony, suggests Wong, is "[go ahead, in your stubbornness] become like the idols who have eyes but cannot see, who have ears but do not hear" (2008, 26). Furthermore, Wong notes G. K. Beale's (1991, 258-60) comparison of these people with the idols of Pss 115:5-7 and 135:16-17, who have mouths, eyes, and ears but do not speak, see, or hear.

So, in their stubbornness of heart, God's people have become so insensitive to God's covenantal demands that Isaiah's preaching "continued to desensitize them as they responded negatively to the message" (Chisholm 2002, 26). In this sense only can we speak of divine hardening.

■ **11** Isaiah's anguished response is to cry out, **For how long, O *Sovereign*** [*'ad mātay 'ădōnāy*]? Is Isaiah's question: **How long** will this people continue to reject? Or **How long** must I go on preaching to such a rebellious people? In this cry we hear a plea for mercy, for leniency on God's part, and for the people's calloused rejection not to be permanent. But, the Sovereign's reply is not what his prophet hopes to hear. He must continue to preach, and God's people will continue to reject. And even beyond his own lifetime of ministry, as other prophets take up the message, rejection will continue, **until** there is nothing remaining but **cities** that **lie ruined**, empty of **inhabitant**, **houses** that **are left deserted**, and **fields ruined and ravaged**.

■ **12** How is this to happen? ***Yahweh will send everyone away***, a way of expressing exile or deportation. This practice was begun by the Assyrians, who from 734 BC onward wreaked havoc upon the northern kingdom, leading to mass population deportation of Israelites to the far reaches of the Assyrian Empire in 722 BC (2 Kgs 17). In 701 BC the Assyrians brought a most severe defeat upon the southern kingdom, of which Isaiah was a witness (Isa 36—37). With the fall of the Assyrian Empire in 612 BC, the Babylonians continued the practice of deportation. From 605 BC onward the Babylonian army wreaked havoc throughout the southern kingdom, resulting in the destruction of Jerusalem in 587 BC, with masses of Jews deported eastward to Babylonia (2 Kgs 24:1—25:21; Jer 52:1-30). Thus, "Isaiah is alerted to the fact [of exile] but not to its timing" (Motyer 1993, 79).

■ **13** The syntax of this verse is difficult and many suggestions have been made, including emendations of the Hebrew text. But, leaving the text as it is, the intent seems to be: ***Even*** **though a tenth *only* remains in the land, *and though that tenth should*** **again be laid waste, *just*** **as the terebinth and oak leave stumps when they are cut down, so the holy seed will be the stump in the land.** Thus judgment is not God's final word. It never is. There is always the hope of salvation. Just as the stumps of certain trees will put forth new growth "at the scent of water" (Job 14:9), so there will be **holy seed** ready to put forth new growth. The **holy seed**, on the one hand, may point toward the remnant, those who return repentant from exile from 538 BC onward, ready to rebuild the temple and be a new people of God. On the other hand, it may well point further into the future to a messianic descendant of David: "the stump of Jesse; . . . with righteousness he will judge . . . [and] with justice" (Isa 11:1, 4).

FROM THE TEXT

Though the text does not indicate so, perhaps Isaiah was in the habit of visiting the temple on a regular or daily basis. And, upon visit after visit, nothing unusual happened. Yet he continued to come, to give an offering or a daily sacrifice, to carry out the "duties" of a faithful worshipper. Isaiah, though regularly attending worship at the holy temple where the holy God is always present, sees but does not perceive. Thus he is no different (at this point) than those to whom he will be commissioned to continue to preach (Isa 6:10). And so God waits. Perhaps, just perhaps, on one of his visits to the temple Isaiah's spiritual eyes may be open, so that God may invite him in for an audience. And then it happened. God was already there, larger than life! And Isaiah, with eyes open to perceive, was drawn into God's presence, transformed, and sent forth recommissioned.

Just so, we attend worship experiences week after week, and often our worship seems so routine. We ask, "Where was God today?" Yet our holy God is *always* present in the holy sanctuaries of our land, and it is *we* who do not perceive his presence. But, as God's servants, we are not to grow weary of faithful attention to matters of regular gathering with others to worship our holy God. It just may be that on one (or more) of those occasions, enabled by God's Spirit, our eyes will perceive God's presence; and invited into his presence in a new and glorious experience, he will work in us a transformation previously unimagined. We surely would not want to miss such an occasion.

This passage also speaks to those of us who preach the word, time upon time, often to ears that seem closed to the gospel of repentance and acceptance of God's forgiveness. We, too, ask, "How long?" And, just as Isaiah must have been tempted to soften the truth of God's demands that he might see his people turn "to God from idols to serve the living and true God" (1 Thess 1:9), we, too, often are tempted to lessen God's demands for high ethical standards, and his calls for justice and integrity. But we must not. At the same time, our presentation of God's demands must be done "with the most sincere and earnest love for the people to whom [we are commissioned] to minister" (Young 1965, 262).

E. King Ahaz: Trust God or Assyria? (7:1-25)

Chapter 7 gives an insight into Isaiah's prophetic ministry and counsel to the Judean royal house, during the time when a coalition of Syrian and Israelite forces made war against Judah and Jerusalem (in 734 BC; compare 2 Kgs 16:5; 2 Chr 28:5-8). The resistant response to Isaiah's message, promised in Isa 6, is highlighted in his counsel to "ask **Yahweh** your God for a sign," which Ahaz, grandson of King Uzziah (referenced in ch 6), roundly rejects (vv 11-12).

Along with this theme of rejection, ch 7 speaks of one who is to be called Immanuel (**God is with us** [v 14]), and thus more directly introduces the theme of messianic hope, begun in 4:2 and 6:13.

Chapter 7 divides into three units: vv 1-9, 10-17, and 18-25.

1. Hearts Shaken but Do Not Lose Heart! (7:1-9)

BEHIND THE TEXT

Second Kings 16 provides information that a coalition of the forces of Syria and Israel "besieged Ahaz, but they could not overpower him" (v 5). Thus, in advance of what is recorded from Isa 7:2 onward, we the readers know what Ahaz at the time did not know, that, though his city would be besieged, it would not be attacked nor broken into.

The 2 Kgs 16 account informs us that the forces of Rezin and Pekah had already invaded Judah. Rezin's army, however, had given Jerusalem a reprieve for the time being, bypassing her and moving to the far south to occupy Judah's Red Sea port Elath (v 6). This account in 2 Kgs 16 gives us additional details concerning Ahaz's response to this invasion, details that are not given in the Isaiah account. In fear, Ahaz sent an urgent message for help to the big player on the world scene, the Assyrian king Tiglath-Pileser III, in which he characterized himself as "your servant and *your son*" (*binkā*, "vassal" [v 7]). To present himself as "son" in ancient Near Eastern diplomatic parlance, however, is, in fact, tantamount to an offer to place himself under the Assyrian king as a vassal. With his message Ahaz sent a significant gift from the royal treasuries and the Jerusalem temple to seal the deal (v 8). Happy to comply, Tiglath-Pileser III attacked and captured Syria's capital, Damascus, killed Rezin, and, as was Assyria's practice, deported its inhabitants to Kir (location unknown).

IN THE TEXT

■ 1 Isaiah gives a brief summary overview of a political event that occurred within the first or second year of the reign of **Ahaz . . . king of Judah**, **King Rezin of Aram [= Syria]** *along with* **Pekah son of Remaliah king of Israel marched up to** *make war* **against Jerusalem, but**, adds Isaiah, **they could not overpower it**.

The Syrian-Israelite siege of Jerusalem had been broken off, with no actual attack against the city itself. The probable reason was that Rezin's army, and Rezin himself, if he was physically with his army, must have returned quickly to defend Damascus against an impending Assyrian attack (→ Behind the Text, above).

Who Was Tiglath-Pileser III?

The biblical Tiglath-Pileser is the third Assyrian ruler to bear this name, so we append III after his name. Ruling from 745 to 727 BC, he led a resurgence of Assyrian influence, centered in the region of Nineveh, initiating her most powerful period of military and political might. He conquered the Aramean/Chaldean peoples of Babylonia to the south, took the Babylonian throne, and assumed the throne name Pulu ("Pul" in 2 Kgs 15:19; 1 Chr 5:26).

After conquering the kingdom of Urartu to the north, he turned his armies against the kingdoms to the west. In 743 BC he nipped in the bud an anti-Assyrian coalition in northern Syria. By 738 BC, as recorded in Tiglath-Pileser III's own annals, he had taken tribute from, among others, Rezon (= Rezin) of Damascus, Menahem of Samaria (= Israel), and Hiram of Tyre (Pritchard 1969, 283). Not only were these tribute-taking campaigns, but also they were intended to be permanent conquests, incorporating these entities into the Assyrian Empire. Thus, when a subject people rebelled, Tiglath-Pileser III deported the rebels to other areas of the empire, incorporating their kingdoms as Assyrian provinces.

As early as the thirteenth century BC Tiglath-Pileser I mentioned taking "hostages" from conquered towns. In the first half of the ninth century BC Ashurnasirpal II mentions both taking "hostages," and, in the case of "the Luhuti country," he "settled natives of Assyria in it." Then, in the latter half of the ninth century BC Shalmaneser III records that from the towns of the country of Hattina, "14,600 I brought away as prisoners of war" (ibid., 274-78). It was Tiglath-Pileser III, in the eighth century BC, however, who elevated hostages and prisoners of war to the category of mass deportations, the cause for doing so being rebellion, but with the intended result to create multiethnic populations in each region of the empire, thus making the empire easier to govern.

■ **2** Now the house of David *had been* told (*wayyugad*), that is, the news of a military alliance between **Aram** (= Syria) and **Ephraim** (= Israel). This news bulletin *precedes* the summary Isaiah gives in v 1. Perhaps no imagery could better picture the fear of Ahaz and his people than **hearts** shaking **as** [the leaves of] **the trees of the forest are shaken by the wind**. Such fear immobilizes, if one is trusting only in human understanding and solutions. In the face of the strength of two kingdoms from the north, what chance did small Judah have of surviving an invasion? From a human viewpoint, very little chance. Again, from the 2 Kgs 16 account we learn that Ahaz, from the time he came to the throne at the age of twenty, "did not do what was right in the eyes of **Yahweh** his God" (v 2). So, it was not habit for him, in times of national distress, to turn to God for help. Self-sufficient Ahaz would find his own human solution!

■ **3** In view of the impending Syrian-Israelite siege (see above), it seems that King Ahaz, and no doubt a cadre of construction engineers, were outside the city walls checking on the city's water supply at the **Upper Pool**, somewhere south of the city where apparently the **Launderer's Field** was located (Burrows 1958, 227; Wildberger 1991, 295). In case of a siege, the city's survival depended on its water supply.

It was on this occasion that **Yahweh** commanded his prophet **to meet Ahaz at the end of the aqueduct**. Isaiah was not to go alone but was to take along his first **son Shear-Jashub**, who must have been several years old, to accompany his father on a mission to meet the king (Wildberger 1991, 297). Why should Isaiah take along his son? Most likely because of the meaning of his son's name (*šĕ'ār yāšûb*, "A remnant shall return," with **Shear** in the emphatic position, i.e., preceding the verb, rather than following, as is the usual Hebrew indicative pattern). This suggests perhaps that "*only* a remnant shall return" or "*indeed*, a remnant shall return!" Either meaning would resonate with the lament of 1:7-9, esp. v 9: "Unless **Yahweh Sebaoth** had left us some survivors, we would have become like Sodom . . . [and] Gomorrah," and 6:11-13, esp. v 13: "so the holy seed will be the stump in the land." Thus, when Isaiah met King Ahaz, the presence of Isaiah's son, an "acted oracle, a visual aid" (Motyer 1993, 81), would have prophetic meaning for Ahaz and would add prophetic impact to Isaiah's words of warning.

■ **4** The message Isaiah is to give to Ahaz begins with a series of four imperatives: (1) **Be careful**, (2) **keep calm**, (3) **don't be afraid**, (4) **do not lose heart**! At this point, does Isaiah possess insider information that Ahaz and his advisers, the "house of David" (vv 2, 13), are considering an end run around the two powers to the north, to send for help from the world's big player, Assyria? One cannot know for sure, but elsewhere Isaiah indicates close relationship with persons in high places (8:2; 22:15). So, **Be careful** may be Isaiah's warning to Ahaz not to forget who he is: as a king of the "house of David" he is the inheritor of God's promises to the Davidic dynasty (2 Sam 8; Ps 132).

In establishing his "house," Yahweh committed to David to "be his father" and David "his son" (2 Sam 7:14). Thus each succeeding Judean king from the line of David would be considered to be in a "son" relationship with Yahweh. For Ahaz to offer himself to Tiglath-Pileser as a son (2 Kgs 16:7; → 7:1 above) would be tantamount to abrogation of his son relationship with Yahweh, thus declaring a son relationship not only with the Assyrian king but also with his deities. We learn from 2 Kgs 16, in fact, that as a result of refusing to heed Isaiah's warning, Ahaz did bring into the Jerusalem temple an altar constructed according to Assyrian design (vv 10-16).

The remaining three imperatives are in regard to the impending invasion and/or siege of the Syrian-Israelite coalition.

These two smoldering stubs of firewood is an expression of contempt describing **Rezin** and **the son of Remaliah**, heads of the kingdoms of **Aram** and **Ephraim**. The metaphor is that of a campfire that has effectively burned itself out, leaving only the smoking stubs of a couple of sticks, no longer burning, soon to be only two piles of cold ash. Isaiah's title for the head of Ephraim here also carries an element of contempt. By not citing his given name (Pekah), he is simply **the son of Remaliah**. Perhaps Isaiah is signaling nonrecognition of the legitimacy of Pekah's rule of the northern kingdom, since, as a military officer of high rank in the northern kingdom, in 740 BC he had seized the throne after assassinating King Pekahiah (2 Kgs 15:25-27).

■ **5-6** Yes, Ahaz, these two burned-out flames have **plotted your ruin** (Isa 7:5). They are planning to **invade Judah**, and they do intend to **tear it apart** (v 6). Moreover, they intend to remove you as king and place on your throne one named **the son of Tabeal**. Here again is a note of contempt in that Isaiah mentions no given name. The MT spelling **Tabeal** (*ṭābĕ'al*) means "good for nothing." The NIV follows the LXX spelling, **Tabeel** (*ṭābe'ēl*), meaning "the goodness of God." This would-be usurper of the Judean throne was probably Aramean.

■ **7** To this situation of fear and trembling, Isaiah gives assurance: Ahaz, what you fear (the dismembering of your kingdom, the siege of your city), **it will not happen**. Just as other OT prophets insist they are privy to information that the ordinary person does not have (compare Jer 23:18; Amos 3:7), Isaiah has received advance information from **Sovereign Yahweh**, himself.

■ **8-9** The two name sequences are listed in declining order, kingdom, capital, head of state: **Aram/Damascus/Rezin** (v 8) and **Ephraim/Samaria/Remaliah's son** (v 9). The divine word is meant to assure Ahaz that, though the two kingdoms, **Aram** and **Ephraim**, appear overwhelming when allied against him, behind each was ultimately merely a human being, **Rezin** and **Remaliah's son** (Clements 1980, 85). Therefore, as the plans of these two men unraveled, so would the threat against Ahaz's kingdom.

The prophetic promise in Isa 7:8*b*, that **within sixty-five years Ephraim** would cease **to be a people**, raises an interpretive/historical problem. Samaria, Israel's capital, was captured, and the kingdom of Israel made an Assyrian province in 722 BC, only some twelve or thirteen years later than when this prophecy was given in ca. 734 BC. Ezra 4:2, however, mentions the Assyrian king Esarhaddon's (reigned 680-669 BC) resettling foreign groups of peoples in the area of Samaria. Esarhaddon gives extensive description of his campaigns against the "12 kings from the seacoast," and mentions marching through "the region of Samaria" (Pritchard 1969, 290-92). Additionally, the MT of Ezra 4:10 mentions the Assyrian king "Osnapper" (most likely the NIV's "Ashurbanipal" [reigned 668-627 BC], son of and successor to Esarhaddon) deporting (from) and settling "other people . . . in the city of Samaria." These two events could well be that to which the Isaiah prediction points; these later deportations and resettlements would effectively bring to an end any hope of continuance of the northern tribes' identity as Ephraimites or Israelites.

In Isa 7:9*b* there is a wordplay on two forms of the Hebrew root *'mn*, the causative "to believe," and the passive, "to be established." Therefore, Isaiah's summary challenge to Ahaz and his ruling entourage is: **If you** [pl.] **do not believe** [stand firm in your faith], ***indeed*** [*kî*, NIV omits] **you** [pl.] **will not remain established** [stand at all]. Ahaz is to believe the word of the Sovereign and of his prophet (v 7). Undergirding this word is the covenant made with the house of David (→ v 4), of which he, Ahaz, is a recipient and bearer.

FROM THE TEXT

This moment between king and prophet on the road to the Launderer's Field (v 3) concludes with the implied question: Ahaz, will you trust in the sovereignty of the Sovereign God, the one who rules over and controls all nations and has the welfare of your own kingdom in view? Or will you abandon the security offered through faith in Sovereign Yahweh for the unsure, shaky fickleness of promised security in liaison with Assyria? Decision hangs in the balance.

Perhaps we are not so different from Ahaz, in that it takes courage to risk faith, especially when it seems that the circumstances of worldly events loom larger and more real than God's word, which says "wait and see what I am about to do," when it seems that God is doing nothing. Moses' faith was tested when the Israelite leaders accused him of not having helped their cause any by coming back to Egypt. In turn, he accused Yahweh of sitting on the sidelines and doing nothing to help. Yahweh replied that he was about to act against Pharaoh with his "mighty hand" (Exod 5:21—6:1). Habakkuk's faith was stretched to the point that he accused the Lord of not listening to his continual cries for help to right the violence and injustice in Judah. To this the Lord told Habakkuk to "look" and "watch," for he was about to act in a way that even Habakkuk would find difficult to believe (Hab 1:2-5).

We, too, often wait with impatience for God to act for us or for others for whom we have concern, or for a change of circumstances. The message of Isaiah for us is no different than it was for Ahaz: Believe, stand firm, and watch for God to work in his timing, not in ours.

2. The Sign of Immanuel (7:10-17)

BEHIND THE TEXT

Isaiah confronts Ahaz a second time, probably at a later time and different place, though the content links it with the preceding confrontation (7:3). Isaiah challenges Ahaz to test God by requesting a sign. This challenge appears to have taken place before Ahaz sent his plea to Tiglath-Pileser III for Assyrian help.

The main interpretative problem in this passage centers on two questions concerning Yahweh's "sign" (v 11): (1) Who is "the virgin" who births "a son *called* Immanuel"? (2) Who is "Immanuel" (v 14)?

IN THE TEXT

■ 10 *And* again *Yahweh* spoke to Ahaz: though reference to Isaiah is omitted, this word surely comes through Yahweh's prophet.

■ 11 Thus Isaiah instructed Ahaz, **Ask *for yourself* a sign *from Yahweh* your God.** We find in the biblical narrative records of God giving solicited or unsolicited signs to initiate faith in his power and confirm his word to those who have lack of faith (see Gen 15:5; Exod 4:1-9; Judg 6:17, 36-40; John 20:30-31). The hyperbole **deepest depths or . . . highest heights** gives Ahaz the widest possible options for asking from the deity very familiar to him: **your God.**

■ 12 But, under the facade of piety (see Deut 6:16), Ahaz **will not ask.** Unwilling or perhaps unable to recognize that it is he, himself, who is being tested, Ahaz declares that he **will not put *Yahweh* to the test.** The text clearly implies that Ahaz's refusal to ask for a sign that God initiated was a clear evidence of his unbelief; he was determined to follow the political decisions he had already made.

■ 13 Isaiah addresses his words, **Hear [pl.] now, O house of David!**, to both Ahaz and his royal supporters. **House of David** reminds them that the king is still the bearer of the earlier divine covenant between Yahweh and David; that covenant promised Yahweh's faithfulness in return for the king's loyalty and trust. With Ahaz's refusal to trust, however, Isaiah's terminology changes: it is now no longer "your God" (v 11), as Isaiah sharply rebukes Ahaz for *also wearying* **my God.** Yahweh now becomes a foreign deity to Ahaz.

■ 14 In response to Ahaz's refusal to request of the Lord a sign, the **Sovereign** himself now **will give** Ahaz and his royal household **a sign.** The aspects of the sign are: (1) **the pregnant young woman** (*hā'almâ*, **virgin**); (2) a yet-to-be-born **son**; (3) the naming of the son, **Immanuel** (*'immānû 'ēl*, "God is with us"). The interpretive history has focused on two questions: (1) Who is the *young woman*? (2) Who is **Immanuel**? Looking through the rearview lens of Matt 1:23, which quotes the LXX (*parthenos*, "virgin," for *'almâ*), traditionally, the Christian interpretation has been that the *primary* interpretation of Isaiah's prophecy is that the **virgin** is Mary and **Immanuel** is Jesus, despite the fact that Jesus is never called Immanuel in the NT. Because the LXX translators used a Greek word clearly meaning "virgin" for *'almâ*, however, one must ask, what is the meaning of the Hebrew *'almâ*? Specifically, does *'almâ* exclusively refer to one who is a **virgin**? With the exception of its debated meaning in Prov 30:19, all other references to an *'almâ* in the OT do appear to be unmarried women, and thus by cultural expectation, virgins. The focus of the term, however, is not on virginity, but on reproductive maturity, one who can now bear a child (Motyer 1993, 84-5; Oswalt 1986, 209-11).

Additionally, the traditional interpretation generally fails to recognize that, for the **sign** to have any meaning for Ahaz and his present situation, the "plain sense of the text" (Oswalt 1986, 208), requires that its *primary* fulfillment had to occur within the time period of Ahaz's rule. Therefore, the identity of the *young woman* and, relatedly, that of **Immanuel,** must be found within the more immediate context of Isaiah and Ahaz. That said, however, these identities have successfully eluded all scholarly suggestions, though most commentators ultimately settle upon one or another possibility, though their conclusions are speculation at best.

Immanuel, "God is with us," surely was intended to give positive assurance to Ahaz, that, in spite of his refusal to "test" (= trust) God (Isa 7:12), God would stand by his promise related to Aram and Ephraim in vv 8-9, reaffirmed in v 16. And, **Immanuel** points even beyond this crisis event, beyond Ahaz's refusal to trust God, to the son who bears God's covenant commitment with the "house of David"; **Immanuel** points to the "expectation of one who is the [true] Son" (10:33—11:9) (Kaiser 1972, 105).

Immanuel will occur again in 8:8 where he is possessor of the land ("your land, O Immanuel") and in 8:10 in a wordplay translated "for God is with us." This larger context will give some clarification of how the **sign** of **Immanuel** was understood messianically.

■ **15-16** These two verses speak to a time frame, measured by Immanuel's age, in which Aram and Ephraim **will be laid to waste**: that is, **before the boy** [Immanuel] **knows enough to reject the wrong and choose the right** (v 16). This time frame is vague but seems to refer to the concept of moral accountability, though Smith suggests that here is an implication that Immanuel will reject the wicked ways of Ahaz and rule with justice (2007, 214). In any case, within three years of this prophecy, Assyria had taken Damascus/Aram, and within thirteen years, Samaria/Ephraim, both well within the time frame of a child's reaching accountability.

Curds and honey (v 15), which Immanuel will eat in the period before he reaches accountability, can be a symbol of poverty amid devastation (negative) or a symbol of blessing as in a land "flowing with curds and honey" (positive). Here, it seems to be both, pointing forward to vv 21-22, when, in the midst of the devastation following Assyria's invasion (negative), even a single cow and a couple of goats will produce enough milk that the survivors who remain in the land will eat an abundance of "curds and honey" (positive).

■ **17** But, the sign of Immanuel has negative implications for Ahaz as well, for when **the king of Assyria** finishes wasting the lands of Aram and Ephraim, **Yahweh will bring him upon you** [= Ahaz] **and on your people and on *your father's house*** (*bēt 'ābikā*). A *bēt 'āb* (a ***father's house***) most often in the OT is a technical term for "the extended family" (Ross 1979, 62), at the head of which is the most senior or authoritative male member. Thus the consequences of Ahaz's refusal to trust God will extend outward to his entire royal family, and, ultimately, to all the people of his kingdom.

FROM THE TEXT

This portion of text focuses on God's offer to Ahaz, through Isaiah, to ask for a sign as evidence that he would keep his covenant promise of protection and security. It is a simple request, or so it seems. Yet the offer is refused. The present political circumstances seemed to Ahaz more concrete and real than the ancient promise of an unseen God. Perhaps Ahaz was out of touch with history, unfamiliar with the acts of God on behalf of those who ruled before him, back to forefather David, and even long before that, back to the wonderful acts in the early days of Israel's formation. Without spiritual memory of the past, Ahaz is unable to grasp hold of the spiritual reality of the present and believe that the God who stood by Israel in the past can and will stand by his kingdom in the present.

But Ahaz is not alone in this. We, too, often through ignorance of the past or sometimes through simply setting aside what we do know of God's faithfulness to our "fathers," in fear of the present, elect to go it alone and resolve present threats and difficulties in our own wisdom. We place our trust in the "seen" rather than in our God whom we do not see. Oswalt observes that what a person "trusts in place of God will one day turn to devour him" (1986, 214).

3. In that Day: Only Briars and Thorns (7:18-25)

BEHIND THE TEXT

A characteristic phrase of this passage, "in that day" (vv 18, 20, 21, 23), brings together a "mosaic of oracles" (Motyer 1993, 88) that possibly were given at varying times but now, together, give substance to the threat hinted at in v 17. This threat is the coming invasion of "the king of Assyria" (v 20). The land will be depopulated, and cultivated fields will return to wilderness.

IN THE TEXT

■ **18-19** Though humans strategize the invasion, behind all such actions is **Yahweh**, who **will whistle** for the great powers to come against Judah (v 18). Wherever one might attempt to hide from the overwhelming presence of the armies of **Egypt** and **Assyria**, they will be there, just as one cannot escape from swarms of **flies** or swarming **bees**. In 735 BC, however, Egypt has weakened and is not a threat, but even a resurgent Egypt could be a threat without trust in God's protection. The imminent threat is Assyria.

■ **20** It is Ahaz who had **hired . . . the king of Assyria**, Tiglath-Pileser III, with a significant gift (2 Kgs 16:7-8), to come to his rescue from the Syrian-Israelite threat. Now, however, the **Sovereign** will use this *hireling like a razor to shave*

the hair of the head and legs [*raglāyim*] ***and also the beard***. Regarding *raglāyim* ("legs, feet"), there is no textual evidence, OT or otherwise, that this is a euphemism for **private parts** (→ 6:2). Such complete shaving of body hair subjects one to complete humiliation. So Judah will be overwhelmingly humiliated.

■ **21-22** In the aftermath of the Assyrian invasions of northern Israel in 722 BC, and of Judah between the time of this prophecy and 701 BC, both the human population and domestic livestock will be greatly reduced. A farmer will be reduced to ***keeping*** alive [***only***] **a young cow and two goats** (the negative aspect [v 21]). Yet, because of the **abundance of the milk** (v 22) produced by the few milk-producing animals throughout the land, both the farmer and the few inhabitants **who remain in the land will eat curds and honey** (the positive aspect; → v 15).

■ **23-25** The negative depiction of the aftereffects of the Assyrian invasions continues. With the human depopulation, the valley **land** (v 24) and the **cultivated** (v 25) sides of the **hills** return to wilderness; now, instead of golden fields of grain or luscious **vines,** one finds only **briers and thorns**. Now, only hunters come with **bow and arrow** (v 24), or herders to let their **cattle** and **sheep** forage (v 25). The land outside the cities has become a place of **fear**.

FROM THE TEXT

Ahaz's unbelief in God's ability to protect in the impending crisis brings disaster upon his entire kingdom. His people, for several generations, had worked hard to build up agricultural farms and herds of livestock. They had poured their resources into these enterprises, only to see it all dissolve before their eyes, through no fault of their own: they had trusted in the wisdom of their king, only to discover that he was trusting in his own worldly wisdom.

Because of their unwise and unbelieving king, the people's world was changing and would remain forever changed. The dominant power in their backyard would now be Assyria, succeeded by Babylon. A few later kings would attempt to bring Judah back to worship and trust in Yahweh, such as Hezekiah and Josiah, but it was now too late. God's plan for his people would inevitably move toward that day when they would be largely removed from his holy land. His larger plan, however, would use a later world power, Persia, to return a remnant of his people to his holy land for replanting and rebuilding (compare Isa 44:26-28; Jer 1:10; 24:6; 31:28).

F. The Flood Waters of Assyria (8:1-22)

BEHIND THE TEXT

Traditionally divided into six units (Isa 8:1-4, 5-8, 9-10, 11-15, 16-18, 19-22), ch 8 is linked to ch 7 through key terms: "Damascus" and "Samaria"

(8:4), "Rezin" and "Remaliah" (v 6), "the king of Assyria" (vv 4, 7), and "Immanuel" (vv 8, 10). Thus the historical/political context continues to be the Syrian-Israelite threat and its aftermath.

Three times Isaiah says, "**Yahweh** spoke to me" (vv 1, 5, 11). In v 17 he says, "I will wait . . . I will . . . trust," and in v 18 he mentions "I, and [my] children." These first-person reflections give the chapter an autobiographical flavor.

The implication that Isaiah's soon-to-be-born child will serve as a sign to the people of Judah is featured in unit 1 (vv 1-4), paralleling the child sign theme of ch 7. But Isaiah's child is not Immanuel, for, in unit 2 (8:5-8) "Immanuel" is addressed in the context of "your land," that is, as the owner of ("Lord of" [Childs 2001, 73]) the land of Judah. Thus an eschatological, messianic expectation is introduced.

The chapter concludes (vv 19-22, unit 6) on a negative note: a dispute between Isaiah and unspecified persons who "consult mediums and spiritists" (v 19) and thus are challenging "this word" (v 20) of the prophet as the best/only means of discerning God's will.

IN THE TEXT

1. Quick to the Plunder, Swift to the Spoil (8:1-4)

■ 1 The interaction has shifted from personal interaction between Isaiah and Ahaz to Isaiah and the wider public, probably in Jerusalem.

Yahweh commanded Isaiah, **Take a large *tablet*** [*gillāyôn*] **and write on it**. Since this was to be **large**, apparently so that the public could easily read it, it probably was not a leather or papyrus **scroll**. It may have been a wax-covered wooden board similar to some wax-covered ivory tablets found at Assyrian Nimrud (dating to ca. 707-705 BC) or wooden writing boards, most likely covered with wax, used by the Hittites in an earlier period (Wiseman 1955, 3, 11). Isaiah was to write on it the Hebrew words **Maher-Shalal-Hash-Baz**, meaning something like "swift to come is the spoil, speedy is the prey." The billboard, with its writing, was apparently to function as a sign, though no prophecy or prediction was spoken.

■ 2 Two well known, **reliable** persons are called as **witnesses** to this sign. **Uriah the priest** is most likely the same Uriah who built and officiated at the Assyrian altar in the Jerusalem temple at Ahaz's command (2 Kgs 16:10-16). **Zechariah son of Jeberekiah** may be the Zechariah who was the father of Abijah/Abi, wife of Ahaz and mother of Hezekiah (2 Kgs 18:2; 2 Chr 29:1). The taking of two witnesses conforms to the Law (Deut 17:6; 19:15). Isaiah needs witnesses no doubt to confirm, months or years later when the implications of the sign were completed, the time when it was first made public. The significance of this action-sign will be revealed only at a later time.

■ **3** There is no reason to believe that **the prophetess**, to whom Isaiah **made love**, was not his wife. Having **conceived**, after an implied nine months, she birthed **a son**. At **Yahweh's** command Isaiah named him the same name he had earlier written on the public billboard: **Maher-Shalal-Hash-Baz.**

■ **4** At the time of naming his son, Isaiah gives a prophecy, with its completion to be before the child can speak, **"My father"** or **"My mother."** Within that time frame, **the wealth of Damascus and the plunder of Samaria will be carried *before*** [*lipnê*, not the NIV's **off by**] **the king of Assyria**. An example of this is a monument from the ninth century BC called the Black Obelisk, showing Assyrian king Shalmaneser III sitting on his throne, receiving tribute brought *before* him by Israel's king Jehu son of Omri (Pritchard 1958, plates 100a, b).

Within a short time Isaiah's prophecy is fulfilled. In 733 BC, as claimed in his annals, Tiglath-Pileser III deported many inhabitants and possessions of the House of Omri (the Assyrian name for northern Israel) and incorporated its territories as Assyrian provinces. In 732 BC he conquered and brought to an end the long dominance of Damascus (Pritchard 1969, 284).

2. Immanuel! (God Is with Us!) (8:5-8)

■ **5-6** **This people** (v 6), the people of Judah/Jerusalem, **has *scorned*** the **gently flowing waters of Shiloah**. Their action denies them the right to be addressed as "my people." The **waters of Shiloah** refers to a canal through which flowed water from the Gihon spring to pools on the southeastern side of Jerusalem. The inhabitants of the city depended upon this **gently flowing** water for their existence. Just so, for their continued existence and protection, they were to depend in faith upon the quiet, steady word of God through his prophet Isaiah: trust God, not Assyria. But Ahaz and his advisers have ***scorned*** this word; following their lead, the people are ***rejoicing*** over the defeat of **Rezin** of Syria and **Remaliah** of Israel.

■ **7** But their rejoicing would be short-lived. In contrast to the gentle waters of Shiloah, the **Sovereign** will **bring against them the mighty floodwaters of the Euphrates, which annually *overflows* . . . all its banks**. The Euphrates is a metaphor for **the king of Assyria**.

■ **8** Therefore, the Assyrian king, the one in whom Ahaz had placed his trust and to whom he had offered his allegiance as a son (2 Kgs 16:7), after putting down the Syrian-Israelite rebellion, will now **sweep on into Judah**, like a flood **reaching up to the neck**. But God's Assyrian judgment upon Judah is limited because, as Isaiah exclaims at the conclusion of Isa 8:8, **Immanuel! *God is with us!*** Childs suggests this to be a wordplay on "the mysterious child of the promise" of 7:14, now appearing as the messianic "Lord of the land of Judah" (2001, 73).

3. With Us Is God! (Immanuel!) (8:9-10)

■ **9-10** The message is sent out to the **nations** (*'ammîm*), to those in **every distant land**: Take a lesson from the ultimate fate of Assyria (v 9). Though you may **prepare for battle**, though you may **devise your strategy** (v 10), though you may carefully **propose your plan**, whatever **war cry** (v 9) you **raise** against Yahweh's land, ultimately you will not succeed. Why? It is because **with us is God** (*'immānû 'ēl*), even amid judgment.

4. Fear Yahweh! (8:11-15)

■ **11** This passage continues in the context of the pending Syrian-Israelite threat against Judah, causing great fear in Jerusalem. The message is directed to an inner circle of Isaiah's faithful followers.

For thus Yahweh said to me. Isaiah does not say how he received this message; he does, however, give a cryptic "code" (Wildberger 1991, 357), **as the seizing of the** hand. This would be the same **hand** of **Yahweh** that was upon both Ezekiel and Jeremiah when they received a "word" from Yahweh (Jer 15:16-17; Ezek 1:3; 3:14). To be seized by **the** hand of Yahweh is to be temporarily possessed by God in some way out of the ordinary, a prophet's experience. The message was a personal **warning** to Isaiah **not to follow the way of this people**. **This people** could well be pejorative here, in that God does not say "my people." These would be the citizens of Judah in general, and more specifically the inhabitants of Jerusalem. Their **way** is not to be Isaiah's way.

■ **12-13** In these two verses Isaiah is addressing an inner circle of followers (**you** is pl. [v 13]), identified in v 16 as his "disciples." The content (and of vv 14-15) is the essence of the warning message Isaiah had received from Yahweh.

One can imagine the following scenario. Rumors of the impending Syrian-Israelite invasion from the north fly from house to house throughout the city. Talk spreads of this prophet fellow Isaiah advising King Ahaz against seeking help from Assyria: might he actually be in cahoots with the northern alliance seeking to depose Ahaz to put Tabeal on the throne? Meanwhile, someone in a back alley whispers: **conspiracy** (v 12). The whisper becomes talk, until the talk becomes a shout: **CONSPIRACY! CONSPIRACY!**

Isaiah's prophetic message to his inner circle is: Don't believe the **conspiracy** theory of **this people**. There is no need to **fear what they fear**, no need to **dread**. For the prophetic word that I spoke earlier still stands: "It will not take place" (7:7); **With us is God** (8:10).

There is **one**, however, **you are to fear**: this is **Yahweh Sebaoth** whom **you are to regard as holy** (v 13). To succumb to conspiracy theories is to deny the sovereignty of God, who does not deal in conspiracy. Oswalt notes, "That which is holy is distinct from the common or ordinary" (1986, 234). He then draws us back to Isaiah's vision of God "high and exalted" (6:1), in power, character and essence. It is in this that God is holy. Thus **to regard** [God] **as holy** is to demonstrate by attitude and behavior that God is not "helpless, indifferent, and unimportant" (ibid.).

■ **14-15** For those of **Israel, Judah,** and **Jerusalem** who, ignoring the cries of the conspiracy mongers, come before God in trust, regarding him as holy, God **will be** for them **a holy place** (*miqdāš*), a place of refuge and safety (v 14). But for those who, by their lifestyle of carelessness and indifference, treat him as though he is powerless and does not matter, God will be in their path **a stone** that, in their darkness, **causes** them **to stumble** and **fall**. In the coming Assyrian invasion, especially in the northern kingdom, by implication only a few will find refuge in God the **holy place**. But **many of them will stumble** (v 15) upon God the **rock that makes them fall** (v 14), and **captured**, they will be led away into exile (v 15).

5. Bind Up the Testimony (8:16-22)

■ **16** Motyer keenly points to the contrast of attitudes in this passage: Isaiah, who in "patient faith" says, "I will wait for *Yahweh*" (v 17) and the people's, who in "impatient unbelief" (1993, 95) "curse . . . their God" (v 21).

My disciples is ambiguous as to whose they are: God's or Isaiah's? Most commentators take them to be Isaiah's (Motyer 1993, 96, is an exception). These **disciples**, however, would not necessarily be persons in a student/teacher relationship in an established prophetic school, as is often suggested. Rather, they would be a group of Isaiah's "trusted companions" (Wildberger 1991, 367), followers who believe in and trust the word of the prophet.

The MT of v 16 reads simply, ***Bind testimony*** [*tĕ'ûdâ*], ***seal instruction*** [*tôrâ*] ***among my disciples***, without defining ***testimony*** and ***instruction***. *Tĕ'ûdâ* and *tôrâ* are used elsewhere, however, of God's revelation (compare Deut 4:44, 45; 1 Kgs 2:3; Ps 119), both generally and in the written word. Here, Isaiah would be including his earlier admonition against an alliance with Assyria, and his urging Ahaz to trust his word that the Syrian-Israelite alliance against Jerusalem will fail. He is putting in written format **among** [**his**] **disciples** his confidence in God's revelation for the future; he is urging them to that same confidence. The written word will be evidence for them of God's revealed word in the future.

■ **17** In this time of uncertainty and approaching darkness (v 22), when **Yahweh is hiding his face from the descendants of Jacob** (both Israel and Judah), he is withholding the blessing of grace and peace that are present when he "make[s] his face shine on" them (Num 6:25). Yet Isaiah **will wait** *patiently* in **confident** trust until the time God chooses to act in both judgment and salvation toward his people.

■ **18** It is not Isaiah alone who waits, but he along with his two **children**, Shear-Jashub and Maher-Shalal-Hash-Baz, whose names are known to all **in**

Israel. In their waiting, their names, and perhaps also (as Oswalt [1986, 236] suggests) Isaiah's name ("Yahweh saves"), stand as **signs and symbols**. Their names point to the predicted fall of Damascus and Israel and both the judgment upon Judah and the still held out offer of repentance and salvation (Kaiser 1972, 121).

■ **19** There appear to be some, perhaps the same as those crying "conspiracy" (v 12), who do not share Isaiah's "***confident*** trust" in God (v 17). In opposition to him, they are urging others to turn to the practitioners of the occult: **mediums** ['*ōbôt*] **and spiritists** (*yiddĕōnîm*, from *yd'*, "to know" [v 19]). An *'ōb*—in the case of the witch of Endor, for instance—was both a living person said to be able to contact the dead and the spirit in the realm of the dead through which the living person gained access to the dead. The purpose of this access was to obtain information on behalf of the living (1 Sam 28:7-8). The *yiddĕōnîm* are those spirits in the realm of the dead thought to have "inside knowledge," to be "in the know" about the future. The consultation of **mediums and spiritists** is forbidden in Lev 19:31; 20:27; and Deut 18:11. Oswalt notes the irony of the LXX translation of *yiddĕōnîm* as "ventriloquists," indicating the Jewish translators' concept of the true source of the ***whispering and muttering*** (1986, 237).

■ **20** No, one does not discern God's will by consulting the occult. The only sure and authoritative source is **instruction** (*tôrâ*) and **testimony** (*tĕ'ûdâ*) given by God through his prophet. But Isaiah's voice would not be the only voice heard in the streets of Jerusalem. There would be others propagating a message, but their message was not **according to this word**. For them, persisting in their refusal to heed **God's instruction**, there can only be a deepening darkness with **no light of dawn**, a "metaphor for a hopeful future" (Motyer 1993, 97).

■ **21-22** The outcome of turning to the occult for guidance (v 19), which operates in the dark corners while rejecting the light of God's Word (v 20), offered to all in the open, is inevitable **darkness**, which leads to **utter darkness** (v 22). While ***roaming*** **through the land** (either in the aftermath of the Assyrian destruction or on their way to exile), they become **distressed and hungry**, in fact, **famished** (v 21). Unable to detect the spiritual defect within themselves, **enraged**, they can only **curse their king** [perhaps Ahaz, who refused to trust God] **and their God** (whom they, themselves, had refused to trust).

FROM THE TEXT

The focus of Isaiah's message in this chapter is Immanuel (v 8), whether in judgment or salvation. We may not know just how God is going to work out the details of our future, but in time God will reveal his future for us, as we trust him and rest in his care for us in the now; for, in fact, "God is with us" (v 10). We will wait, says Isaiah, to see the outcome of Ahaz's distrust of God and misplaced trust in Assyria. Not so, say the "conspirator" party. We will not wait. We do not see the evidence of God's presence among the living, so we will search for direction for our future among the dead, through our mediums and spiritists. Down with the prophet and his prophecy!

And so, Isaiah the prophet and the "conspirator" party are at an impasse. In time, insists Isaiah, God will carry out his plan of judgment and reprieve. In time, the word of the prophet will be vindicated. For Israel, vindication will begin with Tiglath-Pileser III's first invasion of the Galilee region in 735 BC and will conclude in 722 BC with Israel's downfall and the exile of multitudes of her inhabitants to the far reaches of Assyria. For Judah, vindication will result from the several Assyrian military campaigns southward, until the 701 BC invasion of Assyrian Sennacherib; though Jerusalem miraculously will escape through God's intervention, her towns and countryside will be left devastated.

Isaiah's, however, is not the only prophet's voice speaking during the reign of Ahaz. Micah's voice, too, is heard, preaching to both Samaria and Jerusalem (Mic 1:5). His message, too, is that, because of the sin of idol worship/prostitution (v 7), not only is God's judgment to fall upon Israel, but "disaster has come from **Yahweh**, even to the gate of Jerusalem" (v 12).

There are yet even other prophets' voices heard in the streets of both north and south, countering the voices of both Isaiah and Micah. Isaiah mentions "prophets who teach lies" (Isa 9:15 [14 HB]). Micah notes those prophets who, perhaps in mockery of Isaiah's "Immanuel/God is with us," are declaring, "Is not **Yahweh** among us? No disaster will come upon us" (Mic 3:11). But Micah, as does Isaiah, looks beyond the 701 BC reprieve to a time when "Jerusalem will become a heap of rubble" (v 12), which indeed was brought about by the Babylonians in 586 BC. From these who reject God's word, says Micah (as does Isaiah), God "will hide his face" (Mic 3:4; see Isa 8:17); for them there will be no sun of the day but only the darkness of night, shamed and disgraced (Mic 3:6-7).

G. Unto Us a Child Is Born (9:1-7 [8:23—9:6 HB])

BEHIND THE TEXT

The passage speaks of a people, oppressed and in darkness, whose darkness is lifted by the *dawning* of "a great light" (v 2 [1 HB]). This condition of "light" is made possible: (1) *because* (*kî*) the slaver's "yoke" has been "shattered" (v 4 [3 HB]); (2) *because* (*kî*) "battle" weapons have been burned (v 5 [4 HB]); and (3) *because* (*kî*) "a child is born," whose name signifies a coming messianic ruler whose qualities for ruling far exceed those of any mere human ruler.

With this passage Isaiah's brings to a close his prophetic messages at the time of the Syrian-Israelite crisis and the Assyrian threat to Israel and Judah.

IN THE TEXT

■ **9:1 [8:23 HB]** Isaiah concluded the previous section with "distressed and hungry" people, cursing both king (most likely Judean Ahaz) and God, groping about in "fearful gloom" (8:21-22). But, now, **no more gloom for those who were in distress**. Isaiah's concern is for more than Judah and Jerusalem, for he now directs his message to the northern kingdom's **Zebulun** and **Naphtali**. Isaiah presents two contrasts: **In the past he humbled** (*hēqal*, "make light of," "treat as of no account," causative of *qll*, "to be light") . . . **but in the future he will honor** (*hikbîd*, "make weighty," "treat as of much worth," causative of *kbd*, "to be heavy"). The **he** of both verbs is unspecified, but the first **he** must surely refer to Tiglath-Pileser III. In his campaigns of 734-733 BC, he conquered these northern Israelite territories and deported many Israelites to Assyria (2 Kgs 15:29; Aharoni and Avi-Yonah 1993, 110), while bringing other settlers in from distant parts of the empire. Subsequently, in 733-732 BC, these territories were annexed as Assyrian provinces. The second **he** must surely refer to God, for it is only God who can dispel the **gloom**, replacing it with "light" (v 2 [1 HB]).

There is no agreement among scholarly attempts to give exact identifications to Isaiah's **Galilee of the nations**, **Way of the Sea**, and **beyond the Jordan**. The area north of the Jezreel valley between the Sea of Kinnereth/Sea of Galilee and the Mediterranean Sea, however, is the general area to which Isaiah refers. The international roads providing interchange and trade between the peoples of Mesopotamia to the east, Anatolia to the north/northwest, and Egypt to the southwest passed through this territory. Thus, over time, the travelers, languages, and cultures of **the nations** (*haggôyim*) of the biblical "world" intermingled, until this area truly became a **Galilee of the nations**.

Thus Isaiah sounds a note of hope and with it "introduces a new idea, the involvement of the Gentiles [peoples of nations other than Israel/Judah] in the time of hope" (Motyer 1993, 100).

■ **2 [1 HB]** The enigma in this verse is to determine upon whom **a light has dawned**, who it is that has **seen a great light**. Isaiah says, **The people,** *the ones* **walking in darkness**. One possibility is that they may be those who, in their rebellion, had persisted in choosing sin but now desire to turn away from their sin (Oswalt 1986, 242). A second possibility is that they may be the faithful remnant, remaining steadfast, **walking/living** in expectant hope, yet are caught in the **darkness** of national calamity (Motyer 1993, 100). A third possibility is a combination of the above two, that this salvific message is here given to those who were thrust into the judgment of "utter darkness" (8:19-22), a word of grace and hope in the midst of judgment to both the faithful and the unfaithful in the land.

Whichever is the possibility, the **great light** that **has dawned** can be none other than God himself, who is both Creator of light and light itself (Gen 1:3-4; Ps 139:11-12; Isa 42:16; John 1:4, 5, 9; 2 Cor 4:6). The two verbs of Isa 9:2 [1 HB], **have seen** and **has dawned**, are in the perfect tense, signaling action completed. Isaiah here appears to be using prophetic perfects, that is, the prophet looks forward, with God-given surety, as though the events have already taken place. (→ From the Text for 9:1-7 [8:23—9:6 HB], below, for more on the **great light**.)

■ **3 [2 HB]** It may be the faithful remnant (v 2 [1 HB]), the few, who have been living in oppressive darkness or all the people who live in darkness who wait expectantly for the light of God's favor to shine upon them. When that happens, when their Messiah comes like the dawning light, their *rejoicing* will be uncontainable. This will be so because **the nation** will become so **enlarged** the land itself will be unable to contain them. Isaiah 49:8-23 gives an expansive description of God calling and bringing his captive people, "those in darkness" (v 9), together in such numbers that it will be said, "This place is too small for us" (v 20).

Harvest is seen as God's reward for one's faithful labor, **plunder** was God's gift for victory in battle. Both required dependence upon him; both give cause for *rejoicing*.

■ **4 [3 HB]** Freedom from the **oppressor** is the reason for the people's rejoicing. Isaiah highlights three symbols of oppression; (1) **the yoke** [*'ōl*] *of his burden* (*sōbel*, related to *sēbel*, "forced labor") is generally a symbol for a slave's servitude (e.g., Jer 30:8); here, it indicates the added symbolism of foreign domination (e.g., Isa 47:6); (2) **the *pulling* bar** [*môṭâ* (emended) instead of MT's *maṭṭēh*, as in Isa 58:6, 9; Wildberger 1991, 386] *of his shoulder*, suggestive of prisoners of war pulling heavy loads; and, (3) **the rod** [*šēbeṭ*] **of *the taskmaster*** (*nôgēś*; compare Exod 3:7; 5:10, 13, 14), symbolizing the *scepter* of the conquering ruler. All these Yahweh has **shattered**.

The historical reference, **as in the day of Midian's defeat** (compare Judg 6—8), occurs last in the Hebrew sentence. It is surely intended to bring to mind: (1) the location of the historic Midianites' oppression: the area of "Asher, Zebulun and Naphtali" (Judg 6:35); (2) the victory over the Midianites and their allied "eastern peoples," "thick as locusts" (v 33; 7:12) was clearly to be credited to God alone (vv 2-14), not to human military power; and (3) the sudden shattering of night's darkness with the light of three hundred torches (vv 19-21). Thus, if God could deliver his people from foreign oppression in the past, indicates Isaiah, he certainly can do so in both the present and future.

■ **5 [4 HB]** Yahweh's historic defeat of Midian on behalf of his people serves as a symbol of God's acts yet to come: (1) Jerusalem's overnight deliverance and destruction of Sennacherib's Assyrian army in 701 BC (Isa 37), and (2) an ultimate universal abolishment of war. **Every warrior's boot** and **every** [warrior's] **garment rolled in blood**, symbolizing all weapons of war, are consumed in fire. One is reminded of Ezekiel's war imagery, in which Yahweh vanquishes the enemies of his people, declaring that he will be known among "the nations" as "the Holy One in Israel." His people will "use the weapons [of the defeated enemies] for fuel" (Ezek 39:7, 9). The psalmist sings of Yahweh, that he "makes wars cease to the ends of the earth," shattering and burning all war weapons (Ps 46:9 [10 HB]).

■ **6 [HB]** The first half of Isa 9:6 [5 HB] focuses on an announcement of **a child . . . born** and **a son . . . given**. It is not said who the **child/son** is. But, he is someone destined to rule, for it is said, **government will be *upon* his *shoulder***, thus, in a wordplay, releasing the "shoulder" of the oppressed from pulling heavy loads (v 4 [3 HB]).

The focus in the second half of v 6 [5 HB] is upon the child's name and the name's significance: **And *his name*** [*šĕmô*, not the NIV's **he**] **will be called**. ***Name*** is singular. At the center of the name is the theophoric element *'ēl gibbôr*, **Mighty God**. In 10:21 *'ēl gibbôr* clearly refers to Yahweh. Thus it is most plausible that here *'ēl gibbôr* also refers to Yahweh. The full translation of the name would be: [*A*] **Wonderful Counselor** [*is the*] **Mighty God**, [*the*] **Everlasting Father** [*is a*] **Prince of Peace** (Firth and Williamson 2009, 244-45). **Wonderful Counselor** anticipates Isaiah's later description of Yahweh as one who ***makes wonderful counsel*** (28:29), while **Everlasting Father** looks back to Isaiah's earlier description of Yahweh as one who "reared children and brought them up" (1:2).

■ **7 [6 HB]** This "child/son" of v 6 [5 HB] will govern from **David's throne**, that is, he is presented as a descendant of David. But, from the description of his **kingdom**, Isaiah envisions no ordinary human ruler, but someone greater than any Ahaz-like king God's people have ever seen. He envisions the breaking into history of Yahweh himself, who ushers in a **government** of **peace**, of which **there will be no end**, a reign that is characterized by **justice and righteousness**. Here is an echo of 5:16 and an anticipation of 11:1-5. This child/son ruler is the ultimate Immanuel, the ideal Davidic king, whom the NT finds fulfilled in Jesus Christ (→ From the Text, below, for more on Jesus as Yahweh of the OT).

It is because of God's intense love, his **zeal**, for his people, that, against the opposition of human and spiritual darkness, the light of spiritual and physical freedom can be realized. It is ***Yahweh*** **Almighty** who **will accomplish this**.

FROM THE TEXT

The fuller understanding of Isaiah's "great light" (v 2 [1 HB]) and of Israel's ongoing messianic hope comes only when Jesus, going about "in the area of

Zebulun and Naphtali . . . began to preach, 'Repent, for the kingdom of heaven has come near.'" This, observes Matthew, was "to fulfill what was said through the prophet Isaiah" (Matt 4:13, 17, 14; compare Isa 9:1-2 [8:23—9:1 HB]).

When announcing to Mary the child she would birth and the child's name, Jesus, the angel Gabriel ascribed to the child sonship of the Most High, rulership, and a kingdom with no end (Luke 1:32-33). Gabriel was clearly alluding to Isa 9:6-7 [5-6 HB]. Furthermore, Zechariah's prophecy about his son, John, alludes to what God has said "through his holy prophets of long ago," and describes John as a prophet going "before the Lord to prepare the way." While this echoes Mal 3:1, his description of "the Lord" as "the rising sun [that] will come to us from heaven to shine on those living in darkness . . . to guide our feet into the path of peace," is clearly allusion to Isa 9:2 and 7 [1 and 6 HB] (Luke 1:70, 76, 78-79). Luke clearly sees Zechariah's prophecy (and Isaiah's) as applying to Jesus.

Thus, Hartley states, "Jesus was the light that penetrated the thick darkness that had sealed the world from a knowledge of God. As God incarnate, he was uniquely the theophany of Yahweh." He then cites John 1:4-5, in which Jesus is identified as "The light [that] shines in the darkness," and 14:9-10, in which Jesus says to Philip, "Anyone who has seen me has seen the Father. . . . I am in the Father, and . . . the Father is in me . . . it is the Father, living in me, who is doing his work." That "work," God's peaceful reign over all creation, established in Jesus' first coming, has yet to be consummated in his second coming (1982, 216-17).

H. Yahweh's Upraised Hand (9:8 [7 HB]—10:4)

BEHIND THE TEXT

This section is structured around the four occurrences of the phrase "his hand is still upraised" (9:12, 17, 21 [11, 17, 20 HB]; 10:4). The mixture of perfect and imperfect tense forms throughout the passage do not allow for easy interpretation of historical references. Do the oracles here speak of events that have already happened in the past, are still to happen in the future, or a mixture of both? Are the oracles directed against the northern kingdom, Ephraim (Israel), or against the southern kingdom (Judah)?

Oswalt concludes that, though the passage is addressed to Ephraim, its message applies to the whole of Israel, both north and south (1986, 250). Childs suggests that it is best not to attempt to locate the historical events vaguely referenced, but to discern the theological function of the oracles in the larger literary context. This function is to "trace the historical effects of the divine word, unleashed against Israel, . . . past . . . present and . . . future," and to show that these "historical calamities . . . do not serve to bring Israel to repentance." Rather, Israel's response is continued arrogance (2001, 84). Childs further observes that the general tenor of the passage is that Ephraim has already historically received her punishment, while Judah's final destruction has not yet occurred (ibid., 85).

IN THE TEXT

■ **8 [7 HB]** *A word* [*dābār*] **Sovereign** [*'ădōnāy*] **has sent.** *A word* (*dābār*) occurs first, indicating the emphasis of the Hebrew sentence. *Dābār* also means "event," and, in Hebrew conception, God's word and event are not separated; that is, God's word spoken begins a process that concludes with what the word predicts coming to pass (compare Isa 55:11). Motyer suggests that the ***word*** the **Sovereign has sent** refers to the preaching of Amos and Hosea **against Jacob**, the northern kingdom, from 760 BC onward (Hosea uses the name Jacob/Ephraim three times [Hos 10:11], Amos six times [Amos 3:13; 6:8; 7:2, 5; 9:8]). Motyer further points out that the Hebrew verb form of **will fall** can be translated as a habitual happening, "and it kept falling" **upon Israel** (compare Amos 4:6-11), that is, God, in mercy, kept pleading for them to repent (1993, 106).

■ **9 [8 HB]** Here, too, the first Hebrew verb form allows for a past habitual practice. ***The people continually knew, all of them***. They could not plead ignorance of God's requirements. **Ephraim** (the chief tribe of the northern kingdom) and **Samaria** (the kingdom's capital) represent the whole of the northern kingdom. At the core of their continual resistance to God's word was **pride and arrogance of heart**. In Hebrew thought, the **heart** was the seat of will, attitude, and decision. And from that haughty **heart**, out of the mouth (**who say**) came the defiant boast of Isa 9:10 [9 HB].

Samaria

Samaria (its Greek name), mentioned 190 times in the OT, was a residence of the kings of the northern kingdom (Israel) during the divided monarchy. In ca. 884 BC Omri, king of the northern kingdom (Israel) purchased a small settlement named Shemer, located on a hilltop in the central mountains of Ephraim, overlooking the main coastal road that ran from the Jezreel valley southward toward Egypt. Omri was the first to build a royal residence on this hill surrounded by a fertile valley (see Isa 28:1, 4). He named it *šōmĕrôn* (1 Kgs 16:24), from the Hebrew word "to watch"; the city's name means "watching point" (the name Samaria is the English rendering of the Greek LXX spelling, *semerōn*). Omri then moved his royal capital to Samaria from Tirza, located to the east. King Ahab enlarged the town. A temple to Baal was built in Samaria, though no remains have been found. An important archaeological find was a cache of sixty-five broken pieces of pottery with writing on them, from a storehouse dating to the time of Jeroboam II (reigned 783-741 BC). They were like "invoices" detailing quantities of oil and wine delivered to royal officials. Samaria remained as the capital of northern Israel until 722 BC. During the reign of Israel's last king, Hoshea, Assyrian general Sargon II captured the city, exiled masses of Israelites to Assyria (2 Kgs 17:6), and demoted Israel's status from an independent kingdom to an Assyrian province.

■ **10 [9 HB]** The *mud brick walls* have fallen down, but we will rebuild with dressed stone; the *sycamore* fig *beams* have been *hewn to pieces* [*gd'*], but we will replace them with *cedar beams*. Wildberger points out that elsewhere cedars and squared stones are paired as expensive building materials (1 Kgs 6:36; 7:11) (1991, 231-32). Moreover, mud bricks (air/sun dried and perhaps somewhat strengthened with straw) are inferior, and cedar wood was imported (usually from Lebanon), as opposed to a plentiful supply of beam material from the natively grown sycamore fig. Additionally, *gd'* means both "to cut down/fell" and "to hew into pieces" (Zech 11:10, a rod; Ezek 6:6, altars). So, whether the destruction of their houses is from natural causes (perhaps the earthquake of Amos 1:1; 4:11) or from an invading army, from the prophets' point of view, God being the instigator of either, they say they are equal to the challenge. Out of human strength alone they would prevail.

■ **11-12 [10-11 HB]** Human arrogance, however, is confronted with the biblical **But Yahweh** (v 11). Behind the scenes God is still sovereign. It is he who moves the pieces on the playing board of political and national entities. **Rezin's foes**, an apparent allusion to Assyria, at Yahweh's bidding, is also a threat to the northern kingdom. **Arameans from the east and Philistines from the west** (v 12), Israel's historic enemies, represent adversaries rising up from all sides like some great cosmic war machine advancing with **open mouth**. In arrogance and pride, blindly believing in her self-sufficiency, Israel is **devoured**, until the siege and fall of Samaria in 722 BC to the Assyrians.

Yet for all this implies Israel's continual nonrecognition of God's call for repentance and turning to him. So, **his hand is still upraised**. Yahweh stretches out/upraises his hand over his people in both protection and deliverance (compare Deut 4:34; 5:15; Ps 136:11-12), and in punishment, as here. **His anger** at Israel's intransient resistance **is not turned away**.

■ **13-17 [12-16 HB]** The people (*hā'ām*) in Isa 9:13 occurs first in the Hebrew sentence for emphasis. *Hā'ām*, while generally referring to a whole ethnic people, such as "the people of Israel," sometimes clearly refers to a specified group of persons in leadership (e.g., Josh 24:1-2). Here, the term appears to specify leaders, **the elders and dignitaries . . .** [and] **prophets** (Isa 9:15 [14 HB]), those who are responsible to **guide this people** (v 16 [15 HB]). **This people** (*hā'ām hazzeh*) refers to the general population of the northern kingdom, who rely on their leaders to teach them God's truth; instead they have been taught **lies**, and have been *misled*/**led astray** (v 16 [15 HB]). Thus the defiance and arrogance of the leaders so permeates the general population that **everyone** is ungodly and *practicing evil* [ptc.] *and* every mouth *speaking* [ptc.] **folly** (*nĕbālâ*). Oswalt observes that folly "is not harmless triviality but rather that perversion of truth which makes good evil and evil good ([Isa.] 5:20; Ps. 14:1)" (1986, 255). See also Amos 5:14-15. Indeed, Ps 14:1 depicts the "fool" (*nābāl*) as one who believes he can live as though "there is no God."

The response of **Yahweh** (Isa 9:14 [13 HB]) the **Sovereign** (v 17 [16 HB]) to this pervasive evil and rejection of his prophets' message, and living as though he does not exist, will be swift and severe. **In a** [metaphorical] **single day** (v 14 [13 HB]) his judgment will fall, with no exceptions, upon all: the leaders, the ***choice ones*/young men, . . .** [*even*] **the fatherless and widows** (v 17 [16 HB]) will be caught up in the Assyrian invasion and destruction, and consequent deportation and exile of 722 BC.

■ **18-21 [17-20 HB]** These four verses expand on the "folly" of v 17 [16 HB]. A small **fire** of the field, at first ***consuming*** only the **briers and thorns** (compare 5:6; 7:23-25), if uncontained soon spreads to the **forest thickets** and sets them **ablaze**, until nothing remains but **a column of smoke** (v 18). Just so, **wickedness** pervasively advances among God's people, if unchecked. But **the wrath of Yahweh Sebaoth** at this unchecked, spreading evil also ***scorches*** the **land** (v 19). Thus it is both the people's pervasive evil and God's responsive judgment that constitutes the fire that **consumes** the nation.

Additionally, this increasing, ***devouring*** evil summarizes the long history of northern tribal civil strife, and inter-kingdom rivalry: **Manasseh** and **Ephraim**, the two largest northern tribes, **feed on** each other (v 21). But they are never **satisfied**; their hunger for more persists (v 20). So, uniting, they **turn against Judah** (v 21).

■ **10:1-2** Whereas 9:15-16 [14-15 HB] spoke of the leaders' misleading in a generalized way, these verses are very specific: they legislated **unjust laws** and **oppressive decrees** (v 1), specifically **to deprive the poor**, the **widows**, and **the fatherless** from obtaining **justice** and their **rights** in the law courts (v 2). **Prey** and **robbing** imply enrichment of themselves at the expense of the powerless. These acts of injustice constitute the prime illustration of pride and arrogance, of living as though God has no place in one's life. The law governing justice for the defenseless in Israel (the poor, the foreigner, the fatherless, and the widow) was to mirror God's character: "For **Yahweh** your God . . . defends the cause of the fatherless and the widow, and loves the foreigner residing among you" (Deut 10:17-18; compare Exod 23:6-9; Lev 19:15; Deut 16:19; 24:17).

■ **3-4** One can live as "the wicked" of Ps 73: in their "pride" and arrogance they "threaten oppression" from their "callous hearts"; their "mouths . . . say, 'How would God know? Does the Most High know anything?'" (vv 3-11). But, indicates Isaiah, God has the final word. There will be a **day** when the **Sovereign** (of Isa 9:17 [16 HB]) arrives for a **reckoning** (*pqd*), and with him, **disaster** [*šôʾâ*, "violent storm"] . . . **from afar** (10:3). As in 5:26-28, Isaiah has in mind the Assyrians, whose invading army will be this violent storm. Wildberger reminds us, however, that only "as the tool of the wrath of God" was Assyria enabled to bring this judgment against Israel (1991, 215). Isaiah indicates this to be so in 10:5.

And when (not if) this storm suddenly overtakes the nation, **to whom**, asks Isaiah, **will you run for help?** (v 3). **You** is plural and is directed at the oppressive, unjust leaders, the aristocratic level of society, as evidenced by the reference to **your riches**, the wealth they have gained through exploitation of the poor. You will **run**, indeed, here and there, but from **whom** can help be expected? Not from other leaders, not from the king, and certainly not from God, now no longer the expected refuge, but the initiator of the **disaster**. Perhaps there is an intended pun in the added question, **Where will you leave** [*ʿāzab*] **your riches?** *ʿĀzab* could mean "to leave/hide (in safekeeping)" or "abandon," as when one flees in the face of danger, taking nothing, there being no time for either. Neither position in society nor wealth gives protection. When the battle is finished, some leaders find themselves ***cringing*** **among the captives** (v 4), to be marched off to exile; others are found ***fallen*** **among the slain**, destined for burial.

FROM THE TEXT

As noted above (→ 9:8 [7 HB]), Motyer suggested that Isaiah may have been alluding to the preaching of Amos and Hosea as God's past attempts to bring Israel to repentance, and a change of her evil ways. Isaiah four times repeats "his hand is still upraised" (9:12, 17, 21 [11, 17, 20 HB]; 10:4), expressing Yahweh's response to Israel's continued refusal to heed his "message" (9:8 [7 HB]). This echoes Yahweh's plaintive "yet you have not returned to me," occurring five times in Amos 4 (vv 6, 8, 9, 10, 11).

In Amos, Yahweh's "message" comes not only through the prophet's preached word but also through Yahweh's direct interventions: famine (v 6), thirst (vv 7-8), agricultural damage (v 9), enemy invasion/death (v 10), and divine fire (v 11). Added to these direct interventions was Amos' call that they seek Yahweh in whom is found true life (5:4, 6), as replacement for continual religious pilgrimages to the sanctuaries at Bethel, Gilgal, and Beersheba (v 5). At these sanctuaries they gave burnt, grain, and fellowship offerings, accompanied by feasts, songs, and musical instruments (vv 21-23). Amos urged them to give up doing evil and turn to doing good (v 14); he pled with them to return justice to the city courts (v 15).

All this, however, served only to deepen the resistance of Israel's leaders. Their response was to multiply injustice (Amos 5:7), through imposing heavy taxes on the poor (v 11), and the taking of bribes (v 12). Thus the response of Israel's leaders to the warnings of Amos is the same as to the warnings of Isaiah: they continue living as though God has no relevance to what they do or say. Yet God will have the final say: in "the day of disaster" they will be sent away into exile (v 27; 6:7).

Oswalt reminds us that "it is not Assyria's overwhelming power that dictates the future of Ephraim and Judah; it is their failure to submit to God and to live in accordance with his principles" (1986, 260).

I. The True Sovereign and the Arrogant Assyrian (10:5-34)

BEHIND THE TEXT

This passage continues to highlight Assyria. There are three major units. In unit 1 (vv 5-19) Assyria, in the pride and arrogance of her kings, is bent on worldwide domination. Isaiah shows, however, that Assyria is simply an instrument in God's hand, appointed to execute his judgment upon Israel and Judah. Unit 2 (vv 20-27) sets up a contrast between the claimed divine sovereignty of Assyria and the historically demonstrated divine sovereignty of **Sovereign** [*ădōnāy*] **Yahweh Sebaoth** (v 24): Isaiah cites God's actions on behalf of Israel in Egypt (v 24) and upon "Midian at the rock of Oreb" (v 26). Based on the past, God's people can rest in the confidence that God will rescue a remnant out of Assyria's captivity. Unit 3 (vv 28-34), in a manner parallel to 5:26-29, presents an invincible army, a seemingly unstoppable Assyria, advancing on Jerusalem, bent on her utter destruction. But the God of history, **the Sovereign** [*hā'ādôn*] **Yahweh Sebaoth** (10:33), will intervene, bringing about Assyria's fall, metaphorically depicted as Lebanon (v 34, compare Ezek 31:3).

IN THE TEXT

1. Arrogant Assyria, a Tool in God's Hand (10:5-19)

■ **5-6** In 10:1 "woe" was pronounced against the rulers of Israel for acts of injustice and oppression, with the announcement of judgment coming soon "from afar" (v 3), that is, from the Assyrians. Now Yahweh, as "King" (compare 6:5), has given his **rod** and his **club**—both symbols of his royal power—into the **hand** of **the Assyrian** king to carry out this mission of judgment against Israel (10:5). Israel is characterized here as **a godless nation** (*gôy* [v 6]; no longer *'ammî*, "my people"). What a shocker! Was Israel now more **godless** than Assyria, which, though having many gods, never recognized Yahweh, the Creator of the universe? Yes, relatively so, "because she has had more light to reject" (Oswalt 1986, 263). But, if Yahweh has commissioned Assyria to **loot**

... **plunder,** and **to trample** his people **like mud in the streets** (v 6), why is a **woe** pronounced against her (v 5)? This is answered in v 7.

■ **7** Isaiah indicates that the Assyrian king (**he** represents Assyrian rulers generally) is oblivious to the limits of Yahweh's commission to judge Israel and Judah. Rather, **in his heart** is his own plan that goes far beyond Yahweh's intentions. Isaiah describes Assyria's intention: **to annihilate** and **to exterminate** [Wildberger 1991, 415-16] **nations, not** [**just**] **a few** (*gôyim lo' mĕ'āṭ*), a Hebrew way of emphasizing the great number of peoples who had already fallen victim to Assyria's insatiable appetite for vast territorial control.

■ **8-11** These verses depict Isaiah as privy to the boastful thoughts of the Assyrian king, who boasts of the capture of a number of the great city-states of Syria (v 9). They are listed not chronologically but geographically from north to south, bringing the Assyrians right up to the northern border of Judah, poised to take **Jerusalem** (v 11).

Cities of the Assyrian King's Boast in Isa 10:8-9

Kalno, most likely the "Kalneh" of Amos 6:2, located in northern Syria, was taken by Tiglath-Pileser III in 738 BC. **Carchemish**, located on the middle Euphrates, was destroyed by Sargon II and its citizens deported in 717 BC. **Hamath**, located on the Orontes river in Syria, was subdued three times in the second half of the eighth century BC—by Tiglath-Pileser III in 738 BC, by Sargon II in 720 BC, and by Sennacherib in 700 BC. **Arpad**, always mentioned with Hamath, was conquered by Tiglath-Pileser III in 740 BC, and again by Sargon II in 720 BC. **Damascus**, capital of Aram, was captured by Tiglath-Pileser III in 732 BC, following the request for help by Ahaz of Judah (→ 7:4; compare 2 Kgs 16:7-9). **Samaria**, the capital of the northern kingdom (Israel), whose last king (Hoshea, ruling as a vassal of Assyria) rebelled upon the death of Tiglath-Pileser III in 727 BC. Shalmaneser imprisoned Hoshea and besieged Samaria, which was finally subdued by his successor, Sargon II, in 722 BC.

There is an underlying implication of the Assyrian boast: it is that, though the captured **kingdoms** were **kingdoms of . . . idols** (v 10), none of their **idols** or **images** could protect their territories from the more powerful Assyrian deities that guided the Assyrian **hand** of conquest. And, **Jerusalem** (v 11) is placed in the same category: she is nothing but a city that worships **images** that cannot save her.

In an interesting turn, what begins in the mouth of Isaiah as a woe oracle against Assyria for going beyond God's commission concludes with an indictment of fact in the mouth of the Assyrian ruler: **Jerusalem** indeed has become a city that serves idols (2:8, 18, 20).

We hear an echo of this Assyrian boast in the mouth of Sennacherib's military commander in the later 701 BC siege of Jerusalem, against King Hezekiah: Sennacherib is "the great king [*hammelek haggādôl*], the king of Assyria" (36:4, 13). The "gods" (36:18, 19, 20; 37:12) of **Hamath**, **Arpad**, and **Samaria** (10:9; 36:19; 37:13), among others, were incapable of delivering their cities out of his "hand" (36:18, 20). Likewise, he says, neither would Jerusalem be delivered! (36:20).

■ **12** The Assyrian king's boast is interrupted with the prophet's observation that says two things. (1) The ***punishment*** that the ***Sovereign*** has in store for the **king of Assyria**, though seemingly delayed, will surely happen in the ***Sovereign***'s own time (compare Ps 73:11, 18-19). (2) The **work against Mount Zion and Jerusalem** will happen under the sovereign judgment of God, not as an outworking of the **willful pride** of the Assyrian king.

■ **13-14** The Assyrian's most arrogant boast is the appropriation of the title **mighty one** (*'abbîr* [Isa 10:13]), a title given to God in 1:24; 49:26; 60:16 (compare Gen 49:24). **By the strength of my hand I have done this** (Isa 10:12) looks back to v 10, "my hand seized the kingdoms," and the list of cities in v 9. (Tiglath-Pileser III records: "At the command of my lord Ashur, I was a conqueror [lit.: my hand conquered]" [Pritchard 1969, 275].) This outward show of **strength** (v 13), according to the Assyrian's boast, was the outworking of his own inner **wisdom** and **understanding**. This anticipates ch 11, in which Isaiah speaks of the coming of the ideal messianic Ruler, "a shoot . . . from the stump of Jesse . . . a Branch . . . the Root of Jesse" (vv 1, 10), a king who exemplifies true "wisdom" and "understanding" (v 2). In this time of messianic rule, the "***Sovereign*** will reach out his hand" and take back "his people" from all boastful, grasping monarchs (v 11).

In boasting of ***removing*** **the boundaries of the nations** (10:13), the Assyrian king is certainly speaking of the standard Assyrian policy of mass deportation and importation of conquered ethnic and national populations and the establishing of new provincial boundaries. This they did to pacify the vast reaches of the empire and to reduce the options for future rebellion. But the establishment of "boundaries for the peoples" of "all mankind" was the prerogative of God, "Most High" (Deut 32:8). Thus the Assyrian kings had arrogated to themselves that to which only the Creator had a right. And gathering up the **wealth** (*ḥêl*) of these conquered ***peoples*** (*hā'ammîm*), boasts the Assyrian, was as easy as ***gathering*** **abandoned eggs** from an unprotected **nest**.

■ **15** It appears that Isaiah is appropriating wisdom imagery here: **the ax . . . the saw . . . a rod . . . a club**, each is simply a tool whose ability and strength to carry out a task is derived not from within itself but only from the "strength of **the** hand" and the "wisdom" and "understanding" (Isa 10:13) of **the person who . . . uses it**. Likewise, the Assyrian king, who dares to transfer from the Creator to himself the title "mighty one," is only a tool in the hand of the true "Mighty One" (→ v 13).

■ **16-19** Therefore, because the Assyrian king(s) gave no recognition to **the Sovereign** [*hāʾādôn*] **Yahweh Sebaoth** (compare Pritchard 1969, 275-89, for the numerous times the Assyrian kings refer to Ashur as "king of the gods" or "my lord Ashur"), Yahweh's judgment will fall upon Assyria. Isaiah mixes two judgment metaphors: (1) **a wasting disease upon his . . . warriors** (lit. *a leanness upon his fat ones* [v 16]). Seitz suggests that it was possibly a deadly disease that killed 185,000 of Sennacherib's Assyrian soldiers in one night in Judah in 701 BC (compare 37:36) (1993, 94); and (2) **a fire**, which is the **Light of Israel**, God himself, **their Holy One** (10:17). The Assyrian Empire, the dominant world power for over two hundred years, appeared invincible. Yet it will seem as though **in a single day** [→ comments on the "single day" concept at Behind the Text for 2:6-22] . . . **it will *be* completely *destroyed***, just as when a sick person wastes away (10:18). ***Consumed*** will be its small ones, symbolically **his thorns and his briers** (v 17), and its great ones, symbolically **his forests and fertile fields** (v 18).

The Demise of the Assyrian Empire

The mighty Assyrian Empire disappeared in the short period of less than two decades. In 627 BC, under the leadership of Nabopolassar, a Chaldean, the province of Babylon gained independence and by 623 BC had formed an alliance with the Medes against Assyria. In 614 BC the Medes captured the key city, Asshur. In 612 BC Median and Babylonian forces joined to capture the capital city, Nineveh. Retreating westward to Haran, the remnants of the Assyrian forces were driven out from there by Babylonian forces in 610 BC. They retreated further westward to Carchemish, where, in 609 BC, though Egypt attempted to assist them to stem the Babylonian advance, they were finally crushed. The Assyrian Empire was no more (Aharoni and Avi-Yonah 1993, 120; Bright 2000, 315-16).

2. A Remnant Will Return (10:20-27)

This section speaks to all God's people, north and south. The names "Jacob" and "Israel" (vv 20, 21, 22), often applied to the northern kingdom, highlight the concept of the "return" of "a remnant" (vv 21, 22). The name "Zion" (v 24), often implying the whole of the southern kingdom, highlights the promise of God's deliverance from the oppression of the Assyrians (v 24). The phrase "in that day" (vv 20, 27) offers a word of hope to the faithful core that salvation, not judgment, is God's final word.

■ **20 In that day** is a reference to the period of the Assyrian invasions that took place from 734 to 722 BC against both Israel and Judah. The northern kingdom (**Jacob/Israel**), against the encroaching threat of Assyria, had turned to an alliance with its longtime enemy, Aram/Damascus, which Isaiah refers to here as the one **who struck them down**. Now, however, Aram/Damascus has been destroyed (in 732 BC) and is no longer a reliable political or military partner. **Israel**, too, will meet her doom at the hands of Assyria (in 722 BC), but out of this devastation will emerge **survivors**, a **remnant** who will learn the foolishness of reliance on human power and **will truly** [*be'emet*, *in truth*] rely on *Yahweh,* **the Holy One of Israel** (*yhwh qĕdôš yiśrā'ēl*).

■ **21** Lest there be any confusion as to the number of "survivors" (v 20), for emphasis, the Hebrew places **remnant** (*šĕ'ār*), without an article, before **will return**. This implies that *only* a remnant will return . . . **to the Mighty God** (*'ēl gibbôr*), "the Holy One of Israel" (v 20). Isaiah here is not speaking of an eventual "return" of survivors from Assyrian captivity but a "turning back," a "repenting" from an old way of living as though God does not exist, to now recognizing God's hand in all of life (compare 1:27 concerning those in Zion who repent).

■ **22-23** In fact, it is in the very midst of the **destruction** that **the *Sovereign*** [*hā'ādôn*] ***Yahweh Sebaoth*** (compare 10:16) has **decreed upon the whole land** (v 23) that **a remnant will return** unto God, as they see the ***righteousness*** of his judgment. The reference to **your people . . . like the sand by the sea** (v 22) indicates Isaiah's conviction that God's ancient promise to Abraham concerning his descendants (Gen 22:17; 32:12) still stands. It is now restricted, however, by God's judgment (Oswalt 1986, 271; Childs 2001, 95), indicated by the NIV's insertion of **only** (Isa 10:22).

■ **24-27** *Sovereign* [*'ădōnāy*] ***Yahweh Sebaoth*** now speaks a word of comfort and hope to **my people who live in Zion**, representing the beleaguered remnant in the southern kingdom (v 24). **Therefore** refers to the "destruction decreed" in v 23. **My people**, as opposed to "this people" (8:6, 12), speaks of a continuing covenant relationship that provides God's protection to the faithful core. Isaiah indicates that ultimately the southern kingdom will lose its independence, and large numbers of its inhabitants will be deported (6:11-12; by the Babylonians in 587 BC). The faithful of his day, however, need **not be afraid of the Assyrians** (10:24), who, indeed, will soon be at the gates of **Zion** (in 701 BC; compare chs 36—37). But ***Yahweh of Hosts*** (v 26) in an earlier time had delivered his people from the oppression of **Midian** (Judg 7:25) and **Egypt** (Exod 14:13-18). Just so, he will deliver his people from the **Assyrians**: both **burden** and **yoke** (Isa 10:27), symbols of subjugation (compare 9:4 [3 HB]), will be **lifted/broken**. God's **anger against** his people **will end** and be *redirected* to the **destruction** of the Assyrians (10:25).

The last line of v 27 is difficult to translate, and thus to make any sense of it; the NIV's **because you have grown so fat** is a conjecture.

Midian and the Rock of Oreb

In the time of the Judges, the Midianites, oppressing central Israel, were encamping in the land "like swarms of locusts" (Judg 6:5). God raised up Gideon, who, with only three hundred Ephraimite soldiers, miraculously routed the Midianites from the Jezreel valley near the hill of Moreh, with the deception of torches and trumpets. Chasing the fleeing Midianites eastward across the Jordan River, they captured Oreb and Zeeb, two of the Midianite leaders, killing Oreb at a rock and Zeeb at a winepress, each location subsequently named after them (Judg 7).

3. Assyria Felled (10:28-34)

■ **28-32** Pictured in these verses is most likely Isaiah's imaginative vision of a combination of invasions of Judah yet to take place (taking the verbs as prophetic perfects). Isaiah is depicting the seemingly unstoppable southward advance of an invincible army, exemplified by the arrogant Assyrian. With a swiftness that catches the inhabitants of **Ramah, Gibeah, Gallim, Laishah, Anathoth, Madmenah,** and **Gebim** by surprise (vv 29-31), so that they take **flight** in all directions, this arrogant army **will halt at Nob**, just to the north of Jerusalem (v 32). There **they will shake their** [collective] **fist** (lit. "swing its hand") at Yahweh's beloved **Daughter Zion**, which sits on the elevated **hill of Jerusalem**. Her location on a **hill** implies that possibly it is Jerusalem's well-defended position that will protect her.

■ **33-34** But, no, it is neither Jerusalem's location nor her high and thick walls that will stop this unstoppable enemy. Rather, it is **the Sovereign** [*hā'ādôn*] **Yahweh Sebaoth** (v 33), bearing the name **Mighty One** (*'addîr*, lit. "noble one" [v 34]), who, with his metaphorical **ax**, will decimate the Assyrian army, here depicted as a metaphorical forest. God **will lop off the boughs . . . , will fell lofty trees**, and **will bring low** the tall ones (v 33). Thus the arrogance of Assyria will be brought under God's judgment and silenced. Oswalt points out that, although this prophecy does not specify the results of Sennacherib's 701 BC invasion of Judah and siege of Jerusalem, "the spectacle of the decimated Assyrian camp, . . . must have brought Isaiah's words back to the Judeans' minds with a great deal of satisfaction" (1986, 275-76).

FROM THE TEXT

The focus of this passage (10:5-34) is on Assyria, the one seemingly invincible world power of Isaiah's time, and the Assyrian king's boasting that pits himself and his kingdom against God and his kingdom. In this passage the titles of God are **the Sovereign, Yahweh Sebaoth** (vv 16, 23, 24, 26, 33), "the Light of Israel" (v 17), "**Yahweh**, the Holy One of Israel" (v 20), "the Mighty God" (v 21), and "the Mighty One" (v 34).

Of these titles for God, "the Light of Israel" (*'ôr yiśrā'ēl*) is of special significance when viewed in the context of Isaiah's previous announcement (9:2) of the dawning of "a great light" upon God's people, who are wandering in "deep darkness." In the latter part of Isaiah (60:1-2), the prophecy announces a "light," Yahweh himself, who comes and dispels a "thick darkness" that covers both earth and peoples. To this light both nations and kings will be drawn. Thus God himself is depicted residing at the very center of his restored people in the messianic kingdom, a people through whom now "the reality of God's salvation is displayed to all the earth" (Oswalt 1998, 534).

John, when identifying "the Word," at Jesus' first Advent (John 1), picks up on this Isaianic theme of the coming of the light: "the light of all mankind" (v 4), "the light [that] shines in the darkness" (v 5), "the true light that gives light to everyone" (v 9), light that "the darkness has not overcome" (v 5). Moreover, testifies John, this light, "the Word became flesh and made his dwelling among us," and, as the "one and only Son, who came from the Father," evidenced true "grace and truth" (v 14).

Additionally, when depicting the messianic kingdom at Jesus' second Advent (Rev 21), John speaks of the light that radiates from God and the Lamb (= Jesus) who dwell in the center of restored Jerusalem (v 23), making it possible for nations and kings to "walk by its light" (v 24). This is now made possible because Satan and his evil powers, having deceived and enslaved the nations and kings (13:14; 17:2), have been removed from the earth. Now, "the whole earth worships the one true God and walks in his light" (Witherington 2003, 272). John views history concluding with the final destruction of "Babylon" (Rev 18), the representative of all arrogant earthly powers, just as Assyria stood as that representative for Isaiah.

J. The Branch from Jesse (11:1-16)

BEHIND THE TEXT

This sixteen verse segment, in the final edited version of Isaiah's book, is set immediately following Isaiah's prediction of the coming utter obliteration of the Assyrian Empire, the world power of Isaiah's time. Assyria's pride, depicted metaphorically as "forest thickets" having been "cut down . . . with [God's] ax" (Isa 10:34), would be left as "nothing but a field of stumps" (Oswalt 1986, 278), never to rise again. Also, in 6:11-13, as a response to the pride and corrupt practices of Judah's rulers, epitomized in Ahaz's actions, Isaiah had predicted God's judgment on his own people: their near destruction. Only "stumps" would remain, among which would be "the holy seed . . . the stump in the land" (6:13), which would one day sprout, and God's people would live again. Thus judgment was not God's final word for his people.

These sixteen verses consist of two segments: 11:1-9 (poetry) and vv 10-16 (vv 10-11, prose; vv 12-16, poetry).

The first segment (vv 1-9) picks up the theme of 6:13 ("stumps," "stump in the land") with "the stump of Jesse," from which will come "a shoot" from whose "roots" will issue "a Branch" (v 1) whose mode of rulership will issue out of his very character of "righteousness" and "justice" (v 4). Under this messianic king, all creatures can live in absolute security.

The second segment (vv 10-16) is linked with the first by the designation of this king as "the Root of Jesse," who becomes the rallying point, the "banner" to which "the peoples" (*'ammîm*), "the nations" (*gôyim*), and "the surviving remnant of his people" (*'ammô*) will gather (vv 10-11). This theme of regathering of "the exiles" (v 12), and the voluntary flowing of the others to this messianic king, links this passage with Isaiah's vision in 2:1-4, in which he sees the "nations" streaming to "the mountain of the LORD's temple" (v 2), and with his vision in 4:2-6 of "Zion" as a place of safety for the "survivors in Israel."

IN THE TEXT

■ **I** As Isaiah views the Judean ruling family, Ahaz's rejection of God's protection in the face of the Syrian-Israelite threat, and his turning to Assyria for help, has caused God to turn his back on the house of David. Though God will not abrogate his promise to David that a succession of his descendants will continue to sit on the Judean throne, the Davidic monarchy is all but dead.

There will yet be a few God-fearing kings (e.g., Hezekiah, Josiah), but following Ahaz, the Davidic kings will lead Judah on a downward path until her demise in 587 BC. Yet God's promise to David is not dead. Going back to David's very **roots**, the **stump of Jesse**, "a reminder of David's humble beginnings" (Childs 2001, 102), Isaiah declares that in a future time, from that **stump** a new **shoot will come up**, **a Branch**. It is clear from what follows that this **Branch** is more than human; he is God's Messiah, a King who rules over a "new messianic society" (ibid., 106). This Messiah King will indeed be a descendant of David (compare 16:5; 55:3-4; Jer 23:5; 33:15).

■ **2** This new King, the Messiah, is one upon whom **the Spirit of *Yahweh* rests**. God's **Spirit** endows him with three pairs of divine characteristics:

(1) **Wisdom** is the ability to make wise judgments based on **understanding** (or ***discernment***) of the rightness or wrongness at the heart of issues (compare 1 Kgs 3:9).

(2) **Counsel** (or ***strategy***) is the capacity for determining a correct course of action, but ***power*** is needed to carry it to completion.

(3) **Knowledge** is "truth grasped and applied to life" (Motyer 1993, 122). A person cannot truly "know" another person apart from a long, intimate, and enduring relationship. The **fear of the LORD** is an OT expression for just such a relationship, a relationship that requires a deep knowledge of God's moral requirements and living a life conformed to them.

■ **3-5** In the OT four groups of defenseless persons are often listed together as those oppressed and robbed of their possessions by the ruling class and deprived of their rights in court by the judges. These are the alien, the fatherless/orphan, the widow, and the poor/needy (compare Exod 22:22 [21 HB]; Deut 10:17-19), all of whom have Yahweh as their Defender.

Here Isaiah speaks of two of these defenseless classes, **the needy** (*dallîm*) and **the poor of the earth** (*'anwe 'āreṣ*) (Isa 11:4). From the OT contexts in which the term *dallîm* occurs, **the needy** are most likely those of the poor peasant farmer class, not totally impoverished but still economically defenseless before the cruelty and oppression of the rich and powerful of society. **The poor** (*'ănāwîm* and its synonym *'ăniyyîm*, "oppressed" [10:2]) are those who have been "humbled" either under the pressure of circumstances or through exploitation leading to impoverishment (VanGemeren 1997, 1:951; 3:454-55).

The merely human ruler (king or judge), when giving ***judgments*** on behalf of **the needy** or **decisions** on behalf of **the poor**, unless endowed with special God-given insight, is limited by the knowledge he takes in physically through **his eyes** (11:3) and **his ears**. But the Messiah King is endowed with the "Spirit of . . . knowledge" (v 2) to see, hear, and know that which is revealed only by God's Spirit. As Judge, he will bring a corrective to the oppressive behavior of Israel's leaders, implied in 1:15-16 and highlighted in 3:5, 14-15 and 5:7. **Righteousness** (*ṣedeq*) and **equity** (*mîšôr*), which will characterize the Messiah's rule, extend even to **the wicked** (*rāšā'*): ***equity*** requires that he **slay** them with **the *scepter*** [*šēbet*] **of his mouth** and **the breath** [*rûaḥ*] **of his lips** (11:4). Note the metaphors of the king striking down his enemies with a "***scepter*** [*šēbet*] **of iron**" in Ps 2:9, and Yahweh, "by the breath [*rûaḥ*] of his mouth," setting the stars in their places at the dawn of creation (Ps 33:6).

Metaphorical reference to various items of a person's clothing points to the consistency between the fundamental inward character and outward actions of that person, for either evil or good. Goldingay notes that "the clothing . . . thus mirrors the person" (2001, 84). For instance, "necklace" and ***clothing*** represent the "pride" and "violence" of the "arrogant/wicked" (Ps 73:3, 6), while "robe," "turban," and "clothing" represent Job's "justice" and "righteousness" (Job 29:14; see also Ps 132:9, 16, 18; Isa 59:17; 61:10; Eph 6:14, 17; 1 Thess 5:8).

Isaiah presents the Messiah King with a **belt** and **sash** representing his **righteousness** (*ṣedeq*) and **faithfulness** (*'ĕnûnâ*, from *'mn*, "to be reliable, dependable, true") (Isa 11:5). *'Ĕnûnâ* emphasizes "a way of acting which grows out of inner stability," that is, one's "inner attitude and the conduct it produces" (*TDOT* 1:317). The term often occurs as the opposite of *šeqer*, "falsehood, deception, lying" (VanGemeren 1997, 1:431) (e.g., Prov 12:22). Wildberger points out that Isaiah's connecting *'ĕnûnâ* (**faithfulness**) with *ṣedeq* (**righteousness**) indicates that he is still depicting the Messiah in his function as a judge of "absolute reliability which a person might count on when in need of help in obtaining justice." This rock-steady justice will characterize the messianic community.

■ **6-9** Though there is no mention of the Messiah King in this passage, Isaiah's description of universal peace that includes both the animal and human world is set within an eschatological context of security and safety that can only be brought about through the rule of a truly righteous ruler (Childs 2001, 104; Oswalt 1986, 283). Some interpreters have seen this description as a literalistic return to the supposed idyllic innocence of Eden, but, as Oswalt points out, this would require, for example, a change in the basic carnivorous nature of the lion. He further concludes that a figurative interpretation allows one to see the "single, overarching point" of the passage: in the reign of the Messiah King, both individuals and the entire world no longer need live in a context of "fears associated with insecurity, danger, and evil" (ibid., 283).

All my holy mountain (*qol har qodšî* [v 9]) must surely refer to Zion/Jerusalem and not only to the "mountain" on which was located **Yahweh's house** (*har bēt yhwh*). To this location "all nations will stream," seeking to be taught God's "ways" that they might truly "walk in his paths" (2:2-3). It is in Zion/Jerusalem, under the rulership of the corrupt Davidic kings, that Isaiah has said no citizen can find justice (*mišpāṭ*) or righteousness (*ṣedeq*) (1:17, 21-23; 3:8-9, 15; 5:7). But, under the rule of the Messiah King, no longer will the weak need to fear the powerful, for **they will neither *do evil* nor *will they corrupt***. Moreover, God's **holy mountain** extends not only to all of Jerusalem but, under the rule of Messiah King, to the entire **earth**. And because Messiah King will be endowed with the "Spirit of . . . knowledge" (11:2), **the knowledge** [*dē'â*, from *yd'*, "to know"] **of *Yahweh***—in abundance **as the waters cover the sea**, even ***filling* the earth**—will be accessible to all.

In the OT, "to know," among its many levels of knowing, is used to describe the deepest of human relationships: the covenant of marriage and the consummation of that covenant through sexual relations. It is, then, used to describe the most intimate of covenant relationship between God and humans: to know God is often cast in marital terms (e.g., Hos 2:20 [22 HB]). Knowing God in the world of the messianic community implies a covenant relationship with God. This relationship, Jeremiah says, enables the displacement of "unrighteousness" (*lo' ṣedeq*) and "injustice" (*lo' mišpāṭ*) with "right" (*mišpāṭ*) and **righteousness** (*ṣĕdāqâ*): to defend "the cause of the poor and needy." "Is that not what it means to know [Yahweh]?" asks Jeremiah (22:13-16).

■ **10-11 In that day**, opening each verse, indicates that what is depicted in vv 10-16 happens during the reign of the Messiah King who rules with "righteousness" and "justice" (vv 1-9). There is to be an ingathering of two groups: **peoples** (*'ammîm*)/**nations** (*gôyim*) (v 10), and the **surviving remnant of his** [i.e., God's] **people** (*'ammô*) from those nations (v 11). The focus is on **the Root of Jesse** (the Messiah King) who **will stand as a banner for peoples** (*'ammîm*, indefinite) (v 10). These **nations** [*gôyim*, indefinite] **will *seek*** [*drš*, meaning "to inquire of"] **him**. Thus, suggests Motyer, "The leading idea is Gentile incorporation" (1993, 125). Compare 42:1, 4 where "the islands" (i.e., Gentiles) are said to be *waiting in hope* for Yahweh's "servant" who "will bring justice [*mišpāṭ*] to the nations" (*laggôyim*).

The focus shifts to the **Sovereign** (*'ădōnāy*) who **will reach out his hand a second time** (11:11). The focus and reference point for the **second time** may be upon God's *reaching* **out his hand** (the first time) at the great Exodus event when he brought the Israelites out of Egypt with a "mighty hand" (Exod 6:1; 13:3; Deut 6:21; compare Exod 3:19-20; Ps 44:2 [3 HB]). Or the focus may be upon the "banner" of Isa 11:10, which Yahweh first raised (5:26) as a call to Assyria to bring judgment upon Israel, now reversed and used as a symbol of his salvation. The reference to Yahweh's future act to "dry up the gulf of the Egyptian sea" (11:15) in this great future ingathering would argue for the historical Exodus being the first referent. **His hand** represents Yahweh's power to **reclaim the surviving remnant of his people** (*'ammô*) from their worldwide dispersion, that is, from among the "peoples" (*'ammîm*) and "nations" (*gôyim*) (v 10), which are powerless to hold them. The names listed are representative of the kingdoms of Isaiah's world: to the northeast, **Assyria**; to the south, **Egypt** and **Cush** (Ethiopia); to the east, **Elam** and *Shinar* (**Babylon**); to the north, **Hamath**; to the west, **the islands of the** *sea* (**Mediterranean**). These figuratively represent "the four quarters of the world" (v 12), suggesting "that God is able to restore his people from *everywhere* [emphasis original]" (Oswalt 1986, 287).

■ **12** Again, the Sovereign/Yahweh (v 11) **will raise a banner**, and again **the nations** (*haggôyim*) are included in the great future messianic ingathering. Moreover, "his people" (v 11) are now more specifically **the *scattered ones* of Israel** and **the scattered *ones* of Judah**. Thus, suggests Oswalt, "The remnant will be a restoration of the whole" (1986, 288).

■ **13-14** The historic **jealousy** and *hostility* between the northern and southern kingdoms, symbolized in the two tribal names **Ephraim** and **Judah**, will **vanish** (v 13). There will be peace among God's people as they are again a united kingdom under the reign of the Messiah King. Moreover, Israel's historic enemies—**Philistia, Edom, Moab**, and Ammon (v 14), representative of all enemies of the Messiah King—will be brought into submission under the Ruler who rules with justice and righteousness, as envisioned in vv 1-9.

■ **15-16** In these two verses we hear echoes of the historic Exodus from Egypt, so that what God will do in the messianic age to come, when he gathers the nations and the remnant of Israel/Judah out of the nations, can be viewed as a second great Exodus. Using terms associated with the first Exodus (**dry up, Egyptian sea** [i.e., Red Sea], **scorching wind, will sweep his hand** [v 15]), Isaiah creates the figurative image of a second Exodus. This second Exodus, however, is worldwide, suggested in the use of **Euphrates River** and **Assyria** (v 16), both geographically located opposite from Egypt, on the northern extremity of Isaiah's world. Paralleling his action making it possible for the Israelites to cross the barrier of the Red Sea in the first Exodus, God will remove all barriers, whether **sea** or **river**, which prevent **his people** from assembling at his "holy mountain" (v 9). God even figuratively constructs **a highway** so that they may more easily make the journey **from Assyria**, with **Assyria** representing all places from which God's **people** will be gathered.

FROM THE TEXT

Concerning the Messiah, Isaiah says, "The Spirit of **Yahweh** will rest on him" (11:2). The OT gives a number of instances in which "the Spirit of **Yahweh**" comes to rest upon persons to empower them for certain assignments: Saul to prophesy (1 Sam 10:6), and (implied) for kingship, since "the Spirit of the LORD" left Saul later in his reign (1 Sam 16:14); David for kingship (1 Sam 16:13); Bezalel for craftsmanship (Exod 31:3; 35:31); Gideon and Jephthah for skill in war (Judg 6:34; 11:29); Samson to deliver Israel from Philistine oppression (Judg 13:25; 14:6); Eldad and Medad to prophesy (Num 11:26).

Noted in the commentary above is that "the Spirit of **Yahweh**" (Isa 11:2) empowers the prophesied Messiah to bring "justice" and "righteousness" to the defenseless classes, "the needy" and "the poor of the earth" (v 4). In the closing section of the book of Isaiah, the prophet quotes someone speaking in the first person, saying, "The Spirit of . . . Sovereign **Yahweh** [*'ădōnāy yhwh*] is on me, because **Yahweh** has anointed me to proclaim good news [*baśśēr*] to the poor [*'ănāwîm*]" (61:1). Oswalt points out that the identity of this speaker is to be equated with the Messiah, as depicted in ch 11 (1998, 563). Note the listing of those to whom the speaker is sent: "the poor," "the brokenhearted," "the captives," "the prisoners," "all who mourn," and "those who grieve"; all these are disenfranchised because of injustice. Only One greater than any human king is able to bring to them "comfort," "joy," and "righteousness" (61:1-3). When Jesus turned to and read this passage in the Nazareth synagogue on the Sabbath, there can be no doubt that he understood himself to be the fulfillment of this prophecy, that is, he is the Messiah prophetically spoken of in Isa 11:1-9 and 61:1-3.

K. A Song to the Holy One of Israel (12:1-6)

BEHIND THE TEXT

This song of praise, written in psalm style, divides into two parts (vv 1-3 and vv 4-6), each opening with "In that day you will say." Childs sees this chapter responding to God's acts of "salvation to his people in Zion," as presented in chs 1—11, thus serving as a conclusion to these first eleven chapters

(2001, 107-8). Oswalt (1986, 291) and Motyer (1993, 127) see it serving as a conclusion to chs 6—11.

As indicated by the person and gender of the personal pronouns, there is a change in the addressee throughout this song: in 12:1-2, an individual male is called to "praise"; in vv 3-5, the community of the saved as a whole is called to "praise" and "sing"; in v 6, Zion personified as an individual female is called to "shout" and "sing." The singular masculine/feminine at beginning and end form an inclusio bracketing the plural community, thus depicting "totality . . . [all] alike absorbed in salvation, in its joy and its proclamation" (ibid., 128). The majority of scholars do not deem ch 12 to be from Isaiah. Motyer, however, fittingly views ch 12 as epilogue to chs 6—12; according to Motyer, ch 6 is the prologue. He further suggests that "the whole collection, chapters 6—12, was put together by Isaiah . . . to give heart to a beleaguered remnant of the Lord's people" (ibid., 127-28).

IN THE TEXT

■ 1 **In that day** links this passage with 4:2; 10:20; and 11:10-11, where "in that day" signaled the hope of salvation, in opposition to 2:20; 3:18; 4:1; 7:18, 20, 21, 23, where "in that day" signaled God's impending judgment (Oswalt 1986, 292). **You** (masc. sg.) at the beginning of the song signals Isaiah's call to each male member of the saved community to join this song of praise. The prophet, as herald, lines out the words to sing: **I will praise you, O Yahweh**. Praise (*ydh*) most often occurs in the context of acknowledgment or giving thanks to God for his having resolved a recent crisis. Such acknowledgment was often accompanied by a thank offering (*tôdâ*) (compare Lev 7:12, 13, 15; 22:29; Ps 107:21-22), given in response to God's divine grace (VanGemeren 1997, 2:405-6).

The song expresses the crisis: **You were angry with me**, though it does not give the cause of Yahweh's **anger**. Yet one recalls Yahweh's anger, in Isaiah's own time, at King Ahaz for fearing the Syrian-Israelite coalition and turning to Assyria for help rather than trusting in Yahweh for deliverance (7:2-9, 17-20). As the invading Assyrian army destroyed town after town of the Judean countryside, moving ever closer to Jerusalem, each citizen's heart would no doubt have resonated with the psalmist, "How long, **Yahweh**? Will you be angry forever?" (Ps 79:5; compare Pss 80:4 [5 HB]; 85:5 [6 HB]). But Yahweh withdrew his impending judgment, and the intended Assyrian siege of 701 BC was withdrawn and Jerusalem delivered (Isa 37:36-37). And so the crisis has passed: [but] **your anger has turned away and you have comforted me**. The theme of God's *comforting* his people will recur at 40:1; 49:13; 61:2; and 66:13.

When we read ch 12 in the context of ch 11, after which it has been purposefully placed, this song of comfort also points beyond the historical context of Isaiah's time to "the full eschatological consummation of the kingdom of God" (Childs 2001, 110). It is in the community of the Messiah King that Yahweh's *comfort* will be fully realized.

■ **2** The voice of the male singer continues, twice affirming that **my salvation is God** (*'ēl*), whose name is **Yahweh** (*yhwh*), the self-revealed name of God to Moses prior to the Exodus (Exod 3:13-15). The singer's **salvation** is not in any of the gods of the nations, such as Baal, Hadad, Chemosh, or Molech. Within the restorative assurance of God's "comfort" (Isa 12:1), the singer sings a variation on a line from Moses' song commemorating the Israelites' crossing of the Red Sea (Exod 15:2): **I will trust [in God] and not be afraid** (*lō' 'ephād*), because **God** has proven that **Yahweh, himself, is my strength . . . my song/defense . . . my salvation** (Isa 11:2; note the Exodus event shimmering in the background of Isaiah's words in 11:15-16). That his **salvation** lay in **trust** in Yahweh is what King Ahaz could not bring himself to believe (7:2-9), even though Isaiah had urged him, "Don't be afraid [*'al tîrā'*]" (v 4).

■ **3-5** The verbs of these verses are in the plural; Isaiah is now addressing the "community of the saved" (Motyer 1993, 129) as a whole. They are to **draw water** (v 3), **give praise, proclaim, make known** (v 4), and **sing** (v 5). It is **Yahweh's** name (i.e., his character or attributes) and the **glorious things** that **he has done** (v 4), that the community of the saved are to **make known . . . to all the world** (vv 4-5; compare Exod 34:5-7 where God a second time proclaimed to Moses "his name, **Yahweh**," followed by a listing of his attributes).

The focus is on God's **salvation**, metaphorically likened to fresh **water** continually bubbling forth **from springs** (*ma'ayĕnîm* [v 3]), to which the saved community has abundant access. This imagery invites us to glimpse again the Exodus event shimmering in the background and to recall God's provision of life-giving water in the wilderness (from the "twelve springs" [*'ēnōt*, related to *ma'ayĕnîm* above] of water at Elim [Exod 15:27], and from the rock [Exod 17]). Moreover, God continues to give life, not only for his people but also for **the nations** of **all the world** who are invited to partake of God's **springs** of **salvation** and thus become part of the community of the saved.

■ **6** The two imperatives in this verse (**shout** and **sing**) are feminine singular and are addressed to **Lady Zion** (*yôšebet ṣîyôn*, lit. "female dweller of Zion"). This title is similar to Isaiah's earlier "Daughter Zion" (*bat ṣîyôn*). There, however, Zion's circumstances in the aftermath of the Assyrian invasion of 701 BC gave no cause for rejoicing and singing. There she sat "like a shelter in a vineyard . . . like a city under siege" (1:7-8). There "the Holy One of Israel" was not in their midst because, of their own volition, they had "turned their backs on him" (1:4). Yet God had promised a restoration, "if you are willing and obedient" (1:19), so that in a future day "Zion will be delivered with justice," and again she would be known as "the City of Righteousness, the Faithful City" (1:27, 26).

But, now, **O Zion**, is the time for ***shouting*** and ***singing*** with a **joy** that wells up from within, because our God who is faithful to his promise, **the Holy One of Israel** [is] **among you**. The injustice and oppression that characterized the rulers of Zion, exemplified in King Ahaz and most of those of the house of David who followed him, is now replaced by the "righteousness," "justice," and "faithfulness" (11:4-5) of the Messiah King.

FROM THE TEXT

One of the central themes of this brief chapter is "water" and God's "***springs*** of salvation" (v 3). Water as an image for salvation is used many times in both the OT and NT (compare Pss 42:1-2 [2-3 HB]; 46:4-5 [5-6 HB]; Isa 35:6-7; 44:3; 55:1; Jer 2:13; John 4:15; 7:37-38; Rev 7:17).

One time, while participating in a geographical study in southern Israel during the dry season, our team searched for streams but found none. I glimpsed a gazelle racing across the barren desert hills. Surely there must have been some watering place, perhaps a spring known only to the gazelle, from which, daily, it quenched its physical longing for water. I recalled the psalmist's depiction of the deer longing for "streams of water," with a new understanding of his imagery; my heart joined his in his own longing: "My soul thirsts for God, for the living God" (Ps 42:1, 2 [2, 3 HB]).

Several hundred years after this psalmist, Jesus said to a woman of Samaria at Jacob's well, "Everyone who drinks this water will be thirsty again, but whoever drinks the water I give them will never thirst. Indeed, the water I give them will become in them a spring of water welling up to eternal life" (John 4:13; see vv 4-14). Jacob's well contained water, but it was not living water; Jesus had offered living water, that which can become a never-ending source from within to quench the thirst of our souls.

Jesus' living water has OT roots. Jeremiah records God's deep anguish over the choice his people have made: "They have forsaken me, the spring of living water, and have dug their own cisterns, broken cisterns that cannot hold water" (Jer 2:13).

On another occasion in Israel, my fellow students and I were doing a small archaeological dig with our Israeli professor in the ruins of an Israelite town, dating to just after Prophet Jeremiah's time (early- to mid-sixth cent. BC). Surveying the environs of the town, I came across an ancient water cistern dug in the ground. Would I find thirst-quenching water there? Alas! The plastered walls had long since cracked and broken, the water long since leaked away. There was no life in this cistern, only dirt, stones, a couple of scorpions, and a snake. For just such a broken cistern Judah had turned her back on Yahweh, the Spring of Living Water.

The woman of Samaria, having had five husbands, and the man she was currently living with not her husband (John 4:16-18), did not know of the Spring of Living Water until she met Jesus at Jacob's well. Her life was a "broken cistern," filled with the brokenness of unfaithful and unfulfilling human relationships; she had known the sting of the scorpion-like gossip of the townspeople. Sin, like dirt, filled her "broken cistern." Jesus offered her Living Water. "Sir, give me this water," she begged, and, "leaving her water jar, the woman went back to the town and said to the people, 'Come, see a man . . . Could this be the Messiah?'" (John 4:15, 28-29).

II. YAHWEH, SOVEREIGN OF ALL NATIONS: 13:1—27:13

Overview

Chapter 12 brought to a close Isaiah's prophetic activity during the Syrian-Israelite threat upon Judah during the latter third of the eighth century BC. It also concluded Isaiah's prophecies concerning God's coming judgment upon and future destruction of Assyria, the imperial power broker of Isaiah's world. (But see 14:24-27.)

Chapter 13 marks the beginning of a new section of the book of Isaiah that extends through ch 27. This new section can be viewed in two segments: chs 13—23 and chs 24—27.

The all-encompassing theme of the first segment, chs 13—23, is "the purpose of God in exercising his sovereignty over the nations" (Childs 2001, 173). The segment begins with a "prophecy ***concerning*** Babylon" and continues with prophecies concerning other nations within the OT world: Assyria, Philistia, Moab, Damascus, Cush, and Egypt (chs 13—19). It concludes with an oracle concerning Tyre (ch 23). Between these oracles concerning the nations, ch 20 briefly mentions the 711 BC Assyrian military campaign led by Sargon against Philistine Ashdod and invasion of Egypt and Isaiah's warning to Judah's leaders to put no trust in Cush and Egypt for military assistance against Assyria. Chapters 21 and 22 give four rather enigmatic oracles concerning nonnations and a warning to Judah's royal steward Shebna, that he will be deposed and replaced by Eliakim son of Hilkiah.

The second segment, chs 24—27, has an "eschatological focus" (ibid.), presenting Yahweh triumphant over all nations and peoples, indeed over the whole earth. In his triumph, "***Yahweh Sebaoth*** will reign on Mount Zion" (24:23), from where he will carry out a restoration that now includes "all peoples," who are invited to enjoy "a banquet" prepared "on this mountain" (i.e., Zion). Effective for all is the abolishing of "death," "tears," and "disgrace" (25:6-8). In chs 26—27, Yahweh emerges "to punish the people of the earth for their sins" (26:21). Then, when a great eschatological "trumpet ***is blown***," Yahweh's "perishing" and "exiled" people "will be gathered" from "Assyria" and "Egypt." These two geographical entities represent all the nations of the earth out from which the entire diaspora of God's people will be gathered; they will come to "worship ***Yahweh***" in the place where he reigns supreme, figuratively "on the holy mountain in Jerusalem" (27:12-13).

Excursus: A Theological Basis for Yahweh's Sovereignty over the Nations

In these chapters (Isa 13—27) several of the nations of the world come up before the judgment throne of Yahweh and are found wanting. In one way or another, all have violated, beyond continuance of nationhood, Yahweh's covenant norms of justice, mercy, and respect. These are norms that govern relationships between independent peoples, each of whom is in a subordinate/dependent/vassal relationship with the same overlord/suzerain, Yahweh.

Such violations by one subordinate against another are deemed to be violations against Yahweh, the overlord. Amos calls these *pĕšāʿîm*, "transgressions," "rebellions" (Amos 1:3, 6, 9, 11, 13; 2:1, 4, 6). These are willful violations of known covenant stipulations. From what took place at Mount Sinai between Yahweh and the diverse group of people who escaped from Egyptian Pharaoh's conscripted labor force, it is clear how Judah and Israel could certainly be held accountable to these covenant norms. But how could other nations be brought to book for covenant norms of which they ostensibly know nothing? They were not in covenant with Yahweh! Or were they?

Psalm 96 reflects Israel's view that Yahweh's sovereign authority extends to all nations and peoples, and their gods. This authority requires all nations to conform to that which characterizes Yahweh's rule: "equity" (v 10), "righteousness" and "faithfulness" (v 13) (Brueggemann 1997, 492-93). Psalm 95:1-5 theologically links Yahweh's status as "great King" with his act of creation; that is, all creation belongs to him by virtue of his having brought it into being. Hezekiah links Yahweh's lordship "over all the kingdoms of the earth" with his creatorship of "heaven and earth" (Isa 37:14-20).

This theological view is rooted in Gen 1—11. The first portion (Gen 1—3) declares the origin of humankind to be in the making (*'śh* [1:26]), creating (*br'* [1:27]), and forming (*yṣr* [2:7]) acts of God/Yahweh God, from which origin came all subsequent humans and nations. Brueggemann draws attention to the latter portion (Gen 9:8—11:30), "which bear witness to Yahweh's postflood governance of the nations." The nations, however, reject their status as Yahweh's subjects and refuse his gifts (ibid., 493-94).

A. A Prophecy Concerning Babylon and Assyria (13:1—14:27)

BEHIND THE TEXT

Babylon

From ca. 3000 BC, Babylon (Gen 10:10) was a city located in central Mesopotamia on the Euphrates River. Archaeological levels of the earliest city date from the nineteenth to sixteenth centuries BC. Babylon's influence and power began to spread in the early eighteenth century BC. At its peak under Hammurabi (reigned 1792-1750 BC), this (first) Babylonian Empire stretched from the Persian Gulf to the middle Euphrates and upper Tigris Rivers regions. By the late tenth century BC, however, Babylon became a vassal of Assyria and, by the time of Tiglath-Pileser III (reigned 745-727 BC), was completely under Assyrian control. In 722 BC, however, Babylon's vassal ruler, Marduk-Baladan (2 Kgs 20:12-13; Isa 39:1), revolted and for a brief decade ruled an independent Babylon. Assyrian Sargon put down his revolt in 711 BC.

In 626 BC Nabopolassar freed Babylon from Assyrian control, and under his rule (626-605 BC) and his son Nebuchadnezzar II (reigned 605-562 BC), the Neo-Babylonian Empire expanded to the height of its glory. This imperial rule passed to the Persians in 539 BC under Cyrus. Alexander the Great destroyed Babylon in 330 BC, though it continued to be inhabited, but of little importance. The city's last archaeological mention is on a Babylonian clay tablet dated to ca. 10 BC (*NIDB* 116-20).

Eight of the passages in chs 13—23 relative to various nations, instead of being introduced as "vision" (*ḥăzôn* [1:1]) or **word** (*dābār* [2:1]), are introduced with *maśśā'*. These are: 13:1, "Babylon"; 14:29, "Philistines"; 15:1, "Moab"; 19:1, "Egypt"; 21:1, "the Desert by the Sea"; 21:11, "Dumah"; 21:13, "Arabia"; 22:1, "the Valley of Vision"; 23:1, "Tyre." Commentators translate *maśśā'* variously: "burden," "oracle," "verdict," or "prophecy" (as in the NIV). Some suggest it means "a lifting up of the voice" (e.g., Oswalt 1986, 296; Motyer 1993, 136). While the NIV, and some commentators, add the preposition "against" (e.g., "a prophecy against Babylon" [13:1]), the MT has no preposition. Grammatically, ***of*** or ***concerning*** more correctly expresses the relationship between the two terms: thus, for example, "a prophecy ***concerning*** Babylon."

The introduction of "Babylon" in 13:1 signals the beginning of a new section. Both historically and symbolically, in these chapters "Babylon" epitomizes the "arrogance" and "pride" of the nations (13:11, 19; 16:6 ["Moab"]; 23:8-9 ["Tyre"]. It is this self-exaltation above God, epitomized by "the king of Babylon" (14:4, 13-15), which brings about their downfall. With this theme, chs 13—27 pick up the central theme of chs 1—12.

IN THE TEXT

1. Yahweh Gathers His Worldwide Army (13:1-5)

These verses appear to be set in the context of Yahweh in the midst of his heavenly council (Watts 2005, 246). They reflect the OT concept of holy war, with a worldwide call to arms (Motyer 1993, 137).

■ 1 In the time of **Isaiah son of Amoz**, **Babylon** was a vassal province in the Assyrian Empire. Though a vassal, it exerted powerful influence throughout the southern Mesopotamian area. Marduk-Baladan, a powerful Aramaean prince, seized the throne of Babylon in 722 BC (the same year that Samaria fell to the Assyrians), holding power for twelve years. In this section of Isaiah (chs 13—27), however, **Babylon** represents both the historical city and the empire that it later became, wielding power from the Eastern/Lower Sea (Persian Gulf) to the Western/Upper Sea (Mediterranean Sea). In the **prophecy . . . that Isaiah son of Amoz saw** (*ḥāzâ*), **Babylon** is symbolic of the nations' "arrogant self-sufficiency" (Motyer 1993, 136). The name Babylon, for several generations to come, will call to mind the very "spirit of . . . world power" (Young 1965, 413). Calvin speaks of the Babylonians as those "who gave themselves up to deeds of dishonesty and violence, and despised all law both human and divine" (1850, 317).

■ 2-3 The speaker in these two verses speaks in the first person: the **I** (v 3) is emphatic, placed first in the Hebrew sentence. Verse 4 reveals this speaker to be **Yahweh Sebaoth**. Whom Yahweh is addressing is not stated, but possibly heavenly messengers (compare Ps 104:4; Zech 1:11-12; 6:5-8) or prophets (compare Judg 4:6). They are to **raise a banner** [*nēs*; compare Isa 5:26; 11:10; Jer 51:27] **on a bare hilltop** for clear visibility; they are to **exalt** [**their**] **voice** for clarity of hearing; they are to **wave** [**their**] **hand** for signaling direction (Isa 13:2). **Them** refers to those whom Yahweh (as General of his army) has **commanded** (v 3): they are **my separated ones** (*měqudāšāy*)/**those I prepared for battle**; they are **my warriors of my wrath** (*gibbôray lĕ'appî*); they are **my exulting ones of arrogance** (*'allîzê gā'ăwâ*). These are the ones being summoned **to enter the gates of the nobles** (v 2), possibly referring to the military encampment or government center where they assemble for the coming march to Babylon.

■ **4-5** In these verses we "hear" an auditory description of the ***tumult*** and **uproar** of a great ***army*** **mustering . . . for war** (v 4). This **great multitude** of soldiers is assembling from the **nations** and **kingdoms** of the world, **from faraway lands** (v 5), even **from the ends of the heavens** (the horizon, the line where earth and sky appear to meet; compare Deut 28:49, "the end of the earth" [NRSV]). This is no ordinary gathering of troops, for it is **Yahweh Sebaoth** who gathers this **army for war** (*ṣĕbā' milḥāmâ* [Isa 13:4]). The purpose is for the destruction, not only of Babylon, but of **the whole *earth*** (*kol hā'āreṣ* [v 5]). Here is anticipated **Yahweh's Day**, as introduced in v 6.

2. Yahweh's Day of Burning Anger (13:6-16)

■ **6 Wail!** (*hêlîlû*, impv.) is an often used term for calling people and other personifications to lament in the face of impending disaster (compare Isa 14:31; 23:1, 6, 14; Jer 4:8; 25:34; 49:3; Ezek 31:17; Joel 1:5, 11, 13; Zeph 1:11; Zech 11:2). Here the impending disaster is **Yahweh's Day** (*yôm yhwh*), which is said to be **near**. This **day** is **like destruction** [*šōd*] **from the Almighty** (*šadday*) (Joel 1:15 employs the same description). Scholars have not determined the original meaning of *šadday*, but it is an ancient title for God associated with the patriarchs (Gen 49:24-25). The LXX and Vulgate preserve a traditional meaning of "omnipotent," hence the long-standing translation **Almighty**. Whereas the name normally would give a sense of comfort, here (and in Joel 1:15), in a wordplay based on sound, *šadday* is associated with *šōd*, **destruction**, and would call up the opposite image of God: he is now the ***destroyer*** (in Isaiah, of all that Babylon represents; in Joel, of Judah).

■ **7-8** These verses depict the peoples' reaction in the face of the impending "day of **Yahweh**" (v 6): **terror** in such magnitude that **all hands will *become enfeebled*** and **every *human* heart will melt** (v 7). The **hands** (outer) and **heart** (inner) represent one's total being, hence, total paralysis in the face of incomprehensible destruction. The imagery of a **woman in labor** (v 8) is a simile for "that which is sudden, inevitable and inescapable; the end result of a process that cannot be stopped (1 Thess. 5:2-3)" (Motyer 1993, 138).

■ **9-13** Again the prophet speaks of the eschatological **day of Yahweh**, truly a **cruel day** (v 9). This **day** will bring Yahweh's **punishment** that will affect **the [*whole*] world** because of the **evil** and **sins** (v 11) of its inhabitants: **the sinners** (v 9) and **the wicked** (v 11). The primary sins are **arrogance** and **pride**. In ch 2 also, because of these same two sins, God's people had turned away from him to worship "idols . . . the work of their hands" (v 8). In ch 2 God is given the title **Yahweh Sebaoth** (as here in 13:13), and, in his day of judgment "rises to shake the earth" (2:12, 19, 21). Here, in ch 13 also, Isaiah says that in Yahweh's eschatological judgment, both **the heavens tremble** and **the earth will shake from its place** (v 13). The **constellations** and the **sun** (*šemeš*), even the **moon** (*yārēaḥ*), all worshipped as deities in the idolatrous cults surrounding Israel, and often incorporated by Israel herself, will cease to **show their light** (v 10). Oswalt suggests that, since these heavenly bodies are but reflections of God, who is light (1 John 1:5), the extinguishing of these lights indicates "God has withdrawn his blessing from the world" (1986, 306). The effect of the resulting darkness, says Wesley, is that humankind "shall have no comfort or hope" (n.d., 3466).

■ **14-16** The world's inhabitants are now **likened** to the dispersing of a herd of **gazelles** when **hunted** or to the scattering of a flock of **sheep** with **no shepherd** to keep them together (v 14). One can imagine them *fleeing* a major city, perhaps Babylon, in the face of the Day of Yahweh: those who have migrated to the big city for the better life, better jobs, new opportunities, or those who have been brought as deportees. Refuge is sought in a **return . . . to their native land**. Yet some have no hope of escape from the invading army. Those overtaken still in the city, **before their *very* eyes** (*lĕ'ênêhem* [v 16]), see their **infants . . . dashed to pieces . . .** , **their houses . . . looted** and their **wives *raped***, all common consequences of war.

3. Babylon Overthrown (13:17-22)

■ **17-18** Only now does the prophet reveal whom God is summoning to attack the still unnamed city: **the Medes** (v 17), a people inhabiting the Zagros Mountains, east of Mesopotamia (Curtis 2009, 67). They cannot be bought off with **silver** or **gold** (compare Zeph 1:18). Their single-minded cruelty is graphically depicted: their **bows**—their "weapon par excellence" (Wildberger 1997, 29, citing Herodotus and Xenophon)—*dash in pieces* **the young men** (Isa 13:18). They show **no mercy on *fruit of the womb*** [*pĕrî beṭem*] **infants**, perhaps referring to the practice of ripping open pregnant wombs and destroying the fetus (compare 2 Kgs 8:12; 15:16; Hos 13:16; Amos 1:13). ***Their eye shows no pity*** on **children**.

■ **19** For Isaiah, **Babylon** symbolizes the central city, the Babylonian Empire, and the nations of the world, all who live in arrogance and pride without regard for God. **Babylon** is depicted here as a **jewel of kingdoms** (compare Isa

47:5, "queen of kingdoms"), yet her **overthrow**, and that of the nations of the world, will be as complete as that of paradigmatic **Sodom and Gomorrah**.

■ **20-22** And, like Sodom and Gomorrah, when the Day of Yahweh comes, Babylon and the kingdoms of the world will experience a complete reversal of civilized, settled life: cities no more **inhabited**, **tents** of the **nomads** and **shepherds** with **their flocks** seen no more for all succeeding **generations** (v 20). In the place of humans and domestic animals will be a plethora of wild animals: **jackals**, **owls**, **wild goats**, and **hyenas** (vv 21-22), "animals which inhabit dark and lonely settings." One now hears only "the hoots and howls of the night-dwellers" (Oswalt 1986, 310).

This will all happen in **her time**, which is said to be **at hand** (lit. **near to come** [v 22]). In pointing toward the future demise of Babylon, Isaiah is speaking of "God's time . . . In full confidence, long before its demise is revealed for all to see, the prophet pronounces the imminent end of the oppressor." In doing so, the future demise of Babylon is "a demonstration of God's sovereignty over the nations" (Childs 2001, 125).

4. Yahweh's Compassion on Jacob (14:1-2)

■ **1** This verse opens with *kî*, **for** (omitted in the NIV), suggesting that the future demise of Babylon in ch 13 is because **Yahweh will have compassion** (*yĕraḥēm*) on his people. To **have compassion** is the verbal form of the noun *reḥem*, "mother's womb" (from the root *rḥm*). While in the womb a child is utterly helpless and dependent upon its mother's care and protection. As such, "the womb is a metaphor of divine compassion" (VanGemeren 1997, 3:1097). The idiom here, then, could be translated, **Yahweh will womb [helpless]** Jacob (compare 49:10; 54:8, 10).

Moreover, in an echo of the first Exodus, just as Yahweh chose his people while in Egyptian bondage, **again** [*'ôd*] **he will choose** them while in bondage in Mesopotamia. The parallel use of **Jacob/Israel** (compare 10:20; 27:6) includes all God's people. And, just as the purpose for bringing them out of Egypt was to bring them into the land of Canaan, again Yahweh **will give them rest** [*hinnîḥām*] **in their own land** (*'admātām*).

Also in parallel with the first Exodus, just as **a great mixture** (Exod 12:38) came out of Egypt with the descendants of Abraham, so in this future return from Mesopotamia, **foreigners** [*gēr*] **will unite with the house** [*bêt*] **of Jacob**. Here is a theological play on *gēr*, a "resident alien," who was to receive special protection in Israel (Deut 14:21, 29; 16:11). This concept was based partly on Israel's previous status as aliens in Egypt (Exod 23:9; Deut 10:19). Ultimately, though, they were to mirror Yahweh's very character in their treatment of the alien (Deut 10:18). Here, again, in spite of having been oppressed in Mesopotamia, Yahweh's people, when brought home again, were to emulate Yahweh's "compassion" even for their oppressors, welcoming them equally as **descendants of Jacob**.

■ **2** Here is seen a reversal of roles. The **nations** who had been Israel's **oppressors** will now **bring** God's oppressed people back to their homeland. They will, in fact, become **servants** of God's people.

5. A Taunt against Babylon's King (14:3-21)

■ **3-4a** This brief section serves as an introduction to Isa 14:4b-21. Isaiah now speaks directly to God's people, concerning **the day Yahweh gives you rest** (*hānîaḥ*) (v 3). This is the same "rest" promised in 14:1. They will no longer endure **suffering and turmoil** and **harsh labor** (*hā'ăbōdâ haqqāšâ*), descriptive of the oppression of a tyrant. *'Ăbōdâ*, "labor/slavery," describes Israel's former condition in Egypt (Exod 1:14; 2:23; 5:9, 11; 6:9). So, here again, the prophet—in drawing an analogy with the long ago Egyptian experience, out of Israel's "salvation history"—finds "strength . . . to believe and to hope" for the future (Wildberger 1997, 50).

Taunt (v 4a) is *māšāl*, "to compare." It generally describes a proverb, a synonym, or a parable and, on occasion, can describe a negative example, that is, something or someone that one should not emulate. In Num 21:27, those skilled at such sayings are called *mōšĕlîm*, **taunters** ("poets" [NIV]). **The king of Babylon**, on the one hand, may be one of the Assyrian kings of Isaiah's day, since Assyrian kings from Tiglath-Pileser III onward took the title King of Babylon. On the other hand, this title also is a representation of the "arrogance" and "pride" of the "haughty" and "ruthless" rulers of Isa 13:11 who, in the end, will pass off the world's scene.

■ **4b-8** Shipp describes this unit, a *mashal* (→ v 4a above), as a coherent literary poem, whose author has borrowed its themes from ancient Near Eastern funeral lament forms. The images, however, have been transformed to mock and taunt a dead king, who in life arrogantly tyrannized the world of Isaiah's day. This king's actions and pride suggest his desire to rise to divine status, but which instead brought him to the "lowest possible pit in Sheol" (2002, 160-66). Though the identity of the tyrant referenced in this poem cannot be identified with certainty, Ginsberg cogently argues that it is Sargon II (reigned 721-705 BC); he bases this on an Akkadian text, which reads: "Sargon . . . was not buried in his house," which he (with others) understands to mean that Sargon's body was abandoned on the battlefield (1968, 50).

The downfall of the **oppressor** is the theme of this paragraph. The **oppressor**, possibly Sargon II, also represents all **wicked ones**, all imperial rulers, who, **in anger smite peoples** (*'ammîm* [v 6]) and **in fury subdue** nations (*gôyim*). He/they have **come to an end** (v 4) because **Yahweh** has intervened and **broken** (v 5) his/their power (**rod/scepter**). This gives cause for great rejoicing, as **all the earth**, now *quietly resting*, in unison **breaks** into singing (v

7). Even **the cedars of Lebanon,** harvested often by Assyrian kings for use in palace construction, personified, ***rejoice:*** ***no longer does the woodcutter ascend*** [*ya'ăleh;* note the use of *'lh* in v 13] ***upon us!*** (v 8).

The Trees of Lebanon and the Assyrian Kings

The Assyrian kings' tree-gathering campaigns to Lebanon are well documented. Tiglath-Pileser I (reigned ca. 1116-1078 BC) records: "At the command of Anu and Adad, the great gods, my lords, I marched to the Lebanon Mountains *[missing text in the original]* its (their?) plunder I carried off and brought to my land." Again: "Its cracks I smoothed over, with cedar and *[missing text in the original]* -logs, (for) which, at the command of Assur and Anu, the great gods, my lords, I went [to the Lebanon Mountains] (where) I cut down, and (whence) I brought these splendid beams of the temple of *[missing text in the original],* where the great gods, my lords, continually abide" (Luckenbill [1926] 1968, 94, 96-97).

In an inscription of Ashurnasirpal II (reigned 884-860 BC) we read:

I made my way to the slopes of Mount Lebanon . . . I climbed up to Mount Amanus (and) cut down logs of cedar, cypress, *daprānu*-juniper, (and) *burāšu*-juniper. . . . I transported cedar logs from Mount Amanus and brought (them) to *Ešarra* to my temple the shrine, a joyful temple, to the temple of the gods *Sîn* and *Šamaš,* the holy gods. (Grayson 1991, 218-19)

In the time of Isaiah, Tiglath-Pileser III (reigned 745-727 BC) boasts concerning the construction of the rooms of his palace in Calah:

I put more work upon them (than was put) on (any) of the palaces of (other) lands. With long (*lit.,* tall) cedar beams, whose fragrance is as good as that of the cypress tree, products of Amanus, Lebanon and Ammanana (Anti-Lebanon), I roofed them over, and brought (them) to faultless completion. (Luckenbill [1926] 1968, 288-89)

Concerning the construction of his elaborate palace in Nineveh, Sennacherib (reigned 705-681 BC) twice mentions: "Beams of cedar, the product of Mt. Amanus, which they dragged with difficulty out of (those) distant mountains, I stretched across their ceilings. . . . Great cedar beams they felled in Mt. Amanus, dragged them to Nineveh and roofed (my palaces with them)" (Luckenbill 1924, 96, 132). Isaiah 37:24 (= 2 Kgs 19:23) records Yahweh's rebuke of Sennacherib's boast:

By your messengers you have ridiculed the **Sovereign** [*'ădōnāy*]. And you have said, "With my many chariots I have ascended the heights of the mountains, the utmost heights of Lebanon. I have cut down its tallest cedars, the choicest of its junipers. I have reached its remotest heights, the finest of its forests."

Beyond Isaiah's time, Nebuchadnezzar II (reigned 605-562 BC) reports: "I constructed a straight road for the . . . mighty cedars, high and strong, of precious beauty and of excellent dark quality, the abundant yield of the Lebanon" (Pritchard 1969, 307).

■ **9-11** This paragraph takes us to **Sheol** (→ 5:14 sidebar, "Sheol in the OT"), to which, in death, the great "oppressor" (14:4) has now come. Already resident in **Sheol** are other departed earthly beings, former **leaders of earth**, **kings of nations** (v 9), called **rephaim**. Scholars have not determined the origin of the term *rĕpā'îm*, though a consensus is that its meaning is best rendered as "shades." That is, the OT belief is that the life of a human person continued to exist beyond the death and decay of the physical body in a "shadowy" existence in **Sheol** (compare Job's plea to God, "Oh that you would hide me in Sheol . . . I would wait until my release should come. You would call, and I would answer you" [Job 14:13-15 NRSV]).

These shadowy **leaders** and **kings** are depicted as seated upon **thrones**, retaining their previous status as **kings** on earth, a concept seen in Egyptian, Mesopotamian, and Syro-Palestinian literature (Shipp 2002, 126). The arrival of the tyrant **makes them rise from their thrones** (*kis'ōtām*; note Isa 14:13) as though to honor him. The implication may be that he had once ruled over some of them on earth (Wildberger 1997, 61). But, instead of a welcome of honor, we hear their mocking chant: **Even you! Weakened you have become, just as we are! Yes, like us you have become!** Your **pride** and the **music of your harps** mean nothing here (v 11). (Such music characterized great palace festivals and would have accompanied a king's funeral bier to his grave.) There is not even a **throne** for you here in **Sheol**. Your decomposing, rotting body lies on a bed of **maggots**, and **worms cover you**.

■ **12-15** Isaiah now takes us from the depths of the underworld to the heights of **heaven**. Drawing on terminology that appears to parallel that found in Canaanite myths discovered at Ugarit in 1927 (McKay 1970), the taunt song speaks of **morning star, son of the dawn**. The prophet is not speaking of the fall from heaven of Satan or any angelic being but is drawing an analogy with "the oppressor" of v 4, the tyrant **who once laid low the nations** (*gôyim* [v 12]). The passage is about the arrogance and futility of human pride, the creature challenging the rightful place of the Creator.

We are given a glimpse into the innermost aspirations of this tyrant, who **said in his** heart, "I will ascend [*'e'ĕlâ*; note the use of *'lh* in v 8] **to the heavens, I will exalt my throne**" (*kis'î*; note v 9), not necessarily higher than God (*'ēl* [v 13]), but at least equal with **the Most High** (*'elyôn* [v 14]). *'Elyôn* is possibly derived from the root *'lh*, "to ascend" (Wildberger 1997, 67). The combination of the two epithets (*'ēl 'elyôn*) means "God the high one" or "God Most High." It is this title by which God was known to both Melchizedek and Abram: "God Most High, **Possessor** [*qōnnēh*; "Creator" (NIV)] of heaven and earth" (Gen 14:19, 22). And so, "the oppressor" who wished to make himself **like the Most High** and sit upon his **throne in the heavens** is not only **cast down to the earth**

(Isa 14:12) by the one who possesses both **heaven** and **earth**, but beyond to the underworld, *to Sheol* (vv 12, 15).

■ **16-20a** Isaiah now turns from heaven in which "the oppressor" had coveted to place his throne and from Sheol where his "shade" now exists in shadowy darkness. We are taken to the desolate field of battle, the site of the tyrant's defeat. The clash of swords and rumble of chariots has ceased. The only sound is of those who have come to identify those **slain** in battle (v 19). There, they discover the slain tyrant's **corpse** lying abandoned, to be **trampled underfoot**. Having been stripped of his royal robes by conquering soldiers, his only covering now is a pile of other decaying corpses, those **pierced by the sword**.

Isaiah has put words of mockery into the mouths of **those who see** and **stare** at the tyrant's corpse: "Surely this couldn't be **the man who shook the earth . . . *overthrowing*** its cities and ***refusing to*** let his captives go home!" (vv 16-17). Isaiah further observes that the tyrant's corpse will remain homeless; there will be no **burial** for him in a tomb as would befit a benevolent king. But this king did what no king should ever do: **you . . . destroyed your *own* land, *you slayed* your *own* people** (v 20).

■ **20b-21** Verses 20b-21 consist of a curse pronounced against the deceased tyrant ruler. This curse echoes an ancient Near Eastern practice, often invoked whenever a ruler was overthrown. His entire family was wiped out so none from his family line could ever again regain power. One threat concerning an Aramaic ruler reads: "The gods of this treaty will all snatch away . . . Matti'el and his son and his grandson and his descendants" (Wildberger 1997, 73). Such a practice is also noted in 1 Kgs 15:28-30 and 2 Kgs 10:17. In the case of the present tyrant, two things are wished to ensure that his family line does not again **rise to inherit the land**: (1) *may there be no calling out* [i.e., naming/mentioning] *of* **the offspring of the wicked *one for eternity!*** (Isa 14:20b) and (2) **prepare a place** *of* **slaughter** *for* **his children** (v 21). Thus his evil royal line was to be obliterated forever!

6. Babylon's Name Wiped Out (14:22-23)

■ **22-23** We now see that the taunt of the previous verses (vv 3-21) is against more than a single tyrannical ruler, "the king of Babylon" (v 4). It is a taunt against Babylon itself, in which **Yahweh Sebaoth** declares, **I will rise up against them** (v 22). Yahweh's means of removing Babylon is not that of chariots and horses, but of a simple **broom** (v 23), bringing to mind the image of someone *sweeping* away the dust from the floor. Just so, with impunity, **Yahweh Sebaoth**, with a swish of his **broom of destruction**, will forever remove from history **Babylon's name and survivors, her offspring and descendants** (v 22)—all that she represents. In Yahweh's plan of world history, Babylon is but a mere "speck of dust on the scales" (40:15 NASB). Where once there was a thriving city, ruling far reaches of the world, there will be nothing but a **swampland**

(14:23) inhabited by wild animals. Oswalt observes, "Never far from Isaiah's consciousness is the direct involvement of God in history. . . . when Babylon comes down, it will be because God did it" (1986, 326).

7. Yahweh Will Break Assyria (14:24-27)

■ **24-27** The promise contained in these verses is based on the one who **has sworn**, the one who has **purposed**. It is **Yahweh Sebaoth** (vv 24, 27) who will **break Assyria** (v 25). In vv 3-23, Isaiah has been using "Babylon" as representative of all imperial powers in general; here, he (re)turns to the specific imperial ruler of his own day: **Assyria**. In so doing, he echoes 10:23-27: in both passages it is **Yahweh Sebaoth** who promises to remove Assyria's **yoke** and **burden** from his people (14:25); in both passages Yahweh's overthrow of Assyria serves as the model for his **plan determined for the whole world** (v 26; compare 12:5; 13:5; 25:8; 28:22; 29:5-8). Wildberger suggests that Isaiah is "the first prophet who works with the equation: history = world history," and this is because of his vision of Yahweh as the King whose "glory" fills "the whole earth" (6:3) (1997, 85). Isaiah's reference to Yahweh's **hand stretched out over all nations** (14:26) is the same hand stretched out in punishment in 5:25; 9:11, 16, 20-21; and 10:4.

FROM THE TEXT

In 13:1—14:27, Isaiah speaks of God's future worldwide judgment upon human arrogance and pride. This is symbolized in his judgment upon the Mesopotamian empires, Assyria and Babylon, whose rulers epitomized the magnitude of human arrogance and pride. Through the symbolical singling out of one tyrannical ruler who desired to elevate himself "to the heavens . . . above the stars," to become "like the Most High" (14:13-14), Isaiah depicts the desire of all humankind that resides deep within our beings.

This desire is what the serpent placed before Eve, and Eve before Adam, both representative of all humankind, in the garden of Eden at the dawn of human creation. There, the serpent suggested that if they were to disobey their Creator they would become "like God" (Gen 3:5). Thus, suggests Hamilton, the serpent offers humankind "the possibility of being more than [they are] and more than God intended [them] to be." But, rather than gaining more, the first human couple lost all: kicked out of the garden, they experienced no more that sweet daily fellowship with God they once enjoyed (1990, 190, 208).

The eschatological occasion in which God will dispense punishment for the world's evil, putting an end to human arrogance and pride (Isa 13:11), is what Isaiah calls the Day of Yahweh (vv 6, 9). When this great day comes, all creation (inclusive of humankind, earth, heavens, stars, constellations, sun and moon) will be affected. In what is depicted as a reversal of creation, a great shaking and trembling of earth and heavens will be accompanied by the stars, sun, and moon no longer giving light, and an emptying of the earth of humanity (vv 9-13).

In Matt 24, Jesus' disciples ask him what the sign will be "of your coming and of the end of the age" (v 3). They were referring to the future time when the Son of Man would return to earth to terminate the current system of human government and to establish God's reign over the whole earth. In his reply, Jesus spoke of a cosmic upheaval in which the sun, moon, and stars will cease to give any light to the earth (v 29), echoing Isa 13:10 (compare 34:4; Ezek 32:7; Joel 2:10). Jesus also says that, "the powers of the heavens will be shaken" (Matt 24:29 NASB), perhaps pointing "to the overthrow of the cosmic and demonic powers often associated in paganism with the sun, moon, and stars" (Blomberg 1992, n.p.).

Revelation 6:12-17 likewise echoes Isa 13:10-13, as John witnessed the opening of the sixth seal at the time of what he calls "the great day of their wrath" (Rev 6:17), that is, of the one "who sits on the throne and . . . the Lamb" (v 16). On this day, metaphorically, the universe seems to undo creation as the sun and moon darken, stars fall, and the sky recedes like a rolled-up scroll. So terrified are the world's rulers (kings and princes) and military leaders (generals) that they flee to the caves, pleading that the rocks and mountains would hide them "from the wrath of the Lamb." Here, too, we hear echoes of Isaiah's portrayal of the Day of Yahweh: in great terror, people will attempt to find safety in caves and rocks (Isa 2:10, 19-20). On that day, says Isaiah, "every heart will melt with fear" at the impending "destruction from the Almighty" (*šadday*) (13:7, 6). Both "the heavens" and "the earth" will experience "the wrath of **Yahweh Sebaoth**, in the day of his burning anger" (v 13).

In the context of the Matt 24 passage, Wesley reminds us that, since "ye know not what hour your Lord doth come" (v 42 KJV), a wise servant is one who is "every moment retaining the clearest conviction, that all he now has is only entrusted to him as a steward" (n.d., 80). Therefore, at the coming of our Lord, we must be ready to give an account of all entrusted to us.

B. A Prophecy Concerning Philistia (14:28-32)

BEHIND THE TEXT

The context for Isaiah's prophetic **oracle** (*maśśā'*) here to both the Philistines (v 29) and by inference to the new Judean king, Hezekiah, is soon after the death of King Ahaz (v 28). Envoys have come from Philistia to Jerusalem, possibly under the pretense to offer sympathy for King Ahaz's death. The larger context, however, is the continuing threat from Assyria. Earlier, in 734 BC, the Philistine city of Gath had withheld tribute from the Assyrian overlord and had been roundly chastised. In 720 BC an attempted alliance of Philistia with Egypt against Assyria had resulted in Sargon II defeating Egyptian forces at Gaza and capturing the Philistine cities of Ashkelon and Gath (compare 20:1-6). Now, it seems, the Philistine envoys may be suggesting that Judah join them, perhaps with renewed Egyptian backing, in a new anti-Assyrian alliance.

IN THE TEXT

■ **28** **The year King Ahaz died** is not certain, as the writer of 2 Kings does not give the number of years of his reign when noting his death (16:20) and the beginning of Hezekiah's reign. Moreover, 2 Kgs 18:1 states that Hezekiah's reign began in (Israelite) King Hoshea's third year (compare vv 9, 10), which we know to be 727 BC, while v 13 states that Sennacherib's attack on Jerusalem, which we know was in 701 BC, occurred in Hezekiah's fourteenth year. This would make the first year of his reign 715 BC. The year of King Ahaz's death depends on which date Hezekiah began to reign.

■ **29** Who is the **rod that struck** the **Philistines**, now **broken**, giving Philistia cause for *rejoicing*? Perhaps it is Assyria's king Tiglath-Pileser III, who died in 727 BC, under whom "the Philistines experienced the harshest treatment from the Assyrians" (Wildberger 1997, 93). It might be Judah's king David, as Motyer insists, saying, "No other king was so consistently victorious over the Philistines." The rejoicing comes now that Ahaz, the last of David's successors to hold power over Philistia, is **broken** (1993, 147-48). It is possible that the **broken rod** is not any single ruler, as Oswalt suggests, but a "general Assyrian weakness" during the ten-year period following Shalmaneser V's death in 721 BC (1986, 332).

But, warns Isaiah, **do not rejoice, all you Philistines**, for this Assyrian weakness would be only for a time; the **broken rod** would be followed by the strike of a **viper**, a **venomous serpent**. Historically, this would be epitomized rather immediately by Sargon II (reigned 721-705 BC). Isaiah 20:1-6 appears to reflect a Philistine plan for rebellion against Assyria's overlordship, with Egypt's support, as the reason for Sargon II's attack and capture of Ashdod and defeat of Egyptian forces in 713-711 BC. Later, the **viper** will strike again, and again, as Sennacherib (701 BC) and Esarhaddon (674-671 BC) continue to enforce Assyrian rule over the kingdoms along the eastern Mediterranean seacoast.

■ **30** Within this verse is depicted a contrast of peace and destruction. On the one hand are **the poorest of the poor, the needy**, imaged here as sheep, some *grazing* (*rʻh* I), some **lying** down [*rbṣ*, "stretch out"] **in** *security*, far from any battlefield or army. As indicated in v 32, these are the Judeans, the inhabitants of "Zion" (Oswalt 1986, 332). On the other hand are those, most likely the Philistines, whom Yahweh says, **I will destroy by famine**, right down to their **root**, that is, "nothing will remain of them to spring up again" (ibid.). **Famine** calls forth the image of an enemy army surrounding a city, allowing no one in or out, until its inhabitants die of hunger.

■ **31** The triple command, **Wail, you gate!** [compare 13:6] **Howl, you city! Melt away/*Despair* [*of heart*]**, is addressed to **Philistia, all of you**, that is, to the five cites that composed the Philistine kingdom. It is the **gate** that is first attacked, and if breached, the **city** will be overrun, and its inhabitants will find no escape. The **cloud of smoke** envisioned is that rising from the towns set on fire by the Assyrian army as they advance **from the north** toward Philistia. The Assyrian invaders would advance either via Phoenicia, southward along the coastal plain (Tiglath-Pileser III, 734 BC), or from Damascus, southwesterly through the Galilee/Jezreel valley to the coastal plain (Shalmaneser V and Sargon II, 724-712 BC) (Aharoni and Avi-Yonah 1993, 111, 114).

■ **32** Judean king Ahaz had remained a loyal vassal of the Assyrian Empire, against Isaiah's advice (→ 7:1-25). Ahaz has now died. **Envoys** have come from Philistia to Jerusalem, possibly to investigate the forming of an anti-Assyrian alliance. Sargon II notes in his memoirs that "the king of Ashdod had schemed not to deliver tribute anymore and had sent messages (full) of hostilities against Assyria, to the kings living in his neighborhood." He later mentions that he put down a rebellion of Ashdod, the rulers of Palestine, Judah, Edom, Moab, and the islands (in the western Mediterranean Sea) (Pritchard 1969, 286-87).

Isaiah's response to the **envoys** is a resounding No! Jerusalem/Judea will join in no such alliance. Not because she will continue to trust in Assyria, as in the days of Ahaz, however. No, the inhabitants of Jerusalem will trust in **Yahweh** who **has established Zion**. Earlier, Isaiah had affirmed that "Mount Zion" is the dwelling place of **Yahweh Sebaoth** (8:18). Where God dwells, there **his afflicted people** [*'ăniyyê 'ammô*] **take** refuge (compare Ps 10:12, 18, where God is the protector/defender of the helpless and the oppressed).

FROM THE TEXT

Amos cites an Israelite memory, that the Philistines migrated "from Caphtor" (Amos 9:7) to their biblical location southwest of Judah on the Mediterranean coast. Caphtor was a more ancient name for the island of Crete, located south of Greece in the Mediterranean Sea. Several Indo-European tribal groups were pushed out of their Aegean Sea homelands (north-central Mediterranean) by an inward migration of Dorian Greeks in the thirteenth to twelfth centuries BC. These Indo-European tribal groups then migrated eastward, some by land across Anatolia, others by sea, passing through/past the islands of Caphtor/Crete and Cyprus.

Those groups that came by sea, whom the Egyptians called Sea Peoples, attempted an invasion of Egypt in ca. 1168 BC. Though Pharaoh Ramesses III defeated them, he allowed them to settle along Egyptian-controlled south-western Canaan (Dothan 1992, 13-28). These groups, known as the Philistines, gave their name, Philistia, to the area. Archaeological remains show that the Philistines "enjoyed a technologically advanced standard of living. . . . From the . . . ruins of the great Philistine cities, we catch glimpses of the vibrant, advanced culture that they transplanted from their old to their new homeland" (ibid., 258-59).

When Joshua was old and had fought his battles of conquest, "all the regions of the Philistines" are in the list of the land yet to be possessed (Josh 13:1-2). The Philistines remained a battle enemy and source of irritation and oppression throughout the judges period and into the monarchy. In Samuel's time, high priest Eli's sons lost their lives, and the ark of Yahweh, in a battle with the Philistines in the plain between Ebenezer and Aphek, in which Israel lost thirty thousand foot soldiers (1 Sam 31—2 Sam 1). Not until the days of Judah's king Uzziah (reigned 791-740 BC) was the power of Philistia broken, though she remained in existence. The Chronicler narrates that Uzziah fought the Philistines, broke through the fortifications of Gath, Jabneh, and Ashdod, and built Judean settlements throughout Philistine territory (2 Chr 26:6).

In addition to Isaiah, four other prophets speak words of judgment concerning the Philistines: Jeremiah (25:15, 20), Amos (1:6-8), Zephaniah (2:4), and Zechariah (9:5-6). They specifically mention Gaza, Ashdod, Ashkelon, and Ekron: they will be forsaken, uprooted, drink from Yahweh's wrathful wine cup, perish, and their inhabitants replaced with foreigners.

What covenant violation had the Philistines committed against Yahweh, the covenant maker, such that Yahweh would declare through Amos that his judgment against them would not cease "till the last of the Philistines are dead" (Amos 1:8)? The charge is that "she took captive whole communities and sold them to Edom" (Amos 1:6). "Sold them to Edom" is literally "imprisoned them to Edom," implying the whole process of kidnapping, deporting, and selling into slavery. Within Israel's legal system such an act is forbidden on the penalty of death (Exod 21:16). Since Yahweh is ruler/overlord over all, rooted in his creatorship of all nations (Gen 1—11), Philistia has violated Yahweh's covenant norms of justice, mercy, and respect, to which all nations are held accountable (→ section II overview excursus, "A Theological Basis for Yahweh's Sovereignty over the Nations").

Assyria was to be God's prime agent to bring judgment against the cities of Philistia. Tiglath-Pileser III (745-727 BC) captured Gaza in 734 BC. He records:

> As to Hanno of Gaza . . . who had fled before my army and run away to Egypt, [I conquered] the town of Gaza, . . . his personal property, his images . . . [and I placed (?)] (the images of) my [. . . gods] and my royal image in his own palace . . . and declared (them) to be (thenceforward)

the gods of their country. I imposed upon th[em tribute]. (Pritchard 1969, 283)

Ashdod, a popular caravan stopover city on the route between Gaza and seaport Joppa, was at one time taken by Judean king Uzziah but did not remain under Judean control. Sargon II (reigned 721-705 BC) records his response to Ashdod's scheme to involve her neighbors in an anti-Assyrian rebellion:

> I besieged (and) conquered the cities Ashdod, Gath, Asdudimmu; I declared his images, his wife, his children, all the possessions and treasures of his palace as well as the inhabitants of his country as booty. I reorganized (the administration of) these cities (and) settled therein people from the [regions] of the East which I had conquered personally. I installed an officer of mine over them and declared them Assyrian citizens and they pulled (as such) the straps (of my yoke). (Ibid., 286)

Ashkelon, a seaport located halfway between Gaza and Ashdod, is listed twice in the memoirs of Tiglath-Pileser III (reigned 745-727 BC) as having paid him tribute. In the second instance, he writes:

> [. . . (as to) Mitinti from] Ashkelon (who) had [violated] the oath sworn to me [and had revolted], (when) he learned about [the defeat inflicted upon] Rezon he [perished] in in[sanity]. [Rukibtu, son of Mitinti] sat (himself) upon his throne. (Ibid., 283)

Ekron, the northernmost of the royal Philistine cities, was located on the border of Judah and Dan (Josh 15:11; 19:43). It is listed among Sennacherib's (reigned 704-681 BC) conquests, of which he writes:

> The officials, the patricians and the (common) people of Ekron—who had thrown Padi, their king, into fetters (because he was) loyal to (his) solemn oath (sworn) by the god Ashur, and had handed him over to Hezekiah, the Jew . . .—(and) he (Hezekiah) held him in prison, unlawfully, as if he (Padi) be an enemy—had become afraid and had called (for help) upon the kings of Egypt . . . I assaulted Ekron and killed the officials and patricians who had committed the crime and hung their bodies on poles surrounding the city. . . . I made Padi, their king, come from Jerusalem . . . and set him as their lord on the throne, imposing upon him the tribute (due) to me (as) overlord. (Ibid., 287-88)

Later, both Esarhaddon (reigned 680-669 BC) and Ashurbanipal (reigned 668-627 BC) claimed Ekron as their vassal (ibid., 291, 294). In time, Yahweh's word against Philistia came to completion: Philistia ceased to exist.

Judah, too, later ceased to exist as an independent kingdom in 587 BC under Babylonian dominance. Jeremiah will say that this will happen because both king and people have ceased obeying God's word (Jer 25:3-11). Meanwhile, however, in the face of the Philistine challenge to put their trust in a political-military alliance with her neighbors, in what may have appeared humanly foolish, Isaiah urges the Judeans to trust in "**Yahweh** [who] has established Zion" (Isa 14:32).

C. A Prophecy Concerning Moab (15:1—16:14)

BEHIND THE TEXT

"Moab" is the ancient name of the territory on the east side of the Dead Sea. Its northern border was generally considered to be the Arnon River, at about the midpoint of the Dead Sea. Often, however, the Moabite ruler claimed the land northward to above the Dead Sea, including the city of Heshbon. Moab's southern border was the Zered River, at the south end of the Dead Sea. Its northern neighbor was Ammon, its southern Edom.

This prophetic **oracle** (*maśśā'* [15:1]) is a "lament" (v 5; see v 8) revolving around an attack that has brought disaster upon the Moabites, resulting in a multitude of "fugitives" (vv 5, 9) fleeing for their lives. It is not said who has perpetrated the attack, nor what was the historical occasion of the attack.

Some of the textual portions of this lament are also found in Jer 48, suggesting that both prophets were possibly drawing from the same core of lament terminology concerning Moab.

This **oracle** can be divided into three units, plus a double conclusion: Isa 15:1-9 laments a sudden disastrous attack upon Moab, resulting in a multitude of fugitives; 16:1-5 is a request that the fleeing Moabites seek "shelter" (v 4) from Daughter Zion (= Judah [v 1]); vv 6-12 speak of "Moab's [former] pride" and the **emptiness** of "her pride" (v 6); vv 13-14 are an interpretation of the oracle, giving a time frame for its application.

IN THE TEXT

1. The Attack on Moab and Its Effects (15:1-9)

There are seventeen place names mentioned in 15:1-9, all within territory claimed by **Moab**. They extend from the cities **Heshbon and Elealeh** (v 4) north of the Dead Sea, to the city **Zoar** (v 5) just south of the Dead Sea. Thus the entire kingdom is effected by and laments the sudden ("in a night" [*bĕlêl*]) destruction of **Ar-Moab** and **Kir-Moab** (v 1), the two chief cities in the central area of greater Moab.

■ **1** (On the meaning of **prophecy** [*maśśā'*] *concerning* and the grammatical construction of this phrase, → Behind the Text for 13:1—14:27.)

■ **2-4** With a small emendation on the basis of Jer 48:18, a possible reading that makes sense of the Hebrew of the first half of Isa 15:2 is: **Daughter** Dibon [Wildberger 1997, 107; compare "Daughter Zion" (1:8; 10:32)] **ascended the** high places to weep; *upon* Nebo and *upon* Medeba *Moab wails. Daughter Dibon* would imply the inhabitants of Dibon. The city **Dibon** was the home city of Mesha, king of Moab, in the time of Ahab, king of Israel. In the Mesha Stone, Mesha records: "I made this high place for Chemosh in Qarḥoh as a [place of de]liverance because he delivered me from all assailants" (*ISBE* 3:396). Now, however, Chemosh, the chief deity of Moab, has failed to protect his people. **High place** (15:2), with its occurrence again in 16:12, forms an inclusio, signaling that 15:1—16:12 is intended to be read as a unified passage.

Standard public signs of mourning, accompanying *wailing* and **weeping** are the *shaving* of *heads*, *cutting* off of *beards*, and *wearing* of sackcloth.

■ **5-9** In v 9 the I who *brings* still more upon Dimon, causing **the waters** to be **full of blood**, can be none other than Yahweh, for it is he who brings judgment upon Moab. This, then, identifies the speaker of v 5 who mourns: **My heart cries out over Moab**. Yahweh is the mourner of vv 5-9. Even Yahweh is stricken with grief when judging the nations for "pride" (16:6) (Motyer 1993, 151). Yahweh's **heart** mourns as he watches Moab's **fugitives** *fleeing* southward to **Zoar** (15:5), perhaps intending to seek refuge in Judah to the west of the Dead Sea (16:1). Their thirst is left unassuaged at **Nimrim**, for the **waters . . . are dried up**; their hunger left unsatisfied, for **the vegetation is gone** (15:6).

As with refugees in all times fleeing the ravages of war, value still is placed on **the wealth they have acquired**, which **they carry away** (v 7). But there will be no security in **wealth**, for still to come will be **a lion** ['*aryēh*] **upon the fugitives of Moab** (v 9) (compare Jeremiah, who likens both the Babylonians and Assyrians to lions that devour and crush [Jer 4:7; 50:17]). **Lion** ('*aryēh*) is a pun on '*ărîēl* ("lion of god"), a term describing "Moab's two mightiest warriors" (*šĕnê 'ărîēl mô'āb* [2 Sam 23:20; 1 Chr 11:22]). Motyer comments, "Did they [the Moabites] boast of lions? Lions they shall have!" (1993, 151).

15:5—16:1

2. Asylum Requested (16:1-5)

■ **1** **Sela** (*sela'*, "rock") is a place name in Edom (Judg 1:36; 2 Kgs 14:7), most likely the rock fortress Petra, the later capital of the Nabateans, far to the south of Moab. **The mount of Daughter Zion** (*har bat ṣîyôn*) is Jerusalem. **Across the desert** (*midbārâ*) indicates a direction of travel. One can visualize a possible contingent of Moabites, perhaps government officials, escaping the devastation depicted in 15:1-9, finding temporary safety in **Sela**. Among these Moabite refugees in **Sela** a suggestion is made: **send lambs as tribute to the ruler of the land**. We know that King Mesha of Moab, a keeper of large herds of sheep, at one time was under obligation to send King Ahab of Israel a large tribute of sheep and wool (2 Kgs 3:4). So, it would appear that the Moabite leaders recognize the more powerful status of the **ruler of the land** (of Judah) by sending a **tribute** . . . **across the desert** to Jerusalem (v 1) with a request for asylum for Moabite "fugitives" (v 3).

■ **2** The **Arnon** River is the ancient northern boundary of Moab. Ar and Kir are locations south of the Arnon, representing the Moab that has been "destroyed in a night" (15:1). The fleeing **women of Moab**, representative of all the war refugees fleeing the devastation, **like fluttering birds** are bunched up at **the fords of the Arnon**, waiting to cross northward into what would be considered Judean territory. Will they be granted asylum?

■ **3-4a** The Moabite ambassadors bring their leaders' request to the "ruler of the land" at Jerusalem. Don't delay your **decision** on our request for protection: *put* your [= Judah's] **shadow** over us, **like** the full darkness of **night** that would protect from the burning sun **at high noon**, when shadows are at their shortest (v 3). ***Let the banished ones of Moab sojourn*** [*yāgûrû* from *gwr*, "to live as a resident alien" (VanGemeren 1997, 1:836)] ***among*** you (v 4a). Resident aliens (*ḥaggēr*) are those who, usually for economic or political reasons, can no longer live in their homeland and have been given refuge in another. In Israel, such a resident, just as the native-born Israelite, is under Yahweh's full protection (Deut 10:18; Ps 146:9) (ibid., 1:837-38).

■ **4b-5** The Judean response to the Moabite request is that, in the future, **in love** [*baḥesed*, "in loyalty," "in mercy"] **a throne will be established**, presumably on Mount Zion. From the ***tent*** [*'ōhel* = family/descendants] **of David** will come one who will sit upon that throne **in faithfulness** (*be'emet*, "permanently," "in truth"). Characterizing his **judging** will be ***seeking*** **justice** and ***speeding*** . . . ***righteousness*** (Isa 16:5). When he comes, **the oppressor**, *the trampler* of all disenfranchised persons, including the sojourner (*ḥaggēr*), **will vanish from the earth** (v 4b).

The invitation to the Moabites, then, in the spirit of 2:1-4, is open: come up to the "mountain of **Yahweh**" and learn "his ways," "his paths." In so doing, accept Yahweh's **love**, his protection. Oswalt observes that "Moab's hope is identical with Judah's. Both wait for the [messianic] King of Israel" (1986, 343). One is reminded of Ruth the Moabitess, who, in complete humility, found refuge within the protection of Yahweh's "wings" (Ruth 1:16; 2:12).

3. Loss of Raisin Cakes Bewailed (16:6-7)

■ **6-7** These two verses reflect Isaiah's evaluation of the cause of the earlier devastation that had befallen Moab: **pride, arrogance, conceit** (all variations on the *g'h*, "to be high"), and **insolence** (Isa 16:6). (Compare Zeph 2:9-10: as a consequence of her "pride," Moab will become "a place of weeds and salt pits.") Also here is perhaps a reflection of Moab's refusal of Judah's gracious offer to come under Yahweh's protection, which would require a turning away from their Moabite gods. But no, they still **wail**, . . . **lament and grieve for the raisin**

cakes, an essential component of their religious rituals (Isa 16:7). (Compare Hos 3:1 where "turn to other gods" is paralleled with "Love the sacred raisin cakes.")

4. Isaiah/Yahweh Laments for Moab (16:8-12)

■ **8-12** Commentators are divided as to whether the first-person speaker of this passage (Isa 16:9, 10, 11) is the prophet Isaiah or Yahweh. But such a distinction is unnecessary. Fretheim points out that the OT prophet so absorbs "the heart and mind of God . . . that the prophet becomes a veritable embodiment of God." Thus, "to hear and see the prophet was to hear and see God" (1984, 149-54). Isaiah, then, so embodies Yahweh's suffering that it is Yahweh's deep sorrow for Moab's collapse that we witness: **I weep, . . . I drench you with tears** (v 9), **my heart** [lit. *belly*] [my inmost being] **laments for Moab like a harp** (v 11).

A people whose entire economy was dependent upon agricultural production and exportation find their **fields** and **vines** . . . **trampled** by **the rulers of the nations** (v 8). No longer do **shouts of joy** at the **harvests** ring out across the fields; no joyous ***singing*** is heard in the **orchards** or **vineyards** (vv 9-10). Yahweh admits, of course, **I have put an end to the shouting** (v 10); it is **I** who has stirred up **the rulers of the nations** (v 8). Yet, observes Fretheim, "once the judgment has occurred, God joins those who mourn" (ibid., 133). He mourns, not only over Moab's devastation, but because of her rejection of his gracious offer of protection. **Moab** still **appears at *his*** **high place**; there, ***at his*** **shrine**, one (= the individual Moabite) still ***prays*** to Chemosh (→ 15:2-4) or to one's individual god. But, says Isaiah/Yahweh, **it/*he avails nothing*** (16:12). **High place** (v 12), with its previous occurrence in 15:2, forms an inclusio, signaling that 15:1—16:12 is intended to be read as a unified passage.

5. The Fulfillment of the Prophecy (16:13-14)

■ **13-14** Isaiah now adds a summary statement concerning the prophecy of 15:1—16:12: **This is the word** *which Yahweh had* spoken *formerly* [*mēʾāz*] *to* **Moab** (16:13). This could indicate that some parts of the prophecy were given concerning Moab even before Isaiah but are drawn upon by the prophet for the present occasion. ***And/*But** [the conjunction *wĕ* can be either] now **Yahweh has spoken** *[again]*: "Within three years" the judgment will come. "**Moab . . . will be very few and feeble**" (v 14). The historical event within the lifetime of Isaiah that brought about this judgment cannot be determined. It may be that Moab allowed itself to be enticed to join one of the rebellions against the ruling overlord of the time, only to find its kingdom punished nearly to the death.

Moab in the OT

Since ancestral Moab was the offspring of Lot by his older daughter, Moab was considered a relative of Israel (Gen 19:30-38). The relationship between Israel/Judah and Moab, however, was generally that of a long history of enmity. The Israelites' first encounter with the Moabites occurred while they were journeying from Egypt to Canaan. After defeating Sihon (king of the Amorite kingdom of Heshbon) and Og (king of Bashan) and taking possession of their territories (Num 21:10-35), the Israelites encamped north of the Dead Sea in the plains of Moab (22:1). While there, the women of the Moabite town of Peor invited the Israelite men to join them in making sacrifices to their gods. This involved bowing down before these gods and eating the sacrificial meal, concluding with sexual intercourse with the Moabite women. "So Israel yoked themselves to the Baal of Peor" (25:3). For this violation of their earlier Sinai covenant vows to serve Yahweh only, twenty-four thousand Israelites died of a plague (vv 1-9).

During the time of the judges, King Eglon of Moab subjugated the central area of Israel for eighteen years (Judg 3:14), after which the left-handed Benjamite Ehud won their freedom (vv 15-30). In the time of the monarchy, Moab's king Mesha delivered to Israel's king Ahab a tax of wool from one hundred thousand lambs and one hundred thousand rams. After Ahab's death, however, Mesha rebelled against Israelite overlordship (2 Kgs 3:4-5).

Israel's subjugation of Moab is also recorded in the Moabite/Mesha Inscription, the only inscription presently surviving in the Moabite dialect (a Canaanite dialect related to those spoken by the Israelites, Edomites, Ammonites, Aramaeans, and Phoenicians). From this inscription, written by or on behalf of King Mesha, we learn that Israel's subjugation of Moab began under Israel's king Omri, Ahab's father, continuing for forty years (Albright 1969, 320). Ahab's son Jehoram, with the assistance of Judah's king Jehoshaphat and a king of Edom, put down Mesha's rebellion (2 Kgs 3:6-27).

In addition to Isaiah, the prophets Zephaniah (2:9-10), Jeremiah (48:4, 9), and Ezekiel (25:8-11) prophesied Yahweh's judgment against Moab because of her pride, boastfulness, and taunting of God's people. It is Amos, however, who cites a specific violation of Yahweh's covenant with the nations, a violation by one vassal (Moab) against another vassal (Edom) that would require the intervention of the overlord/suzerain, Yahweh (→ section II overview excursus, "A Theological Basis for Yahweh's Sovereignty over the Nations"). The charge is that "he [i.e., Moab's king] burned to ashes the bones of Edom's king" (Amos 2:1). A sovereign suzerain would view such an act of desecration by one vassal king against another vassal king as a gross violation of their common covenant. Such a blatant violation of covenant agreements would be punishable by armed invasion and overthrow. For this violation Yahweh vows to destroy Moab's fortresses, ruler, and officials (vv 1-3).

FROM THE TEXT

It is the ravages of war that will bring an end to Moab. "Moab will *die* in great tumult" (*ûmēt běšā'ôn mô'āb* [Amos 2:2]) personifies the nation as an individual. The king's "officials," too, participated in this vile desecration of a covenant partner. The crime, then, is a national sin, "and the nation will die, so completely that it will be like the death of an individual" (Niehaus 1992, 358).

The message to Moab is clear: nations and individuals that resort to violence and inhumane treatment of others cannot expect to escape the judgment of God, the sovereign Judge of all nations/individuals in the world.

D. Prophecies Concerning Damascus and Cush (17:1—18:7)

BEHIND THE TEXT

Isaiah begins this collection of prophecies with a message concerning the certainty of the demise of Damascus/Aram (Isa 17:1, 3) to the north of Israel/Judah. He concludes with what at first appears to be a message via envoys directed to Cush (18:1) to the south of Egypt in Africa but, in fact, is directed to all "people of the world" (v 3). Isaiah also speaks of Ephraim, the Israelites (*běnê yiśrā'ēl*, **sons of Israel**), and Jacob (17:3-4), all designations of the northern kingdom, which too will disappear.

There is a thematic unity in these prophecies spoken to Judah at some time in the lifetime of Isaiah. This thematic unity is that the nations to the north and to the south, no matter how strong or promising they may seem as political/military protectors, are not to be trusted. The only one to be trusted is **Yahweh Sebaoth** (17:3; 18:7), "**Yahweh**, the God of Israel" (17:6), "the Holy One of Israel" (17:7).

Damascus

Abraham's chief servant Eliezer's origin is mentioned as Damascus (Gen 15:2). Outside the OT, in the extant literature, the earliest mention of Damascus is in a list of the conquests of Pharaoh Thutmose III (reigned 1504-1450 BC). Control of the city passed back and forth between the Hittites and the Egyptians until ca. 1350 BC, when the Arameans invaded, settling Damascus and its immediate territories. In ca. 1000 BC King David conquered Damascus, so that during his time and that of his son Solomon, the Aramean territories were part of the kingdom of Israel.

In Solomon's latter years, however, one named Rezon, from ca. 930 BC, founded a strong Aramean kingdom centered in Damascus, throwing off Israelite control (1 Kgs 11:24). There followed periods when Aram overran and subjugated the northern kingdom (Israel), times when the Israelite kings opposed the Aramean kings, and times when the two kingdoms joined in opposition against the common enemy, Assyria. For a brief time, Jeroboam II (reigned 783-741 BC) "recovered for Israel both Damascus and Hamath" (2 Kgs 14:28). Rezin/Rezon (reigned ca. 750-732 BC), however, reestablished Aramean independence, only to be overrun by Tiglath-Pileser III's Assyrian forces in 732 BC. According to 2 Kgs 16:9 he attacked and captured the city of Damascus, killing Rezin. Tiglath-Pileser records that he deported 2,100 Aramean inhabitants and destroyed

"592 towns . . . of the 16 districts of the country of Damascus" (*ISBE* 1:852-54; Pritchard 1969, 283).

IN THE TEXT

1. The Demise of Damascus and Ephraim (17:1-6)

The mention of both Damascus with Ephraim in this passage is a reference to the failed anti-Assyrian Aramean-Israelite coalition of 735-732 BC (→ Behind the Text for 7:1-9).

■ **1** Isaiah opens with **a prophecy *concerning*** [*maśśā'*] **Damascus**, the capital city of Aram (→ Behind the Text for 13:1—14:27 for the grammatical construction of *maśśā'* as ***concerning***). Once dominant, powerful **Damascus** has so completely **ceased** (*mûsār*, pres. ptc., indicating a present state of being) that, among the powers of the biblical world, it ***is* no longer** to be considered **a city**; rather, it is now simply **a heap of ruins**.

■ **2 The cities of Aroer** were not within the sphere of Damascus' control but were cities in Moab (Jer 48:19) to the south. Here, Isaiah is depicting their condition, **deserted** (pres. ptc.), in the aftermath of invasion, as a comparison: this is what Damascus, too, is like, a place fit only for the grazing of domestic **flocks**.

■ **3** Wildberger finds here a contrastive play on the two phrases **the *fortress is ceased*** from Ephraim and the ***monarchy*** [*is ceased*] from Damascus (1997, 167). Samaria, on the one hand, represented the first, a ***fortress*** (of **Ephraim**) requiring a three-year siege by Assyrian Shalmaneser V to conquer. Within its walls, however, was an unstable monarchy whose dynasties changed in quick succession. Within the walls of Damascus, on the other hand, ruled a stable **monarchy** consisting primarily of one dynasty unchanged for two hundred years. Israel could possibly survive without its monarchy, but **Aram** without its monarchy was doomed. For **Aram**, however, Isaiah envisions a **remnant**, though its number is compared to the diminishing **glory of the Israelites** (*kĕbôd bĕnê yiśrā'ēl*).

■ **4-6 The glory of Jacob** speaks of the northern kingdom (not the whole of Israel as the people of God). Its **glory** is false, a facade, self-made. **In that day** (v 4), when **Yahweh, the God of Israel** (v 6), allows judgment to come, all that Israel idealized herself to be **will fade** away. Isaiah illustrates this three ways: (1) as a person once **fat,** without food, **will waste away** (v 4); (2) as a field, once filled with standing grain, is left with only **gleanings** (v 6) for the poor when the **reapers** (v 5) have completed their work; (3) as an **olive tree**, once with **fruitful boughs**, now bare except for **two or three olives**, perhaps **four or five** that the pickers could not reach (v 6).

2. The Holy One of Israel: Maker, Savior, Rock (17:7-11)

■ **7-8** Using creation language, Isaiah speaks of a new attitude of **humankind** (*hā'ādām*) as a result of the judgments spoken of just previously: **in that day**. No longer will **humankind** reject **the Holy One of Israel** (v 7) as having any jurisdiction over their way of living, but **will gaze** [*š'h*] **upon** him as their **Maker** (*'ōśēh* from *'śh*). In so doing, they will no longer **gaze** [*š'h*] **upon** the **work** (*ma'ăśēh* from *'śh*), which they have made with **their hands** and **their fingers** (v 8; compare Ps 8:3 [4 HB]). Thus they will turn away from their humanly "created" **altars**, **Asherah poles**, and **incense altars** (Isa 17:8) to the true Creator, **the Holy One of Israel** (v 7), who is humankind's Helper and Redeemer/Savior (41:14; 43:3; 49:7). One is reminded of Paul's commendation of the Thessalonian believers for having "turned to God from idols to serve the living and true God" (1 Thess 1:9).

Asherahs

In Israel the Asherahs were most likely living trees (not "poles" as usually translated), representations of fertility goddesses, as seen in depictions from Egypt, Babylon, Mari, Canaan, and Phoenicia (Taylor 1995, 40-44). The Canaanites appear to have borrowed the worship of the fertility goddess Asherah from Assyria. In the Canaanite mythology Asherah is the consort of the supreme deity El, and later of Baal, with whom she is associated in the OT.

■ **9** The meaning of this verse is not clear. As translated by the NIV, however, **their strong cities** may signify some of the cities of Israel that the former Canaanite inhabitants (**they**) had *abandoned* when the Israelites entered the land under Joshua's leadership. Having taken over these empty **cities**, the Israelites (re)built them. Now, however, when Yahweh's judgment comes, these **cities** will again be **abandoned** and **all will be desolation**.

■ **10-11** The **you** throughout these two verses is feminine singular. Most likely Jerusalem, representing God's people, is the recipient. They have **forgotten/not remembered** their **God** who is their **Savior**, their **Rock**. It is he who is truly their *refuge* (Isa 17:10), rather than "their strong cities" (v 9) in which they have put their trust.

The cult of Adonis, a Syro-Phoenician vegetation deity, has been suggested as the practice in the background of the agricultural activity in these verses. In the Adonis fertility cult, potted plants were force-bloomed but allowed to quickly die within a few days (de Vaux 1971, 210-14). The mention of **strange** [*zār*] **vines** (v 10) may point to this Adonis cult or to some other Canaanite cultic practice that promises a quick and bumper **harvest** (v 11). In fact, however, it is not clear to what kind of **plants** and **vines** (v 10) Isaiah is referring. The implication does seem to be, though, that God's people have placed their trust in some type of exotic gardens with sacred significance, thus to ensure a good harvest; the results, however, are only **disease and incurable pain** (v 11).

3. Chaff Driven before the Wind (17:12-14)

The background of this three-verse section may be the Assyrian threat against Judah beginning in 745 BC and culminating in Sennacherib's threat against Jerusalem in 701 BC (chs 36—37). It is applied here, however, to demonstrate that no nation can stand before the "wind" (*rûaḥ* [17:13]) of Yahweh.

■ **12 Ha!** (*hôy*) is an exclamation of derision. **Many nations** (*'ammîm rabbîm*) may indicate Sennacherib's multinational imperial army approaching Jerusalem. The sound of its horses, chariots, and marching soldiers is likened to the **roaring** of the **sea/great waters** in a fierce storm.

■ **13** In the context of creation, the psalmist says of Yahweh, "at your rebuke [*g'r*] the waters fled [*nws*]" (Ps 104:7, see vv 5-9; compare Job 26:11-12; Ps 89:9-10 [10-11 HB]). In an analogy with the chaotic, raging waters, Isaiah says here of **the peoples** (*'ummîm*, i.e., the Assyrians) that **he**, Yahweh, exercises his authority over them, and **when he rebukes** [*g'r*] **them they flee** [*nws*] **far away**. In a sudden change of imagery, however, the power of the Assyrians turns to illusion. They are nothing but **chaff** that is **before the wind** (*rûaḥ*) or a **tumbleweed before a whirlwind** (*sûpâ*). In Nah 1:3, in the context of punishing the guilty, Yahweh's "way" is said to be "in the whirlwind" (*sûpâ*). Isaiah's **whirlwind**, then, is Yahweh himself, who scatters the Assyrians **on the hills**. And might Isaiah's *rûaḥ* that disperses the **chaff** be more than a mere **wind**? Perhaps here is an allusion to the Spirit.

■ **14** Even while one sleeps circumstances may radically change: **At the time of evening, behold terror**; yet, **before the morning**, that is, even before one awakes, Yahweh removes the cause of such terror: **he** [i.e., the Assyrian] **is not**. The one who came up to **loot us**, to **plunder us**, has vanished. Us must be Jerusalem. The circumstance that gives historical flesh to this is Sennacherib's intended siege of 701 BC: **when they arose in the morning, behold! all of them, dead bodies!** The death of 185,000 Assyrian soldiers, slain at the hand of "the angel of **Yahweh**," convinced Sennacherib and the remainder of his army to return to faraway Nineveh (37:36-37).

4. Yahweh's Message to the People of the World (18:1-7)

■ **1** This verse opens with **Ha!** (*hôy*) **The Land of the Beetle of Two-wings** (*'ereṣ ṣilṣal kĕnāpāyim*). The first word, *'ereṣ*, is readily understood as **land of**; the last word *kĕnāpāyim*, a dual form, is clearly **two wings**. It is the middle word, *ṣilṣal*, which has given translators and commenters, including the Greek LXX and Aramaic Targums, much difficulty in understanding its meaning. Some have opted for something to do with the sails of the "papyrus boats" mentioned in v 2, or the boats themselves that whiz up and down the Nile

River. Some opt for **whirring**, suggestive of the sound of some kind of insect, based on the one other occurrence of this term (in Deut 28:42), where the *ṣilṣal* ("swarms of locusts") destroy trees and crops.

Lubetski has convincingly demonstrated that *ṣilṣal*, both in Deut 28:42 and Isa 18:1, should be translated "beetle," referring to the two-winged dung beetle or what the Egyptians called the "sack carrier." This insect appeared to carry a sack, but actually rolled and carried a ball of its dung with its hind feet as it moved along (2000, 11-12; 2008, 104-10). Thus Isaiah is referring to the ***Land of the Beetle of Two-wings***, "the emblem of the unified Egyptian kingdom" (ibid., 2008, 111). The beetle symbol, with wings spread, giving protection to the two parts of Egypt, in many instances replaced the winged solar deity Horus (Gardiner 1944, 53). Its dung ball represented the sun that Horus was thought to roll daily across the sky. In the time of Isaiah, the last half of the eighth century BC, both upper and lower Egypt were ruled by pharaohs from Nubia, that is, ***from beyond*** [*mē'ēber*, not NIV's **along**] **the rivers of Cush**. Lubetski suggests that Isaiah's Judean audience would have had no trouble identifying their southern neighbor, Egypt, as the country associated with Isaiah's ***Land of the Beetle of Two-wings*** (2008, 103-12). Archaeological evidence demonstrates extensive cultural contacts between Egypt and Israel. For example, the Israelites even adopted the Egyptian system of measures and weights (Aharoni 1966, 13-19).

■ **2** **Which sends** continues the sentence of the previous verse; **which** refers to the ***Land of the Beetle of Two-wings***, that is, Egypt. Thus it is the Nubian/Cushite pharaoh of Egypt who **sends envoys by sea**. The international situation may well be that to which ch 20 alludes. The Egyptians have decided to resist the encroachment of Assyrian military might and apparently have sent **envoys** to the various Canaanite kingdoms, including Judah, eliciting their alliance and promising Egyptian protection against the Assyrians.

In the second half of v 2, however, Isaiah turns the tables on the Egyptian emissaries. Instead of counseling the Judean king (Hezekiah?) to accept Egyptian protection, he commands **swift messengers**, either those who have come from Egypt or his own from Judea: **go . . . to a people tall and smooth-skinned**, a reference to the Egyptians, with a message from his God, Yahweh.

■ **3** Isaiah's message, though sent in reply to the Egyptian pharaoh, is actually to **all *the world's*** [*tēbēl*] ***inhabitants and earth's*** [*'āreṣ*] ***dwellers***. Employing the symbolism of a call to war, if they are watching, **when a banner is raised**, they **will see it**, and, if they are listening, **when a trumpet sounds**, **they will hear it**. This will be the time for Yahweh (vv 4-6) to intervene decisively in the course of history.

■ **4** ***Yahweh*** has spoken a word to his prophet Isaiah. This word is that he, **Yahweh**, will not support Judah's joining the rebellion against Assyria. He will allow the present big powers to exercise their might against each other, as he sits *quietly* in his **dwelling place**. The rebellion will fail. For the present, Assyria will prevail. Egypt, in fact, was kept at bay, and those Palestinian kingdoms that had fomented rebellion suffered the full crushing Assyrian might under Sargon's (721-705 BC) armies (Pritchard 1969, 284-85).

■ **5** The **harvest** referred to could be Sennacherib's expectation of the capture of Jerusalem in 701 BC. But, **before the harvest** could take place, indeed "before the morning" (17:14), with his **pruning knives** Yahweh **cut off** the Assyrian army in a single night (37:36-38).

■ **6** The slaughter of 185,000 Assyrian soldiers by "the angel of **Yahweh**" (37:36) at Sennacherib's siege of Jerusalem would certainly leave an abundance of corpses on which the **birds of prey** and the **wild animals** would feast for, at least hypothetically, a **summer** and **winter**.

■ **7 At that time** seems to bear both an Isaianic time frame and a futuristic view: Yahweh will act, both in the more immediate Assyrian crisis on behalf of his people in Jerusalem and on the larger scene of world history. When he does, the world's great powers, represented here by **a people tall and smooth-skinned** (the Egyptians) will come to him, bearing **gifts**. Here, Isaiah envisions **Yahweh Sebaoth** residing/ruling from **Mount Zion** (Jerusalem), the place he chose as a dwelling for his **Name** (compare Deut 12:11; Isa 45:23-24).

FROM THE TEXT

Isaiah concludes this section (17:1—18:7) with the depiction of the peoples of the world, in a time of world peace, streaming up to Mount Zion, bearing gifts to the Sovereign of history, **Yahweh Sebaoth**.

This draws us back to previously depicted scenes. In 2:2-4 it is to this same mountain of Yahweh's temple that, "in the last days," the nations and peoples stream, seeking to learn Yahweh's ways. It is from this mountain that Yahweh judges between nations, so that war has ceased and is no more. In 4:2-6 Jerusalem/Mount Zion "in that day" will be "a shelter and shade, . . . a refuge and hiding place" for those who have been washed/cleansed.

We are urged forward to later depictions in the book of Isaiah. In 45:14-17 peoples who once had been Israel's oppressors, of their own volition now come to Jerusalem, bearing tribute and acknowledging the sovereignty of Israel's God and his activity in history. In 45:23 "every knee will bow" to Yahweh and "every tongue will swear" that "in *Yahweh* alone are deliverance and strength" (in both Rom 14:11 and Phil 2:10-11 Paul draws on this passage). In Isa 60:1-14 is depicted an assembling of peoples from all directions to the "City of **Yahweh**, Zion of the Holy One of Israel" (v 14). They come bearing "the riches of the nations" (v 5): camels from Midian and gold from Sheba (v 6), wood supplies from Lebanon (v 13), and more. All this, says Yahweh, is "to glorify the place for my feet" (v 13). In 66:23 the book of Isaiah concludes with the affirmation that one day "all mankind will . . . bow" before Yahweh. In Rev 15:3-4 this affirmation is reflected in the "song of God's servant Moses and of the Lamb."

E. A Prophecy Concerning Egypt (19:1—20:6)

BEHIND THE TEXT

On the Assyrian scene, the great Tiglath-Pileser III has died; the northern kingdom (Israel) has fallen (in 722 BC) to Shalmaneser V. Shalmaneser V has also died, and now Sargon II is the Assyrian king. Upon his ascension to the throne, Sargon was immediately confronted with rebellions in Babylonia and elsewhere in the empire, which took his attention from the Syrian/Palestinian part of the world for nearly a decade. In 712 BC, however, Sargon had to send his army to put down a rebellion in the Philistine city of Ashdod, noted in Isa 20:1.

In Egypt, there had come a resurgence of the appearance of strength, with the uniting of Upper and Lower Egypt under one ruler, an Ethiopian named Piye. This was only an apparent strength, however, as much strife and struggle for power continued internally during the latter half of the eighth century BC.

In Judah, meanwhile, King Ahaz has died, and his son Hezekiah has assumed the throne in Jerusalem. Hezekiah instituted sweeping religious reforms, reversing many of his father's evil practices (2 Kgs 18:3-6; 2 Chr 29—31). Hezekiah, then, in some manner rebelled against the Assyrian king, refusing to serve him (2 Kgs 18:7). But now, subsequent to the Ashdod rebellion, there is an increasing threat of Assyrian encroachment upon the quasi-independence of Judah. The question that is in the background of chs 19 and 20 is: Should/will Judah turn to Egypt for protection against Assyria?

Chapters 19 and 20 record Yahweh's response to this question through his prophet Isaiah, a prophecy concerning Egypt. The prophecy is not directed to Egypt, however, but to Judah, advising how foolish it would be to place trust in the wisdom and military protection of Egypt in the face of this increasing Assyrian threat.

The two chapters can be viewed in three main segments: 19:1-15, in which Yahweh undermines Egypt's religious system, economic support, and wisdom teachers; 19:16-25, in which Yahweh makes himself known to the Egyptians; and, 20:1-6, in which trust in Egypt would be a cause of dismay and shame.

Motyer aptly shows that Egypt's coming social, economic, and political problems "have a spiritual causation. They are the outworking of the divine purposes and are directly traceable to the hand of God" (1993, 164).

IN THE TEXT

1. Consulting Idols and Mediums Results in Confusion (19:1-4)

■ 1 *Look!* (*hinnēh*) urges Isaiah's Judean audience to see with spiritual eyes something beyond that which can be seen with normal, everyday human perception. Your leaders are contemplating a treaty with Egypt. But here is a **prophecy *concerning* Egypt**. It is from **Yahweh**, the one who **rides on a swift cloud** (the "sky rider" who helps you [Deut 33:2, 26; Judg 5:4] and who exercises power over earth's peoples [Ps 68:34]). And, just as once long ago he entered Egypt to do battle with the pharaoh and his deities to free his people, so, again *he enters* [*bā'*, ptc.] **Egypt** to confront **the idols** ['*ĕlîlîm*, "nothings"] **of Egypt**, which **tremble** ["quiver," "totter"] **before him**. The very *heart of Egypt will* melt *within it*. The singular Hebrew *it* points to the core of national Egypt, which will be in disarray.

■ 2 The *stirring* up of *Egypt* against *Egypt* is the action of Yahweh, the one who holds sovereignty over all peoples. The two Egypts, Upper and Lower, had a long history of vying for control over both Egypts, and Isaiah anticipates the present unity under the Ethiopian rulers to fracture. Judah dare not place her trust in a nation that will erupt into civil strife, **kingdom against kingdom**.

■ 3 The result of the civil strife will be that the very *spirit of Egypt in its inner being will be drained away*. Why? Again it is because of Yahweh's action behind the scene: **I will *confuse its*** [i.e., Egypt's] *plan*, that is, the rulers' plan for national unity and military defiance of Assyrian expansion. In desperation, Egypt's rulers and strategists will **consult** not only **the idols** and the deities they represent but also **the spirits of the dead**, through those who communicate with them, **the mediums and the spiritists**.

■ 4 But none of these religious actions will do any good, for again **Yahweh, Yahweh Sebaoth**, in exercising his sovereignty over all nations, **will hand Egypt over** to be ruled by a **cruel master**. The ruler who fulfilled this prophecy cannot be historically determined. It may have been Ethiopian Piye (715 BC), Assyrian Sargon II (ca. 711 BC), Sennacherib (701 BC), Esarhaddon (680 BC), Ashurbanipal (668 BC), or Persian Artaxerxes III Ochus (343 BC).

2. The Nile Will No Longer Support National Life (19:5-10)

■ 5-10 In these six verses, the Nile is referred to nine times by name and synonyms. Without the Nile, the Egyptian society would never have existed, as the Nile is what has sustained life and industry from ancient times. Depicted here is a complete demise of the life support of ancient Egypt because of the failure of annual flooding of the Nile. As the runoff from the southern mountains diminishes, **the riverbed** [the main northward flow of the river] **will become parched and dry** (v 5). This will affect (1) **the waters of the *sea*** (*hayyām* = the appearance of the Delta at flood stage), which **will dry up** (v 5); (2) **the** [irrigation] **canals**, which receive water from the main river or from reservoirs; they **will stink** because of a lack of water (v 6); and, (3) **the streams of Egypt** (= the divisions of the Nile throughout the Delta) **will dwindle and dry up**. The **reeds and rushes** (v 6) that produce **combed flax** die out, so that **the weavers of fine linen** and **the workers in cloth** are no longer **wage earners** (vv 9-10). The farmers who grow crops in the **sown fields** along the **canals** that carry water out from the Nile no longer are able to produce because the very soil is ***blown away*** (vv 6-7). The **fishermen** who depend on an abundance of fish from the Nile lose their livelihood (v 8).

Though Yahweh is not said to be the cause of the Nile's failure, in the broader context of this passage, Isaiah surely intends his audience to catch the utter failure of the Nile to support life in Egypt to be the result of Yahweh's "***entering*** Egypt" (19:1).

The Nile River

The OT word *yĕ'ōr*, a borrowed Egyptian word for "river," is used primarily of the Nile. The river begins its flow from Africa's Lake Victoria on the equator and flows northward to the Mediterranean Sea, a distance of some 2,500 miles. From the torrential springtime rains in Ethiopia far to the south, the Nile annually floods, reaching its northernmost point, the Delta in Egypt, by about the first of July. The flooding waters bring an abundance of fertile sediment from the mountains. If the annual flood does not come, then Egypt's life support begins to diminish. If the flooding should fail for several years (as in Gen 41), disaster prevails. In Egyptian religious thought, Hapi was the Nile deity, a hermaphrodite, both male and female. Offerings and prayers were given to the Nile for the benefits that he/she gave through the annual flooding.

Flax and Linen

Linen is both the thread and the textile produced from the flax plant, which was abundantly grown in Egypt in both the natural marshy areas of the Nile and in irrigated areas. Egyptian linen products were exported widely, and thus imported by well-to-do Israelites (Prov 7:16). However, flax was also grown and linen produced in Canaan from very early times, as shown from archaeological linen textile finds in caves near Jericho in the southern Jordan Valley, and near En Gedi on the western shore of the Dead Sea. The Israelite calendar months of Adar-Nisan (March-April) are mentioned in the Gezer Calendar (from ca. 900

BC) as the time for pulling flax. After pulling the flax, there were basically four steps in the process to produce linen: (1) the flax stalks were soaked to soften and separate the fibers; (2) the stalks were then laid out in the sun to dry and to bleach, often on rooftops (Josh 2:6); (3) the linen fibers are "combed" from the stalks and spun into thread; (4) the threads are woven into linen cloth. The noble wife of Prov 31 maintained a linen textile producing industry in her home (vv 13, 24); "clans of the linen workers at Beth Ashbea" are mentioned in 1 Chr 4:21. Both linen outerwear and underwear were the garments prescribed for Israelite priests (Lev 6:10 [3 HB]) (King and Stager 2001, 148-52).

3. The Stupidity of Pharaoh's Political Advisers (19:11-15)

■ 11 The pharaohs of the twenty-first and twenty-second dynasties (mid-eighth cent. BC) constructed **Zoan**, an important city located in the northwest part of the Nile Delta. The **officials** [*śārê*] **of Zoan** served as counselors to the Egyptian **Pharaoh**, and though convinced in their own eyes to be **wise counselors**, Isaiah insists they are, in fact, nothing but **fools** (*'wl*, lit. "to be a fool"; but compare v 13). How? Because the **advice** they give is ***stupid*** (*b'r*, from *b'yr*, lit. "cattle"; Wildberger 1997, 251), thus nothing but "animal thoughtlessness" (Motyer 1993, 166). They each say, **"A son of wise men I am, a son of ancient kings." Son** in this context means pupil or member of a group who studies under a **wise** teacher, who teaches wisdom handed down from ancient times. But the **advice** these **officials of Zoan** give **Pharaoh** shows they have learned nothing of value to offer him. The theological understanding here is that when they do not know Yahweh, the giver of true wisdom, their "wisdom" can only show them to be **fools**. (Compare Jer 4:22: "***Because*** my people are fools, they do not know me. . . . They are ***wise*** in doing evil, ***in knowing*** not how to do good.")

■ 12 Then, figuratively addressing Pharaoh, Isaiah challenges him to demonstrate the wisdom of his **wise men**. Can they **make known** what **Yahweh Sebaoth** has **planned *concerning*** Egypt? The implied answer is: Of course not! How can they when they do not even know Yahweh? (compare Isa 41:22-23; 43:9, 12; 44:9; 45:21; 48:14).

■ 13 Isaiah says that the pharaoh's counselors in **Zoan have become fools** (pass. of *y'l* I). Similarly, the **officials** [*śārê*] **of Memphis are self-deceived** (pass. of *nš'*-2, the same verb used of the serpent's deception of Eve [Gen 3:13]). **Memphis** (Heb., **Noph**) was another important city, located in the south part of the Nile Delta, an alternate location from which the pharaohs ruled during Isaiah's time (Kitchen 1973, §324-26). The self-foolishness and self-delusion of these **officials** in these two chief pharaonic cities in turn extend to the **cornerstones of her peoples** (lit. *chief rulers of tribal territories* [Wildberger 1997, 253]); they, in turn, **have led Egypt astray** (compare Isa 3:12 and 9:15 where Israel's leaders likewise led God's people astray). Wildberger suggests that these leaders "allowed themselves to be misled by their faulty analysis of the situation" (ibid., 256).

■ **14-15** Here, Isaiah pulls back the veil to reveal Yahweh still active behind the screen. Unknown to the Egyptian officials and tribal leaders, **Yahweh has brewed within her** [i.e., Egypt] **a spirit of dizziness**. This "brew," imbibed by Egypt's counselors, infects all of **Egypt**. The imagery of a **drunkard staggering around in his vomit** is meant for Isaiah's Judean audience. The implication is that Judah, too, would be just as self-foolish and self-deluded as Egypt if she were to put her confidence in an Egypt in such political and religious disarray.

4. Yahweh Makes Himself Known to the Egyptians (19:16-25)

■ **16-17** The concluding section of ch 19 (vv 16-25) includes five oracles, each introduced with the phrase **in that day**. This first **in that day** (v 16) prefaces an oracle judgmental in tone, it and may be linked to Yahweh's act in v 1 when he enters Egypt riding "on a swift cloud." Yahweh's swift entrance, with his **uplifted** [or **swinging**] **hand**, signifying the brandishing of a battle weapon, instills **shuddering** fear in the **Egyptians**, who will become like **women** (weaklings) (*nāšîm* can mean either "women" or "wives"). Their **fear** will be like that of **wives** left alone in their homes, with no defenders to protect them when the enemy invades.

In this same context the prophet envisions that just the mention of **the land of Judah** (v 17) will remind **the Egyptians** of Judah's God, **Yahweh Sebaoth**, and what he **is planning against them**. Their response can only be **terror**.

■ **18** This second **in that day** oracle begins to describe Egypt's eventual turning to Judah's God, **Yahweh Sebaoth**. But the interpretation of its meaning remains "impenetrable" (Motyer 1993, 168). Scholars have proposed every historical possibility for the identity of the **five cities** that take up speaking **the language of Canaan** (most likely Hebrew is intended [Wildberger 1997, 270]), with no glimmer of agreement. The nearest agreement is that **the City of the Sun** most likely refers to Heliopolis ("Sun-City"), the Greek name for the city of On, where the deity Re (the Egyptian sun god) was worshipped. Oswalt suggests that the prophet is speaking metaphorically of small beginnings that represent "Egypt one day turn[ing] to God in a radical way" (1986, 377).

■ **19** This third **in that day** oracle (vv 19-22) contains echoes of exodus terminology. **An altar** and **a monument** will be constructed within Egypt; these items, however, are not represented in the original exodus event. Both will be dedicated **to Yahweh**. Who will construct them is not stated, but the overall intent of the passage would signify that it is not Jews who have returned to live in Egypt, but Egyptians who have experienced conversion to Yahweh.

■ **20** The function of the altar and pillar is clear: they **will be a sign and witness to Yahweh Sebaoth**, inside Egypt, just as, following their exodus, the

Israelites set up reminders outside Egypt as a sign and a witness to Yahweh's deliverance (Josh 4:6; 24:26-27). The Israelites had once cried out to God for deliverance from their Egyptian taskmasters (Exod 2:23); likewise, the now believing Egyptians know that, when they **cry out to *Yahweh*** for deliverance from **their oppressors**, just as he sent Moses earlier, Yahweh will send them **a savior and defender, and he will rescue them**.

■ **21** In Exod 5—14, the theme of "knowing" who Yahweh is through his acts related to delivering his people from Egyptian bondage occurs eleven times. Of these eleven occurrences, seven times it is said that the Egyptians or Pharaoh "will know" (7:5, 17; 8:10, 22 [6, 18 HB]; 9:14; 14:4, 18; the other four are Moses and the Israelites [5:2; 6:3; 10:2; 11:7]). Yet from the text of Exodus the Egyptians and the pharaoh never "know," that is, never acknowledge the superiority of Yahweh. In our passage here, however, we see a reciprocal "knowing": ***Yahweh* will make himself known** [causative pass. of *yd'*] **to the Egyptians, and *the Egyptians* will *know*** [active of *yd'*] ***Yahweh***. This "knowing," this experiential relationship with Yahweh, will result in acts of **worship** (**sacrifices, offerings,** and **vows**).

■ **22** As incongruous as it may seem to us, ***Yahweh* will strike Egypt**, both ***striking and healing***. But the intention of such discipline is that the Egyptians **will turn to *Yahweh***.

■ **23-25** The book of Isaiah speaks of a metaphorical "highway" (*měsillâ*) provided for God's people, on which to return to Jerusalem from exile in Assyria, Babylon, and other parts of the diaspora (Isa 11:16; 35:8; 49:11). A different metaphorical "highway" (*měsillâ*) is provided for God, as King, upon which either to come to the rescue of his people in Babylon or to travel to Jerusalem to receive them when they arrive from Babylon (40:3).

In these fourth and fifth **in that day** passages (19:23, 24), a metaphorical **highway** (*měsillâ* [v 23]) connects **Egypt to Assyria**. Though the text does not explicitly say that the **highway** will pass through Israel/Judah/Jerusalem, the context implies so. The purpose of this metaphorical **highway** is to freely facilitate **worship** of historical enemies, the **Egyptians and Assyrians . . . together** worshipping Israel's God. Yet all three—**Israel, Egypt,** and **Assyria**, as one entity—will be a **blessing *in the midst of*** the earth (v 24). So, Israel, too, is a worshipping partner with both of her historical enemies. On the one hand, Childs suggests that this "strikes a resonance with the promise of the nations' assembly in 2:2-4" (2001, 144), where the nations stream to Jerusalem. On the other hand, Wildberger suggests that, "the expectation here is not for the 'peoples' to stream to Jerusalem." Rather, "Zion was [not] the only place where Yahweh could be worshiped." He compares this with Zeph 2:11 and 3:8-10 (1997, 279), where the nations worship Yahweh, each in its own land.

The theological understanding of this passage is, then, that **Egypt** and **Assyria** represent the oppressors of this world, while **Israel** represents all peoples who are oppressed (compare Isa 27:12-13). **In that day** Yahweh will bring a reconciliation in which all peoples, with deep respect for each other, can worship the same God together.

Chapter 19 concludes with a blessing from **Yahweh Sebaoth** upon this worshipping triad. The shocker is, however, that the lover's title, **my people** (v 25)—always considered reserved for Israel/Judah alone (compare Exod 6:7, plus twenty-four more times in both the OT and NT)—is now applied to **Egypt**, Israel's former oppressor. Surely Isaiah's Judean audience would have been as shocked by this audacious assertion as was Amos' northern Israelite audience when he declared that, just as they were ***brought up*** people "from Egypt," so were their two archenemies, "the Philistines from Caphtor and the Arameans from Kir" (Amos 9:7). That is, their God, Yahweh, had a hand in the migrations of their enemies also! How dare he? But, yes, because Yahweh is the Creator of all peoples and nations, he dares to name even Israel's former oppressor, now turned to him, as **my people** (Isa 19:25).

5. Isaiah's Shocking Behavior (20:1-6)

Sargon II and the Ashdod Rebellion

Sargon II, who ruled Assyria from 721 to 705 BC, tells in his annals of a succession of troubles in the Phoenician seacoast city of Ashdod, a city in vassal relationship with Assyria. The initial hint of trouble was that Ashdod's vassal king, Azuri, "schemed not to send tribute" any more to Assyria, and urged other kingdoms "in his neighborhood" to do the same. In response, Sargon replaced Azuri with his younger brother, Ahimiti, as Ashdod's king. But the Ashdodites, hating Ahimiti, deposed him, putting on the throne an illegitimate king, one named Yamani, an Ionian/Greek. Yamani, too, withheld tribute, encouraging rulers of other Palestinian kingdoms, including Judah, Edom, and Moab, to join him in this rebellion. He even "sent bribes to Pir'u king of Musru" (i.e., Egypt), which Sargon says "belongs (now) to Ethiopia," meaning that Egypt is ruled by foreign southern Nubian kings at the time of the Ashdod rebellion (Pritchard 1969, 286-87).

■ **1 Sargon king of Assyria** could not tolerate insubordination by a vassal. The historical context of 20:1 is Sargon's response to Ashdod's insubordination and rebellion: "I besieged (and) conquered the cities Ashdod, Gath, [and] Asdudimmu" (Pritchard 1969, 286). This siege and capture of Ashdod occurred in 712 BC (Tadmor 1958, 79-80). Even before the arrival of Sargon's army at the gates of Ashdod, however, King Yamani fled to Egypt, seeking asylum. But, the fear of an invasion by Sargon took all the bravado out of "the Ethiopian king," who extradited Yamani and "brought him to Assyria, a long journey" (Pritchard 1969, 286). To further punish Ashdod, Sargon carried out the classic Assyrian population exchange, carrying away many Ashdodite citizens and importing people from other areas of the empire.

■ **2-6** Here a narrator explains why Isaiah shockingly goes about among his people **naked** and **barefoot for three years** (v 3). The message is directed to Judah and King Hezekiah: do not trust in fallible, weak Egypt. Continue to trust in our God, **Yahweh**, because just as Ashdod had met the fate of deportation at the hands of powerful Assyria (v 1), so, **in that day** (v 6) Egypt will be led away **stripped and barefoot . . . , with buttocks bared** (v 4).

At some point earlier (**at that time**), presumably the time of the sacking of Ashdod referred to in v 1, **Yahweh had spoken to** Isaiah, commanding him to remove his **sackcloth** and **sandals** (v 2). In obedience, **he** *had done* so. This left him *naked* and **barefoot**. Scholars debate the purpose of Isaiah's **sackcloth** (*śāq*). It may have been the coarse, hairy garment that one put on as a sign of mourning, either beneath an outer garment, next to the skin (2 Kgs 6:30) or over one's outer garment (19:1). In such case, Isaiah would have been in mourning about something, possibly the recent destruction of northern Israel, begun in 722 BC with the capture of Samaria by Assyrian Shalmaneser and completed in 720 BC by Sargon II when he deported 27,290 Israelite citizens (Oswalt 1986, 385; Bright 2000, 275; Pritchard 1969, 284). Or the **sackcloth** may have been a prophet's regular outer garment (e.g., Elijah [1:8]). It is also not clear whether **naked** (*'ārôm*) means completely naked or lightly clothed.

In any case, Isaiah, in going about **naked** and **barefoot for three years**, carries out a prophetic symbolic action, **a sign and portent** *concerning* **Egypt and Cush** (v 3). The message in this symbolic action is for Judah and perhaps other neighboring kingdoms.

The message is this: just as you see Isaiah, stripped and barefoot, so will you see **the king of Assyria** carrying off **Egyptian captives and Cushite exiles, with buttocks bared** (v 4). So, if you **trusted in Cush and boasted in Egypt** (against Assyria, with the Ashdod rebellion), with **Egypt's shame** you, too, will be **put to shame** (v 5).

Verse 6 is an **in that day** reflection on the foregoing that may, in fact, be applied at any time subsequent to the Egyptian-Ashdod-Assyrian crisis of Isaiah's time. It is a call to God's people at any time to reflect upon this moment in history and know that to trust in one ungodly world power against another ungodly world power is to court disaster. One's only ultimate hope is to trust in God, the Creator of the universe, who has all world powers in his hand.

FROM THE TEXT

This two-chapter unit, 19:1—20:6, opens with Yahweh entering Egypt, swiftly, riding on a cloud (19:1), to bring general confusion throughout the land. Isaiah depicts Yahweh as working behind the scenes in a way that the wisest of Pharaoh's counselors, believing in the truth of their own counsel, cannot discern the cause of the nation's confusion. Yet, somewhere along the way, as the road of history unfolds, Isaiah, in echoes reminiscent of the long ago Israelite exodus, sees Egypt coming to acknowledge Yahweh's supreme lordship. Thus that intimate, erotic covenant term **know** (v 21) will be given even to the idol-worshipping Egyptians: they will know and be known by Yahweh (v 21). This will necessitate a casting aside of their "idols of silver and idols of gold, which they made to worship" (2:20).

The most astonishing and most difficult concept for the hearts of God's people to grasp and accept is that in this reciprocal act of knowing, Yahweh now gives to the Egyptians the coveted title "my people" (19:25). After all, Israel has been to Yahweh especially "my people," having been rescued from the cruel oppression of these very Egyptians. And to add to the difficulty of acceptance, Yahweh titles Assyria "my handiwork," also reserved for Israel since the day Yahweh brought them out of Egypt to create them as his special people.

This text is a powerful reminder to us about the wideness of God's grace, which knows no geographical, ethnic, cultural, religious, or political barriers or boundaries. The fact that God embraces the enemies of his covenant people issues a challenge to the people of God to recognize the truth that in God's kingdom there are no insiders or outsiders. The church should not overlook the missional challenge we find in this text and the universality of the gospel of salvation.

How difficult it is sometimes for us even today, when we, who have for a long time enjoyed a special walk with the Lord, see those persons who have so vigorously opposed us and our Lord come into the kingdom. And now they, too, right along with us, are God's "people." We see them enjoying the blessings of the Lord, just as we are, and resentment may well up. But such ought not to be. In our Lord's wisdom, he will call whomever he wishes "my people."

F. Prophecies Concerning Babylon, Dumah, and Arabia (21:1-17)

BEHIND THE TEXT

Chapter 21 consists of three units: "a prophecy *concerning* the **Wilderness of** the Sea" (vv 1-10), "a prophecy *concerning* Dumah" (vv 11-12), and "a prophecy *concerning* Arabia" (vv 13-17). The declaration that "Babylon has fallen, has fallen!" (v 9) indicates that the overall focus of the chapter is on some historical catastrophe that has come upon that great city, and that all three suboracles are related to that historical reality.

Assyrian Sargon II defeated Babylon and its rebellious ruler Marduk-Baladan in 710 BC and again in 703/2 BC. Marduk-Baladan, however, in further rebellion, returned again to Babylon, but Assyrian Sennacherib defeated him in 700 BC, then devastated the city in 689 BC. After this, Marduk-Baladan disappeared from history (*ISBE* 1:385-86).

Assyrian power began to wane during the final third of the 600s BC. From 625 BC, a new batch of rulers, the Chaldeans, arose in Babylon, reconstructing the city and rebelling against Assyrian rule. In 612 BC, allied with the Medes, they captured the Assyrian capital, Nineveh, and two years later crushed the vestiges of the Assyrian imperial army at Haran and Carchemish. Thus arose the Neo-Babylonian Empire, the biblical world's power broker until Persian Cyrus captured Babylon in 539 BC (ibid., 338; Aharoni and Avi-Yonah 1993, 126).

The question is, is one of the above-mentioned defeats of the city of Babylon the possible historical context for understanding Isaiah's oracle(s) in this chapter? The older view has been that it is one of the defeats of Marduk-Baladan at the end of the eighth century BC. The most prevalent view among today's critical scholars is that the Persian overthrow of the city in 539 BC best fits.

For the historical context of Isa 21:1-17, Sweeney argues most clearly for Sennacherib's final campaign against Marduk-Baladan in 700 BC, his defeat of Arabian tribal groups in the northern Syrian and Arabian desert in 691-689 BC, and his destruction of Babylon in 689 BC (1996, 280-82). This is the view followed in this commentary.

IN THE TEXT

1. A Prophecy Concerning the Wilderness of the Sea (21:1-10)

■ 1 ***Wilderness of* the Sea** is *midbar yām*. *Midbar* can refer to pasture, steppe, wilderness, or desert (*HALOT* 547), that is, areas outside of or on the borders of settled land, and "does not exclude a marshy region" (Sweeney 1996, 280). The Babylonian rule of Marduk-Baladan in the final decade of the eighth century BC provides the best context for understanding the meaning and location of ***Wilderness of* the Sea**. Brinkman notes that Marduk-Baladan belonged to the *bal kur tam-tim*, which translates from the Akkadian as "dynasty of the Sealand" (*kur*, "land"; *tam-tim*, "sea") (1964, 35-36, 41). *Kur* is equivalent to Hebrew *midbar*, in that *kur* also refers to the borders of settled land. Akkadian records also refer to the swampy area in southern Babylonia as *mat tamti*, "Land of the Sea," through which the confluence of the Tigris and Euphrates Rivers flows as it empties into the Persian Gulf (Sweeney 1996, 280). An inscription of Tiglath-Pileser III also designates Marduk-Baladan as *šar tam-tim*, "king of the Sea(land)" (*CAD* 2006, 18:155). Thus, concludes Sweeney, "*midbar yām* (***Wilderness of* the**

Sea) is an appropriate Hebrew designation for the *kur tam* ruled by Merodach-Baladan" (ibid., 281).

The Hebrew text says only that ***it/he* comes** [*bāʾ*] **from the *wilderness*** (*mimmidbār*). What/who is it that **comes**? Is it Yahweh, often depicted as coming on the winds of the storm (Pss 18:10 [11 HB]; 104:3)? Is it Sennacherib in his 700 BC attack against Marduk-Baladan and his 689 BC destruction of Babylon? Or perhaps is it both Yahweh and Sennacherib. Isaiah's view is that Yahweh is the ultimate force behind Assyria's destruction of Babylon. The attack that is coming is metaphorically **like whirlwinds *in* the southland**: unstoppable, terrifying!

■ **2** Verses 2-4 describe Isaiah's personal reaction to the news of Sennacherib's attack. This news has come to Isaiah in the form of a **vision** (*ḥāzût*) that, he says, **has been *told/reported*** [*hugad*] **to me** (v 2). A **vision** is usually something that God reveals to the prophet's inner perception, something that he describes as seeing. To receive it aurally is unusual. Yet, in v 3, he will speak of both hearing and seeing this vision.

The one whom Isaiah designates **the treacherous one** [*habbôgēd*], **the destroyer** (*haššôdēd*) appears to be Assyria, coming against Babylon and Marduk-Baladan. Commentators usually interpret the war shouts (**Elam, attack! Media, lay siege!**) as commands to Elamite and Median forces, supposedly allied with Assyria, to attack besieged Babylon. The Assyrian documents, however, show Elam to have given Marduk-Baladan military aid in 720, 703, and 700 BC against Assyrian forces (Brinkman 1965, 164-65). Moreover, the verb translated **attack!** (*ʿălî*) literally is ***go up!***, which could be a call to **Elam** to resist the invading Assyrians. The verb translated **lay siege!** (*ṣûrî*) could, as in Judg 9:31, express the act of instigating **Media** into hostility toward Assyria (Sweeney 1996, 281; VanGemeren 1997, 3:791; compare Exod 23:22-23; Deut 2:9, 19; Esth 8:11). Perhaps Watts, however, gives the wisest counsel: that the text does not define the role of **Elam** and **Media** in the conflict, "whether for or against Babylon, but it does establish their participation in the struggle" (2005, 328).

The final phrase of this verse is ambiguous: **I will bring to an end all the groaning**, or ***her* groaning** (grammatically, the form can be read either way). Who is **I**? It is certainly not the prophet. Possibly it is Marduk-Baladan promising to relieve Babylon from Assyrian oppression (Motyer 1993, 174). Or, more likely in the larger context, it is God promising to put a stop to Babylon's groaning, "although not in quite the way Babylon hoped" (Oswalt 1986, 392).

■ **3-4** ***Therefore*** (*ʿal kēn*) (omitted in the NIV) opens Isa 21:3, linking Isaiah's visceral response to the news revealed to him in his vision of v 2: he "is all but undone by anguish and dismay" (Seitz 1993, 158). He centers his physical ***anguish*/pain** in his ***loins***, likening it to the intensity of the **pangs . . . of a woman giving birth** (v 3). The auditory (**what I hear**) and the visual (**what I see**) aspects, he says, create only **bewilderment**. Even **my heart** (v 4) is affected: it **staggers** or **wanders about**. We might say, my heart is out of rhythm.

■ **5** In vv 5-10 Isaiah gives vignettes of scenes that come to him in his vision, all relating to the central theme of v 9: the succumbing of Babylon to her enemies. Four cryptic terms depict **officers** (*śārîm*) in the act of feasting: *arranging the table, spreading the rug, eating,* and *drinking* (v 5). Two potential historical settings have been suggested for this feast: (1) a possible banquet at the Judean capital, welcoming Marduk-Baladan's envoys (Motyer 1993, 175) who, under the guise of sympathy for Hezekiah's recent illness (39:1-2), have come seeking Hezekiah's alliance against Assyria (ca. 703-702 BC); (2) Belshazzar's feast (Dan 5) at the time of Persian Cyrus' capture of Babylon (539 BC) (Oswalt 1986, 389, 393). An alternate suggestion is that it is not necessarily an actual historical feast but a "description of smug complacency" referring "to the ineffective resistance of the anti-Assyrian coalition" of Marduk-Baladan and his allies (Childs 2001, 152).

The command to the **officers** to **anoint** [*mišḥû*] **the shields**, in preparation for battle, may refer to some long practiced ritual, the meaning now forgotten, but in an earlier time intended to endue magical powers of protection on the weapon. Compare 2 Sam 1:21, where the same may be implied: "the shield of Saul—no longer **anointed** [*māšîaḥ*] with oil" (Wildberger 1997, 320-21).

■ **6-7** *For* (*kî*, omitted in the NIV) begins Isa 21:6, giving further explanation for Isaiah's reaction to his "dire vision" (v 2), **thus the Sovereign said/had said** [the Hebrew does not distinguish] **to me** (v 6). Within his vision Isaiah had been ordered to **post** [*an imaginary*] **lookout**, requiring of him that *that which he might see, he would* **report**. What he was to watch for were **horses, donkeys,** and **camels**, with **riders** (v 7). That these would be the Assyrian army advancing, not toward Babylon, but returning from its victory over Babylon, is not revealed until v 9.

■ **8-9** The **lookout** suddenly *called out*, avowing his faithfulness: **day and night** I *have been standing* on the watchtower; . . . I *have been stationed* at my post (v 8). His faithfulness is rewarded: **Look!** *It came* (that which he had been instructed to watch for [v 9]): *A troop of men* (*HALOT* 1233), **teams of horses**, apparently on march away from Babylon, for one of the soldiers announces to the watchman an astonishing piece of news. The formula that introduces his announcement, **he gives back the answer** (*wayya'an wayyō'mer*, *he answered and said*), is an interpretation response to an implied question, "What is the meaning of what I am seeing?" (This Hebrew response formula [*wayya'an wayyō'mer*] is the same in Zech 4:4, 6.)

The meaning is in the content of the announcement: *Fallen, fallen is* **Babylon,** *and* **all the images of** *her* **gods** *are* **shattered on the ground!** The marchers are most likely military personnel returning from the sacking of Babylon. The most appropriate historical occasion for this announcement would be Sennacherib's sacking of Babylon in 689 BC, about which he recorded: "I had destroyed Babylon, had smashed the gods thereof, and had struck down its people with the sword" (Luckenbill 1926, §438).

But what Isaiah is seeing and hearing is visionary, and in a vision events are not necessarily bound to a single historical event. Thus this announcement echoes the finality of the destruction of Babylon and her idols depicted in Isa 13—14 and Jer 50:2; 51:8, 44, 47. Moreover, it anticipates God's future final overthrow of that "great city" (Rev 17:18) that represents the ultimate of human pride, of which an angel announced, "Fallen! Fallen is Babylon the Great!" (18:2; compare v 21).

■ **10** This section of Isaiah's vision (Isa 21:1-10) concludes with a word of encouragement for God's people. These history-changing events (wars and rumors of wars, armies on the march, cities overthrown) do not happen at the mere whim of humans; they are the actions and will of **Yahweh Sebaoth, . . . the God of Israel**. Though God's people **are crushed** and will yet be crushed like grain **on the threshing floor**, over which the threshing sledges are dragged, **Yahweh Sebaoth** is still their God. Isaiah assures them that what he has reported to them is not of his own imagination; rather, that which he has **heard** is from **the God of Israel**.

War Crime in the Ancient World

Isaiah 21:10, 2 Kgs 10:32 and Amos 1:3 make reference to a cruel and atrocious war crime committed by nations in the ancient Near East. In the latter half of the ninth century BC, Aram carried out several border invasions and territory expansions against Israel; the Israelite narrator reports that Aram "made them [Israel's people] like the dust at threshing time" (2 Kgs 13:7). Some forty years later, Amos (ca. 760 BC), looking back at this devastation, spoke a charge against Damascus (Aram): you "threshed Gilead [in Transjordan] with sledges having iron teeth" (Amos 1:3). The language of the narrator of both 2 Kings and Amos suggests a nonmetaphorical description of actual war crimes, in which the Aramaeans physically dragged threshing sledges over prostrate, captured Israelite soldiers, and Israelite citizens of Gilead (Niehaus 1992, 341).

In the normal agricultural life of ancient Israel, farmers brought harvested grain, still on the stalk, to the threshing floor for separation from the stalk (threshing) and then removal of chaff from the grain by the wind (winnowing). To separate the grain from the stalk, oxen (Deut 25:4) or donkeys were used to drag a heavy sledge (about 3 x 7 feet) upon which the farmer rode again and again over the grain stalks. For cutting, teeth of flint, basalt stone, or iron were embedded on the underside of this sledge. Thus, if the 2 Kings and Amos references noted above to dragging threshing sledges over prostrate Israelites are nonmetaphorical, skin and flesh would be ripped from the bodies over which these sledges were dragged. These kinds of terrorist activities (see also Amos 1:13) induced fear among the powerless nations defeated by superior military powers.

2. A Prophecy Concerning Dumah (21:11-12)

■ **11-12 Dumah** (v 11) has been identified as the desert oasis Adummatu in Assyrian documents (which often prefix *A-* to proper names), also known as Dumat al-Jandal. Located midway between Babylon and Syria, with its abundance of water and orchards, it was the most important stop for trading caravans and other travelers in all of North Arabia (Eph'al 1982, 119-22). Tema (Isa 21:14) and Kedar (vv 16-17), both also located in Arabia, appear along with Dumah in a list of names in Gen 25:13-15.

Seir is a name for Edom, the area to the southeast of Judah (east of the Wadi Arabah). Judean political involvements and life of the everyday Judean citizen were not independent of what was happening between the great city Babylon and the Assyrian power broker far to the east. News of those eastern happenings would come along the Arabian trade route via Dumah. So, says Isaiah, in his visionary imagination, **someone calls to me from Seir**, addressing him as **Watchman** (v 12); twice he (Isaiah) is asked his prophetic view on the length of the **night** of oppression at the hands of the Assyrians, who are wreaking havoc in the east. Both the question and answer, however, are meant as a message for Judah, not for Seir/Edom. Isaiah's response appears to be that there is no news from Dumah, indicating that this important center has evidently fallen. Yet **morning *has come***, that is, dawn is on the horizon ("the change in fortune is already a reality, . . . significant cracks on the stage of world history were now showing up" [Wildberger 1997, 337]). But there will still be further **night** before God, in his own timing, brings the full light of salvation. When will that be? It is not for the prophet to know God's timing. One will need to **ask . . . yet again**.

3. A Prophecy in/within Arabia (21:13-17)

■ **13a** The superscription, **A prophecy *in/within* Arabia,** is structured differently from previous ones in ch 13 onward, with the addition of the preposition *bĕ*, "in, within," prefixed to the name **Arabia**. Thus the verses following concern actions taking place within Arabia, not with Arabia as a whole.

■ **13b-15 Caravans of Dedanites** (v 13*b*) are apparently returning to Dedan, their home base, located south of **Tema** (v 14) in northwestern Arabia. They would be traveling from a northeasterly direction, most likely from Babylon. For some reason, they do not **camp** in the normal caravan shelters but in the **thickets** (v 13). Though there are grammatical difficulties, it is most likely that these ***Dedanite caravaneers*** are the **fugitives** (v 14) who are ***fleeing*** from the **sword**, the **bow**, and the **heat** [*kōbed*, "heaviness," "vehemence" (BDB 458)] of **battle** (v 15). It is to these **thirsty** (v 14) and hungry travelers, that ***the inhabitants of the land of*** Tema are urged to show desert hospitality by ***bringing water*** and **food**.

■ **16-17** It is the ***Sovereign*** (*'ădōnāy*) who again speaks to Isaiah, with an additional word: **the splendor** [*kābôd*] **of Kedar will** [*soon*] **come to an end**. *A year* (the Hebrew lacks a number) is enigmatic, representative of an indeterminate time period (v 16). *Kābôd* "expresses the acquisitions, both tangible and intangible, which give a lifetime significance and importance" (Oswalt 1986, 402). The ravages of war will nearly annihilate the Kedarite fighting men. Only a few **survivors** of the **archers** and **warriors** will remain (v 17).

Kedar is the general area in northwestern Arabia in which Dedan and Tema are located. Kedar (along with Tema) is mentioned in the records of Assyrian Tiglath-Pileser III, Sargon II, Sennacherib, and Ashurbanipal, and, Babylonian Nebuchadnezzar and Nabonidus, in regard to paying tribute to them and revolting several times against their control, from at least 738 BC to the early sixth century BC (Kaiser 1974, 134-35). Perhaps the immediate context that links this passage with the two previous prophecies concerning Dumah and Babylon is Assyrian Sennacherib's campaigns against the Arabs (which may have included the Kedarites) in the deserts to the west of Babylon between 691 and 689 BC (Eph'al 1982, 118).

This prophecy of the coming decimation of Kedar was meant for the ears and hearts of God's people in Judah, and especially for Judah's king Hezekiah. Kedar was allied with Babylon against Assyria. Babylon's king Marduk-Baladan appears to have been urging Judah to make an alliance with Babylon against Assyria. Isaiah is saying to Hezekiah: Don't do this! Allow God to use Assyria to bring about his judgment upon Babylon.

I have this word, says Isaiah, on the authority of **Yahweh, the God of Israel** who **has spoken**.

FROM THE TEXT

In 21:10 Isaiah speaks of God's people "crushed on the threshing floor," a metaphorical description of the suffering of Israel and Judah from attacks by the Assyrian army.

Isaiah's judgment speech in 21:1-10 against Babylon clearly contains a condemnation of inhumane treatment of political prisoners by any nation, ancient or modern. Such acts would be deemed violent crimes against human beings made in the image of God. These crimes would be violations of Yahweh's basic covenantal requirement of mercy. The "threshing sledge" metaphor occurs in Isa 41:15-16, in the context of Yahweh addressing exiled Israel in Babylon, on the eve of her impending rescue and return to Jerusalem. The Hebrew syntax of vv 15-16 allows a conditional translation (Watts 2000, 641-42): "*If I had made* you into a threshing sledge, . . . you *would* thresh the mountains and crush them." Indeed, Yahweh could have made exiled "Israel/Jacob," the "descendants of Abraham" (41:8), into a military machine, a threshing sledge wreaking devastation upon his enemies. It could have been Israel cutting to bits the military and political powers of the world. If so, the glory of victory would be claimed by Israel, rather than be given to Yahweh.

Since the tables are now turned, and Israel is no longer the victim of the nations' threshing, Israel is to "rejoice in **Yahweh** and **sing praises** in the Holy One of Israel" who brings deliverance to her from her enemies (41:16). Note that it is not *to* Yahweh but *in* Yahweh that God's people (including us in this twenty-first century) are to rejoice and sing praise, for Yahweh is the basis, the reason for our existence. Here is an OT parallel to the NT expressions "in Christ," "in the Lord," "in the Spirit" (e.g., Eph 1:1; 5:8; 6:18).

G. Two Cases of Divine Grace Flaunted (22:1-25)

BEHIND THE TEXT

This chapter clearly divides into two oracles, Isa 22:1-14 and vv 15-25. The first concerns the leadership and inhabitants of "the City of David"/"Jerusalem" (vv 9, 10); the second concerns two individuals, Shebna (v 15) and Eliakim (v 20). In the first, the inhabitants of Jerusalem publicly flaunt God's grace by feasting and revelry in the aftermath of God's miraculous deliverance of the city from invasion and destruction, rather than engaging in soul-searching leading to repentance (vv 12-13). In the second, Shebna flaunts God's gracious appointment to the divine calling as "steward" (*sōkēn* [v 15]) by privately using his office to attempt to immortalize himself with a rock-cut tomb, apparently in Jerusalem.

There is no question among scholars that the first oracle (vv 1-14) speaks of a military threat against Jerusalem, for which the leadership had made frantic preparations to protect the city. Moreover, there is no question that the author of the oracle is not pleased with this show of self-trust, rather than trusting in God. Scholars, however, question the identity of the author of the oracle as it now stands in our text of Isaiah. Some view the author to be Isaiah, speaking within the context of an event of his own time at the end of the eighth century BC, when Assyria was the biblical world's power broker; yet he speaks with a prophet's forward view of Jerusalem's final demise at the hands of Babylon in 587 BC. Others view the author to be an editor, working with the text following Jerusalem's destruction in 587 BC, when Babylon had replaced Assyria as the biblical world's power broker. This editor, while working with Isaiah's original material, added his own reflections from Babylonian exile; thus the text now points primarily back to the disaster of 587 BC.

Wildberger points out that the main point of this oracle speaks to Isaiah's earlier theme (compare 5:12 and 7:3-13), a call to the citizens of Judah to return to Yahweh, rather than trusting in their own ability to defend themselves (1997, 357). From this, and other factors of the text, he concludes that Isaiah is the author of the oracle (ibid., 358). Childs concludes "that there are no clear signs of a major editorial reinterpretation," yet allows that "canonically speaking the text functions prophetically toward the future," that is, it foreshadows the 587 BC destruction of Jerusalem (2001, 159).

Regardless of authorial view, this oracle (22:1-14) cannot be interpreted in isolation from the larger context of the Isaiah text. Within the text's presentation of interchange between Isaiah and King Hezekiah, the two great powers, Babylon and Assyria are very much in view. Chapter 39 details the visit of Babylonian king Marduk-Baladan's emissaries to King Hezekiah. Scholars suggest (though the text does not say so) the behind-the-scenes purpose of the emissaries to have been a request for Judah to ally with Babylon against Assyria. After the departure of these emissaries, **Yahweh Sebaoth**'s word is revealed to Isaiah that the final demise of Jerusalem will be at the hands of Babylon, not Assyria (39:5-7). Thus there is no reason why Isaiah, in this present oracle, could not be speaking prophetically to both the present and the future.

The military presence threatening Jerusalem in Isaiah's present, however, is Assyria. But, which Assyrian invasion event is in the background, if, in fact, any one event can be identified? Suggestions have ranged from invasions of 722/21, 711, 705, 703, and 701 BC. On the one hand, some of the allusions in the oracle appear best to point to Sargon's 711 BC attack on Ashdod and the capturing of Judea's southern city of Azekah. On the other hand, other allusions seem best to point to Yahweh's deliverance of Jerusalem from Sennacherib's siege of Jerusalem in 701 BC. In reality, however, it is impossible to identify the specific invasion event. It seems that Isaiah is presenting an oracular collage of perhaps the 711 and 701 BC threat events as the backdrop for condemning Judah for a lack of trust in Yahweh's protection.

Scholars have also questioned why the oracle concerning Shebna and Eliakim is placed in the text at this particular point. Childs interprets the pairing of these two oracles as an "analogy." The first (vv 1-14), a "public display of unbelief," and the second (vv 15-25), a "private abuse of a divine calling," are intentionally paired, an analogous demonstration of "the full intensity of God's judgment" (2001, 162).

IN THE TEXT

1. A Prophecy Concerning the Valley of Vision (22:1-14)

■ **1a** The **Valley of Vision** apparently is picked up here from v 5 to give a title to this oracle.

■ **1b-3** The prophet addresses a **town/city** (using second feminine singular pronouns), identified in v 10 as Jerusalem. He opens his address with a question of reproach: **What *is it with* you now, that you have *ascended, all of you, to* the roofs?** (v 1). The flat rooftops of houses were used for various purposes: for sleeping in the warm months (1 Sam 9:25-26; 2 Sam 11:2; 1 Kgs 17:19), as places of worship (2 Kgs 23:12; Jer 19:13; 32:29), or as places of public mourning in times of disaster (Isa 15:3; Jer 48:38). Here, however, they are being used for celebration: *a tumultuous city, an exultant town*. Why are they celebrating? Assyrian Sennacherib's sudden withdrawal from his 701 BC threat against Jerusalem gives a possible reason (2 Kgs 18—19 // Isa 36—37).

But celebration is not the order of the day; rather, a turning to God in repentance, seeking his face, should consume them. Why? Because of the despicable actions of **your leaders**, who, abandoning the citizens to possible invasion, *together* fled the city, but *together* were taken prisoner (Isa 22:3). These **leaders** are those whom Isaiah designates **your *profaned ones*** (*ḥălālîm*; **your slain** [v 2]). The root Hebrew form *ḥll* (most likely from two different original roots) carries two meanings: one, "profaned"; the other, "pierced," "slain" (*HALOT* 319-20). Isaiah is making a pun: **not . . . sword-*profaned/pierced*** [*ḥallê ḥereb*] **nor . . . battle-*dead***, that is, not profaned "in the sense that a dead body is thought of as profaned" (Watts 2005, 337), but *profaned* by their own immoral actions. Some commentators suggest that Isaiah is speaking of a siege by Sennacherib and its effects on the inhabitants of the besieged city. For example, Oswalt speaks of "the streets littered with bodies of those starved in the siege" (1986, 409). This is pure imagination, however, since neither the biblical account nor Sennacherib's own account indicates any siege of Jerusalem being undertaken (Millard 1985, 69-70).

■ **4** **Therefore** (*'al kēn*), says Isaiah, **let me weep bitterly . . . over the destruction of *the daughter of* my people** (*bat 'ammî*), a metaphor usually understood to refer to Jerusalem. Jerusalem, however, received no destruction at the hands of Sennacherib. The cities and towns of Judah, on the contrary, suffered the full fury of Sennacherib's army (compare 1:7). It is for this broader destruction that Isaiah ***weeps***. Sennacherib claims to have conquered forty-six of Hezekiah's cities, taking 200,150 of their inhabitants, along with countless domestic animals, as war booty, apparently deporting them to Assyria (Pritchard 1969, 288). Moreover, it may be that Isaiah's prophetic eye looks beyond the present situation to that final **destruction** that Yahweh yet has in store for Jerusalem. His bitter weeping also is because God's people fail to understand that it is the Sovereign who directs both the present eighth-century BC Assyrian threat and (as yet unknown to them) Babylon's coming sixth-century BC devastation of Judah and Jerusalem.

■ **5** This verse opens with *kî*, **For** (omitted in the NIV), clarifying that this present Assyrian threat against Jerusalem was not planned by mere humans at the helm of a world empire; rather, it ***was/is* a day *belonging to the Sovereign***

Yahweh Sebaoth. Indeed, it was a frightful **day**, with **tumult and trampling and terror in the Valley of Vision**. **Valley of Vision** is most likely a metaphor for the Valley of Ben Hinnom, located to the south of the city's walls. It seems that Sennacherib's "field commander with a large army," having come from the siege and capture of the southern Judean city of Lachish, approached Jerusalem from the south/southwest. His messengers challenged Hezekiah's administrators on the wall at "the aqueduct of the Upper Pool, on the road to the Launderer's Field" (36:2), which was located in the Valley of Ben Hinnom. The **battering down** of **walls** does not refer to those of Jerusalem but to the destruction that the Assyrian army wreaked on the Judean towns prior to, and including, the taking of Lachish.

■ **6** Listed together in this verse are four, noninfantry entities of an Assyrian army, whether engaged in open battle or siege of a city: (1) those who ***take*** up **the bow** (i.e., archers), (2) ***manned chariots***, (3) **horses**, for both drawing the chariots and some mounted archers, and (4) those who ***uncover*** **the shield**. The last can refer to two types of shield bearers: (1) There are those who protect chariot-riding archers with arm-held shields as they (the archers) shoot from either the chariot platform or from a disembarked standing position; (2) There are others who remove (***uncover***) large siege shields from the rear of the chariot for strategic placement, facing a city's walls; the archers, in turn, give them covering protection while they perform this task, then the archers, in turn, shoot from behind the siege shield (De Backer 2009, 29-47; 2012, 436).

The most plausible explanation for the mention of **Elam** and **Kir** in the context of Sennacherib's 701 BC western campaign is that Assyrian kings required conquered peoples to supply contingents of fighting men for their standing armies (Wildberger 1997, 364). Elam supported Babylonian Marduk-Baladan in his revolts against Assyria, and in his campaigns against this rebel, Sennacherib may well have taken into his army Elamite archers, who were known as some of the best (ibid.). The location of **Kir** is still unknown, but possibly somewhere near Elam. It is mentioned in Amos 9:7 as the place from which the Aramaens originated, but in Amos 1:5 and 2 Kgs 16:9 as the place to which the Aramaens will be/were returned in exile.

■ **7** The **valleys** leading up to Jerusalem are filled with multitudes of **chariots**, the bulk of the forces held in reserve. In the vanguard are **horsemen**, which have been strategically **posted at *its* gates**, lest any from inside should attempt to escape.

■ **8-11** As Sennacherib's forces capture town after town of Hezekiah's kingdom, and the strategic southern cities of Azekah and Lachish fall, a move upon Jerusalem appears more imminent. To prepare for this eventuality, the king and inhabitants of Jerusalem make frantic efforts to strengthen the city's defenses.

The Assyrian War Chariot, Archers, and Shield Bearers

The Assyrian war chariot consisted of two six- to eight-spoked wheels attached to an axle, upon which was mounted a framed platform, usually with sides. A yoke attached to the forward end of a horizontal pole enabled two to four horses to pull the chariot at significant speed into battle. There were (usually) four men in the chariot: the driver, an archer (usually, though sometimes a javelin/spear thrower), and (usually) two shield bearers. The archer stood behind/beside the driver, with a shield bearer on each side, with raised arm-held round shields to protect him as he shot his arrows. The reliefs depict the archer shooting both forward (while advancing) and rearward (while retreating). The forward "siege" chariots, moreover, carried large shields at their back, providing protection from the rear. Upon arrival close to the walls of a city to be sieged, one shield bearer disembarked, removing the siege shield. The archer disembarked with him, providing him protection, while the other shield bearer provided protection to the archer with his arm-held shield. Once the large siege shields were set up, archers could shoot from behind them at defenders on the city's walls (De Backer 2009, 29-47; 2012, 436; King and Stager 2001, 242-45).

These verses form a unit defined by the Hebrew root *nbṭ*, **you looked** (v 8) and **you did not look** (v 11), which forms an inclusio. The unit describes preparations for withstanding a possible siege. One of the applications of *nbṭ* is in contexts where "people are to look to, i.e., fix their eyes on, and thus guide their lives according to the will of the Lord as their only help (Ps 34:5[6]; Isa 51:1, 6)" (VanGemeren 1997, 3:9). The noun form of this root is applied to those who "trusted" (i.e., "hoped expectantly for") Egypt's and Cush's promised help to Ashdod in its 711 BC rebellion against Assyria (Isa 20:5-6). The implication is that their trust/hope was misplaced, as Egypt's help did not materialize.

Verse 8 states simply that ***he/someone*** [Heb. 3rd masc. sg.] ***uncovered the covering*** of **Judah**. Who it is that does the uncovering is left unstated. Wildberger suggests that just as Samaria was the "fortified city" of the northern kingdom (→ 17:3), without which Israel could not continue, so Jerusalem is Judah's last defense. Sennacherib, having taken such a vast number of Judah's towns, has left Jerusalem now "exposed." If she should fall, Judah has no future.

In that day (22:8), the day when you became aware that Sennacherib might soon approach Jerusalem, says Isaiah, **you looked** (*tabbēṭ*), first, **to the weapons in the Palace of the Forest**. This was the building Solomon built, using cedars from Lebanon for columns, beams, and ceiling paneling (1 Kgs 7:2; compare 10:17, 21). By Hezekiah's time it was apparently used to store armaments.

Isaiah 22:9-11*a* describes five actions that convey the city's frantic preparations: **You saw . . . broken . . . walls; . . . you stored up water . . . You counted the buildings . . . *you* tore down houses . . . you built a reservoir**. The implication is that peoples' (mud-brick) houses were destroyed to repair the breaches in the walls. The water preparations were to ensure access to water inside the city walls, since Jerusalem's main water source, the Gihon spring, was outside the eastern wall. A siege would prevent their access to that water supply. We know from 2 Kgs 20:20 and 2 Chr 32:30 that King Hezekiah, at some time during his reign, dug a tunnel through which to channel the water from the Gihon spring to the inside of the city wall. Whether or not it was in preparation for this impending siege cannot be determined.

The grand error on the part of Hezekiah and his people in the midst of the present situation, says Isaiah, was not in preparing the city to withstand siege; that would be expected of any sensible and wise king. No, the error was that, in the midst of these preparations, they did not recognize that behind the movements of armies and the rise and fall of kingdoms is *the Maker* and *the Planner of it* (v 11; *it* = the present situation), **Sovereign, Yahweh Sebaoth** (v 12). To him **you did not look** (*lō' hibbaṭṭem*), *for* [*him*] **you did not** have regard (*lō' rĕ'îtem*) (v 11). Trust in strengthened walls and redirected water was misplaced trust. Only ultimate trust in Yahweh, who directs and turns history in mysterious ways, would suffice to turn back the threat of an Assyrian army (compare 39:33-35).

■ **12 On that day** refers to Yahweh's "day" of 22:5, when the threat of Sennacherib's possible siege was very real. It was the same **Sovereign Yahweh Sebaoth** (of v 5) who called for the rituals of repentance: *weeping* and *mourning* and *baldness* and *putting* on sackcloth.

■ **13** But, no, the prophet's call was blatantly ignored: instead there was **joy and revelry** in the city (compare v 2). Why? Perhaps they are celebrating the sudden withdrawal of Sennacherib's forces (compare 37:37). Or perhaps the **slaughtering of cattle and killing of sheep, eating of meat and drinking of wine** is happening even while Sennacherib's army is at the very gates of the city. This may be indicated by the well-known saying, found in various forms throughout the ancient Near Eastern and Mediterranean literature (compare the quotes in Wildberger [1997, 373-75]; even Paul quotes it [1 Cor 15:32]), that Isaiah puts into the mouths of the Jerusalemites: **eat and drink . . . for tomorrow we die**. Since there will be no **tomorrow** for us, and we will have no future need of these **cattle** and **sheep** (brought inside the city to keep safe from the enemy), we might as well live it up!

■ **14** This act of rejection of trust in Yahweh's provision for "tomorrow," says Isaiah, **this *iniquity*** [*he'āwôn hazzeh*] **will not be atoned for. Till your dying day** points forward to the final destruction of Jerusalem, which will occur in 587

BC. This word, affirms Isaiah, is on the authority of **the Sovereign Yahweh Sebaoth,** who **has revealed this in my** *ears*.

2. Yahweh's Word Concerning Shebna and Eliakim (22:15-25)

This latter half of ch 22 concerns (1) the ousting of Shebna from the position of "palace administrator" (vv 15-19), and (2) the elevation of "Eliakim son of Hilkiah" to Shebna's position, then his removal (vv 20-25).

■ **15** Someone, presumably Isaiah, has received a command from **Sovereign, Yahweh Sebaoth** to confront **Shebna,** identified as **this steward** (*hassōkēn hazzeh*), **the palace administrator** (*'ăšer 'al habbāyit,* **who is over the house**). The term *hassōkēn* appears only here in the OT. A number of cognates, however, appear in other Semitic languages, signifying a high government official, or a "representative" (Wildberger 1997, 384; Watts 2005, 347). The phrase *'ăšer 'al habbāyit* first appears in King Solomon's list of officials (1 Kgs 4:6) but does not indicate an especially high rank. By King Hezekiah's time, however, the position appears to be that of one second to the king, what we today might call a "prime minister" (Oswalt 1986, 418).

■ **16** Whether or not there is personal animosity, or a difference of political view, in the background of the confrontation between Isaiah and Shebna (which some commentators imaginatively suggest), cannot be ascertained from the text. The issue is Shebna's apparent misuse of bureaucratic position to attempt to immortalize his person and name by **hewing** *his* **grave on the height**. Though the text does not identify the location, it surely must have been a prominent place near the Jerusalem precincts. A number of rock-hewn tombs, from the time of the Judean kingdom, still exist today on a hillside east of the Kidron Valley. It may have been in that location that Isaiah confronts Shebna with the challenge: **What** *do you have* **here and** *whom do you have here, that you have* **cut out a grave for yourself here?** (Note the thrice-repeated **here** in contrast with the twice-repeated "there" of Isa 22:18.) Isaiah may be questioning Shebna's ancestral burial history **here** (as a commoner, you have none, and thus have no right to a tomb **here**!); or he may be asking why Shebna is **here,** when at this time the very existence of the nation hangs in the balance, and he, as "prime minister," is not tending to more crucial matters.

■ **17-18** The grammar of these two verses is not easily translated. The general sense is, however, that **Yahweh** will **take firm hold** of Shebna, who considers himself to be a **mighty man** (*gaber*), and, as though he were **a ball, hurl** him **into a** *broad* **country,** most likely Assyria. **There,** declares Isaiah, **you will die,** never to be entombed in your beautifully cut Jerusalem tomb; moreover, **there** *your glorious* **chariots** *will be* (vv 17-18). Fancy chariots were the privilege of kings or those to whom the king granted such privilege (compare Gen 41:43; 1 Sam 8:11; but compare 2 Sam 15:1, where Absalom usurped this privilege).

Isaiah, implying that Shebna has usurped this privilege, cannot resist a final scathing comment: (*You are*) **a disgrace to your master's house**! (Isa 22:18).

■ **19** On the one hand, we read nothing more of Shebna's deportation to a distant country. Some scholars (e.g., Sweeney [1996, 298]), however, suggest that Shebna may have been the "messenger" in Sennacherib's account following his breaking off his intended siege of Jerusalem: "Hezekiah . . . In order to deliver the tribute and to do obeisance as a slave he sent his (personal) messenger" (Pritchard 1969, 288). According to this theory, then, it is Sennacherib who deports Shebna.

On the other hand, in 36:3, 22, and 37:2, at the time of Sennacherib's challenge to Hezekiah's officers on Jerusalem's wall, a Shebna appears as "the secretary" (*hassōpēr*), along with Eliakim son of Hilkiah "the palace administrator" (*'ăšer 'al habbāyit*, "who is over the house"). Is this the same Shebna as here in ch 22? Seitz argues that he is not, since his conduct (in chs 36—37) is in keeping with Isaiah's call in 22:12, exemplified in the wearing of sackcloth (37:2) (1993, 160). Other commentators, however, suggest that Isaiah's word to Shebna in 22:19, **you will be ousted from your position**, has already been implemented; by the time Sennacherib's troops arrive at Jerusalem's walls, Shebna has been demoted from prime minister to scribe (e.g., Wildberger 1997, 389; Oswalt 1986, 421).

■ **20-22** We do not know if **Eliakim son of Hilkiah** (22:20) is to be elevated from some other lesser official position or if he is selected from some well-placed Judean aristocratic family. In any case, he is now to wear Shebna's **robe** and **sash** (v 21), both symbols of **authority** of the office of prime minister. Apparently in contrast to Shebna, he will **be a father**, exercising protection, care, and concern for the inhabitants of **Jerusalem** and **Judah. The key to the house of David** (v 22) surely has symbolic meaning here, but may well include authority to determine who to admit into the presence of the king.

■ **23-24** Yahweh *drives* (v 23) Eliakim **like a** *tent* **peg** [*yātēd*] **into a firm place**, to hold steady **the house of his father** (*bêt 'ābîw*). But this will last only for a while, for his new **seat of honor** will become a burden beyond the burdens of the office: all the **vessels** (v 24), **the bowls**, **the jars** (symbolizing the nephews, nieces, cousin-brothers, cousin-sisters and shirttail relatives) will want a piece of the **glory**.

■ **25 In that day,** when demands of family become too heavy, Eliakim, now a ***wall*** **peg** (*yātēd*), will be unable to bear **the load** any longer. Like a **peg**, he **will be sheared off and will fall**. And so, Eliakim was not so different in high office than Shebna (who attempted to use his position for his own personal aggrandizement), in that he turned his position into "a maintenance system for his family" (Motyer 1993, 188).

FROM THE TEXT

In this chapter, Isaiah has put together two seemingly unrelated facets of life in Jerusalem at a time of great peril, when the very continued existence of the city seemed in doubt.

The first facet reveals the response of the general populace of the city, in the depiction of their revelry and feasting (vv 2, 13) while their enemy's army fills the valleys and his soldiers are at the city's gates. Their resignation of despair and hopelessness is revealed in the quote that Isaiah puts in their mouths: "'Let us eat and drink,' you say, 'for tomorrow we die!'" (v 13). Their response reveals a complete absence of any recognition that God might just still be working behind the scenes and that deliverance may be possible. Even fear seems to be absent. Rather, their actions reveal belligerence and arrogance: "In the brief time we have left to live, we will live only for ourselves, without God." As their "leaders fled" (v 3), possibly including spiritual leaders, the people were left with no one to infuse them with spiritual grace and faith. Here is a striking reminder to us, the church, in a society of declining faith in the Creator God and his requirements: we must be the infusers of grace and faith to a faithless and confused people.

The second facet is that of a government official, Shebna, who, in this time of national crisis, is found occupied with concerns primarily for himself. In his seeking to ensure for himself a burial place of some prominence, he was seeking to somehow ensure that he be remembered in death by those still living. Yet we all know from experience that only a very few persons (out of the billions who live and die) achieve a lasting place in the memories of the living. Such an attempt is an effort in futility. How much more memorable it is that we live out our brief life spans doing the deeds that Yahweh requires: "to loose the chains of injustice . . . to set the oppressed free . . . to share your food with the hungry . . . the naked, to clothe them" (58:6-7). Isaiah adds a postscript: "Then you will call, and the LORD will answer; you will cry for help, and he will say: Here am I" (v 9).

H. A Prophecy Concerning Tyre (23:1-18)

BEHIND THE TEXT

This chapter clearly divides into two units. The first unit (vv 1-14) is cast in lament form concerning devastation of the Phoenician international merchant cities Tyre and Sidon, and a decline of the Phoenician sea trading business in general. Blenkinsopp, however, notes that "the poem is not a lament but rather an ironic injunction to others to lament" (2000, 344). Lessing defines the poem as a "satirical city-lament" (2003, 91). The devastation of

Tyre and Sidon is credited to a command of Yahweh (vv 11-12). The second unit (vv 15-18) is a prophetic announcement that, sometime in the future, Tyre will be restored to her world trading activities, at which time she will dedicate her profits to Yahweh's service (v 18*b*).

The question concerning the first unit is whether Isaiah has in view specifically one of the known military campaigns subduing the Phoenician coastal area, which would have included attacks against Tyre and Sidon: Assyrian Ashurnasirpal II (876 BC), Shalmaneser II (842 and 839 BC), Tiglath-Pileser III (743 and 738 BC), Sennacherib (701 BC), Esarhaddon (678 and 672 BC), Babylonian Nebuchadnezzar (585-573 BC, thirteen-year siege of Tyre), Persian Artaxerxes III Ochus (348 or 343 BC), and Macedonian Alexander the Great (332 BC).

Eiselen has concluded from Tiglath-Pileser III's inscriptional accounts of his western expeditions, that, by his time (reigned 745-727 BC), Tyre had achieved superiority over Sidon and the other cities of southern Phoenicia. Moreover, the king of Tyre was also the king of Sidon, but he kept his royal residence in Tyre (1907, 47-48). Sennacherib's account of his 701 BC campaign against Sidon, his third to "Syria," corroborates this. He recounts capturing eight walled cities belonging to one named "Elulias king of Sidon," after which Elulias fled "from the midst of Tyre to Yatnam [Cyprus] which is in the midst of the sea." After Elulias' flight to Cyprus, Sennacherib put on the throne of Tyre/Sidon one named Tubahal (Smith 1878, 53-54) and handed over to Sidon Tyre's land empire, one hundred miles of coastal area stretching south to the Mount Carmel peninsula (Markoe 2000, 43). That the king of Sidon fled from Tyre after all the cities of southern Phoenicia had been captured is important: it indicates Tyre as the ruling seat of power in southern Phoenicia.

Sweeney, for example, concludes "that Phoenicia's capitulation to Assyria [noted above] provides the historical setting for 23:1b-14" (1996, 309). The problem with this conclusion, however, is that Sennacherib did not devastate the island city of Tyre, any port on Cyprus, or the port of Tarshish, as Isaiah's poem appears to indicate, if taken as historical prediction. By the time of Sennacherib's son Esarhaddon, Tyre had regained its southern coastal holdings and had rebuilt its political and economic power base (Markoe 2000, 43). Tyre was not destroyed until Alexander the Great built a causeway linking shore to island city in 332 BC.

We must conclude, with Oswalt, "that Tyre here, . . . is being used in a representative way" (1986, 427). In Isaiah's time, "Tyre was the central city of human commerce" (Young 1965, 121), and, in large measure, commanded the economic dependence of nations both east and west, including Israel and Judah. In this poem Isaiah is saying to Judah that someday God will give a command, and this whole economic structure will come crashing down.

IN THE  TEXT

1. Devastation of Southern Phoenicia (23:1-14)

■ **1a** The superscription, **A prophecy *concerning* Tyre**, identifies the overall focus of the oracle.

■ **1b** The first command, **Wail** [*hêlîlû*], **O ships of Tarshish**, is addressed to large merchant ships, able to travel across open sea, away from shoreline. These **ships** were of Phoenician origin, plying their trade all around the Mediterranean Sea. Their westernmost destination was **Tarshish**, possibly Tartessos in southern Spain (→ 2:12-17 sidebar, "Lebanon, Bashan, and Ships of Tarshish"); their homeports were located on the Phoenician/Canaanite seacoast, including Tyre and Sidon. Why are they commanded to lament? ***Because devastated*** [*šuddad*] ***is Mbyt Harbor*** (MT, *mibbayit mibbô'*). The NIV's **harbor** represents an emendation of *mibbô'* ("while coming/entering") to *mābô'* ("entrance"/"port of entry"), an emendation proposed by Barré (2004, 118, n. 20; *mābô'* [in plural form] also occurs in Ezek 27:3 in a lamentation concerning Tyre, where the NIV translates "gateway"). Barré moreover suggests that the MT's vowel pointing, *mibbayit*, represents a misunderstanding of the term as "from/without a house" (thus NIV). Yet the MT does preserve the correct original consonants, which possibly represent "the name of a port city on the Phoenician trade routes (probably on Cyprus). . . . of whose name no trace has been preserved in the historical record" (ibid., n. 21). The reading here follows this suggestion of ***mbyt*** as the name of a port city or harbor.

Word of the devastation of ***Mbyt Harbor*** in some way **has come to them** (i.e., the **ships of Tarshish**) **from the land of *Kittim*** (= Cyprus). Cyprus, the easternmost island in the Mediterranean Sea, would be the last port of call on the homeward journey for these great **ships**, or the first port of call if outbound.

■ **2** The second command, again ***wail*** (*dōmmû*), now turns from ships at sea to those in the homeports. The NIV's **be silent** misunderstands the verb *dmm*, which derives from two different roots: one, "to be silent," the other, "to wail"; the latter is attested in both Akkadian and Ugaritic (*HALOT* 226) and in this poem functions as a synonym of *hll*, "wail" (Isa 23:1, 6). In the home ports are the ***inhabitants*** of the ***coastland*, merchants of Sidon, *whose messengers have crossed over the sea*.** Sidon is the name of both the city and, in Sennacherib's account of his 701 BC military sweep through Phoenicia, the entire southern Phoenician area. Here, in Isaiah's view, Tyre would be included. Ezekiel 27 depicts a detailed account of the Phoenician (Tyrian) trading partners and goods exchanged that would involve extensively ***crossing the*** [Mediterranean] ***sea***.

■ **3** Isaiah 23:3 continues the thought of v 2, concerning the traveling merchants: ***yes, on water, in great numbers*** (Wildberger 1997, 404). **The Shihor** is a synonym for **the Nile**, so that **the grain** and **the harvest** also are synonyms. These were the abundant agricultural products of Egypt paid to the Phoenicians in exchange for goods from other ports of call. Thus this lucrative trade resulted in ***her*** [= Sidon's] **revenue. Yes, she became the marketplace of the nations.**

■ **4** The third command, **be ashamed**, is addressed directly to **Sidon** (representing the area of southern Phoenicia, compare v 2). But, why **be ashamed**? It is ***because*** **the sea has spoken, *the haven/harbor*** [*mā'ôz*] **of the sea**. The noun *mā'ôz* is derived from the root *'wz*, "to seek refuge" (Barré 2004, 117-18, n. 17; the NIV confuses the root with *'zz*, "to be strong," thus, **fortress** [compare vv 11, 14]). The content of ***the sea's*** speech gives the cause for shame: the metaphor is that of a barren wife, unable to bear children, who brings shame upon her husband. Just so, "I have become barren," declares **the sea and *Sidon's harbor***. As a result of the devastation of her **harbors**, Phoenicia's merchant activity on **the sea** will no longer be productive (Wildberger 1997, 426).

■ **5** The sea still is speaking. **Egypt** (compare v 3) is one of Phoenicia's chief trading partners. Thus, **when *the report* comes to Egypt**, that is, **the report** *concerning* Tyre [of the devastation of Phoenicia's ports and seafaring merchant business], **they will be in anguish. Egypt's** prosperity was in large measure tied to that of **Tyre.** Moreover, a military takeover of **Tyre** may well place **Egypt** next in line for the same.

■ **6** The fourth command is double: **Cross over to Tarshish**, and **wail** (*hêlîlû*), addressed to ***those who inhabit the coast***. The poet is satirically urging the inhabitants of the southern Phoenician coastal cities to flee to far-off **Tarshish**. It would be unlikely, however, that a mass evacuation of Phoenician refugees would be undertaken to **Tarshish**, because of its location at the western extremity of the Phoenician merchant world.

■ **7a** The poem continues with a satirical question: ***Could*** **this *have happened to you*, O *exultant one*, [*the one who*], *her origin is from days of old*?** Though the term **city** is not in the Hebrew text, the feminine pronominal suffix (***her***) does imply a reference to a **city**, apparently Tyre (v 8). Tyre was indeed a very ancient city. Herodotus, researching/writing in ca. 450-420 BC (Strassler 2007, x), traveled to Phoenicia and related that he was told there that Tyre "had been inhabited for 2,300 years" at his time (ibid., 137 [Herodotus 2:44]). This claim to antiquity is corroborated by archaeological soundings in the 1970s at the island city of Tyre that reveal initial settlement there in the third millennium BC (Markoe 2000, 17).

■ **7b** The question continues: [***the one who***], ***her*** **feet have *carried*** her to **sojourn** [*lāgûr* from *gwr*] **among far-off lands?** This refers to the so-called Phoenician colonies, established around the Mediterranean Sea for purposes of trade. These included ports at points along the southern boundaries of Europe and along the coast of North Africa. At the eastern end of the sea was the archaeologically and epigrapically confirmed settlement at Kition (*kittîyîm* [v 12]) on Cyprus, dating from about the mid-ninth century BC. On the western extremity of the sea, the archaeological record confirms the presence of Phoenicians in the Andalusian coastal plain of southern Spain, east of Gibraltar, from the eighth century BC onward. The impetus for establishing their presence there was Spain's rich deposits of gold, copper, tin, and silver ores, metals that formed the core of the Phoenician "world-wide" mercantile trade (Markoe 2000, 170-85).

■ **8-9** When Tyre and her "world-wide" mercantile business should be brought down in the future, the response of nations and governments will be to analyze the crash from all political and economic angles. What went wrong? Whose fault was it? Isaiah's response is to satirically ask the same question: **Who planned this against Tyre?** (v 8). And, as a prophet to whom "Sovereign **Yahweh** . . . **reveals** his plan" (Amos 3:7), he rhetorically responds, **Yahweh Sebaoth** planned it (Isa 23:9). Why? It is **to profane [human] pride of all splendor**, not only of Tyre, but to **dishonor all earth-honored ones** (compare 2:11, 17; 5:15; 13:19; 14:12-20).

■ **10** The Hebrew of his verse has made little sense to translators. Barré, on the basis of the LXX's reading and a redivision of the Hebrew words, however, makes good sense of it in the context of the previous commands of the poem. He translates as: "Cross (back) to your own land, for Tarshish has perished, (for) the harbor/port city is no more" (2004, 116-17).

This verse, then, contains the fifth command of the poem: **Cross over, back to your own land**, that is, back to the Phoenician seacoast from Tarshish (to which the Phoenician inhabitants had been advised to flee in 23:6]. But, since **Tarshish has perished** it cannot provide a place of refuge or a haven for the "ships of Tarshish" (vv 1, 14), since **the port city is no more**.

■ **11-12a** As noted in v 10, here, too, **Yahweh** (v 11) is active behind and in the outworking of the events of history. It is **Yahweh [who] has stretched out his hand over the sea**; it is he who **has caused** kingdoms **to** tremble; and, it is he who **has given an order concerning Canaan** [Phoenicia] that her **harbors** [*mā'uznêhā* from *'wz*; → v 4*b*; compare v 14] **be destroyed**.

Virgin Daughter Sidon (v 12) normally would be a title of endearment, but here it is used ironically. This is how you think of yourself, but (Yahweh) has said, **No more . . . reveling, O crushed one!**

■ **12b** Isaiah gives his sixth command: **Arise, cross over to Kittim** (Cyprus), and thus brings us back full circle to v 1, "land of **Kittim**," from which the news of destroyed harbors first comes to the ships of Tarshish. But to believe that one will find **rest** there is "but an illusion" (Wildberger 1997, 432).

■ **13** Isaiah calls upon the Phoenicians to **look** to the east, to the interplay between **Assyria** and **the land of the Chaldeans** (Babylonians). Of the Baby-

Ionians he says, ***this is the people which is not***. While in the above satirical prophecy of Yahweh's destruction of Phoenicia's mercantile "splendor" (v 9), Isaiah has the distant future in view; here he is speaking of the recent campaigns of **Assyria** against Babylon. In those campaigns, **Assyria**, as God's agent of judgment, nearly wiped out the city of Babylon. Sargon's 710 BC campaign and Sennacherib's 689 BC campaign would be well known to both Isaiah and the Phoenicians. When ***Yahweh Sebaoth has planned*** (v 9) and then "has given an order" (v 11), neither Babylon nor Tyre nor any other great world center, in all its pride and splendor, can escape.

■ **14** The seventh command is given: **Wail** [*hêlîlû*], **O ships of Tarshish, because devastated is your harbor** (*mā'uzzĕkem* from *'wz*; → v 4*b*; compare v 11). This forms an inclusio with v 1. Isaiah's prophecy is that someday, in Yahweh's time, the vast sea-spanning Phoenician mercantile enterprise will grind to a stop. It will be remembered only in brief phrases here and there in the literature of the nations, and will be materially seen only in the bits and pieces of its wares and an occasional structural corner or foundation in archaeological digs.

2. Tyre's Future Restoration (23:15-18)

■ **15-18** In this passage, Isaiah contrasts the concepts of "to forget" (*škḥ*) and "to visit" (*pqd*): ***It shall be in that day that*** Tyre will be forgotten for seventy years (v 15). . . . ***But at the end of seventy years, Yahweh*** will ***visit*** Tyre (v 17). **Visit** implies that **Yahweh** will "remember" **Tyre**, so that her former mercantile trading connections **with all the kingdoms on the face of the earth** will be restored.

The expressions **seventy years** (vv 15, 17) and **the span of a king's life** (v 15) are to be taken as figures of fullness or completeness (Oswalt 1986, 435); that is, when a certain time period is complete (God's time) God will act. A nonbiblical witness to the wider ancient Near Eastern metaphorical use of **seventy years** as a period for a city to remain in a state of desolation comes from the Black Stone of Esarhaddon. Following Assyrian Sennacherib's destruction of Babylon in 689 BC, Assyrian Esarhaddon says concerning the city: "Seventy years as the period of its desolation he (Marduk) wrote down (in the book of fate)" (Luckenbill 1925, 167).

In **the song of the prostitute** (vv 15-16), **Tyre** is likened to a **forgotten** [*škḥ*] **prostitute** but not necessarily for the immorality of her deeds. Rather, it is because her "splendor" (v 9), once sought by many lovers (= "kingdoms" [v 11]), has been spurned (**forgotten**) for a period of time. As the **prostitute** has ***gone about*** the city (v 16), seeking customers to no avail, so **Tyre** has sought trading partners during this period of God's "time out," but all her partners have **forgotten** (*škḥ*) her (v 15).

As strange as it may seem to our modern-day sensitivities, however, God's grace intervenes: just as the **prostitute** will one day **be remembered** (*zkr* [v 16]), so ***Yahweh will visit*** [*pqd*] **Tyre. She will return to . . . her trade with all the kingdoms** (v 17). **Her** *profits* **and her earnings** will again flow into her treasury. But they will now be put to ***Yahweh's*** use (v 18). Motyer comments, "What a picture then Isaiah gives of transformation: the converted prostitute consecrating all that the old life, now past and gone, had meant and gained" (1993, 193).

FROM THE TEXT

With this chapter concerning Tyre, Isaiah concludes his oracles concerning the nations, which began in ch 13. In that chapter it was the great eastern city of Babylon upon which God was bringing and would bring judgment. In ch 23 it is the great western city of Tyre that God will, in his time, bring to nonexistence. Other nations within Isaiah's world are the concern of the chapters in between, all of which also are under the judgment of God.

The prophecies, while at times appearing to be addressed to the nations themselves, are spoken within the boundaries of Judah, most likely within Jerusalem and probably often at the royal court. Thus the true audience is Judah generally and Judah's leaders specifically.

The historical context within which Isaiah gave the prophecies was a time when Assyria, the power broker of Isaiah's world, seemed invincible, and from a human viewpoint, destined to control this whole "world." As always, however, there were glimmers of other powers rising, with whom it might be advisable to throw in one's lot, in this case with Babylon and/or Egypt, against the greater power or with Tyre/Phoenicia for its commercial strength. Isaiah's message to Judah, however, is not to fall prey to such temptations. Her (and our) protection is not in alliances with the nations but in a continued and deep reliance upon God, ***Yahweh Sebaoth***.

I. Two Cities and Yahweh Triumphant (24:1—27:13)

Apocalypse of Isaiah

Earlier scholars viewed chs 24—27 of the Isaiah corpus as apocalyptic, calling it the "Apocalypse of Isaiah" or the "Little Apocalypse," suggesting that the material was generated in a setting similar to the book of Daniel much later than the time of Isaiah. As such, it was held that the four-chapter segment could be viewed as a unit quite independently from the material that both preceded and followed it. This view did a grave injustice to the canonical flow of the Isaiah corpus as it has come to us. A number of scholars today, however, in varying degrees, see that the themes of chs 24—27 must be interpreted in the context of the themes introduced in chs 13—23. Childs, for example, points out that God's actions in 24:1-3 were first mentioned in ch 13, which "had spoken about 'destroying the whole earth' (v. 5), 'making the earth a waste' (v. 9), and 'punishing the world for its evil' (v. 11)" (2001, 178).

Generally, however, the prophet moves from Yahweh's more specific dealings with individual nations and with Israel/Judah in chs 13—23, to the broader perspective of Yahweh's lordship over the whole earth in chs 24—27. The four chapters can be divided into two units: (1) chs 24—25 focus on "*a* fortified **city**" (*qiryāh bĕṣûrāh*), representative of the entire world, which Yahweh makes "a heap of rubble" (25:2); (2) chs 26—27 focus on "a strong city" (*'îr 'āz*), which opens its gates to the "righteous nation . . . that keeps faith" (26:1-2). This latter city represents a place of salvation, security, and safety to all those who, amid the judgment of the nations, turn to Yahweh, who is both Judge and Savior.

1. The Earth Laid Waste (24:1-23)

BEHIND THE TEXT

Chapter 24 focuses on God as **Yahweh** (vv 1, 3, 14, 15, 21), "**Yahweh**, the God of Israel" (v 15), and **Yahweh Sebaoth** (v 23). **Yahweh** stands as Judge of "the earth" (*hā'āreṣ* [v 1, plus sixteen times]) and "its inhabitants" (v 1), which have "disobeyed the laws, violated the statutes and broken the everlasting covenant" (v 5). Behind this is the Creator's expectation that, from the time of creation, humanity would live in obedience and fellowship with him. In return for such obedient living, the Creator promised life in abundance. As a consequence of continual disobedience, however, such abundant life would ultimately be taken away.

Chapter 24 can be divided into six units: vv 1-6, the earth is devastated; vv 7-12, joy is banished from the earth; vv 13-16*a*, glorify Yahweh!; vv 16*b*-18*a*, terror all around; vv 18*b*-20, earth is violently shaken; and, vv 21-23, Yahweh Sebaoth will reign.

IN THE TEXT

a. The Earth Is Devastated (24:1-6)

■ **1-3** Isaiah's description of the judgment of **Yahweh** against **the earth** is graphic (v 1): **lay waste, devastate,** *twist* [*'iwwâ*] **its face.** Though no reason for judgment is given here, none of **its inhabitants** escape the effects of judgment, which cut across all levels of society and ranks. Boundaries that enabled "permanently differentiated social levels, so detested by God" (Wildberger 1997, 451) will disappear. Those who for long have held power, **priest, master/mistress, seller, lender, creditor** (v 2), will receive no preferential exemptions. Nor will common **people,** *slave,* **buyer, borrower, debtor,** or **creditor** be singled out for enhanced judgment. The prophet confirms that **Yahweh has spoken this word** (v 3).

■ **4-6** These verses speak of the **earth** having become **defiled** because **its inhabitants** have disobeyed/violated/broken the everlasting covenant (*běrît 'ôlām* [v 5]). This results in a **curse** (*'ālâ*) that **consumes the earth** (v 6).

The expression **everlasting covenant** (v 5) is applied to God's covenant with Noah and all living creatures (Gen 9:16), to God's covenant with Abraham, Isaac, and Jacob (Ps 105:9-10), to the Sabbath within the Mosaic covenant (Lev 24:8), and to God's covenant with David (2 Sam 23:5; compare Isa 55:3, where it is given messianic application). Wildberger points out that, in the OT, the concept of breaking **the everlasting covenant** appears only in Isa 24:5. He suggests that the prophet here is mixing the concepts of God's covenant with Noah, an eternal covenant, and consequently could not be broken, and those of God's covenant with Israel at Sinai, a covenant between partners, which could be broken (1997, 480).

In the covenant that God made "with all living creatures of every kind on the earth" (Gen 9:16; see vv 8-17) after the flood, he had promised that "never again will the waters become a flood to destroy all life" (v 15). But, here Isaiah says that **the earth dries up and withers** (Isa 24:4), apparently because **the curse** (v 6) is God's withholding of water, one of the consequences listed for breaking the Sinai covenant (Deut 28:23-24). Thus Isaiah extends earlier covenant terminology to apply to the whole **earth**: because **the [*whole*] earth has been** defiled by its **inhabitants**; . . . a curse consumes the [*whole*] earth (Isa 24:5-6).

Because of the **curse** . . . **earth's inhabitants** *diminish* (*hārû* from *hrh* II, "to decrease," "to diminish in number;" the NIV's **burned up** assumes the root *hrh* I, "to grow hot [with anger]" [*HALOT* 351]). The result of the **curse** is that *those left of humanity* [*'ĕnôš*] *are* very **few** (lit. *a littleness*). These **few** who remain, like Noah, are recipients of God's "grace" (Gen 9:6) (Motyer 1993, 200).

b. Joy Is Banished from the Earth (24:7-12)

■ **7-9** Because the **vine withers** (v 7; just as "the earth dries up" in v 4), there is no **new wine**. On the one hand, wine drinking is associated with times of joy, such as harvests, weddings, and births. Thus is depicted the cessation of human joyfulness at those times of celebration among inhabitants of a healthy community. **The merrymakers** and **revelers** (v 8) are no longer heard, the **timbrels** and **harp** are **silent**, no **wine** (v 9) with **song**. On the other hand, 5:11-12 associates the drinking of wine, accompanied by the sound of musical instruments at banquets, with those who "have no regard for the deeds of **Yahweh**." So, the effect of God's "curse" (24:6) falls alike upon both the just and the unjust. No one escapes (v 2).

■ **10-12** The focus turns from the inhabitants to the **city** itself, which, when viewed in the larger context of the text is not any one specific city but represents the world (Oswalt 1986, 448). Verse 10 describes the city as a *formless* city (*qiryat tōhû*, "nothing-city" [Wildberger 1997, 487]) that **lies broken**. The term *tōhû*, the opposite of order and stability, describes the chaotic condition of the heavens and earth before God made earth habitable for humanity (Gen 1:2). So, the **city** (= the world), following God's judgment, has reverted to a condition unfit for habitation. The prophet notes that **shut up is every house from entering**, denoting the pervading atmosphere of fear of the few remaining inhabitants.

Isaiah 24:11 describes the disappearance of joy from the streets of the city. Where there is no **wine,** the imagined **joy** that it produces **turns to gloom**. The prophet adds, **There remains in** the city [only] **horror,** [its] **ruined** gate **crushed** (v 12). This depicts both defenselessness and inactivity. We see no elders sitting at the gates, deciding important matters of community life; we neither hear the sounds of the hustle and bustle of commerce, nor observe the comings and goings of locals and visitors.

The Timbrel and the Harp

The *tōp*, translated as "timbrel" (see 24:8) or "tambourine" (e.g., ESV, NASB) in the OT, designates many kinds of handheld percussion instruments, struck with the hand. One simple kind is the frame drum, consisting of a piece of goatskin stretched over a frame of wood. These were frequently played by women while dancing in greeting and celebration, as they did when David returned from killing the Philistine (1 Sam 18:6).

The *kinnôr* is translated as "harp" (Isa 24:8) or "lyre" (e.g., ESV, NRSV) in the OT, though lyre is probably more accurate. This is the most often mentioned stringed instrument in the OT. This instrument had a wooden sound box at its base with two arms extending upward from each end; a yoke (bar) extended across the top, joining the two arms. The instrument was strung with four to eight strings from base to yoke, which were plucked with the right hand. The *kinnôr* was associated with joyous occasions. Thus the Jewish captives in Babylon hung theirs on "the poplars," refusing to sing "the songs of Zion" (Ps 137:2-3).

c. Glorify Yahweh! (24:13-16a)

■ **13** The prophet confirms that "city" in vv 10 and 11 refers to "the world": **For** so it will be **in the midst of** the earth [*'āreṣ*] **in the midst of the peoples** (*'ammîm*). God's judgment will be worldwide. The metaphor, **as when an olive tree is beaten,** that earlier predicted Israel's condition following God's judgment (17:6), is here applied to **the earth/the peoples**. After the harvest, a few only remain. But, Isaiah turns despair to hope, for suddenly the **gleanings** are being gathered (Motyer 1993, 202).

■ **14** This verse opens with the emphatic pronoun **they** (*hēmmâ*), which Motyer translates as "*These are* they *who*," identifying them with the "gleanings" of v 13 and the "few" of v 6 (ibid.). These are the ones who, **from the** west (*miyyām*, "from [the Mediterranean] Sea"), **raise their voices, *sing* for joy, [*and*] in Yahweh's majesty *rejoice*.** The Mediterranean Sea represents the western extremity of the "world" of Isaiah's time.

■ **15** As Isaiah, in his prophetic imagination, hears the singing from the west, he commands **the east** (*'urîm*, "region of light" [*HALOT* 25], where the sun arises), to join in with an antiphonal response: **honor Yahweh!** (*kabbĕdû yhwh*). Then, let **the islands of the sea** join in this festal response to **the name** [= power] **of Yahweh, the God of Israel.**

■ **16a** This verse summarizes the worldwide choir: **from the ends of the earth we hear singing**, the survivors of the worldwide judgment, making their way to Zion, singing **Beauty** [*ṣĕbî*] **to the Righteous One.** Perhaps here Isaiah depicts the start of the pilgrimage of the nations to Zion, pictured in 2:2-4 (Kaiser 1972, 27; 1974, 188).

d. Terror All Around (24:16b-18a)

■ **16b-18a** God's worldwide judgment and the rejoicing of the survivors, however, still lie far in the future. The cry, **I waste away, I waste away! Woe to me!** (v 16b), reveals the prophet's deep anguish at what he knows is still in store for **the inhabitants** of the earth (v 17). Humanity's practices of treachery and **terror** perpetrated against one another continue unabated.

e. Earth Is Violently Shaken (24:18b-20)

■ **18b-20** The ***windows*** **of the heavens** (v 18b) is the same expression as in Gen 7:11. Here, along with the great outpouring of water from above comes a violent shaking of **the foundations of the earth.** This combination causes **the earth** to **split asunder** (Isa 24:19). The cause for this total collapse of earth's structure is earth's inability to any longer bear the weight of humanity's **rebellion** (v 20). So, there is a moral cause for bringing this world to an end: humanity's continued living as though God does not exist, or if he does exist, he has nothing to do with how we live (compare Ps 73:11).

f. Yahweh Sebaoth Will Reign (24:21-23)

■ **21 In that day** obviously refers to that future culminating time when the total collapse of earth's structure brings an end to this world and its historical process. At that time Yahweh **will punish** both **the powers in the heavens above** and **the kings on the earth below.** The first **(powers in the heavens)** may have embryonic reference to created angelic beings that oppose God, though this is a much later development in Jewish theological thought (compare *1 En.* 6—10). The second **(kings on the earth)** echoes Isa 14:12-21 in which the haughty world leader is "brought down to ***Sheol***" (v 15), there to join other "kings of the nations" (v 18).

■ **22** The powers in heaven and the kings on earth who opposed God will be dealt with in two stages. First, they will be rounded up and **shut up in** prison for a period of time. Then, **after many days, *they will* be punished**. The time that elapses in prison before their punishment is carried out is not stated. Wildberger, however, suggests that here may be the earliest hint at what will later develop "into the concept of a [two-phase] drama at the end time," and draws attention to Rev 20:1-10. There, Satan is imprisoned in the Abyss for one thousand years, after which he is released for a while, then executed (1997, 508; also Blenkinsopp 2000, 357).

■ **23** The prophet does not use the astronomical terms for **the moon** and **the sun** (though he does in 13:10 in a similar context: *yārēaḥ* and *šemeš*), which, in the cultures surrounding Israel, often grant them the status of deity to be worshipped. Rather, he designates **the moon** as "the white one" (*hallĕbānâ*) and **the sun** as "the glowing/hot one" (*haḥammâ*). In doing so, he deprives them of any status as deities; they are simply created objects that give light, but whose light is derived from the Creator. In that final day, to be "unmasked" [as nondeities] and their "meaninglessness exposed" can only cause them to **be ashamed** (Wildberger 1997, 510).

Isaiah foresees that ***Yahweh Sebaoth* will reign on Mount Zion and in Jerusalem, and *opposite* [*neged*] *his* elders**. The Hebrew text has ***his* elders**, though one expects **its** [i.e., Jerusalem's] **elders** (which the NIV and Oswalt [1986, 440] have opted; but compare Wildberger [1997, 504] and Kaiser [1974, 192]). It appears that in the background here is the theophany on Mount Sinai when "seventy elders of Israel" accompanied Moses to its top, and there "they saw God, and they ate and drank" (Exod 24:9, 11). Yet this scene appears again in Rev 4:4, 9-11, where "twenty-four elders," sitting on thrones, surround God's heavenly throne, giving "glory" to "our Lord and God." These elders are not designated elders of Israel; they appear to belong to God's entourage. So, perhaps Isaiah has purposely chosen his pronoun: the **elders** on **Mount Zion**, in whose ***presence* [*neged*] *Yahweh Sebaoth* reigns**, are ***his* elders**.

In the final (Heb.) phrase of this verse, the absence of a verb or preposition preceding the final word, *kābôd* ("glory"), troubles translators. Thus most add words for intended clarification, such as the NIV's **with great glory**, though there is no grammatical justification for doing so. Motyer suggests that the Hebrew here is exclamatory: "and before his elders, glory!" (1993, 207). (Compare Ps 29:9 where the final Hebrew word, *kābôd*, is clearly exclamatory: "Glory!"; also, in Ps 73:24, the psalmist cries, "And afterward, ***Glory! you will receive me.***")

FROM THE TEXT

At the conclusion of ch 24, Isaiah makes a metaphorical play on the inadequacy of the light of the moon and sun in that final day of humanity's judgment, when Yahweh's "reign on Mount Zion, in Jerusalem," is made manifest (v 23). Because of the overwhelming brilliance of the "glory" of **Yahweh Sebaoth**, the light of the sun and moon, though originally appointed by God to "give light on the earth" (Gen 1:15), will no longer be needed.

John, in developing his testimony to Jesus as "the Lamb of God, who takes away the sin of the world" (John 1:29), begins at the point of "light." This Lamb, John says, is "the light [*that*] shines in the darkness" (v 5), "the true light that gives light to everyone" (v 9). With the Lamb as light, John associates "glory": "We have seen his glory, the glory of the one and only Son, who came from the Father, full of grace and truth" (v 14). Moreover, says John, his glory was seen as he "became flesh and made his dwelling among us" (v 14). Here John is speaking of Christ's first coming to dwell among humanity.

In Revelation, John visualizes Christ's second coming to dwell among humanity. He speaks of a "Holy City, the new Jerusalem, coming down out of heaven" as the place where God will dwell "among the people" (21:2, 3). Some commentators understand the new Jerusalem "as a symbol of the church in its perfected and eternal state" (Mounce 1977, 370). This eternal kingdom, this "city does not need the sun or the moon to shine on it, for the glory of God gives it light, and the Lamb is its lamp" (v 23). Moreover, in this eternal kingdom, "the nations" do continue in existence, for, says John, they "will walk by its light" (v 24). In some sense, this new Jerusalem, and the dwelling of God and the Lamb within it, symbolizes a return to the conditions of pre-fall Eden: the absence of evil (v 8), the tree of life now available "for the healing of the nations" (22:2) and especially the removal of the "curse" (22:3).

In the new Jerusalem, the eternal kingdom, just as Isaiah saw **Yahweh Sebaoth** together with those who serve him (***his* elders**) in each other's presence on "Mount Zion . . . in Jerusalem" (Isa 24:23), so does John: "The throne of God and of the Lamb will be in the city, and his servants will serve him. They will see his face, and his name will be on their foreheads" (Rev 22:3-4). To see someone's face is to be in that person's presence, to be face-to-face. These "servants" are we "who are victorious," says John; we "will inherit all this" (21:7).

Concerning **Yahweh Sebaoth** of Isa 24:23, Wesley observes, "The Messiah . . . shall come in the flesh, and set up his kingdom, first in Jerusalem, and afterward in all other nations" (n.d., 3512).

2. Yahweh Sebaoth's Banquet (25:1-12)

BEHIND THE TEXT

This twelve-verse song can be divided into three units. The first (vv 1-5), sung in the singular ("my," "I" [v 1]), is a paean of praise to **Yahweh**, who "has been a refuge for the poor [and] the needy" (v 4). The second (vv 6-8) builds on the theme of 24:21-23, which declared the future establishing of the "reign" of **Yahweh Sebaoth** on "Mount Zion"; now, "on this mountain **Yahweh Sebaoth**," in celebration, "will prepare a feast of rich food for all peoples." The third (25:9-12), sung in the plural ("our," "we," "us" [v 9]), *rejoices* in the "salvation" of **Yahweh**. **God's** judgment, however, still goes out against the "pride" (v 11) of the nations, exemplified in "Moab" (v 10).

Motyer makes note of the worldwide song of 24:16, there titled "**Beauty** to the Righteous One." He observes that in ch 25 we now hear that song in detail, "as the world pilgrimage arrives in Zion," where the city has been made ready and a feast prepared (1993, 207).

IN THE TEXT

a. Yahweh, a Refuge for the Poor and Needy (25:1-5)

■ **I** The singer claims a personal relationship with **Yahweh**: **you are my God**. **Yahweh** is not a deity detached from the realities of the singer's everyday life. **Name** is a metaphor for God's character and reputation, which calls forth personal response: **I will exalt you**; *I will* **praise your name**. Why? Because of the **wonderful things . . . you have done, . . . things planned long ago**. These include not only those wonders God does in the grand scheme of the universe but also **things planned** even for me, help that I have personally experienced. **In perfect faithfulness** you do not forget me.

■ **2** It is within God's action of making *a* **city a heap of rubble** that the singer views God's individual faithfulness of v 1. The **city** and the **fortified town** are the same here as in 24:10-13, not any specific city, but representative of human power and pride in the world. In the midst of God's judgment on human arrogance, the singer holds steady in God.

■ **3** The MT has the singular: *a* **strong** *people* and *a* **city** of **ruthless nations**, a reference to the "nothing-city" of 24:10 (Wildberger 1997, 487). The singular represents the "world structured without reference to God" (Motyer 1993, 208). In response to God's humbling judgment, the leaders of this "world city" **will honor** and **will revere** Israel's God. Motyer points out, however, that this does not require that we understand that they "have come to faith in the Lord," but only that the overthrow of their system demands "respect" and "fear" (ibid.).

■ **4-5** **The poor** (*dāl*) and **the needy** (*'ebyôn* [25:4]), in combination elsewhere in the OT, are the oppressed (compare Exod 23:3-6; 1 Sam 2:8; Pss 72:13; 82:4; 113:7; Isa 14:30; 25:4; Amos 2:6-7; 4:1; 8:6). Here most likely they refer to Israel, Yahweh's faithful community, for whom Yahweh has **been a refuge** (*mā'ôz*, "a stronghold," "a fortress"). God as a **refuge** is further characterized as **a shelter from the storm** (*zerem*, "cloudburst," "inundation"), and **a shade from the** [dry, exhausting] **heat**. The sudden **storm** that can sweep one away in the desert ravines and the **heat** that can bring one to death's door with thirst, though they are contrastive extremes, metaphorically express the totality of danger from which God protects his own from **the breath of the ruthless**. Within Yahweh's **refuge**, beneath his **shelter, the song of the ruthless is stilled** (v 5).

b. Yahweh Sebaoth Prepares a Banquet (25:6-8)

■ **6** The prophet returns us to **this mountain**, pointing to Mount Zion of 24:23, on which **Yahweh Sebaoth's** reign will be revealed. Here, **Yahweh Sebaoth will prepare a feast of rich food**. We hear echoes of Moses and the elders of Israel, representing all Israel, on the top of Mount Sinai, enjoying a meal with God (Exod 24:9-11). But, now, on Mount Zion, the **banquet** that God will prepare will be **for all peoples**. This will include regathered Israel and those from out of all nations who have survived God's judgment because they have turned in faith to Israel's God.

■ **7** Both Isa 25:7 and 8 begin with *bl'*, "to swallow," in the intensive form, with the extended meaning, "to swallow completely." Thus Yahweh Sebaoth will *swallow completely* the shroud that *shrouds* all peoples, the *covering that covers all nations*. Verse 7 anticipates v 8: **the shroud/the** *covering* of v 7 is equated with "death" in v 8.

■ **8 Death**, resulting from humanity's rebellion against God in Eden, affects "all peoples" (v 7). Yet "on this mountain" (v 7), that is, on Mount Zion, God **will swallow** *completely* **death**. Oswalt observes that before human beings "can experience the joy of God's great feast [of v 6]," this "universal curse" would need to be dealt with. This, he further observes, has been accomplished in the death and resurrection of Jesus Christ on Mount Zion. "Death has been defeated once and for all, for all the peoples of the earth" (1986, 454).

The prophet now speaks of God as **Sovereign Yahweh** who, in his reign from Mount Zion, in conjunction with abolishing death, **will wipe away the tears from all faces** (v 8). Because death is no more, mourning and sorrow for departed loved ones also will be no more (compare Rev 21:3-4).

One final benefit of God's reign from Mount Zion is promised: **he will remove his people's** [= Israel's] **disgrace from all the earth**. **Disgrace** resulted from both Israel's refusal, at times, to obey God's requirements, and at other times from her refusal to compromise those requirements, living as a people unique among her neighbors. In God's reign from Mount Zion, **his people's disgrace** for her failures and on account of the derision from the nations will be no more.

c. Rejoicing in Yahweh's Salvation (25:9-12)

This portion is a call to the community of those from the nations who have made the pilgrimage to Zion. They are to take up the song as part of the banquet that Yahweh Sebaoth is giving on Mount Zion (v 6).

■ **9-10a** **In that day** (v 9) looks both back to "that day" in 24:21, when Yahweh punishes the powers of both heaven and earth, and forward to the judgment upon Moab in v 10*b*.

They will say (v 9) is singular in the Hebrew (*wĕ'āmar*), implying **he** or **one** or, perhaps best, **And each will say**. What **each** says, together, becomes the unified chorus of the believing community. In unison they sing, **Behold our God! This one!** (*hinnēh 'ĕlōhênû zeh*; Waltke and O'Connor [1990, 310] explain this function of the demonstrative pronoun *zeh*). **We *waited in hope for* him, and he saved us. This one! Yahweh! We *waited in hope for* him**; let us rejoice and *let us* be glad in his salvation. Verse 10*a* answers the unasked but implied question, Why? **Because** [*kî*; omitted in the NIV] **the hand of Yahweh will rest on *the* mountain, *this one!*** (v 10*a*). **Hand** implies strength, ensuring the believing community of Yahweh's protection.

■ **10b-12** **But Moab** is contrastive: there is no protection for her. **Moab** is singled out for her **pride** (v 11), as previously in 16:6. The prophet uses a rather grotesque metaphor to depict Moab's fate: **as straw trampled down in *a watery* manure *pile*** (25:10), from which, though try as she might, she cannot **swim** her way out (v 11). But, in both the context of this chapter, and the larger context of chs 13—27, Moab here represents all the rebellious powers of heaven and earth that refuse to acknowledge the supremacy of Yahweh Sebaoth. The implication is that these rebellious powers will not be included among "all peoples" who joyously participate in Yahweh's "feast" on Mount Zion (25:6).

FROM THE TEXT

Isaiah 25 focuses on God's future reign on/from Mount Zion. Associated with God's future reign is (1) the banquet that he prepares on Mount Zion for all peoples/all nations, and (2) his swallowing up of death forever, while wiping away all human tears (vv 6-8).

Beyond the OT, in the Qumran literature there is the concept of a messianic banquet to be held in the last days when the "Messiah of Israel" appears among the *Yahad* (Community). This banquet, however, is for certain priests and the heads of Israel's clans (1QSa, Col. 2; Wise, Abegg, and Cook 1996, 144, 147). That is, it is not for all peoples, as it is in Isa 25 but is limited to Israel through its representative heads.

In the NT we find several allusions to and imageries of the messianic banquet. Jesus speaks of such a banquet in Matt 22:2-14. Though cast in terms of a wedding feast, certain elements echo Isaiah's feast given by Yahweh: the venue is the kingdom of heaven/the reign of a king; a feast of fattened animals is prepared; the residents of a city are invited; in arrogance and disdain they refuse the invitation; in judgment, the king destroys them and their city, for they "were not worthy" (v 8 NASB).

Jesus makes two other possible allusions to an end-time banquet. In Matt 8:12 he speaks of an ingathering of "many [*who*] will come from the east and the west, and will take their places at the feast with Abraham, Isaac and Jacob in the kingdom of heaven" (compare Luke 13:29). In Luke 22:29-30, to his disciples he said, "I confer on you a kingdom, just as my father conferred one on me, so that you may eat and drink at my table in my kingdom."

In Rev 19:9 John records the words that an angel from heaven commanded him to write: "Blessed are those who are invited to the wedding supper of the Lamb!" The angel then states, "These are the true words of God," an authentication echoing Isaiah's "**Yahweh** has spoken" following his prophecy of Yahweh's coming banquet on Mount Zion (25:8).

Isaiah's concept of Yahweh's abolishing death (v 8) is viewed in the NT as having been accomplished in the death and resurrection of Jesus Christ on Mount Zion. Paul especially makes this argument in 1 Cor 15:12-57. In this passage he argues that because "Christ has indeed been raised from the dead, the firstfruits of those who have fallen asleep. . . . so in Christ all will be made alive." This will happen in "the end" at the time when "he [Christ] hands over the kingdom to God the father." This will happen only "after he [i.e., Christ] has destroyed all dominion, authority and power," and lastly, "death" (vv 20, 22, 24, 26). Near the conclusion of his argument, Paul exclaims with a quote from Isa 25:8, "Death has been swallowed up in victory" (1 Cor 15:54). Paul is surely quoting Isa 25:8 here, though he is giving *nṣḥ* its Aramaic meaning, "victory" (*HALOT* 716), rather than its Hebrew meaning, "forever."

In the Apocalypse John records seeing in a vision the risen Christ, who said to him, "I am the First and the Last. I am the Living One; I was dead, and now look, I am alive for ever and ever! And I hold the keys of death and Hades" (Rev 1:17-18). Later in his vision, when seeing the Holy City, the new Jerusalem descending from heaven to earth, a voice from heaven declared that this signified that in a new way God will dwell among humanity. In doing so, God will act to wipe away all tears from humanity's eyes because death, mourning, and crying will be abolished. This will be possible because of the passing away of "the old order" and the "making [of] everything new" (Rev 21:3-5).

3. In that Day (26:1—27:1)

BEHIND THE TEXT

Scholars differ widely concerning the literary makeup of chs 26—27, especially ch 26. No consensus is discernible; thus, "the present shape of the text" (Oswalt 1986, 470) produces the most fruitful interpretation.

Moreover, chs 26 and 27 must not be interpreted separately from chs 24 and 25. Some of the intertwined themes are: (1) The theme of "city" (*'îr/qiryâ*) is continued in 26:1-2, 5 and 27:10 (compare 24:10, 12; 25:2). (2) There is continued concern for "the earth" (*'ereṣ*) and "the world" (*tēbal*) in 26:9, 18, 19, 21 and 27:6 (compare 24:1, 3, 4, 5, 6, 13, 16, 18, 19, 20, 21; 25:8). (3) The concept of ***waiting in hope*** (*kwh*) for God to act recurs in 26:8 (→ 25:9; compare 25:9 [2x]). (4) God's "salvation" (*yĕšûʿâ*) is an established reality in 26:1 (compare 25:9). (5) God remains sovereign over both his chosen people (Israel) in their present circumstance and the peoples of the world.

The two chapters can be viewed in five units: (1) A city whose gates are open (26:1-6); (2) God makes level the path of the righteous, while the unrighteous reject God's grace (vv 7-15); (3) Israel laments the failure of her witness, yet God brings new life out of the dust (vv 16-19); (4) God's people hide while God punishes the people of the earth for their iniquity (v 20—27:1); and (5) God's vineyard is revisited (vv 2-13).

IN THE TEXT

a. A City Whose Gates Are Open (26:1-6)

■ 1 The opening phrase, **in that day**, links what follows with the previous two chapters (compare 24:21; 25:9). The venue for **this song**, which applies to all of ch 26, is **the land of Judah**. The singers (**we**) are the inhabitants of the **strong city**, which is metaphorically Jerusalem, from which Yahweh Sebaoth has come to reign (compare 24:23, where the singer was an individual). Though the term **God** is not in the MT, the NIV's interpretation is correct: it is only God who can, like constructing strong **walls and ramparts**, with **salvation** guarantee the security of the city.

■ 2 In contrast to "the ruined city" (24:10), whose gates lie crushed (24:12), the singers command the gatekeepers of this city to **open the gates** so that any **nation** (*gôy*) that is **righteous** (*ṣaddîq*) freely **may enter**. Righteousness is further defined as ***keeping*** faith (*'ĕmunîm*). But a nation can be deemed as keeping faith only in terms of the actions of its individual members. Wildberger notes that in the OT faithfulness focuses on an individual's reliability in the realm of ethical behavior (1997, 547). For example, one might ask: Is this person a "trustworthy [*'ĕmunîm*] envoy" (Prov 13:17)? Or is he or she an "honest [*'ĕmunîm*] witness" (Prov 14:5)? Or is one a "faithful [*'ĕmunîm*] person," that is, is one truly who he or she claims to be, one who exhibits "unfailing love [*ḥesed*, 'loyalty']" (Prov 20:6)? In John's vision of the Holy City/the new Jerusalem, "its gates" are always open to "those whose names are written in the Lamb's book of life." Excluded are any who are "impure" or who do "shameful or deceitful" things (Rev 21:25, 27).

■ 3 The righteous nation is further defined as encompassing those citizens who **trust in you**, that is, in God. **Trust**, says Wildberger, "is not just an action that happens by chance, but it is an ongoing, reliable way of life" (ibid.). It is this "way of life" that is indicated by the **steadfast *mind*** (or ***intent***). Thus the person who steadfastly relies on God, God **will keep in perfect peace** (*šālôm šālôm*, "peace, peace"). One is reminded of a common greeting in modern Israel: *shalom shalom*.

■ **4** The "trust" noted in v 3 is now further defined as **trust in Yahweh**. Moreover, **Yahweh** is described as a **Rock**, but not just any rock, in itself a symbol of reliability. **Yah, Yahweh** is a **Rock eternal**, which never changes. Because of God's eternalness, then, we can trust him **forever**.

■ **5-6** In contrast to the "strong city" (v 1) for which God provides salvation, the **lofty city** (v 5) "symbolizes the world organized without God" (Motyer 1993, 214). As such, it represents the pride and arrogance of humanity noted earlier (e.g., 2:9-18; 5:15; 14:12-15; 16:6). Such arrogance cannot stand before the "Rock eternal" (v 4). He **casts it** [i.e., **the lofty city**] **down to the dust** where the tables are now turned: arrogant humanity formerly ground "the faces of the poor [*'ăniyîm*]" into the dust (3:15); now the **oppressed** (*'onî* [v 6]) and the **poor** (*dallîm*) **trample** them into the dust.

b. A Level Path; Rejected Grace (26:7-15)

■ **7-8** The **righteous** (*ṣaddîq* [v 7]) are often equated with the poor and needy, those powerless persons of society whom the powerful oppress (compare Amos 2:6-7, where the powerful trample their heads into "the dust of the ground" [v 7]). The mention of "the feet of the oppressed" in Isa 26:6 leads the singer to speak metaphorically of **the path** (*'ōraḥ* [v 7]), which the feet of the **righteous** take through life's journey, negotiating **the way** [*'ōraḥ*] **of your** [i.e., God's] **judgments** (*mišpāṭîm*). God's *mišpāṭîm* here are both "the individual commandments as well as the summary of the entire law" (*TDOT* 9:94), which God has given to govern how his people are to conduct their lives.

The singer indicates, however, that living according to God's *mišpāṭîm* is an intertwined combination of human **walking** (v 8) and God acting: **O Upright One** (v 7), you go before, **making** all **level** and **smooth**. He acknowledges, however, that along the way there are times when one must **wait** *in hope* (v 8) or **wait expectantly** for God to act. While waiting, the singer says, **the desire** *of one's entire being* (*nepeš*; **our hearts**) is [*to name*] **your name** [*šēm* = "reputation"] **and** [*to invoke*] **remembrance** [*zēker*] **of you**. That is, to recall how you, Yahweh, have acted in the past helps us to know how you will act in the future.

■ **9** The prophet uses two terms as emphatic substitutes for the pronoun "I." Thus he exclaims: ***I*** [*napěšî*, "my entire being"], ***I yearn*** **for you in the night, Yes,** ***I*** [*rûḥî*, "my spirit/breath" (that which enlivens one's entire being)], **in the morning** ***I seek*** **you**. Then, picking up the thought of v 8, he continues: ***For*** [*kî*, omitted in the NIV] **when your judgments** [*mišpāṭîm*] **are on the earth** [*'ereṣ*], **the** ***inhabitants*** **of the world** [*tēbēl*] **learn righteousness**. Only as God's system of law prevails can righteousness be the order of the day in the world's societies.

■ **10** But, there is **the wicked one** (sg., but representative of many), who, **when grace is shown never** [*bal*] **learns righteousness**. Even when he dwells in a **land of uprightness**, a community or society that essentially follows the "judgments" (*mišpāṭîm*) of God, **he continues to act corruptly**. This person **never** [*bal*] **has regard for** [lit. **never sees** (*yir'eh*)] **the majesty** [*gē'ût*] **of Yahweh**. The term *gē'ût* is from *g'h*, "to be high." From this same root is *gē'eh*, "arrogant," "proud," which describes those who oppose Yahweh in 2:12 and 16:6. So, here is a hidden pun: the height of his pride prevents **the wicked** from seeing the height, the **majesty** of Yahweh, who longs to extend to him **grace**.

■ **11** The singer now turns to direct address: **O Yahweh, your hand is lifted high**, apparently in impending judgment, but in their prideful blindness, the wicked **never perceive** [*bal yeḥezāyûn* (from *ḥzh*)] **it**; that is, they may be aware of Yahweh's raised hand, but they have no perception of its meaning for them. Yet the time will come when **they will perceive** [*ḥzh*] **your zeal for your people** and **they will be ashamed** and realize how foolish they have been. But this perception will come too late. **Indeed** [*'ap*, omitted in the NIV], **the fire reserved for your enemies** *will* **consume them**. One is reminded of Yahweh's judgmental "fire," which Amos prophesies will be sent against the citadels of Israel's and Judah's neighbors for gross violation of the terms of Yahweh's covenant with all peoples (Amos 1:4, 7, 10, 12, 14; 2:2, 4).

■ **12** The prophet now affirms his conviction that Yahweh's future actions on his people's behalf will not be different from his past actions on their behalf. **O Yahweh, you** *will* **establish peace** [*šālôm*, "wholeness," "well-being"] **for us, because indeed** [*kî gam*, omitted in the NIV] **all our accomplishments you have done** [*them*] **for us**. Israel has accomplished nothing out of her own abilities, but only as God has intervened on her behalf.

■ **13** In this verse, there is a wordplay on the terms **lords** (*'ădōnîm*) and **have ruled over us** (*bě'ālûnû* [*b'l*]) Wildberger points out, that *b'l* in its noun form (*ba'al*) refers to one who is an owner of possessions, while *'ādôn* is a master over servants (1997, 563-64). These **lords** of the past would include the pharaoh of Israel's bondage, the kings of Israel's neighbors in the period of the Judges, and in Isaiah's own time, the Assyrians. These **lords** considered Israel to be their possession and the Israelites their servants. Yet the Israelites never forgot who was/is their true owner and master. The Hebrew of v 13 reads, **O Yahweh our God, . . . only you, you alone, your name we keep in remembrance**.

■ **14** **The dead who never will live** [*again*], and the **shades** (*rěpā'îm*) who **never will rise**, in the context of the passage, surely refer to the "lords" who formerly ruled Israel (ibid., 564). Yahweh has **indeed** punished [*lāqēn pāqadtā*] **them**, and thoroughly **wiped out all memory of them**. Motyer asks, "Who, for example, is the Pharaoh of the exodus?" (1993, 217). Isaiah's pun here is that it is Yahweh who continues to be remembered (v 13).

■ **15** In spite of other rulers' attempts to reduce God's people to nothing, Isaiah declares (twice) with certainty, **You** [i.e., Yahweh] **have enlarged the nation; . . . you have extended all the borders of the land**. Both verbs (**enlarged, extended**) are perfect (completed) tense, what Oswalt calls "prophetic certitude" (1986, 482). That is, though not yet realized in Isaiah's time, with a prophet's vision, Isaiah speaks of the certain future (compare, e.g., 49:19-21; 54:2-3; Mic 7:11-12). In all this, says Isaiah, **you** [i.e., Yahweh] *are glorified*.

c. Failure in Witness, but New Life from the Dust (26:16-19)

■ **16-18** The grammar and meaning of these three verses have given all commentators extreme difficulty. Different suggestions have been advanced as to how these verses relate to the material just preceding. Smith makes two observations, however, that may give them a historical setting. (1) The primary example of God's discipline on Judah (v 16) in Isaiah's time was Assyrian Sennacherib's attack on Judah in 701 BC. (2) Isaiah's metaphor of Jerusalem as a woman in the pain of childbirth (vv 17-18) is similar to that which Hezekiah spoke in the midst of Sennacherib's attack (37:3). Thus he views the overall historical setting of chs 24—27 to be Sennacherib's 701 BC attack (2007, 410).

The words are addressed to **Yahweh** concerning a time when he has severely **disciplined** his people (26:16). God's most severe act of discipline on Judah in Isaiah's time was the Assyrian Sennacherib's 701 BC invasion of Judah. Judah's towns were sacked from one end of the kingdom to the other, leaving only Jerusalem intact (chs 36—37). The disciplining was so severe that they were left in a condition where they **could barely whisper a prayer** (26:16).

In the midst of that chastisement, **we were in your presence, Yahweh, like a pregnant woman, crying out,** but we gave birth [*as it were, only*] to **wind** (vv 17-18). Through all our history of struggle and **pain** (v 17), all our attempts to **bring deliverance** to the earth (*'ereṣ*) have failed, **and the inhabitants of the world** [*tēbēl*] **have not come to life** (v 18).

■ **19** This verse speaks of resurrection from the dead at some point in the future. The lament of vv 17-18 leads to the question implied in this verse: what happens to **those who dwell in the dust?** "Those saints who have lived and struggled and died" (Oswalt 1986, 485), will they remain **in the dust** forever? This verse answers that question: the **dead will live,** *corpses* **will rise**. The command will come to **those who dwell in the dust: wake up and shout for joy**. And to enable this to happen, **the earth will give birth to her dead**. It is Yahweh's power that gives life to the dead, just as the **dew of the morning** in Palestine provides life to vegetation in the heat of summer when there is no rain.

d. God's People vs. the People of the Earth (26:20—27:1)

■ **20** The title **my people** (*'ammî*) expresses the continuing unique relationship between Israel and Yahweh: "election-love" (Oswalt 1986, 488). God's protection is still available to his **people** during **his wrath** (or "indignation"), but only if they **go, . . . hide** themselves behind **doors** in their inner **rooms**. For this imagery, commentators suggest that Isaiah has in the background the great flood, in which Noah and family were commanded to "go into the ark" (Gen 7:1), while "every living thing on the face of the earth was wiped out" (v 23). *Hiding* implies dependency, waiting until God's **wrath has passed** *over*. The expression **passed** *over* calls to mind that night in Egypt when the Israelites, remaining safely in their homes, were promised that Yahweh "will pass over" their doorways, while destroying all Egypt's firstborn (Exod 12:23).

■ **21** *For* [*kî*, omitted in the NIV] *behold*, which begins this verse, is a call to God's people to look up or pay attention; something phenomenal is about to happen! In the imagery of a theophany, **Yahweh is coming out of his dwelling** (in contrast to his "people," who are hiding in their dwellings). The purpose of Yahweh's **coming out** is **to punish** (*pqd*), not his own people, but **the people of the earth for their iniquity** (*'āwôn*). The deepest level of *iniquity* is bloodguilt, "the type of sin that causes someone's death" (Wildberger 1997, 572). **The earth** will no longer **conceal its blood, . . . its slain**. Here will be the fulfillment of the promise of resurrection in v 19.

■ **27:1** Continuing to depict God's victory over all evil on the earth (26:21), Isaiah uses motifs familiar to him from the myths of the ancient Near Eastern world around him. For example, both **Leviathan the gliding . . . , . . . coiling serpent** and **the sea** (Heb., **Yam**) appear in the Ugaritic (Canaanite) Baal myth as Lotan and Yam (Pritchard 1969, 137-38). Isaiah, however, merely adopts the terminology, not the myth. **Leviathan** and **Yam** represent that evil force that is behind all human evil, which NT John described as "the great dragon . . . that ancient serpent called the devil, or Satan, who leads the whole world astray" (Rev 12:9). To eradicate evil from among his created order of human beings, which the "serpent" (Gen 3:1) brought among us at the very beginning in Eden, the evil force itself must be done away with. This God does with his metaphorical **great and powerful sword**.

4. God's Vineyard Revisited; A Fortified City Desolated; A Great Trumpet Blown (27:2-13)

a. God's Vineyard Revisited (27:2-6)

This is a song celebrating God's vineyard, an allegory in which Yahweh, as loving caretaker, offers salvation to Israel. It is in stark contrast to the earlier vineyard song (5:1-7), given as a parable. There, Yahweh, in judgment upon Israel, had abandoned his vineyard to the ravages of nature and its enemies.

■ **2** The song opens with three exclamatory phrases (in the order of the Hebrew): **In that day**! *A delightful vineyard*! **Sing** *of it*! (Motyer 1993, 222).

■ **3-5** The contrast between the two vineyards can be seen in the following table:

5:1-7	27:2-5
Yahweh removes its protective "hedge" (5:5)	Yahweh watches/protects it (27:3)
Yahweh "commands" no "rain on it" (5:6)	Yahweh waters it continually (27:3)
Yahweh allows "briers and thorns" to "grow there" (5:6)	Yahweh attacks the briers and thorns (27:4)
In his vineyard is "bloodshed" and "cries of distress" (5:7)	Yahweh is a refuge, his vineyard a place of peace (27:5)
A general aura of anger and judgment (5:3-6)	Yahweh's anger is no more, no aura of judgment (27:4)

■ **6** Here, the prophet gives an interpretation of the vineyard allegory: the vineyard/vine is **Jacob**, a reference to the beginnings of God's people; but the name **Israel** is also a reminder that Jacob wrestled with God and prevailed (Gen 32:28). And so, **in days to come**, prior to the end of time when God "comes out . . . to punish the people of the earth" (Isa 26:21), God's people too will prevail. Yahweh will beat back the "briers and thorns" (27:4) so that his people **will take root** and that root **will bud and blossom**. The blossoms of this spreading vine will produce such an abundance of **fruit** that it will **fill all the world** (*ṭēbēl*; compare 37:31; Hos 14:5-7). Oswalt rightly observes that NT teaching includes "all the children of Abraham, Jew and Gentile alike" in the designation "Israel" (1986, 495). Paul declares that any who "stand by faith" are members of God's Israel (Rom 11:20).

b. The Fortified City Desolated (27:7-11)

Here the prophet reflects on God's past acts of judgment upon Israel, inviting his listeners to do the same.

■ **7** The prophet reflects comparatively: Has God **struck** *him* as severely as he has **struck down those who struck** *him*? (the masculine gender here points back to forefather "Jacob" of Isa 27:9). **Those who struck** must refer to the nations who have oppressed God's people throughout their history, upon whom God brings judgment in the larger context of chs 23—27.

■ **8-9** The prophet's response to the above question is: No, God has not struck Jacob so severely as he struck the nations. Rather, *by shooing her away and sending her off* [Motyer 1993, 223; Wildberger 1997, 589] [*God*] *contended* **with her** (the feminine gender now refers to Jacob/Israel as a people). Her removal from the land of Canaan, though certainly a severe punishment for her sins of idolatry, serves to **atone for** Jacob's guilt (*ăwôn* [27:9]) and for **the removal of his sin** (*ḥaṭṭā'ṯ*). The use of the singular pronoun **his** and the terms **guilt** (*ăwôn*) and **sin** (*ḥaṭṭā'ṯ*) here echo Isaiah's own personal encounter with Yahweh in 6:7: "the effect of atonement is primarily individual and personal" (Motyer 1993, 224). But **the full fruit** (27:9) of God's atonement will not be realized until all vestiges of idol worship are removed: when **all the altar stones are crushed to pieces**, and **no Asherah poles or incense altars will be left standing**. (On **Asherah poles** and **incense altars**, → 17:7-8 sidebar, "Asherahs.")

■ **10-11** God's punishment of his people/Jacob, which includes the provision for salvation, is lenient in comparison to God's dealings with **the fortified city** (27:10). This is not any specific city (though Thebes, Babylon, Nineveh, Samaria, and others of Isaiah's time come to mind) but is a symbol of the world city without a consciousness of God, centers of power and oppression (as in 25:2 and 26:5 ["the lofty city"]). God's punishment leaves these centers of power **desolate, . . . abandoned, . . . forsaken** (27:10). Here is fulfillment of Isaiah's earlier prophecy that **Yahweh Sebaoth** will "destroy the whole *land*" and will "make the land desolate" (13:5, 9).

Two images of desolation are given: **calves graze,** *stripping* [*tree*] **branches bare** (perhaps implying that there is no grass); the dried branches then become kindling with which **women come and make fires** (perhaps to cook their meals [27:10-11]). Here is a depiction of the absolute cessation of the vitality of human life.

Why does the **Maker/Creator** *show* **no compassion . . . no favor** (v 11) to the inhabitants of **the fortified city** (v 10)? It is *because* this is a people **without understanding** (*bînôṯ*, "discernment" [v 11]). Paul describes such persons as those who "although they knew God, they neither glorified him as God nor gave thanks to him, but their thinking became futile and their foolish hearts were darkened" (Rom 1:21).

c. A Great Trumpet Is Blown (27:12-13)

■ **12-13** **In that day** (v 12) introduces both verses, which look forward to the eschatological end of time. Though the promise is directed to **Israel**, surely it is to all God's people, who are to be **gathered up one by one**. When the heavenly **trumpet will sound** (v 13), all Yahweh's **perishing** and **exiled** faithful will assemble to **worship Yahweh**, their "Maker" and "Creator" (v 11), whom their oppressors have spurned.

FROM THE TEXT

Chapters 26 and 27 conclude on the ringing blast of the "great trumpet" (27:13), signaling the ingathering of God's people from all over the world. These are the fruit of Jacob, the vine of Yahweh's vineyard that has spread throughout the entire world (vv 2, 6; Motyer 1993, 223). This is the Jacob whose "guilt" has been "atoned for" (v 9). Here, one is reminded that, in Israelite history, Yahweh commanded the trumpet to be blown to announce the Year of Jubilee, which began with the Day of Atonement (Lev 25:9-10).

Zechariah says that when Yahweh "the king" comes to "proclaim peace to the nations" and to establish "his rule . . . to the ends of the earth," as "Sovereign **Yahweh**" he will "sound the trumpet." "**Yahweh** their God will save his people on that day as a shepherd saves his flock" (Zech 9:9, 10, 14, 16).

Matthew records Jesus' words concerning the coming of "the Son Man." At that time, "he will send his angels with a loud trumpet call, and they will gather his elect from the four winds, from one end of the heavens to the other" (Matt 24:30-31).

Paul, in writing to the church at Corinth concerning "the resurrection of the dead," declares that when "the trumpet will sound, the dead will be raised imperishable" (1 Cor 15:42, 52). He reiterates this to the believers at Thessalonica, assuring them that when "the trumpet call of God" is sounded, "the dead in Christ will rise first." Paul was apparently responding to a concern among the Thessalonian believers as to whether or not there was "hope" for "those who sleep in death," "who have fallen asleep in [Christ]" (1 Thess 4:16, 13).

Wesley, in commenting on Paul's view of the coming day of resurrection (in 1 Cor 15), urges his readers to live a life of "cultivating holiness," as we long for that "glorious day." He envisions "millions of voices, after the long silence of the grave," bursting out together in "triumphant song, O death, where is thy sting? O hades, where is the victory?" (n.d., 427).

III. A RIGHTEOUS KING WILL REIGN: 28:1—39:8

Overview

Chapters 28—39 comprise the third segment of the first "book" of the Isaiah scroll (chs 1—39). The first segment (chs 1—12) presented Isaiah's prophetic activity during the Syrian-Israelite threat against Judah during the latter third of the eighth century BC, when Ahaz (reigned 735-715 BC) was Judah's king. At that time Assyria was the great imperial power broker. The second segment (chs 13—27) presented Yahweh's sovereignty and his ultimate triumph over all nations and peoples, culminating in his eschatological/messianic reign from Mount Zion.

This third segment (chs 28—39) returns historically to the time period of the first segment: Assyria is still the world's imperial power broker, but Hezekiah (reigned 715-686 BC), Ahaz's son and successor, is now Judah's king. This third segment concludes with materials that suggest that Assyria's power is waning, while (re)introducing Babylon, on the distant eastern edge of the empire, as inserting itself into Judah's affairs. Thus this third segment (chs 28—39) of the first "book" prepares us for plunging into the second "book," which begins with ch 40. In ch 40 Assyria will be nowhere in sight, having been long gone at the hands of the uprising Babylon of the first "book." (Babylon, with the help of the Medes, captured Assyria's capital Nineveh in 612 BC and by 609 BC had annihilated the remaining vestiges of Assyria's leaders and army, which had escaped westward. From ch 40 onward, however, Babylon itself is on the verge of being displaced/replaced by uprising imperial Persia.)

This third segment of the first "book" may be divided into four units. Unit 1 (chs 28—33) asks the question: Will Judah put her trust in Egyptian power or in Yahweh for deliverance from Assyria? Unit 2 (chs 34—35) is cast in contrastive eschatological imagery; Edom, representing the nations, is turned into a wasteland without human habitant (ch 34); Judah's wilderness, representing "the total world: physical, social, and spiritual, which, human arrogance having destroyed" (Oswalt 1986, 620), is transformed into a Lebanon/Carmel/Sharon-like garden (ch 35). Unit 3 (chs 36—37) details Assyrian king Sennacherib's 701 BC threat against Jerusalem, King Hezekiah's reliance upon Yahweh for deliverance, and Yahweh's miraculous rescue of the city. Unit 4 (chs 38—39) presents Isaiah the prophet (*hannābî'* [39:3]) as counselor to Hezekiah during a near-death sickness and his recovery, and in response to Hezekiah's actions during a Babylonian envoy's visit. Following the departure of this Babylonian envoy, Isaiah gives his prediction of Judah's future Babylonian exile (39:5-7); this prepares the reader for the second "book," from ch 40 onward.

The textual evidence (37:21-22) indicates that Isaiah's prophetic ministry continued at least through Sennacherib's 701 BC threat against Jerusalem, during Hezekiah's reign. The "addendum" mentioning Sennacherib's death (37:37-38), if written by Isaiah, on the one hand, would indicate that Isaiah was still living and ministering as late as 681 BC, the year of Sennacherib's assassination. On the other hand, an editor (one of Isaiah's disciples?) may have added this historical fact following Isaiah's death. In either case, it is a theological declaration based on historical fact: Yahweh, the true "great king" (Mal 1:14), has the final say concerning the destiny of a human who claimed the title "great king" (Isa 36:4), whose god was powerless to save.

A. Will Judah Trust Egypt or Yahweh? (28:1—33:24)

Chapters 28—33 ask the question: In whom will Judah place her trust for deliverance from Assyria: in the promise of Egyptian military power or in Yahweh?

As noted above, chs 28—33 are set against the background of Assyria's increasing threat against Judah/Jerusalem in the latter years of the eighth century BC. Hezekiah is king in Judah. To the southwest of Judah, Egyptian power appears to be strengthening. Perhaps an alliance (*massēkâ*) with Egypt (30:1-2; compare 31:1), promising help against the increasing Assyrian encroachment, would be worth a gamble. No! advises Prophet Isaiah. The Egyptians' promised help will become nothing but **vanity** (*hebel*) and **emptiness** (*rîq*) (30:7). After all, says Isaiah, "the Egyptians are mere mortals ['*ādām*] and not God" (31:3). Moreover, "Assyria will fall by . . . a sword, not of mortals" ('*ādām* [v 8]). Therefore, trust Yahweh, for "**Yahweh** is our king; it is he who will save us" (33:22).

1. Drunken Rulers of Ephraim, Scoffing Rulers of Judah (28:1-29)

BEHIND THE TEXT

Chapter 28 divides into three units. (1) Verses 1-13 describe Ephraim's (the northern kingdom's) drunken leaders and their mockery of the prophet's message. (2) Verses 14-22 speak of Yahweh's judgment upon Judah's leaders for entering into a "covenant with death" (v 15), most likely referring to their treaty with Egypt; at the same time, for those who did not enter into the "covenant with death," God remains "a sure foundation" (v 16). (3) Verses 23-29 consist of a parable of the discriminant "farmer" (v 24) whom "God instructs" (v 26) in how appropriately to bring various grains to fruition. The application of the parable could be: (1) Just so, Yahweh acts wisely in bringing "forth suitable fruits from his creation" (Childs 2001, 211), or (2) "one who is instructed aright will understand the counsel and wisdom of God (28:26, 29)" (Seitz 1993, 209).

The units of this chapter were most likely written/given at different times and for varying purposes. They have been brought together here, however, in the canonical form of the text "not to comment on history so much as to offer a rationale for the way of faith" (Motyer 1993, 228).

a. Woe to Ephraim's Drunken Leaders (28:1-13)

Ephraim (northern Israel) still enjoys the status of an independent kingdom, though its coming fall to Assyrian forces in 721 BC is imminent.

Ephraim's army had earlier suffered a defeat at the hands of Assyria in 735 BC; then, in 732 BC, Damascus (Syria's capital and Ephraim's ally) had fallen to Assyria. Thus Ephraim stands alone, with no northern buffer to deflect the advance of the Assyrian army.

IN THE TEXT

■ **1-4** Though the larger context is a prophetic warning to the leadership of Judah, Isaiah highlights **the *proud wreath* of Ephraim's drunkards** (v 1). The scene is a banquet attended by Ephraim's leaders, **wreaths** of flowers adorning their heads, drinking themselves into oblivion, **smitten** by wine. By the night's end the **fading *flowers*** lie tossed aside as nothing, among the other refuse of the night's partying. In their **pride** (*gē'ût*) Ephraim's leaders refuse to recognize the **Sovereign** [*ha'dōnāy*] **. . . powerful and strong** (v 2), and the partying goes on.

Moreover, the **wreath** depicts Samaria, the **city** of Ephraim's **pride, . . . set on the head of a fertile valley** (v 1). In their drunken defiance, Ephraim's rulers ignore that **the Sovereign** has one (Assyria) on the horizon who soon **will throw** (a Hebrew perfect tense, implying an already determined act) Samaria **to the ground by hand** (v 2). **By hand** is the last Hebrew word of v 2. ***By feet*** is the first Hebrew word v 3: ***By feet will be trampled the proud wreath* of Ephraim's drunkards.** Perhaps here is a bit of Isaiah's humorous imagery of a giant stomping his huge feet, swinging his powerful fists, pulverizing the city (Oswalt 1986, 502). In terms of nature's destructive power, as **the Sovereign's** chosen instrument of judgment upon Ephraim, Assyria's invasion will be **like a hailstorm . . . a destructive wind . . . and a flooding downpour** (v 2).

■ **5-6** **In that day** speaks of after judgment, a time in which hope is offered **for the remnant of his** [i.e., **Yahweh's**] **people** (*lišĕār 'ammô* [v 5]). Even in judgment, **the remnant** of Ephraim is still Yahweh's **people**. **In that day** they will recognize their true king, **Yahweh Sebaoth**. He **will become** for them a **crown of glory** (*'ăṭeret ṣĕbî*), a **wreath** *of beauty* (*ṣĕpîrat tip'ārâ*), and **a spirit of justice** (*rûaḥ mišpāṭ* [v 6]).

■ **7-8** Isaiah now speaks specifically of the religious leadership of Ephraim: the **priests and prophets** (v 7), consumed with drunken partying (**tables covered with vomit** [v 8], ***staggering*** from wine [*yayin* (v 7)] and ***reeling*** from ***strong drink*** [*šēkār*]), have no sense that their minds **are befuddled** [lit. *swallowed up*] *by* wine. The prophet ***errs in vision***, the priest ***stumbles in decision***.

Alcoholic Beverages in the OT

Nine different terms designate alcoholic beverages in the Hebrew Bible, all made from grapes. The most common term is *yayin*, translated "wine." Wine appears to have been served with meals, offered as a sacrifice, and used as a healing medicine. *Yayin* is often paired with *šēkār*, **strong drink** (as in Isa 28:7), which apparently had an alcoholic content much higher than *yayin* (King and Stager 2001, 101-2). Isaiah pronounces a "woe" against "those who rise early in the morning **pursuing strong drink** [*šēkār*]" (5:11).

■ **9** Rejecting prophetic admonitions, the religious leaders turn to mockery of both prophet and message. **Ones weaned from . . . milk, ones taken from breasts** were **children** weaned at about the age of three (compare 1 Sam 1:22-24) (King and Stager 2001, 41). This was the age when the basic teachings for life's journey began. We are not **children**, they insist. We have moved on from mother's **milk**, a child's nourishment, to adult nourishment: wine and beer!

■ **10** Therefore, do not teach us as you would a child! Scholars have made numerous suggestions as to the meaning of the Hebrew words of this verse, with no agreement. The NIV has captured the sense, however, with **Do this, do that** . . . The mockers perhaps intended to make the prophets' teaching sound as nonsense, for indeed, in their drunken hearing, such teaching was nonsense.

■ **11-13** Very well then [*kî*, **indeed**], . . . **God will speak to this people** in a different way (Isa 8:11). **This people** (not "my people") have rejected God's offer of a **resting place** (v 12), a security in God himself. Therefore, it will be through the Assyrian oppressor, through **stammering** lips and a strange tongue ([v 11] how a language sounds to one who does not understand) that this new **word of Yahweh** (v 13) will come to the northern kingdom. The oppressor's commands ("do this, do that" [v 10]) will be as to toddlers who, **while walking, stumble** (fall backward [v 13]) and **are** injured. Yahweh's judgment culminates in the mockers of Ephraim, along with their people, being **snared and captured**, a prophetic word that they face deportation into Assyrian exile (which did occur in 721 BC).

b. Yahweh's Work in Zion: Strange and Alien (28:14-22)

■ **14** It is clear that Isaiah now turns his attention away from the northern kingdom to **Jerusalem** (v 14), the center that influences all Judah. Yet his opening word, **therefore** (*lākēn*), links this prophetic warning to **scoffers/mockers** (*'anšê lāṣôn*, "men of mocking") with the theme of mocking that characterized the priests and prophets of Ephraim (vv 7-13). Proverbs 21:24 says of such a person, "'Mocker' is his name" (*lēṣ šĕmô*): he is "proud" (*zēd*), "arrogant" (*yāhîr*), and prone to **behaving with angry outbursts of insolence** (*'ôśeh bĕ'ebrat zādôn*).

Isaiah then adds a parallel term for the **scoffers** of **Jerusalem** [*mōšĕlê hā'ām*], **proverb-makers of this people** (*mšl* I, "to formulate an expression, show a parable"; the NIV understands the root to be *mšl* II, "to rule," thus, **who rule**) (*HALOT* 647). Isaiah's focus, then, is not upon Jerusalem's political leaders but upon the priests and prophets (parallel with those in Ephraim), teachers and counselors who should be leading **this people** in the wisdom of Yahweh (Kaiser 1974, 250; Seitz 1993, 210).

■ **15** Isaiah accuses these religious leaders of having entered into covenantal agreements with both **death** (*māwet*) and **Sheol** (*šĕ'ôl*). A possible reference to the Canaanite deity Mot, *māvet* is associated here with Sheol, the shadowy underworld abode of the dead (→ 5:14 sidebar, "Sheol in the OT"). Habakkuk 2:5 speaks of *māvet* and *šĕ'ôl* as "never satisfied"; Jer 9:21 [20 HB] personifies *māvet* as entering Judah's fortresses through the windows and snatching children and young men from the streets.

Adding to their covenantal agreements with **death** and **Sheol**, Judah's religious leaders have **made a lie** to be their **refuge**, and *in* falsehood they *have hidden* themselves. Seitz suggests that they "have struck some sort of deal with the forces of death and the underworld" (1993, 210), a kind of gangster world protection from the **overwhelming scourge**, so that when it **sweeps by, it cannot touch us**. How foolish! How self-delusioning! It is Yahweh who sends the **overwhelming scourge**, the imminent invasion of the Assyrian army, not once only, but several times (compare Isa 28:19). Sweeney points out that the imagery **overwhelming scourge sweeps by** is water/storm language and thus alludes to the Assyrian army's coming invasion; Assyria's chief deity Ashur appears to have been a storm deity (1996, 370).

■ **16-19** Death and Sheol are no match for **Sovereign Yahweh** (v 16). They cannot provide protection from his weapons, personified as **hail** and **water** (v 17). The religious leaders' **refuge, the lie** will be *swept* away, their **hiding place** ("falsehood" [v 15]) flooded. Whatever the **covenant** (v 18) and **agreement** consisted of (some commentators suggest a treaty with Egypt, whose impotent promises of military help against Assyria will not materialize), such **will be annulled**; they **will not stand** before the Sovereign of all nations.

Why? Because **Sovereign Yahweh** (v 16) is at work behind the scenes **in Zion**, laying **a sure foundation** for an edifice, with the **measuring line** (v 17) of **justice** and the **plumb line** of **righteousness**. This edifice, suggests Childs, is the believing remnant, "a new creation" emerging "through faith during the period of Israel's judgment" (2001, 209). Thus, **the one who *trusts*** ('*mn*, to *believe* [v 16]) that Yahweh has Jerusalem's ultimate fate, and that of his people, within his larger plan for the nations **will never *act in haste***, for such persons live in God's time. Those who have acted outside of trust in Yahweh in facing the coming **overwhelming scourge** (v 18), however, **will be beaten down** and *carried away* (v 19). The promise that the scourge **will sweep through** again and again (**morning after morning, by day and by night**) aptly describes the several Assyrian military campaigns to the west, ravaging the towns and cities of the kingdoms that bordered the Mediterranean coast. Judah did not escape.

The Plumb Line

Builders use a vertical line with a weight, called a plummet, on the end. Line and weight together are called a plumb line. The plumb line makes use of the earth's gravity to check whether walls under construction are exactly vertical. If not, correction is made. The plumb line is also used to check existing walls of buildings to discern whether or not they need to be repaired and, if beyond repair, torn down. In addition to Isaiah's metaphorical use of the plumb line (28:17; 34:11), Amos uses the plumb line metaphorically to show that the northern kingdom (Isaac/Israel/house of Jeroboam) is not spiritually repairable, and its places of worship must "be destroyed" (Amos 7:7-9). See also 2 Kgs 21:13; Zech 4:10 (*EDB*, §19827).

■ **20** The ***too-short*** **bed** and the ***too-narrow*** **blanket** appear to reflect a proverb, implying the inadequacy of that in which Jerusalem's religious leaders have placed their trust.

■ **21** This verse points back to two historical events in which **Yahweh** came to the aid of his people: **Mount Perazim** (David against the Philistines [2 Sam 5:17-25] and **the Valley of Gibeon** (Joshua against five kings of central Canaan [Josh 10:10-15]). Now, just as he did in those former days, **Yahweh will rise up** again—not against Judah's enemies, but against Judah itself. No wonder Isaiah deems this **his strange work . . . his alien task**.

■ **22** The verbal form of **mocking** (reflexive [*hithpoel*]) points toward the inward character of disbelief, out of which comes the religious leaders' outward act of rejecting the prophet and his message. Yet Isaiah stands by his word, for, in fact, it is not his word: ***For I have heard from Sovereign Yahweh Sebaoth***: **destruction *is* decreed against the whole land**.

c. The Parable of the Wise Farmer (28:23-29)

■ **23-29** These verses, developed in two stanzas (vv 23-26 and vv 27-29), on the surface appear to be simply a wisdom poem about the activities of a peasant farmer. Each stanza, however, concludes with a statement concerning the activities of **God/*Yahweh Sebaoth*** (vv 26, 29).

The peasant farmer knows when to ***plow*** (v 24), how to **sow/scatter/plant** various seeds (v 25), and the correct ways of **threshing** each kind of grain (vv 27-28). In the ways of agricultural farming, he shows great wisdom. In the larger context of ch 28, the simple farmer is set in contrast to the priests and prophets, who refuse to accept/believe God's word and purpose; thus they lack wisdom.

According to vv 26 and 29, **God/*Yahweh Sebaoth*** is the source of the farmer's wisdom in the ways of agricultural farming. Uninformed, and uneducated in matters that concern religious leaders, the peasant farmer nevertheless is presented as wise. In v 26 he is willing to look to **his God** who **instructs** him (*ysr*, "instruct," "chastise," "rebuke") and who **teaches him** (*yrh*; compare Ezek 44:23 where *yrh* is paired with *byn*, lit. "to discern" between right and wrong things). God **teaches** (*yrh*) the farmer **the right way** (*lammišpāṭ*, lit. "good judgment" [Isa 28:26]). This peasant farmer, then, is one whose way of living displays "trust" (*'mn*, to **believe** [v 16]) in the wisdom of Yahweh.

The poem's conclusion (v 29) is a statement about **Yahweh Sebaoth** that suggests that the poem is a parable: the description of the farmer's work is, in the larger context, a parable of God's "strange work," his "alien task" (v 21). The farmer's first task is an act of violence, tearing open the ground by plowing. But this does not last forever. He moves on to the process of planting, cultivating, and harvesting fruit produced by his careful husbandry. So it is with God's act of violence against his own people: judgment is only for a season. Salvation and restoration will follow. The behind-the-scenes work that Yahweh is doing "in Zion" (v 16) will one day produce fruit as he carefully husbands "the remnant of his people" (v 5).

FROM THE TEXT

In the context of Isa 28, Wildberger observes that Isaiah "is a prophet who has been taught by God, no more, but also no less." Thus "he is bound to the word of Yahweh that comes to him," which he must proclaim. From his having been taught by Yahweh there is one observable constant throughout Isaiah's preaching: "He continually summons his listeners to look to Yahweh, simply to believe. This call is balanced by a constant situation within the nature of Yahweh." I understand Wildberger to mean that to **believe** is a response to the very nature of Yahweh, whose "unalterable . . . goal is always the establishment of justice and righteousness" (2002, 61-62).

In ch 28, Isaiah has juxtaposed "**Whoever believes** [*'mn*, also 'to trust,' 'to be faithful,' 'to stand firm'] will never be stricken with panic" (v 16), with "justice" (*mišpāṭ*) and "righteousness" (*ṣĕdāqâ*) (v 17). Yahweh makes justice and righteousness his tools for measuring the integrity of the Zion he is constructing to survive the coming judgment upon Jerusalem (vv 16-17). It is this justice and righteousness, the essence of both Yahweh's nature and the character of reconstructed Zion, that is the "sure foundation" (v 16) that makes it possible for one to **believe** (*'mn*).

In ch 1 Isaiah spoke of "Daughter Zion" (v 8), once the "faithful [*'mn*] city" (v 21) known for her "justice" (*mišpāṭ*) and "righteousness" (*ṣĕdāqâ*) but "now [*a city of*] murderers." Isaiah then speaks of future judgment and restoration: **Sovereign, Yahweh Sebaoth** will turn his "hand against" his "enemies" (vv 25, 24), the faithless "rulers" (v 23) in Zion. When judgment and cleansing are completed, however, Zion again will "be **named** the City of Righteousness [*ṣedeq*], the Faithful [*'mn*] City" (v 26).

In 7:9 Isaiah makes a wordplay when he uses two different verbal forms of *'mn* in his warning to Judah's King Ahaz, who is about to call on Assyria for help against Ephraim's and Aram's aggression: "If you do not **believe** [*ta'ămînû* (causative, *hiphil*)] you will not **be established**" (*tē'āmēnû* [pass., *niphal*]).

In 43:3, Yahweh speaks to the Jewish exiles in Babylon, identifying himself as "**Yahweh** your God, the Holy One of Israel, your Savior." In v 6 Yahweh speaks of "my sons" and "my daughters," "everyone who is called by my name" (v 7). These are "my witnesses" (to Yahweh's coming great rescue of his people out of Babylonian exile [v 10]), declares Yahweh, who will come to "know [*yd'*] and believe ['*mn*] me and understand [*byn*]" that there is no other god, either "before" or "after me."

Matthew 21 presents a confrontation between Jesus and the religious leaders of his time, "the chief priests and the elders of the people" (v 23), concerning those who do believe. Jesus said to them, "[When] John [the Baptist, a prophet] came to you to show you the way of righteousness, . . . you did not believe him, but the tax collectors and the prostitutes did" (v 32). Here is a parallel with Isaiah's confrontation with the priests and prophets of Jerusalem, who refuse to believe in the wisdom and righteousness of God, in contrast to the humble farmer who did believe.

How easy it is for us to become like the Pharisees, thinking ourselves to be somehow more sophisticated than the simple, trusting farmer. In the Pharisee "mode" we cannot receive God's instruction.

2. God's City Ariel, and the House of Jacob (29:1-24)

BEHIND THE TEXT

Though the Assyrians are not mentioned by name in this chapter, its contents indicate a historical time frame in which Judah's leaders anticipate Sennacherib's invasion and intended siege of Jerusalem in 701 BC. Turning southwestward to resurgent Egypt, Judah's leaders either are intending to make or have already made an alliance with Egypt, in which Egyptian military help is promised against the impending encroachment of Assyria.

Isaiah expresses strong opposition to such an alliance, a decision apparently made at the advice of royal counselors, "the wise **ones**" and "the intelligent **ones**" who "hide **counsel** from **Yahweh**" (29:14-15). Why is he opposed? Precisely because the decision to trust in Egyptian help in the face of advancing Assyrian expansion was a decision to believe that Yahweh was not powerful enough to save Judah. This, says Wildberger, was an expression of "atheism," that is, to make one's own plans apart from "the wisdom of God" (2002, 101).

In response to this blind (vv 9-10) disbelief of Judah's leaders, Yahweh will bring against "Ariel" (i.e., "Mount Zion" [vv 2, 7, 8]) the "hordes of all the nations" (a description of the Assyrian army), to "besiege her" (vv 2, 7). But in his "strange" and "alien" way of working (28:21), Yahweh, "suddenly, in an instant" (29:5) will turn away the Assyrian army. And, in that day of Yahweh's salvation, those who have been unable to receive "justice" in the "court" (v 21) ("the humble" and "the needy") "will rejoice" (v 19).

This chapter can be divided into four units: vv 1-14, vv 15-16, vv 17-21, and vv 22-24.

IN THE TEXT

a. Ariel, Ariel (29:1-14)

■ **1** Ariel (*ărî'ēl*) is Jerusalem, as indicated by **the city where David encamped** and its later equation with "Mount Zion" (v 8). But, why is Jerusalem designated **Ariel**? Two possibilities are suggested: (1) It is a reminder of Jacob's designation for Judah in his ancient blessing: a "lion" (*'aryēh* [Gen 49:9]), thus "lion of El" (Oswalt 1986, 526). This would be Isaiah's sarcastic reminder that Jerusalem sees herself as invincible, like a lion. (2) It is the designation for the "altar hearth" (*ări'ēl*) in Ezek 43:15-16 (ibid.), the surface of the altar of burnt offering in the Jerusalem temple (Wildberger 2002, 71). Isaiah 29:1 would thus be referencing Judah's misguided belief concerning the temple: if Jerusalem is metaphorically Yahweh's altar hearth, the presence of his temple, containing the actual altar hearth, within Jerusalem ensures the security of the city (ibid., 72). Under the protection of this presumed security, ignoring the enormity of the Assyrian threat, Jerusalem continues to celebrate the **cycle of festivals**, as though life will continue as usual **year to year**.

■ **2-3** Yet Yahweh **will besiege Ariel** (v 2), an apparent reference to the coming of Sennacherib and the Assyrian army in 701 BC. Indeed, this will cause Jerusalem to **mourn and lament**. The classic symbols of siege are depicted: **encampment** (v 3) of an army **on all sides**, siege **towers** enabling soldiers to reach the top of the walls, **siege works**, earth ramps built against the walls to enable the towers and other machines of war to approach the walls.

Siege Ramps, Battering Rams, and Towers

A siege ramp consisted of a stone foundation with earth piled on top, leading up to near the top of the walls of a city. This would enable an attacking army to move their siege machines upward close to the city's wall. The siege machine was a frame on four or six wheels, with a covering of wood and leather up to a height that soldiers could be inside it as it was moved to the wall. Suspended from the front of the machine by ropes was a wooden ram reinforced with a metal blade. This ram, being swung back and forth with human strength, could be bashed against the city's mud-brick wall with such force that a hole would be broken through. On the top of the siege machine was a tall tower, from which attacking soldiers would shoot arrows at the city's defenders on the wall and even over the wall into the city itself. Such war machinery is mentioned in Isa 29:2-3; Ezek 4:2; and 21:22 [27 HB] (King and Stager 2001, 237-39).

■ **4** The references to **ground** and **earth** (both *'ereṣ*) and **dust** (twice, *'āpār*), out of which Ariel speaks in the aftermath of the threatened siege (Isa 29:2-3), are representations of the underworld (Sheol) where the dead reside (26:19) (*TDOT* 1:399). The brave talk of the "braggarts" (Wildberger 2002, 75), of the "scoffers *of* Jerusalem, *proverb-makers of* this people," those who "boast" of making "a covenant with death [with **Sheol**]" (28:14-15; compare 29:15, 20), is now reduced to a **mumble**, a **whisper**. Their **voice** is merely **ghostlike** (*kĕ'ôb*), like the **whisperings** and **mutterings** of the "mediums" (*'ōbôt*), which Isaiah said were consulted in the days of Ahaz (→ 8:19).

■ **5-6** In a sudden "somersault" (Goldingay 2001, 160), Isaiah depicts the "strange work" of Yahweh (28:21), in that Yahweh, who is the instigator of Assyria's advance against Jerusalem, now turns against Assyria.

Yahweh Sebaoth (v 6) announces that he will pulverize Jerusalem's many enemies (v 5), those encamped all around the city (v 3), so that, **like fine dust [like chaff]**, **the ruthless hordes** are **blown** *away* (v 5; → 17:13; 33:11; compare 40:24; 41:2). (**Ruthless** aptly describes the Assyrians' cruelty and violence against conquered peoples.) This happens when **Yahweh**, unanticipated, **suddenly, in an instant**, **visits** (*pqd*; **will come**) Jerusalem (29:5-6). The powers of nature, which Yahweh controls, at least figuratively, accompany his appearing: **thunder** (*ra'am*; compare Pss 81:7 [8 HB]; 104:7), **earthquake** (*ra'aš*; compare 1 Kgs 19:11-13), **great noise** (*qôl gādôl*; compare Deut 5:22, "loud voice"), **windstorm**/**whirlwind** (*sûpâ*; compare Isa 17:13, "gale"; Amos 1:14, "stormy"; Nah 1:3), **tempest** (*sĕ'ārâ*; compare Ezek 1:4, "windstorm"; Nah 1:3), and **fire** (*'ēš*; compare Ezek 1:4).

■ **7-8** Yahweh's "visit" is both positive and negative. Moreover, the dream imagery of these two verses can be interpreted both positively and negatively.

For Jerusalem, Yahweh's visit will be to intervene on her behalf for good. Jerusalem's inhabitants will go to sleep at night, dreading the intended siege and possible invasion of the city, only to awake in the morning to find **the hordes of all the nations** (Isa 29:7) have vanished. "Were we only dreaming?" In fact, this fits well with Isaiah's later report of the work of Yahweh: 185,000 Assyrian soldiers dead in one night! *How* they died, Isaiah does not say; he is interested only in *what* happened, that this is the mysterious work of Yahweh (via "the angel of **Yahweh**"). So, "when the people got up the next morning—there were all the dead bodies! So Sennacherib king of Assyria broke camp and withdrew" (37:36-37).

For Sennacherib and his Assyrian forces, Yahweh's "visit" is negative. Yahweh intervenes to disrupt the intended siege in progress. The Assyrians' dream is the conquest of Jerusalem, the capture and deportation of its inhabitants, and the carrying away of war booty. Like a **hungry person [*who*] dreams of eating** (29:8), Sennacherib, with his **hordes of all the nations** (v 7), awakens from his dream, only to depart empty from **Mount Zion** (v 8), the city of ***Yahweh Sebaoth*** (v 6).

■ **9-10** These two verses are directed to those who ostensibly receive God's counsel, to be passed on to the political leaders and to the people of Jerusalem. Though given two designations, they are one class: **the prophets/the seers** (v 10). In their refusal to recognize that Yahweh is active in the events transpiring around them (a self-blindness) Yahweh gives them over to their blindness, *sealing* [*their*] *eyes, covering* [*their*] heads, so they become even more **blind** (v 9) and **sightless**. Like one **drunk**, they **stagger** from decision to decision, with no sure word from Yahweh.

■ **11-12** These verses speak of **a scroll** in which **words** are written (v 11). It is not indicated whether these are Isaiah's **words** or those of other prophets, now deemed sacred Scripture and thus preserved in written form. The point that Isaiah is making is that God's message to Judah has become like a message **sealed in a scroll**. Even though presented to one who can read, most likely a scribe, he cannot open it without proper authority (Oswalt 1986, 532; compare Rev 5:1-5). And, in this illustration, he does not care enough to know what the words of the scroll say to seek such authority. In the case of the illiterate person, it would do no good for him to look at the words on the scroll, even if opened, since he cannot read.

Both the literate scribe and illiterate man on the street represent the prophet/seer of Isa 29:9-10. Neither cares a fig for truly knowing God's message.

■ **13-14** The ***Sovereign*** (*'ădônāy*) now speaks concerning the leaders and inhabitants of Jerusalem: when ***worshipping***, **these people** know how to make a good show of it; **their lips** and **mouth** know well the ***humanly-taught catechism*** (*miṣwâ 'ănāšîm mĕlummādâ*), but **their hearts** are away on a **far** journey (v 13).

Therefore, *behold!* Once more I will *be wonderful with* these people (v 14). **Once more** echoes the Exodus event when Yahweh performed **wonder upon wonder** in Egypt on behalf of his people. But now the **wonder** that he will perform will be radically different. This time, Yahweh will cause **the wisdom of the wise *ones*** and **the intelligence of the intelligent *ones*** (the Judean royal advisers) to be of no account: in the outcome of events, when the Assyrian army is at the gates of Jerusalem and the promised Egyptian help is nonexistent, their counsel **will perish, . . . will vanish**. They will be no different from Pharaoh's "officials" and "wise counselors," who give "senseless advice" and thus are shown to be "fools" (19:11-13).

b. The Potter and the Clay (29:15-16)

■ **15-16** These two verses are directed at the "wise **ones**" and the "intelligent **ones**" of v 14. It is they *who go deep from Yahweh to hide counsel* (v 15). **Darkness** implies the secrecy in which they deliberate and decide the counsel they give to the king. The two questions that Isaiah puts into their mouths (**Who sees us? Who will know?**) show their arrogant, cavalier attitude toward Yahweh's counsel and the word of his prophet. Wildberger designates this making of one's own plans in complete defiance of God's wisdom and plans as "atheism" (2002, 101).

The first Hebrew word in v 16 is an accusatory exclamation: **Your perversity!** Judah's royal counselors have a perverse concept of their relationship with Yahweh. Here, Isaiah draws on the apparently well-understood imagery of the **potter** and **pot** (compare Jer 18 and Isa 45:9). To say to Yahweh, the Master Potter, the Creator, **You did not make me,** declares themselves to be self-made, their own creator. To say additionally, **You know nothing**, is to denigrate Yahweh and his work to the same level as the gods of the nations and their idols. It is, rather, they and their work that Yahweh declares to be "less than nothing" (41:24).

In sum, the king's counselors believe themselves to possess wisdom far greater than God, who, in fact, created the entire universe. In this they reject Israel's entire theological understanding of creation.

c. The Deaf Will Hear, the Blind Will See (29:17-21)

The theme of this paragraph is creation, presented as Yahweh's response to Judah's royal advisers, who have denied Yahweh's creatorship. Yahweh's coming action ("In a very short time" [v 17]/"In that day" [v 18]) is to bring about a complete reversal of the oppressive social and religious conditions holding sway in Jerusalem.

■ **17** Isaiah insists that the world is a world of Yahweh's creation. **In a very short time**, an undetermined time span (but compare vv 18-21, which describe a time of salvation), there will come a radical increase in the *fertility* of **Lebanon** and **Carmel**. It is implied that Yahweh who created also controls such increase in luxuriant growth.

■ **18** Likewise, **in that day** (of salvation) the condition of spiritual and judicial **gloom and darkness**, which the religious and political powers have imposed on Jerusalem and its inhabitants of Isaiah's time, will be lifted. This **darkness** will no longer hinder the hearing/seeing (i.e., understanding) of **the words of the scroll**. In this new coming **day** of salvation, **the** [spiritually] **deaf will hear** and **the** [spiritually] **blind will see**. Oswalt suggests that then the words of the prophet "will find lodging in a receptive soil where they can spring up to that luxurious growth spoken of in v. 17" (1986, 538).

■ **19** In this new day of salvation, there will be ***rejoicing*** and ***exultation*** because of a reversal of the circumstances of ***the bowed down*** (*'ănāwîm,* "the downtrodden"), and **the needy** [or "the poorest"] ***of humanity*** (*'ebyônîm 'ādām*). The reason for this reversal is given in the next two verses.

■ **20-21** Here are listed three classes of those in power who have imposed the "gloom and darkness" of v 18. **The ruthless** (v 20) are the oppressors of the "poor" and "needy" in 25:3-5 (compare 13:11; 29:5; 49:25 ["the fierce"]). In Proverbs the ***mocker*** (or "scoffer") is "proud and arrogant" (21:24), the opposite of the "humble and oppressed" (3:34), the opposite of "the wise" (9:8; 15:12; 21:11). **All who *watch to do* evil** are those who hold judicial power, deciding cases **in *the gate*** (the location of the city **court**), ever watching for ways to falsely judge **the innocent** as **guilty** (Isa 29:21). They do this by accepting **false testimony** (compare Exod 23:6-7; Amos 5:12; Mal 3:5). The verb translated here ***watch to do***, in Jer 5:6 describes the leopard "***lying*** in wait" outside Judah's towns, seeking the chance to attack "any who venture out."

The reason for the ***rejoicing*** and ***exultation*** of Isa 29:19 is that in this new day of salvation, these three classes of power, representative of all powers of oppression and deprivation of justice, like the last puff of campfire smoke in the wind, **will vanish, will disappear,** and **will be cut down** (v 20).

d. Jacob Will Accept Instruction (29:22-24)

■ **22** The mention of the name **Abraham**, from whom historically the Israelites descended, is a word of assurance to the present ***house*** of Jacob. When Yahweh appeared to Moses in the midst of a blazing bush, Moses asked for his identification. In response, Yahweh appealed to his previous relationship with Abraham, Isaac, and Jacob. "I am the same God," he is saying (Exod 6:6-16). Thus ***Yahweh*** is assuring **the** (present) ***house*** of Jacob that he is the same God who has watched over Israel from the day of its birth. Yahweh's present word is that the shame **Jacob** bore because of previous lack of faith/belief in Yahweh's work will be removed.

■ **23** The Hebrew text reads, **When *he*** [i.e., Jacob, collectively] ***sees in his midst his*** **children** [*yĕlādîm*], **the work of my hands.** Yahweh's **work** in the new day of salvation is a radical, unexpected increase in the number within the family of **Jacob**. It is **they** who will now hold Yahweh in great sanctity, both his **name** and himself, **the Holy One of Jacob/the God of Israel.**

■ **24** One can make a comparison with the peasant farmer of ch 28, who was open to God's instruction in the ways of farming. Just so, these children of Jacob, formerly **wayward in spirit**, will now no longer **complain**. With a new readiness to be taught by God, they **will gain understanding** and **will accept instruction**.

FROM THE TEXT

At the center of ch 29 is Isaiah's indictment of those who worship God with "their lips" but whose "hearts" are filled only with "human rules they have been taught" (v 13). These "human rules," though considered to be "wisdom" (v 14), are in fact pure foolishness, insists Isaiah, because they shut God entirely out of one's plans and decisions in life. In fact, not only is God ignored, but he is also denied any effective existence: God does not see, God does not know, God has not created (vv 15-16). Such foolishness, which Isaiah satirically calls "wisdom of the wise" and "intelligence of the intelligent," will "vanish" when the "mockers," who have turned God's word to self-serving purposes, are "cut down" (vv 14, 20).

In Mark's Gospel, Jesus, in a confrontation with some Pharisees and teachers of the Law (7:1-13), called them "hypocrites," quoting Isa 29:13. In applying the quote, Jesus insists that the "human rules" (Mark 7:7) are nothing but "human traditions" and not "the commands of God" (v 8). Jesus then slams them with an arrow straight to the heart: "You **nullify the command** of God so that you do not have to 'Honor your father and mother'" (vv 9-12) but rather spend upon yourselves. Jesus then uses this example to teach his disciples that it is from "a person's heart" that such "evil comes" (v 21). Thus the Pharisees worshipped with their lips, but their hearts were away on a far journey.

Lest we become overly judgmental of the mockers of Isaiah's day or the Pharisees of Jesus' time, we must beware of the contents of our own hearts. Do our lips say one thing, to both God and our fellows, but our hearts dictate that our actions take us in ways contrary to God's will? To live in the full recognition that God is our Creator and we his creations, and that he does see and know, will entice us to live and move in the light of his will.

3. Woe to Those Who Form an Alliance with Egypt (30:1—31:9)

BEHIND THE TEXT

The main concern of this two-chapter section is an apparent alliance between Judah and Egypt in the southwest, in which Judah is seeking military assistance against the Assyrian advancement from the northeast. The time frame is the latter part of the eighth century BC. Scholars are divided, however, as to which of two Assyrian incursions are in the background: a several-kingdom (including Judah) revolt against Assyrian dominance and Assyrian Sargon's quelling of that revolt (714-711 BC) or Assyrian Sennacherib's invasion of 701 BC. The overall circumstances depicted in the two chapters appear to tilt the decision to the latter. It is in fear of Sennacherib that King Hezekiah's advisers (though perhaps not Hezekiah himself, as he is not named) have sent emissaries with a large contingent of riches and treasures to the Egyptian pharaoh seeking his protection (30:2, 6). Such an action, insists Isaiah, planned without consulting Yahweh or his Spirit, can only result in shame and disgrace (30:1-3; 31:1). This will be because "Egypt, . . . Rahab the Do-Nothing" will be "utterly useless" to them (30:7). Egypt, along with chariots and the cavalry of Ethiopia (which were, by Sennacherib's description, "an army beyond counting") did, indeed, march out of Egypt, advancing northward on the Way of the Sea, along the Mediterranean seacoast. They made it only as far as Eltekeh, however, just north of Philistia. There, an overwhelming Assyrian force met and defeated them, sending them packing back to Egypt (Pritchard 1969, 287-88; Aharoni and Avi-Yonah 1993, 118).

In the conclusion of this two-chapter section (31:1-9), Isaiah satirically describes Egypt as merely human and not God, implying the foolishness of rejecting Yahweh's help for unreliable human help. Moreover, why fear Assyria? Assyria's end is fully within God's plan: the empire will fall by a nonhuman sword, highlighting God's mysterious involvement in human history.

This two-chapter section divides into six units: 30:1-7; 30:8-14; 30:15-18; 30:19-26; 30:27-33; 31:1-9.

IN THE TEXT

a. Egypt: Rahab the Sitting One (30:1-7)

■ 1 Isaiah speaks a scathing word of **woe** to **obstinate children** (*bānîm*, **sons**), an echo of Yahweh's earlier evaluation of his "children" (*bānîm*), who "rebelled [*pš'*] against me," who "spurned the Holy One of Israel" (1:2, 4). Here (in 30:1) their rebelliousness leads them to **make** plans apart from any listening to Yahweh's **Spirit**. These **sons** refer specifically to those "scoffers" and ***proverb-makers*** of 28:14, and those "who do their work in darkness" of 29:15. Wildberger points out that where there are **sons** there is a father. So Yahweh here is indirectly identified as their Father. And in cultural Israel the son is under the father's authority for as long as the father lives.

Thus, **carrying** out **plans** and **forming an alliance** without consulting Yahweh the Father is a most serious offense (2002, 124). This act of rebellion is described as *ḥaṭṭā't 'al ḥaṭṭā't*, **sin upon sin**. Though *ḥaṭṭā't* usually does not imply rebellion, in this context it apparently does.

Second Kings 18:14 records that King Hezekiah, after Assyrian Sennacherib has attacked and captured many of the cities of Judah, sent a message to Sennacherib, in which he said: "I have done wrong" (*ḥāṭā'tî*), though he does not specify his "wrong." In his response, however, Sennacherib defines Hezekiah's "wrong" as rebellion: "On whom are you depending, that you rebel [*mrd*] against me?" (v 20). Some commentators understand Sennacherib as defining Hezekiah's **sin** from within the context of the terms of the treaty formerly made between King Ahaz and Assyria, which has been violated in Judah's leaders' turning to Egypt. Thus Sennacherib would view this action as Hezekiah, the head of state, ***sinning*** against him, the king of Assyria. This is not, however, how Isaiah defines Hezekiah and Judah's sin.

■ **2** For Isaiah, the sin in Hezekiah's advisers' act of ***going*** down to **Egypt** is in making such plans **without consulting** Yahweh, who has a larger plan for all the nations, including Assyria, Egypt, and Judah (10:12; 14:25-26; 25:1; Seitz 1993, 217).

Judah's leaders' greatest insult to Yahweh, their Father (→ 30:1), is that they are seeking **Pharaoh's protection** and **Egypt's** ***shadow*** (*ṣēl miṣrāyim*) in the place of "the shadow of the Almighty" (*ṣēl šadday* [Ps 91:1]) (Oswalt 1986, 546). This is tantamount to rejecting the entire exodus tradition, of which Yahweh reminded them on several occasions: "I brought you up out of Egypt" (Judg 6:8; compare Judg 2:1; 1 Sam 10:18; 1 Kgs 12:28; 2 Kgs 17:36; Amos 2:10; 3:1).

■ **3-5** Egypt's resurgent power on the world scene, however, is only apparent. Though Judah's **envoys** (v 4) have traveled to the city of **Hanes** with their request, their journey will be for nothing. **Pharaoh's protection** (v 3) and **Egypt's** ***shadow*** will prove to be nonexistent. The Egyptians, insists Isaiah, are **a people** ***of no value to them*** (v 5), that is, worthless, and reliance upon them will result in **only shame and disgrace**.

■ **6-7** These verses describe the journey of Judah's **envoys** (v 6) in terms of the great dangers (**lions** and **snakes**) crossing the **Negev** and (implied) the Sinai to reach **Egypt** (v 7; ibid., 547; Wildberger 2002, 136-37). The irony is that they bring with them **donkeys** (v 6) and **camels** laden with the **riches** and **treasures** of Judah, to be gifted to Egypt, a **nation *of no value***, and **whose help** (v 7) will prove to be ***futility and emptiness***. In a play on the imagery of the mythical fierce chaotic female sea monster **Rahab**, Egypt has been rendered immobile: she is **Rahab the Do-Nothing**. Egypt, the once powerful "Rahab," feared by others, has less bite than the lions and snakes of the desert crossing. So, Judah is buying nothingness! (Wildberger 2002, 137).

Rahab, the Sea Monster

Rahab is the mythical sea serpent that, at the time of creation, Yahweh defeated (Job 26:12; Ps 89:10 [11 HB]; Isa 51:9). Job makes a statement about mythical Rahab (Job 9:13) following a monologue about God's creative power and control over the actions of nature (vv 2-12). In comparison, Rahab's power pales before God's. When God displayed his "anger" (implied from the context: at the time of creation, when God subdued all opposing forces), "even the cohorts of [*'ōzĕrê*, ***helpers of***] Rahab cowered at his feet" (v 13).

b. Isaiah's Message Rejected (30:8-14)

■ **8** This is the second time (compare 8:16) Isaiah has received instructions to **write** down the prophetic message he has received from Yahweh and has been preaching to nonhearing ears. The purpose of the writing, however, is not merely to put a copy in the Judean royal library or to sell copies in Jerusalem's street corner kiosks; the purpose is far-reaching: **that for the days to come it** [i.e., the written record] **may be** *for a* **witness** [to future generations to the truth of Isaiah's spoken message (Wildberger 2002, 143)] *forever.*

■ **9** The **people** to whom Isaiah is preaching are not only **rebellious** (*mrh*) but also **deceitful** [*kḥš*, "false," "lying"] **children, children unwilling to** *hear the* **instruction** [*tôrâ*, "law"] *of* **Yahweh**, their Father (→ v 1). Unwilling (*lō' 'ābû* [*'bh*]) expresses a hardened, recalcitrant attitude of the heart (*TDOT* 1:26). The positive, "if you are willing" (*'im tō'bû*) occurs in contrastive parallelism with "if you **refuse** and rebel" (*'im tĕmā'ănû ûmĕrîtem*) in 1:19-20. In Exod 10:27, "he was not willing" (*lō' 'ābâ*) expresses the attitude of Pharaoh's heart.

■ **10-11** Yahweh's children's refusal to hear their Father's counsel is graphically described. To the **seers** (*rō'îm* [v 10]) and **visionaries** (*ḥōzîm*) they scoffingly jeer: "**No more** of your imaginary **seeing** and **visioning**, purporting to tell us **what is right** (concerning international involvements and treaties). We want **smooth** things, illusions; support us, as any good official prophet (*nābî'*) would do. If you can't do that, be quiet! **Step aside from the path! Get out of our faces** [*mippānênû*] **with the Holy One of Israel**" (v 11).

The counsel of Yahweh, **the Holy One of Israel**, of course, never agrees with their human plans, especially with intention to place national trust in Pharaoh's Egypt. The account in 1 Kgs 22 depicts King Ahab's hatred of Micaiah ben Imlah, "prophet of **Yahweh**" (*nābî' layhwh* [v 7]), whose word from Yahweh never supported the king's plans (v 8). Micaiah was not a member of the king's "four hundred" official "prophets" (*hannĕbî'îm* [v 6]), "yes men" who always supported the king's plans. He reports receiving the "word of **Yahweh**" by seeing (*rā'îtî*, "I saw" [vv 17, 19]), that is, as a "seer" (*rō'ê*), not as a "prophet" (*nābî'*).

■ **12 Therefore** introduces the response of **the Holy One of Israel** to Judah's leaders' arrogant disrespect and disregard. His response is predicated on the leaders' actions: (1) **Because you have rejected/***despised*** this *word*** (specifically, Yahweh's "instruction" of v 9; generally, as Blenkinsopp suggests [2000, 417], the prophetic challenge of chs 28—31 as a whole); (2) (because) **you have trusted in** acts of **oppression and** *perversion.*

■ **13 Therefore** (omitted in the NIV) introduces the ongoing outcome of the leaders' acts of **iniquity** (*'āwôn*). Isaiah uses the metaphor of a **high wall**, not soundly constructed, **cracked and bulging**. One sees the wall's defect but turns away, deluding oneself that the possibility of *collapse* is not reality but only perception. **Suddenly, however, in an instant**, the wall **collapses**, its faulty construction exposed. The Judean leaders' self-delusion that Egyptian help can stop the Assyrian advance into Judah will be just as suddenly shown to be just that: delusion. The Assyrian army will indeed show up at the barred gates of Jerusalem (chs 36—37), after having pillaged the towns of Judah and Philistia and defeating the Egyptian forces at Eltekeh (Pritchard 1969, 288). The Assyrian commander likens dependence upon Egypt's help to a person stupidly leaning on the wrong (sharpened) end of a walking stick and piercing his hand (36:6).

■ 14 The coming complete shattering of the Judean leaders' deluded plans is further reinforced with the metaphor of a **pottery** vessel so **shattered** that no piece is large enough even **for taking coals from a hearth or scooping water out of a cistern**.

c. Yahweh Will Show Compassion (30:15-18)

■ 15 In a satirically presented dialogue between **Sovereign Yahweh, the Holy One of Israel** and the Judean leaders, Isaiah highlights their arrogant, flippant response to the Sovereign's offer. The **Sovereign** asks for a *returning* [or *turning*] *and resting* (instead of hopelessly sending caravans of "riches" down to Egypt [v 6], seeking their help), and, **in quietness and trust** their acknowledgment that God's plan for Judah, as it fits into his larger plan for the nations, is best. If Judah does this, Yahweh will make good on his offer of **salvation** and **strength**. They will have no need to fear Assyria!

■ 16 But Judah's leaders roundly reject Yahweh's offer: "You would have none of it," says Isaiah (v 15). Rather, you have a backdoor plan: If danger becomes too high, **we will ride off on swift horses** (v 16), you say. Indeed, you will, responds Isaiah, with **your pursuers** in **swift** pursuit.

■ 17 Reversing the hyperbolic promise of Lev 26:8 that five Israelites will put one hundred of its enemies to flight, Isaiah predicts that one thousand Judeans will be put to flight by only one enemy (Wildberger 2002, 163). Blenkinsopp notes that Sennacherib, in his account of his Judean campaign, alludes to Judean troops deserting Jerusalem, perhaps a reference to Isaiah's hint of "leaders" fleeing Jerusalem (22:3) (2000, 418; Pritchard 1969, 288).

The motif of the **flagstaff/banner**, visible on the **mountaintop** from a far distance, is a desolate reminder of the remnant of God's people that will still remain (Oswalt 1986, 556; Sweeney 1996, 400). Thus a glimmer of hope shines through in Isaiah's prophecy of Yahweh's coming judgment.

■ 18 *Therefore* [*lākēn*, not the NIV's **Yet**] *Yahweh waits* [*ḥkh*] **to be gracious to you;** *and* **therefore he will rise up to show you compassion.** Why? Because **Yahweh is a God of justice**, who is waiting, "indeed 'longing'" (Wildberger 2002, 172) for the moment when the remnant of his people is ready to receive his grace and compassion (Oswalt 1986, 557). Until that moment arrives, Isaiah's counsel to the faithful remnant is: **Blessed are all who wait** [*ḥkh*] **for him.** So, both Yahweh and his faithful remnant **wait.**

d. Yahweh Will Grace His People (30:19-26)

In these verses the prophet expands in a hyperbolic way on the benefits of waiting for that future time of Yahweh's salvation.

■ **19** Verses 19-22 speak of enhanced benefits personally affecting the faithful. *For a* **people** *shall* **live in Zion** [*kî 'am bĕṣiyôn yēšēb*], **in Jerusalem,** refers to those "who wait for" Yahweh to act (v 18). The Hebrew is idiomatically emphatic: *Weeping, you shall not weep!* (v 19; compare 25:8; Rev 21:4). Why? Again, idiomatically: *graciously he will be gracious to you! The voice of your cry, upon hearing it, he has [already] answered* **you** (Isa 30:19; the verb is perfect tense, signifying completed action; compare Hab 1:2 for the cry of one who waits and waits for Yahweh to answer).

■ **20** Although it is not clear to what the prophet is referring by **bread of adversity** and **water of affliction,** bread and water are the two main staples of life. Perhaps they represent the circumstances of the faithful while waiting for Yahweh's time of gracious salvation. When that time arrives, however, says the prophet, **your *Teacher*** [*môrê*] **will *hide himself* no more.** (Compare 45:15; Pss 27:9; 44:24 [25 HB]; 102:2 [3 HB]; 143:7 where God is hiding himself/his face.) The noun *môrê* (from *yrh*, "to teach/instruct") can be either singular or plural. In the overall context here, however, *môrê* points to the **Sovereign** (*'ădōnāy*) who now intimately reveals himself to the faithful as their **Teacher** (compare Isa 2:3; 28:26 where God "teaches" [*yrh*]). In fact, says the prophet, **your own eyes** *will be [continually] seeing your Teacher*.

■ **21** Not only the eyes of the faithful now see Yahweh clearly and unimpeded, but, says the prophet, **your ears will hear a *word*** [*dābār* (not the NIV's **voice,** which would imply *qôl*)] **behind you, saying.** The prophets often use *word* (*dābār*) to describe how they received a message from Yahweh (Jer 1:4, 11, 13; 2:1; Ezek 6:1; 7:1; etc.). Implied here in 30:21 is that in the time of Yahweh's salvation, God's faithful ones will receive his message directly, without the intermediacy of a prophet.

Moreover, the ***word*** will give instruction for daily living: **This is the way; walk in it:** [giving specific guidance] *that* [*kî*] **you** *should* **turn to the right or** *that* [*kî*] *you should turn* **to the left.** Psalm 25:12 speaks of Yahweh teaching "those who fear **Yahweh,**" that "he will instruct [*yrh*] them in the ways they should choose," and 32:8, "I will instruct [*śkl*, 'give prudence, understanding'] you and teach [*yrh*] you in the way you should go."

■ **22 Idols overlaid with silver** and **images covered with gold** imply expensive household deities, which have held much spiritual (and material) value. Now, with Yahweh before their very eyes and at their shoulders speaking into their ears directions for life's daily journey, these **idols** and **images** will be shown for what they really are: something to be deemed **unclean**. **Desecrate** is the intensive form of the root *ṭm'* ("to be unclean") thus, "to make unclean." And these things, now seen to be **unclean** and of no value, says the prophet, you will **throw them away like [unclean] menstrual stuff**.

■ **23-26** These verses speak of enhanced benefits to the agricultural activities of the faithful, and the enhancements to acts of nature. The **sending** of rain to **enrich the produce of** the land (v 23) is reminiscent of Yahweh's promise in Deut 28:12 (compare Ps 135:7; Jer 10:13; 51:16). One's **cattle** will find themselves **grazing** in **enlarged** meadows (Isa 30:23), implying plenty to eat. One's **working** oxen and donkeys will find their diet improved with **salted** fodder (v 24). Perhaps one could afford salt for one's work animals only in times of economic prosperity.

The meaning of the first part of v 25 is not clear, as no **slaughter** or **towers falling** is mentioned in connection with this day of Yahweh's salvation. The **flowing** of streams of water is to be expected in the valleys and plains. But to flow on the tops of **mountains** and **hills**, is a hyperbolic expression of Yahweh's abundant supply of water for all. Likewise, the **moonlight shining** like the sun, and the sunlight *becoming* seven times brighter is hyperbolic (v 26). No human could withstand the brightness or heat of such strength of the sun. Motyer's suggestion is apropos: that this refers to "the restoration of creation to its true powers, when it also is delivered from the bondage of corruption (*cf.* Rom. 8:21)" (1993, 251). The prophet implies that this restoration of creation is from Yahweh, who **binds up the bruises of his people**.

e. The Name of Yahweh Will Shatter Assyria (30:27-33)

Yahweh's judgment upon "Assyria" (v 31) is the focus of this passage. Isaiah metaphorically depicts **Yahweh** (vv 27, 29, 31, 32, 33) coming as a great storm ("cloudburst, thunderstorm and hail" [v 30]), to "**shake** nations" (*gôyim*) and "peoples" (*'ammîm*) (v 28), to "shatter" and "**smite** Assyria" (v 31).

Isaiah applies anthropomorphisms to **Yahweh** in depicting his "**coming** from afar" (v 27): **nose** (*'ap*, idiomatic for **anger**), **lips**, **breath** (*rûaḥ* [v 28]), **voice** (vv 30, 31), **arm** (v 30), **nose** (again = anger [v 30]), and **breath** (*nišmah* [v 33]).

■ **27-28** God first revealed his **Name** as **Yahweh** (v 27; Yahweh from the root *hwh*, "to be" [*HALOT* 395]: past, present, and future) to Moses (Exod 3:15), when appearing to him as a flame of fire at Mount Horeb. In doing so, God identified himself (1) as none other than the one who appeared long before to the forefathers, Abraham, Isaac, and Jacob (the past [vv 6, 15, 16]), (2) as having "watched over" the Israelites while in Egypt (the present [v 16]), and (3) as the one who will bring the Israelites out of Egypt (the future [v 17]). Thus the **Name** encompasses God's entire character as the one who calls forth, cares for, and redeems. So, as in the past, his **Name** implies a present and future faithfulness to his people.

Yet Yahweh's *coming* is a **wrath-*filled*, anger-*filled*, consuming fire-*filled*** (Isa 30:27) appearance, not against his people, but in judgment upon **nations** and **peoples** (v 28). Here, these are not the kingdoms of the world but represent Assyria (v 31), the ruling world empire. The Assyrian kings conscripted into their army large numbers of soldiers from the various kingdoms that they brought under their control (compare Ashurbanipal, Pritchard 1969, 294). Thus Isaiah can speak of Assyria as **nations/peoples** who invade.

In 8:8, at Yahweh's instigation, Assyria was depicted as "swirling over" (*šṭp*, **overwhelming**) Judah, "reaching up to the neck." The tables are now turned, with Yahweh, *coming* from afar (30:27) to the rescue of his people, depicted as an ***overflowing*** [*šṭp*] **torrent, rising up to the neck** of Assyria (v 28). The imagery is that of the desert riverbed (wadi), dry throughout most of the year, suddenly, as the rainy season begins, becoming an overflowing, rain-fed torrent, as the waters from a torrential rainstorm in the mountains above rush toward the riverbed's outlet. Anyone caught in that riverbed will be swept away. Just as suddenly and unexpectedly Yahweh will intercede for Judah, and Assyria will be swept away.

The imagery of Yahweh ***placing a misleading bridle upon*** the jaws of the peoples (i.e., Assyria) (v 28) indicates that Yahweh is Sovereign even over the movements and destiny of an empire like Assyria and will lead it to destruction. The kings of Assyria believe they are acting according to the will of their supreme deity, Ashur (Pritchard 1969, 276-301).

■ **29-32** A holy festival is introduced in v 29, with God's people *celebrating* on the **mountain of Yahweh**. **Pipes** (v 29), **timbrels and harps** (v 32) accompany this celebration. The occasion for **holy festival** and *celebration* is **Yahweh's** intended *shattering* of Assyria (v 31).

■ **33** The NIV has opted to interpret *topteh* as the proper name **Topheth**, a place located in the Valley of Ben Hinnom on the southwest side of Jerusalem, where apparently children were sacrificed to the deity Molek (compare 2 Kgs 23:10; Jer 19:6 [*hattōpet*]). But sacrifice to a deity is not pictured here, but rather is depicted a judgmental cremation by Yahweh (of Isa 30:32). Thus *topteh* here is a ***place of burning***, **dug deep and wide**. There is **an abundance of . . . wood** stacked nearby. All this **has long been prepared for the final demise of the king**, who represents the Assyrian Empire. All awaits **the breath of Yahweh**, like a stream of burning sulfur to *set* it ablaze.

f. Satire: Egypt Is Merely Human; Assyria Will Fall by a Nonhuman Sword (31:1-9)

■ **1-3** These verses parallel Isaiah's **woe** oracle of 30:1-5. As in the previous oracle, Isaiah again speaks of those **who go down to Egypt for help** without having consulted Yahweh (v 2). The historical context appears still to be Assyrian Sennacherib's 701 BC impending invasion of Judah.

Though Isaiah does not use the word "idolatry," idolatry is precisely the essence of Judah's leaders' action: an outright rejection of **help from Yahweh, the Holy One of Israel**; instead they have substituted **trust** in the apparent military might of **Egypt** (**horses, chariots,** and **horsemen**). This constitutes a denial of Yahweh's victory over Pharaoh and his military might in the Exodus event, in which Yahweh overturned and buried Pharaoh's chariots and horsemen in the sea (Exod 14:26-28). Why should Judah's leaders now believe Yahweh to be less powerful than Pharaoh?

Isaiah's affirmation that **he** [i.e., Yahweh] **is wise** (Isa 31:2) is an in-your-face dig at both Judean and Egyptian counselors, who, believing Yahweh to be a know-nothing deity, advise foolishness (see 5:12; 19:11-15; 28:14-15). In his wisdom, Yahweh **can *cause* disaster *to happen*** (compare 45:7). Though **disaster** did not, in fact, come to Jerusalem during Sennacherib's 701 BC invasion, Yahweh **does not take back his words**. In his own timing, he kept his ***word*** when he sent the Babylonian army to overthrow Jerusalem in 587 BC.

Wildberger suggests that the ***house of evildoers*** (*bêt mĕrē'îm*) refers to the pro-Egyptian counselors at the Judean palace, clan-like sticking together, while the ***doers of iniquity*** (*pō'ălê 'āwen*) are the Egyptians (2002, 210-11). In response to their refusal to acknowledge him, Yahweh **will rise up against** both.

Isaiah continues to confront the Judean leaders with their misplaced trust in the **Egyptians** and their **horses** (v 3). After all, they are mere **mortals** and **flesh**, created beings, just as the Judeans. They are **not God**, the Creator, whom the Judeans have spurned. There may be in the background here a slap at the Egyptian claim that Pharaoh is divine; after all, he is a mere created human too (Wildberger 2002, 213; Blenkinsopp 2000, 427). Moreover, **horses** (from the pharaoh's chariot corps) represent Egypt's military might, and thus represent Pharaoh himself. They, too, **are flesh** [*bāśār*] **and not spirit** (*rûaḥ*), declares Isaiah. Wildberger cites two Egyptian paeans in which the pharaoh is said to be the one who is "'the breath of life,' . . . 'who gives life . . . , the breath for all noses, by which one breathes'" (2002, 213). This is in direct opposition to the OT witness, which affirms that it is the "spirit" // "breath of the Almighty" that gives "understanding" and "life" (Job 32:8; 33:4; compare Ps 104:30).

In response to the foolish wisdom of both the Egyptians and the Judean royal counselors, **Yahweh stretches out his hand**, just as Moses, at Yahweh's command, stretched out his hand over the sea that swallowed up Pharaoh's chariots and horsemen in the exodus event (Exod 14:26-27). And when Yahweh does so, both ***helper*** (the Egyptians) and ***helped*** (the Judeans) . . . **will perish together**.

■ **4** Verses 4-9 speak of Yahweh's deliverance of Jerusalem (vv 4-5) and destruction of Assyria (vv 6-9). Verse 4 opens with **For** (*kî*, omitted in the NIV), indicating that the indictment against "helper" (Egypt) and "helped" (Judeans) that precedes (vv 1-3) is linked with what now follows. Verse 2 says that Yahweh "will rise up against" both the ***house of evildoers*** within the Judean government and the ***doers of iniquity*** of Egypt. Verse 4 restates this as **Yahweh Sebaoth will come down to do battle**. The place from which he will wage war against both is the place of his habitation, **Mount Zion** and its surrounding **heights**. Like a **young** lion defending **its prey**, unperturbed by the **shouts** and **clamor** of a bunch of **shepherds** attempting ***to frighten*** it away, so Yahweh will be undeterred. Yahweh will "not take back his ***word***" (v 2).

Lions in Ancient Palestine

In Isaiah's time the Asiatic lion (*Panthera leo persica*) was present in Israel/Palestine. Samson, in the time of the Judges, is reputed for having killed a lion with his bare hands (Judg 14:6), and Jeremiah speaks of the lion in the Jordan River area (Jer 50:44). The lion has been extinct in Israel/Palestine for many centuries, however. It did survive, though, in the marshlands of the Tigris and Euphrates Rivers until the nineteenth century AD (*EDB*, §15439).

■ **5** Yet, while carrying out his "disaster" (Isa 31:2) against both the evil ones within (Judean treaty makers) and without (Egyptians), in the present Assyrian crisis Yahweh will preserve **Jerusalem**. Like birds ***flying*** overhead, watching for any that would harm their nesting young, so **Yahweh Sebaoth will shield, deliver,** and **rescue** his beloved city. That the rescue will be from the Assyrian threat is made clear in v 8.

■ **6-7** In anticipation of God's deliverance, Isaiah issues a twofold call: to repentance and to a drastically changed way of living. God's people have **greatly revolted against** Yahweh (v 6), the same accusation with which the book of Isaiah begins (1:5). Only in ***returning*** to Yahweh, fully acknowledging his sovereignty and holiness, can God's people then grasp the absolute worthlessness of ***handmade*** idols (31:7). Only in seeing the **One** (v 6, as Isaiah saw **Yahweh Sebaoth**, and then his own sinfulness [6:1, 3, 5]), could they see the ***sinfulness*** of the work of their **hands**. Only then could they allow these **idols** to relinquish their hold, and in that relinquishing, live in the full light of God's guidance.

■ **8-9** Isaiah returns to Yahweh's ultimate overthrow of **Assyria** (v 8). The defeat of the Assyrian army in 701 BC when the Angel of Yahweh slayed 185,000 Assyrian soldiers in one night is certainly one example of Assyria ***falling*** by no human sword (see 37:36). But Isaiah has the longer view in mind. The demise of the Assyrian Empire came with the Babylonian overthrow of its capital Nineveh in 612 BC and the mopping-up destruction of its army remnants over the next three years. Yet, from Isaiah's perspective, the overthrow of Assyria would be Yahweh's doing, with Babylon but a tool in Yahweh's hand. Thus, ultimately, the fall of kingdoms and empires is by the **sword** of God, **not of mortals**.

It was stated in 30:33 that the "fire pit" has been long prepared "for the king." Here, in 31:9, Isaiah points to **Zion/Jerusalem** as the place from which symbolically the **fire** of **Yahweh** burns, his **furnace** in which those nations that oppose him will be devoured. One is reminded of Amos' declaration that it is from "Zion/Jerusalem" that "**Yahweh** roars and thunders" and sends out "fire" to destroy the ruling centers of rebellious nations (chs 1—2).

FROM THE TEXT

Isaiah 30 and 31 present two diametrically opposed parties. On the one side is Prophet Isaiah. He represents Israel's deity, known to him as **Yahweh** (30:1, 18, 27, 30, 31, 32, 33; 31:1, 3, 4, 9), "the Holy One of Israel" (30:11, 12, 15; 31:1), "Sovereign **Yahweh**" (30:15), **Teacher** (v 20), "Rock of Israel" (v 29), "God" (31:3), and **Yahweh Sebaoth** (v 4). On the other side are "people of Zion, **inhabitants of** Jerusalem" (30:19), whom Isaiah labels "obstinate children" (v 1), "rebellious people" (v 9), "deceitful children" (v 9), "his [i.e., Yahweh's] people" (v 26), and "Israelites" (31:6).

From the Judeans' perspective, Judah is at the center of her physical world. At the extreme ends of this physical world are two great powers, Assyria (30:31; 31:8) to the northeast, and Egypt (30:2, 3, 7; 31:1) to the southwest. When Judah's leaders look to the north they see Assyria and its king (30:31, 33), an imminent military threat; when they look to the south they see Egypt and Pharaoh, a potential military help, a "protection" (vv 2-3).

At the center of this physical world, between these two opposing powerful nation empires, Isaiah is a lone voice crying out to God's people that Judah/Jerusalem already has a supreme protector, "Sovereign **Yahweh**, the Holy One of Israel, [*who*] says, 'In repentance and rest is your salvation, in quietness and trust is your strength'" (v 15). Our God offers you **grace** and "compassion" (v 18). But Judah's response is: we will have nothing more to do with your God, Isaiah (v 15). We will trust in Egypt and Pharaoh. If that fails, however, we will fall back on our own resources, employing the best of human wisdom (in actuality, foolishness): we have "swift horses" on which we can "flee"! (v 16).

Paul observes to the church at Corinth that, "the wisdom of this world is foolishness in God's sight" (1 Cor 3:19). To the believers at Rome, Paul speaks of those "who suppress the truth by their wickedness." These are those, who, "although they knew God, they neither glorified him as God nor gave thanks to him." As a result, "their foolish hearts were darkened"; claiming "to be wise, they became fools and exchanged the glory of the immortal God for images made to look like a mortal human being" (Rom 1:18, 21, 22-23).

It is almost as though Paul is reading Isaiah's challenge to those leaders of Judah who have exchanged faith in their Creator for faith in "useless" Egypt (Isa 30:7), and in "idols of silver and gold" (31:7). Yet, says Isaiah, the day will come when God's people will realize that Pharaoh and Egypt are "mere mortals" (v 3) after all, and they "will reject" their "idols" (v 7). Then they "will cry for help," and "**Yahweh**, [*who*] is a God of justice" will **hear** and "will answer" (30:18-19). This is the message of hope we offer to a world that lives by its own foolish "wisdom."

4. Behold! A King Will Reign According to Righteousness (32:1-20)

BEHIND THE TEXT

This chapter divides into three segments. The first (32:1-8) prophesies an era that is in contrast with the conditions in Judea as depicted in the previous few chapters. "Righteousness" and "justice" will be the order of the day for the "king" and his ***princes*** (v 1). The second (vv 9-14) prophesies a desolation of "the land" (v 13) in terms of failed ***harvests*** (v 10) and "deserted ***cities***" (v 14). The third (vv 15-20) prophesies a reversal in which the land abundantly produces through the outpouring of "the Spirit" (v 15), who brings "justice" (v 16) and "righteousness" to "desert" (v 15), "field," and "homes" (v 18).

This chapter contains citations, themes, and key words that have appeared in previous chapters in Isaiah (→ 32:1, 2, 3-4, 5, 9). This suggests a possible intentional summation of Isaiah's previous teaching (warnings and promise), serving as a bridge into ch 33, in which Isaiah depicts Yahweh, having removed all Israel's enemies, reigning as "judge," "lawgiver," and "king" (33:22).

It is not clear from the text of ch 32 whether the prophet is envisioning an era in "real" time or in the messianic age. But this question need not be resolved for the message of the chapter to speak: when God's people are willing to fully live as kingdom people, allowing God to fully rule in their lives, they/we "will live in peaceful dwelling places" (v 18).

IN THE TEXT

a. Princes Will Rule According to Justice (32:1-8)

■ 1 In the new era that is in contrast with present conditions in Judah, there will be **a king** and ***princes*** (*śārîm*) who will administer *according to* **righteousness** and **justice**. At the very beginning of the book, Isaiah depicted Jerusalem as a city in which the administration of justice and righteousness no longer was the rule of the day. Rather, ***princes*** (*śārîm*) were oppressing orphans and widows by taking bribes to subvert their just causes (1:21-23). Even there, however, Isaiah held out the promise that in a future day justice and righteousness would be restored to Zion through a restored, noncorrupt leadership (1:26-27).

■ **2** Each one refers to the *princes* who assist the "king" (v 1). The metaphors—**shelter from the wind, refuge from the storm, streams of water in** the *parched land* (ṣāyôn; compare 35:1), and **shadow of a *heavy* rock**—speak of the protection and provision the king and his officers will provide. These metaphors echo similar benefits of Yahweh's future presence "in that day" on Mount Zion, in the metaphor of a cloud and fire canopy: "shelter," "shade," "refuge," "hiding place" (4:5-6). The concept that people can expect shelter, shade, and provision from their king was widespread throughout the ancient Near East. In one letter from Assyrian Sargon to an official in Que, Sargon urges, "Now eat your bread (and) drink your water (under) the shadow of the king" (quoted by Wildberger 2002, 237). Similarly, Isaiah states that it is "***Yahweh*** our king" who supplies "bread" and "water" for "those who walk righteously" in his presence (33:22, 16, 17).

■ **3-4** The prophet now highlights a transformation of the faculties of seeing (***smeared over*** **eyes** [v 3]), hearing (***nonlistening*** **ears**), inner perception (***hasty/impetuous*** **hearts** [v 4]) and communication (**stammering *tongues***), a transformation made possible in the new society because the king and his officials adhere to righteousness and justice.

In the larger context of the book of Isaiah, surely here is intended a reversal of the closed eyes, dull ears, and calloused hearts that would result from Isaiah's preaching (6:9-10). In the more immediate context, however, this transformation is related to 29:18, where it is promised that the deaf ears and blind eyes of Judah's leaders will someday see and hear ***words of a scroll***, which Wildberger translates as "the scripture" (2002, 238). Yet, Wildberger further suggests, the enabling to see and to hear in this new era is for more than seeing and hearing scripture, though it certainly includes that, but an empowerment "to have correct comprehension and correct insight in general" (ibid., 239). This will be demonstrated in the king and his officers' administrating a society that exemplifies righteousness and justice.

The **heart** (32:4) is perceived as the organ that, if "wisdom" and "knowledge" lodge therein (Prov 2:10; 14:33; 15:14), enables one's "lips" to "speak what is right" (23:15-16) and one's ***mouth*** and "lips" to give out "gracious words" that are "sweet to the soul and healing to the bones" (16:23-24). Thus the **heart** and **tongue** are perceived as intimately connected (Isa 32:4). Therefore, the formerly ***impetuous hearts*** of king and officers, which now grasp, with new ***knowledge*** and new ***understanding***, what their newly opened **eyes** (v 3) and **ears** see and hear, will enable their formerly **stammering *tongues*** (v 4) to speak in new ways. **Stammering** here appears not to refer to physical speech impediments but is a metaphor for the inability to give right and just decisions that benefit society. Transformed, the king and officers' **tongues** now speak ***fluently*** and ***clearly***, without guile, deception, self-interest or favoritism.

■ **5** This verse presents an example of the deceptive hearts and tongues of v 4: the meanings of words have been turned on their heads. In the present, both the **fool** and the **scoundrel** are deemed **noble**, receiving ***high respect***. This implies that the **noble** is deemed a **fool**. Here is an echo of 5:20: "those who call evil good and good evil." But in the new era a fool will be seen to be a fool, and a noble person truly as noble.

■ **6 Fools** here represents Judah's present leaders of 30:1-2 and 31:1, who have refused to seek out the will of Yahweh, Israel's Holy One. In so refusing, they are "the fool [*who*] says in his heart, 'There is no God.' They are corrupt, their deeds are vile" (Ps 14:1). Isaiah's view of **fools** is the same: their rejection of God in the conduct of life is rooted in **their hearts**: it is there that they ***prepare*** [Wildberger 2002, 241] **evil**, out of which they ***speak*** error concerning ***Yahweh***. The implication is that they believe Yahweh is incapable of supplying their daily needs, thus they **withhold** the basic necessities (bread and **water**) from the powerless, leaving them **hungry** and **thirsty**.

■ **7 Scoundrels** is another way of speaking of the "fools" of v 6. It is specifically judicial decisions in cases of the **poor** and **needy** that are singled out here. **Scoundrels** are judges who **use wicked *weapons*, plan** [*y'ṣ*] **evil schemes**, and **lies** to overturn the ***just plea*** of the powerless.

■ **8** In contrast to the "fools" and "scoundrels" are the truly **noble**, who ***plan*** [*y'ṣ*] **noble deeds, and *upon*** [those] **noble deeds they *take their* stand**. That is, they give their time to planning how to do those deeds that will benefit others, and then carry them out, though others may call them fools.

b. Harvest Taken, Cities Deserted (32:9-14)

The term "complacent" (vv 9, 11) illustrates the theme of v 3: eyes that do not see and ears that do not hear. Life will continue as it now is, if one only refuses to acknowledge the political reality of the times. Thus the prophet issues a call to the "women" of Judea, urging them to an awareness of impending invasion and military devastation.

■ **9** Isaiah speaks synonymously to ***wives*** [*nāšîm*, "married women"] **who are complacent** (from the root *š'n*, "to be at ease") and to **daughters** [*bānôt*, "unmarried women"] **who feel secure** (*bṭḥ*, "to trust"). Both ***wives*** and **daughters** represent the Judean population (Wildberger 2002, 249). Isaiah is not necessarily speaking pejoratively here, however, that is, of a carefree, arrogant, don't-give-a-fig attitude; rather, he is speaking of misplaced trust. Security is what one should expect from one's governing leaders; yet one's ultimate trust must be in Yahweh (Oswalt 1986, 585).

The summons **listen** (*šm'*)/**hear** (*'zn*) has been issued previously: (1) to the unjust, bribe-taking "rulers" of Jerusalem (1:23), whose ears were closed to Yahweh's plea for repentance, and (2) to "scoffers," leaders of Judah, who insisted that the "overwhelming scourge" (i.e., Assyria) would not touch them (28:14-19). Here, receiving no positive response from the men of Judah, the prophet turns to the women.

■ **10-14** The prophet predicts that the **grape harvest** and ***gathering*** of other ***crops*** will not be available (v 10). This, along with the takeover of what were once **pleasant fields** (v 12) by **thorns and briers**, a ***palace*** abandoned, and a **noisy city deserted** (vv 13-14), all together speak of war. An invading army will have eaten the food supplies and will have deported inhabitants. All that presently assures security will be gone.

The prophet calls for a general lament: **tremble, shudder, strip *yourselves*, *undress yourselves*, *gird the loins*** (v 11), **mourn!** (v 13). Since the command to **strip** and ***undress*** appears nowhere else in the OT in connection with mourning, Motyer suggests (citing 20:2-3) that here the command to remove clothing is a sign of impending enslavement or captivity (1993, 260).

Commentators have suggested a variety of historical settings for the devastation of 32:13-14, including Assyrian Sennacherib's invasion of 701 BC and its aftermath. Sennacherib recorded in his annals that he devastated forty-six of Judah's towns and cities and deported 200,150 of their inhabitants (Pritchard 1969, 288). Yet it is a ***palace*** that has been **abandoned**, and the busy sounds of a **city**, presumably Jerusalem, that are no longer heard (v 14). This did not happen to Jerusalem during Sennacherib's invasion. So, unless ***palace*** and **city** (both are indefinite) stand generally for Judean towns and their ruling centers, the prophecy looks forward to another day, perhaps to the 587 BC Babylonian devastation of Jerusalem, or beyond.

The **city** spoken of is to become **a wasteland forever**. Goldingay points out that the term **forever** (*'ad 'ôlām*) suggests "something final and permanent." Yet, "Yahweh's commitment to Jerusalem" modifies the permanency of the term, so that "devastation is unlikely to have the last word" (2001, 182). So, **forever** is only ***until*** (v 15).

Mourning in the OT

The acts of mourning were: (1) tearing one's clothes (Gen 37:34), (2) wearing sackcloth next to the skin (2 Sam 3:31; Isa 37:1), a material made of camel or goat hair, (3) fasting (2 Sam 1:12), (4) beating the breasts (Isa 32:12), (5) putting dust/ashes on one's head (2 Sam 1:2), (6) sitting in the dust/ashes (Jonah 3:6), and (7) rolling in dust/ashes. The period of mourning was normally seven days (Gen 50:10) (King and Stager 2001, 372-73; *EDB*, §17448).

c. The Spirit Poured Out; Fertile Fields (32:15-20)

These verses depict a complete reversal of the devastation of vv 9-14, a transformation/restoration made possible by God's "Spirit" (v 15).

■ 15 This verse appears to begin in mid-sentence, **until** (*'ad*), but in fact it continues from the conclusion of v 14. All is a "wasteland forever," but only **until** God's **Spirit is poured out** [*'rh*, "to reveal, "to empty out"] **upon us**. The active work of God's **Spirit** is depicted as transforming the environment, but for the benefit of **us**, defined in v 18 as "my people" ("my" could refer either to God or the prophet, but the prophet so identifies with God that "my" is one and the same).

Two elements of the environment are transformed: (1) **desert** (*midbar*), normally agriculturally unproductive, becomes **fertile field** (*karmel*, **orchard**), and (2) **fertile field** (*karmel*, **orchard**), normally productive, becomes super productive so that it resembles a **forest** (*ya'ar*).

■ 16 Resulting from the Spirit's work, **justice** [*mišpāṭ*] **will dwell** (*škn*) in this transformed **desert** and **righteousness** [*ṣĕdāqâ*] **will inhabit** (*yšb*) the transformed **fertile field**. On the basis of the two verbs, Wildberger observes, "Justice and righteousness would not be guests that visited from time to time, but they would be permanent residents there" (2002, 261).

■ 17-18 As permanent residents in the deserts and fertile fields where **my** [i.e., Yahweh's] **people** (v 18) live and work in the new era, **righteousness** (v 17) and (implied) justice will bring about conditions for **peace, quietness**, and **security** (*beṭaḥ*, "trust"). **Peaceful dwelling places** (v 18) and **secure homes** will be the order of day.

■ 19 This verse, with its negative prediction of both **forest** and **city** destroyed, appears incompatible with the positive idyllic scenes both before and after. Because of this, many commentators bypass it with no useful insights offered or see it as a later misplaced insertion. Blenkinsopp, however, on the one hand, suggests taking the text "on its own terms"; that is, both forest and city will disappear, "leaving only *karmel* (transformed desert and fertile field) as the ideal rural utopia" (2000, 435). Oswalt, on the other hand, suggests that the verse is speaking of the "destruction of Israelite pride which must accompany the restoration of righteousness" (1986, 588).

■ 20 This verse (as a conclusion to the chapter) gives an example of the depiction of peace, security, and rest in v 18. Here is the farmer, representing all God's people, **blessed**, dwelling peacefully in idyllic surroundings. There is no fear of enemies as one cultivates crops wherever there is a source of ***water*** (compare v 2). One's cattle and donkeys graze peacefully nearby, also with no fear of predators, human or animal (compare 11:6; 65:25; compare 30:23). Life's security is maintained by God's Spirit (32:15).

FROM THE TEXT

This chapter speaks of security, dwelling peacefully, sheltering from wind and storm, in both the natural and the human social worlds. Both worlds are so integrally intertwined that both must experience God's redemption, through the transforming activity of his Spirit, for true security and peace to prevail. In commenting on Paul's word to the Romans concerning both "the whole creation" and "we ourselves" "groaning" for "redemption" (Rom 8:22-23), Bence speaks of "the very interconnectedness of the created order" and "this fallen world," in which "God intends for us to be His instruments of righteousness." But, we can be such workers of righteousness only as we live "according to the Spirit" (Rom 8:4), as we allow the Spirit to transform us "into the likeness of God's Son here on earth" (1996, 151).

Thus both Isaiah and Paul speak of a time in the distant future when these intertwined fallen natural and social worlds will experience a transformation that John describes as "a new heaven and a new earth" (Rev 21:1). Of interest is that a benefit of John's transformed/new creation is the making available to those who thirst "the *fountain* of the water of life" to drink *freely* (Rev 21:6), an echo of the "streams of water" in Isaiah's *parched land* (32:2), made available to support the cultivation of crops in Isaiah's transformed natural world (v 20).

5. Yahweh, the King, Forgives Zion (33:1-24)

BEHIND THE TEXT

This chapter lacks specific references to historical contexts or names that enables commentators to date its contents with confidence. Because of this, recent commentators have placed the composition of the chapter in various times: e.g., Isaiah's own time (Motyer, Oswalt, Seitz), Persian times (Wildberger 2002, 271), even as late as the Hellenistic period (Kaiser 1974, 342), a span of some four hundred years. Motyer, with some confidence, sees Assyria "veiled behind the description *destroyer*" as mentioned in v 1, and thus interprets vv 1-12 in the context of "Assyrian times" (italics in original). He interprets the themes of the remainder of the chapter, however, as "eschatological" (1993, 262, 264). Oswalt views vv 18-19 as depicting a real historical situation (→ 33:18-19); he then links this with the references to Assyria in 30:31 and 31:8, which he calls the "literary key" that "tells us that the destroyer is Assyria" (1986, 591-92). Oswalt then interprets the remainder of the chapter against the backdrop of Judah's struggle with Assyria; yet, Judah looks to a distant time when, in fact, "**Yahweh [*who*]** is our king" (v 22), rules. Seitz finds that "chapter 33 gives no convincing signal that would oblige us to seek a historical setting much later than Isaiah's," and identifies the "destroyer" with

Assyria (1993, 233-34). This present commentary interprets ch 33 within the context of the Assyrian period.

The chapter can be divided into four units, all focusing on Zion: vv 1-6, Yahweh's justice and righteousness in Zion; vv 7-12, Zion betrayed; vv 13-16, Zion, both a dreaded place and a refuge; and, vv 17-24, Zion, a peaceful abode.

IN THE TEXT

a. Zion, Filled with Yahweh's Justice and Righteousness (33:1-6)

■ 1 A **woe** (*hôy*) is pronounced against an unnamed **destroyer . . . betrayer**. Applying Oswalt's "literary key" (→ 33:1-24 Behind the Text above), there is no reason why this **destroyer** cannot be Assyria; the annals of the Assyrian kings record their furious destruction of cities and towns as their armies swept westward (Pritchard 1969, 275, 277, 284, etc.). **Betrayer** could well refer to Assyrian Sennacherib who in 701 BC attacked and captured most of Judah's towns, including the heavily fortified southern city of Lachish. Hezekiah sent emissaries to him at Lachish, offering to "pay whatever you demand of me" (2 Kgs 18:14) if only Sennacherib would withdraw. Appearing to agree to this, Sennacherib demanded a large payment of gold and silver, which Hezekiah paid. Yet Sennacherib, betraying his tacit agreement to withdraw, sent an army against Jerusalem (vv 13-17).

The day will come, insists the prophet, when, imperial power waning, Assyria, too, **will be betrayed** and inevitably **will be destroyed**. This betrayal, in fact, did happen when the Assyrian province of Akkad/Babylon, in alliance with the Medes, rose up in rebellion and in 612 BC overthrew Nineveh and by 609 BC brought about the full annihilation of the vestiges of Assyrian leadership and military (Pritchard 1969, 303-5; *EDB*, §18183).

■ 2 The presence of ***their arm*** (*zĕrō'ām*; the NIV's **our strength**) in this verse has given commentators cause for a variety of emendations on the assumption that the pronoun should agree with **our salvation** in the parallel line. One of the Qumran Hebrew texts (1QIsa[a]) also has the pronoun "their" (Oswalt 1986, 589), though other ancient translations (Tg., Syr., Vg.) have "our" (Wildberger 2002, 266). Motyer suggests the correctness of the MT if v 2 is viewed as "a snatch of liturgical form," with leader and congregation engaged in responsive interchange (1993, 263). Verse 2 then would read:

Leader: **Yahweh, be gracious to us**.
Congregation: [**Yahweh**] **We** *wait* **for you**.
Leader: **Be *their arm*** [i.e., **strength**] **every morning**.
Congregation: **Indeed** [*'ap*, omitted in the NIV], **our salvation in *a* time of distress**.

To *wait* for **Yahweh** implies a trust in his plan, in his time to act, an attitude diametrically opposed to that expressed by Judah's leaders in the previous two chapters. Yet implied is a confidence that Yahweh's **grace, strength,** and **salvation** will be extended **every morning**. The writer of Lamentations also expresses that he *waits* for the "every morning" renewal of Yahweh's care: his "love," "compassions," and "faithfulness" (3:22-23). The psalmist expresses that God's help comes "at *dawn*" (lit. *the turning of the morning* [Ps 46:5 (6 HB)].

■ **3-4** The prophet now speaks of **the peoples** (*'ammîm* [v 3])/**the nations** (*gôyim*). As in previous instances (→ 17:12-13; 30:28), **the peoples/the nations** here represent the multi-kingdoms present in Assyria's "army of nations" (Kaiser 1974, 345). The focus is upon the *rising* up of Yahweh, associated with the **sound of an army** (*qôl hāmôn*, lit. **sound of a multitude**; but compare Dan 11:10 where *hāmôn* is parallel with *hăyālîm*, "army"). Thus the prophet speaks of a coming engagement, Yahweh's **army** against the forces of Assyria (the "destroyer" of v 1), in which they will **flee** and **scatter**. The **plunder** (v 4), which Assyria has gathered to itself, when its army flees into oblivion will be **harvested** by the army that Yahweh has sent, like **a swarm of locusts** who devour everything in their path (compare Joel 1:4-7).

■ **5-6** When earthly imperial powers that have exalted themselves against Yahweh (e.g., Sennacherib in chs 36—37 and who in his annals claims that victories are given him by "Ashur my lord" [Pritchard 1969, 287]) have fled and are scattered (v 3), it is **Yahweh** who remains **exalted** (v 5). Though **he dwells on high** (i.e., in heaven: "he stands above all earthly intrigues" [Kaiser 1974, 344]), Yahweh's presence is experienced in **Zion**. He **will** [once again] **fill Zion with** [its former] **justice** (*mišpāṭ*) **and righteousness** (*ṣĕdāqâ*); he will bring to it *stability* (*'mn*, NIV's **sure foundation** [v 6]). Isaiah's earlier word (1:21-27) indicated that Zion, once known as the "faithful ['*mn*] city" (v 21), one day, with "justice" and "righteousness" restored, would again be named the "faithful ['*mn*] city."

In our present passage, all this is predicated upon a relationship, **the fear of Yahweh**, a relationship that draws on the true source of all **salvation and wisdom and knowledge**: Yahweh **exalted** above all other claims (v 5).

b. Zion Betrayed, Treaties Broken (33:7-12)

■ **7** The **brave men** and **envoys of peace** may refer to those messengers that Hezekiah has sent to Sennacherib at Lachish, with the gold and silver tribute intended to secure Sennacherib's withdrawal from Judah (2 Kgs 18:13-17). They **cry aloud** and **weep bitterly** *outside* (*ḥuṣâ*). *Ḥuṣâ* here places them, not **in the streets** but most likely *outside* the city walls/gates as they return from their failed negotiations with Sennacherib. They **cry** and **weep** in response to having been deceived.

■ **8** The character of the "destroyer" (of v 1) is given here: *he breaks covenants, he despises* its witnesses, and *he holds no respect for any person*.

When such an enemy, with his army of nations, is present in the land, **travelers dare not be out and about**; **roads** and **highways are deserted**.

■ **9** **Lebanon** (north), **Sharon** and **Carmel** (along the seacoast), and **Bashan** (east of the Sea of Galilee) all were fertile, productive areas that sustained Israel's life in the land in which God had originally settled them. So intimately intertwined were/are humans and the land, that now, in response to the despicable human actions throughout the land, all fertile land **dries up**, **wastes away**, **withers**, and **drops their leaves** (but compare 35:1-2, where all these areas again become productive in response to seeing "the glory of **Yahweh**"). This imagery is possibly both literal and figurative. Literally, we see the denuding of the land of produce to sustain the Assyrian army as it advances from north to south. Figuratively, we see Judah, dispirited, barren, unfruitful, as it has come to rely on its own wisdom and abilities, rather than that of Yahweh (Oswalt 1986, 597).

■ **10** **Now**, repeated three times, indicates the moment of **Yahweh's** decision to intervene on behalf of his people. **Arise**, **exalted**, **lifted up** emphasize Yahweh's supremacy over the Assyrian "great king" Sennacherib (36:4; Sennacherib claims Yahweh to be powerless [v 20]) and his supreme deity Ashur (Pritchard 1969, 287).

■ **11-12** Although not defined, **you** (v 11) surely refers to the "destroyer" of v 1. Sennacherib's intentions against Jerusalem (to capture, pillage, and deport its inhabitants) are ***conceived*** in the womb of his heart; when ***birthed***, however, they are nothing but **chaff**, blown away by the "wind" of God (Ps 1:4; compare Isa 17:13; 29:5; 40:24; 41:2), or **straw**, which **fire** readily **consumes**.

The imagery of **fire** represents Yahweh's fiery breath upon **the peoples** (*'ammîm* [33:12]), the multi-kingdoms present in Assyria's military forces. They **will be burned to *lime***. Reducing corpses to ***lime*** effectively leaves no substance of that person, denying any possibility of a continued life after death. (→ From the Text following ch 16 for comments on ancient burial practices and beliefs concerning the afterlife.) Thus the intention here depicts Yahweh's judgment bringing a future final and complete end to Assyria.

c. Zion, a Dread for Sinners, a Refuge for the Righteous (33:13-16)

■ **13** Here is a call from Yahweh: **O *distant ones*** [i.e., those outside Jerusalem/Judah], **hear what I have done!** **O *near ones*** [i.e., those within Jerusalem/Judah], **acknowledge my power!** This call looks both backward to 2:2-5, to the call to the nations to ascend to **Yahweh's mountain** (Zion), and forward to 35:9-10, which speaks of "the redeemed"/***the ransomed of Yahweh*** entering Zion. Thus we see those from the nations and from God's people, together entering Zion (Motyer 1993, 266).

■ **14** Sinners (*ḥaṭṭā'îm*) and ***malicious ones*** [*ḥănēpîm*; Wildberger 2002, 286) residing **in Zion**, are singled out for mention. When they see the work and power of Yahweh (v 13), they are ***seized with terror and trembling***. They recognize God to be a **consuming fire**, an **everlasting burning**. Out of their ***terror*** they cry out, **Who of us can dwell** (*gwr*) in the presence of such a God? That is, **who of us *qualifies*?** The verb *gûr* and its noun *gēr* usually are translated "to sojourn" and "sojourner," respectively, with the implication of a temporary stay, without the full rights of a citizen. The terms, however, speak of one who, for various reasons, has given up rights of citizen protection of his home ruler and has placed himself under the protection of another ruler, becoming a "protected citizen" (Wildberger 2002, 288). Thus the question being asked is: Who of us can qualify for protected citizen status in the coming judgment, so that we can survive? The answer is given in v 15.

■ **15** This verse gives the answer to the question asked in v 14. It is the character of one's heart, and the actions governed by that character, that qualifies one to survive God's coming judgment. The undergirding character that governs all is that one must **walk** [*hlk*, a metaphor for life's bent] **righteously** (*ṣĕdāqôt*, lit. ***righteousness***). ***Righteousness*** of the heart is an all-encompassing desire for justice, honesty, integrity, loyalty, and truthfulness in all acts toward others in one's community (*HALOT* 578, 1006). If the heart is right, one will do what is right.

The heart governs the mouth: a righteous person will **speak what is right** (*mêšārîm*, lit. ***uprightness***). Psalm 15:2-3 says that such a person "speaks truth ***in the*** heart" (v 2). If truth is first spoken to oneself *in* one's heart, then "**one's** tongue utters no slander" (lit. ***he does not walk about on his tongue*** [v 3]). Proverbs 23:15-16 links the wise heart with lips that speak righteousness (*mêšārîm*).

The heart governs the **hands**: a righteous person ***rejects wealth gained through*** extortion; that is, ***he shakes his hand from holding on to a bribe***. Exodus 23:8 says that "a bribe blinds ***the opened-eyed ones*** [i.e., judges] and ***subverts*** the words of the innocent."

The heart governs the **ears**: a righteous person ***closes his*** **ears** ***from hearing*** [***about doing***] **bloodshed** (i.e., **plots of murder**). If one does not close one's ears, and thus participates in such acts, so that one's "hands" become stained with "bloodshed," it is Yahweh who hides his eyes from us and does not listen to our many prayers (Isa 1:15).

The heart governs the **eyes**: a righteous person ***shuts his*** **eyes** ***from looking at*** evil (i.e., **contemplating** [***the doing of***] evil).

■ **16** This verse provides a summary of vv 14-15. If one meets the qualifications listed in v 15, then one can be assured of survival in God's coming judgment. The person is even given a new status: not only granted the status of *gēr* ("protected citizen" [v 14]) but also considered a *šākēn* ("a resident," "a settler" [compare v 24]). As such, the person will be given **refuge** and will be entitled to **bread** and **water**, the essentials of life.

d. Zion, an Undisturbed Grazing Place (33:17-24)

This section of ch 33 echoes a number of references concerning Zion/Jerusalem found throughout the earlier chapters of Isaiah. It describes a future time in which Yahweh, himself, ruling from Zion as king, will bring relief from the oppressiveness of foreign rulers. The immediate context is deliverance from Assyrian Sennacherib, but Isaiah is truly speaking of a final day of deliverance from all oppressors (Oswalt 1986, 603). In this "kingdom of Yahweh" (Wildberger 2002, 308) citizens will know security, healing, and forgiveness.

■ **17** Here, **king** is indefinite (*a* **king**) and unidentified, but in v 22 is identified as **Yahweh**. Thus it is Yahweh, **in his beauty** that **your eyes will see**. In 30:20 Isaiah promised that "your ***Teacher*** will be hidden no more; with your own eyes you will see ***your Teacher***." The realm of this king is described as **a land that stretches afar** (33:17), indicating a day when Yahweh will rule all, with no barriers of rivers, seas or mountains.

■ **18-19** In this future time of Yahweh's rule, ***the one who counted*** (*sōpēr* [v 18]) and **the one who *weighed*** (*šōqēl*) will no longer be present. These represent those who had kept the records of Hezekiah's tribute paid to Sennacherib and all others who represent the oppressive demands of foreign rulers. No longer, also, will God's people need to cower in fear because they cannot understand the **obscure, . . . strange and incomprehensible *language*** of their oppressors.

■ **20** Zion is described as **the city of our *appointed times*** (*môʿădēnû*). It is at Zion that, throughout the year at designated times, God's people gathered from near and far to meet Yahweh at the temple. At these appointed times, sacrifices were offered, meals were shared, forgiveness was obtained, and thanks and joy were expressed for Yahweh's benefits. Here is a complete reversal of the conditions of 1:13-15; there, Jerusalem and her inhabitants were keeping the appointed festivals, but because of their sinful ways, Yahweh refused to participate.

Using the imagery of Bedouin **tent** dwelling, which moves from place to place as pasturage was available (according to the seasons), **Zion/Jerusalem** will become the ***immovable*** **tent**, with **stakes** and **ropes** permanently in place. No longer needing to move from place to place, the **city** represents an ***undisturbed grazing place*** (*nāweh*, HALOT 678; compare 32:18).

Tents, Stakes, and Ropes

Tents were sometimes made of cloth but usually of woven goat hair (Exod 36:14) and used as dwellings by shepherds (Isa 38:12) and nomads. When raised, a tent was anchored to the ground by well-placed stakes (Judg 4:21; Isa 33:20), to which strong ropes were attached (Isa 33:20). Large tents were made of several sections, fastened together by clasping loops at the edges (Exod 36:15-18). A flap or screen might cover the entrance (v 37). Sometimes a whole family lived in a single tent (v 8); sometimes a family with servants lived in a cluster of tents (Gen 31:33) (Achtemeir 1985, 1034).

■ 21 Here, Isaiah declares that, against all other so-called deities, **Yahweh is our Mighty One** (*'adîr*). He imagines Zion/Jerusalem as **a place of broad rivers and streams**. Yet no **mighty** [*'adîr*] **ship** of the sea powers will dare **sail** its waters to confront Yahweh. The imagery of the impotency of the sea powers continues in v 23.

■ 22 This verse is an exclamatory interjection of who **Yahweh** (the Mighty One) is: **our judge, our lawgiver,** and **our king**. Because he is **our king, he will save us!**

■ 23 The prophet now picks up his ridicule of the world's sea powers: against the Mighty One (*'adîr*), their mighty (*'adîr*) ships (v 21) are powerless. Their ship's **rigging hangs loose**, their ship's **mast** is not **secure**, and their ship's **sail** catches no wind. They, the great powers, have become so powerless in the seas of the world's trade and political intrigues that **the lame** (representing the powerless of the world) easily **carry off** [*their*] **plunder**.

■ 24 The prophet now returns to those for whom Yahweh is their king, to those who have received Yahweh's salvation (v 22). It is they who have been granted the double status of **settler** (*šākēn*) and **resident** (*yōšēb*). For those who have found security in Yahweh's presence, all sickness and illness will be abolished (compare Rev 21:4). Yahweh's salvation provides conditions of health and wholeness, such that **no one** will need to **say, "I am ill."** Here is a complete reversal of the incurably ill Jerusalem depicted in 1:5-6. In addition to wholeness of physical health, the **sins** of Zion's inhabitants **will be forgiven**. This implies a change of heart attitude, a reversal of the depiction of God's "children" in 1:2-4 where, in complete rebellion, they are not receptive to forgiveness. At the same time, our present passage echoes 4:2-4 where, in the presence of the **beautiful and glorious Branch of Yahweh**, Yahweh himself will wash away the "filth" and "bloodstains" of those who survive and remain in "Zion." Washed and cleansed, they "will be called holy."

FROM THE TEXT

A number of commentators note the similarities between Isa 33:14-16 and Ps 15, but this commentator finds none who bring them together, with Ps 15 adding to our understanding of the fuller qualifications of those who receive God's protection when in his presence. Goldingay does note that in both passages one finds the parallel terms for "dwell" (*gwr* and *škn*). He further observes that the Isaiah passage is the people's acknowledgment "that they cannot fulfill the psalm's prescription and cannot enjoy that dwelling to which the prescription points" (2001, 189).

Among the qualifications in Ps 15 that provide protective dwelling in Yahweh's presence are some that are also taken up in Isa 33. We will look at four: (1) **walking blamelessly** or **with integrity** (*hōlĕk tāmîm* [v 2]), (2) **doing righteousness** (*pō'ēl ṣedēq*), (3) **speaking truth in one's heart** (*dōbēr 'ĕmet bilbābô*), and (4) "not **taking** a bribe [*šōḥad*] against the innocent" (v 5).

(1) The OT's prime example of one who walks **blamelessly** is Job. The narrator declares Job to be "blameless" (*tām* [Job 1:1]), which Yahweh affirms (1:8; 2:3). Job's wife recognizes his "integrity" (*tummâ* [2:9]). Job's friends attempt to search out his failures but find none. All in all, Job is found to be living in accord with what was expected of him by both Yahweh and his fellow citizens.

(2) We turn also to Job as a prime example of one who **does righteousness**. Job declares: "I put on righteousness [*ṣedeq*], and it clothed me; my justice was like a robe and a turban" (29:14 NRSV). He gives examples of his acts of righteousness toward his fellow citizens: "I delivered the poor who cried, and the orphan who had no helper" (v 12 NRSV); "I was eyes to the blind, and feet to the lame. I was a father to the needy, and I championed the cause of the stranger" (vv 15-16 NRSV).

A concrete OT example of one who is **walking blamelessly** is to return to a poor man his pledged cloak daily before sundown (Deut 24:13). In the desert climate of the OT world, night temperature drops significantly, even in the warm season of the year. The poor man who owns no other outer piece of clothing needs his pledged cloak to wrap himself in for warmth through the night. To deprive him of his cloak (and warmth) would be a gross act of unrighteousness! See Amos 2:8 where the prophet brings charges against those who violated this Deuteronomic law.

(3) A definition of **speaking truth in one's heart** is given in the context of Zech 8:3-17. Through this prophet Yahweh speaks of Jerusalem once again (after the exile) becoming known as **the city of truth** (*'îr hā'ĕmet* [v 3]), an echo of Isa 1:26, in which Yahweh promises that Jerusalem someday will again be called "the Faithful [*ne'ĕmānâ*] City." Both *'ĕmet* and *ne'ĕmānâ* are from the root *'mn*, having to do with firmness, that which gives support, that which can be trusted. Thus the future **truthfulness, faithfulness** of Jerusalem will be possible, both because Yahweh again will "dwell" (*škn*) there (Zech 8:3), and because he commands his people: "Speak the truth to one another, render in your gates judgments that are true and make for peace, do not devise evil in your hearts against one another" (8:16-17 NRSV). Thus, **speaking the truth** is speaking words that can be trusted; heart and lips are saying the same thing.

Paul, apparently with Zech 8:16 in the background, advises those of us who are "faithful in Christ Jesus" (Eph 1:1): "Therefore, laying aside falsehood, SPEAK TRUTH EACH ONE OF YOU WITH HIS NEIGHBOR, for we are members of one another" (4:25 NASB). Such truth-speaking can become our natural way of living, however, only as we are "renewed in the spirit of [*our*] mind [*nous*, 'mind,' 'intellect,' 'understanding' = OT 'heart'], . . . created in righteousness and holiness of the truth" (vv 23-24 NASB). And such "truth," says Paul, "is in Jesus" (v 21 NASB).

(4) We find no law against "***taking*** a bribe [*šōḥad*]" in the known cuneiform law codes of the ancient biblical world, though in one case Hammurabi found the bribery of a judge to be morally offensive and confiscated the bribe money. Generally, bribery was a legal transaction often confirmed by witnesses (Finklestein 1952, 79-80). Among Yahweh's people, however, this prohibition was directed specifically to those who made legal decisions, the judges and rulers. Deuteronomy 16:19 insists that, "a bribe blinds the eyes of the wise and ***subverts*** the words of the innocent." Exodus 23:8 further defines the wise as the ***seeing ones*** (*piqḥîm*, "perceptive ones"), whom a "bribe . . . blinds." Any person expecting God's protective benefits of kingdom citizenship "does not accept a bribe" (Ps 15:5).

Psalm 15 gives assurance that "whoever does these things will never be shaken" (v 5). Likewise, Isa 33:16 says to those who live with these qualifiers governing their every action, that they will be assured of the basics of life's sustenance: "bread" and "water."

B. Judgment's Desert, Redemption's Garden (34:1—35:10)

Chapters 34—35 are presented in contrastive eschatological imagery: Edom (ch 34), representing the nations, is turned into a wasteland without human inhabitant; Judah's wilderness (ch 35), representing the physical, social, and spiritual world, having suffered the devastating effects of human power and pride, is transformed into a Lebanon/Carmel/Sharon-like garden.

I. The Earth Is Turned into a Desert (34:1-17)

BEHIND THE TEXT

In ch 34, the earth, with Edom as representative, is turned into a wasteland (v 9) without human inhabitant (vv 5, 6). This wasteland is depicted as *tōhû* ("chaos") and *bōhû* ("desolation") (v 11), terms that depict the earth's condition prior to God's acts of creative ordering (Gen 1:2). This judgment, then, is viewed as a reversal of God's created order. It is the "nations" (Isa 34:1) and their "armies" upon whom Yahweh pronounces his eschatological judgment (v

2). Thus, the "sword of **Yahweh**" (vv 5, 6) comes against all human powers that have set themselves against his sovereignty and those who acknowledge him.

Why is "Edom" (v 5) chosen to represent the arrogance of the world's nations that have pitted their powers against Yahweh? Edom's history of hatred toward Jerusalem and Yahweh's people is reflected in the Jewish exiles' song, composed while in Babylon, as they looked back at the Edomites' reaction to the fall of their sacred city, Jerusalem: "'Tear it down,' they cried, 'tear it down to its foundations!'" (Ps 137:7). Ezekiel 35:5 mentions Edom's "ancient hostility" toward the Israelites. Motyer cites the wars with Edom during the reigns of Saul, David, Solomon, Jehoram, and Amaziah in support of Amos' accusation of Edom's longstanding "hostility" toward Israel (1:11) (1993, 268-69). Oswalt observes that, "from Genesis (25:23) to Malachi (1:2-3), Edom is treated as the antithesis to Israel," and cites Edom's refusal to allow Israel to pass through its territory on their journey from Egypt to Canaan (Num 20:14-21) (1986, 610). Wildberger notes the many threats of judgment against Edom found throughout the OT besides Isa 34 (Num 24:18; Isa 11:14; Jer 9:25-26; 25:15-25; 49:7-22; Lam 4:21-22; Ezek 25:12-14; 35; 36:5; Joel 3:19; Amos 1:11-12; Obad 8-15; Mal 1:4). He then discusses the historical "brotherly relationship" between Edom and Israel, and Edom's violations of that relationship, and concludes that "Edom is not just a nobody; Edom is family" (2002, 326-27).

IN THE TEXT

a. Yahweh Judges the Nations (34:1-4)

■ **1** The prophet issues a twofold call: (1) **nations** (*gôyim*)/**peoples** (*'ummîm*) are called to **come near**, **listen**, and **pay attention** to the message of judgment to be pronounced against them; (2) **the earth** [*'āreṣ*] **and its fullness**/**the world** [*tēbēl*] **and all its offspring** ("all creatures that populate it" [Wildberger 2002, 329]) are called to **listen** as witnesses to this pronouncement of God's judgment. In light of earth's suffering because of people's violation of God's covenant as depicted in 24:4-13, Wildberger suggests that "the earth . . . would be sympathetic to the judgment [of Isa 34] . . . when the wrath of God is poured out upon those who live upon it" (ibid.).

■ **2** Why **Yahweh is angry** is not stated, yet his anger is directed at **all nations** (*kol haggôyim*) and **their armies** (*ṣĕbā'ām*). In his **wrath** Yahweh **has devoted** [*ḥrm*; compare v 5] **them** [i.e., both **nations** and **armies**], [**and**] **has given** them **over to slaughter**. Both verbs are perfect tense (completed action), indicating that Yahweh's judgment has already been decided, though it will not be carried out until sometime in the distant future.

■ **3-4** Both creatures of the earth (v 3) and of **the heavens** (v 4) are affected by God's coming final judgment. To be sure, the prophet gives a hyperbolic depiction of the effects of Yahweh's judgment upon the nations. But, such a description is for what one might in the present day call "shock and awe" effect. When Yahweh's final judgment falls, it will be horrifying: the **slain *flung out*** (v 3), their ***corpses*** left unburied, rotting on **the mountains**, an unbearable ***stench arising***. So much human **blood** flows that even the soil of **the mountains *dissolves***. Similar descriptions of the aftermath of war are found in the accounts of Assyrian Shalmaneser III (reigned 858-824 BC) (Pritchard 1969, 277, compare 279).

Assyrian Descriptions of Corpses on the Battlefield

Shalmaneser III (reigned 858-824 BC) records: "I covered the wide plain with the corpses of his [i.e., the town of Pakaruhbuni] warriors: 1,300 of their battle-experienced soldiers I slew with the sword" (Pritchard 1969, 277). "I slew their warriors [from a coalition of towns, including Carchemish] with the sword, descending upon them like Adad when he makes a rainstorm pour down. In the moat (of the town) I piled them up, I covered the wide plain with the corpses of their fighting men, I dyed the mountains with their blood like red wool" (ibid.). "I slew 14,000 of their soldiers [of a coalition of twelve kings, including Ahab of Israel] with the sword, descending upon them like Adad when he makes a rainstorm pour down. I spread their corpses (everywhere), filling the entire plain with their widely scattered (fleeing) soldiers. During the battle I made their blood flow down the *ḫur-pa-lu* of the district" (ibid., 279).

Even the creatures of **the heavens** are affected by God's judgment (v 4). **The stars in the sky** (lit. ***the host*** [*ṣĕbā'*] ***of the heavens***) point to both the actual **stars** and the many deities which they represented. Most of the world outside ancient Israel, and at times Israel herself, worshipped these **stars** and their deities. In an act depicting a reversal of creation, the **heavens** will be **rolled up like a scroll**, with all those **starry *deities falling*** right and left **like withered leaves** or **shriveled figs**.

b. *Yahweh's Sword Falls upon Edom (34:5-8)*

■ **5-6** It is not Yahweh himself who **descends in judgment on Edom** (v 5), but ***Yahweh's*** [metaphorical] **sword**. The imagery is that of an invisible hand wielding a **sword**, first doing Yahweh's work **in the heavens** against the stars and the deities they represent (v 4). Then, the **sword**, its work finished in the heavens, **descends *upon*** Edom ***and upon*** the people ***whom*** **[*he*] *has devoted*** [*ḥrm*; compare v 2] ***for judgment***. To be ***devoted*** (*ḥrm*) to Yahweh means that all the spoils of war belong exclusively to him (as, e.g., in the destruction of Jericho [Josh 6:17]). Thus, the **great slaughter** (v 6) that ensues **in the land of Edom** metaphorically constitutes ***a sacrifice for Yahweh***. The **blood** with which ***Yahweh's sword is filled*** and the **fat** with which ***it has fattened itself*** are the two parts of the sacrificial animals that, in Levitical sacrificial law, are reserved only for Yahweh (Lev 3:16-

34:5-6

17; 7:23-27). The enactment of **sacrifice/great slaughter** is metaphorically centered in **Bozrah**, the capital of **Edom**, located south of the Dead Sea on the eastern edge of the Arabah Valley (Aharoni and Avi-Yonah 1993, 90). Compare Isa 63:1-6, where Yahweh is depicted coming from Bozrah, his clothing crimson stained with the blood of the nations, whom he alone has trampled in the winepress of his anger.

■ **7** Mentioned together here are **wild oxen**, **bulls**, and **mighty ones**: victims of the slaughter/sacrifice. Of these, only **bulls** (domestic animals) were prescribed for use in sacrifices, yet here even the **wild** animals hyperbolically are included. The last mentioned, **mighty ones** (*'abbîrîm*; great bulls is an NIV interpretation), may be a metaphorical reference to the powerful leaders, specifically of Edom but more generally of the world's nations. The imagery is made even more colorful with the simulation of **their land** as the soil around an altar, **drenched with blood** and **soaked with fat**.

■ **8** Zion's **cause** (*rîb*, "a dispute," "a lawsuit" [*HALOT* 1225]), with which this verse concludes, implies "that Zion is in the right" (Goldingay 2001, 195) in the longstanding controversies with Edom (and with the nations). **Yahweh**, as Zion's defender, takes up her **cause**. The prophet uses two synonyms, *nāqām* and *šillûmîm*, both meaning **vengeance/retribution** (*HALOT* 721, 1511), to indicate that Yahweh's judgment will bring "full settlement" for Zion (Motyer 1993, 271).

c. Edom, a Habitation for Desert Creatures (34:9-17)

Though Edom is not specified in these verses, the use of feminine pronominal suffixes "its"/"it" throughout the passage indicates a continuation of the previous depiction of God's judgment upon Edom.

■ **9-10** Thus *its* streams (*něḥālîm* [v 9]), *its* **soil** (*'āpār*), and *its* **land** (*'ereṣ*) do not escape collateral damage from God's judgment upon the "people" (*'am*) of "Edom" in v 5. These all **will be turned into pitch** and **burning sulfur/brimstone**, and **forever . . . lie desolate** (v 10). Some commentators suggest that here is an echo of God's earlier overthrow of Sodom and Gomorrah (compare Gen 19:24-28; Deut 29:23 [22 HB]; Jer 49:18), cities that were located in what became Edom's territory.

■ **11-15** As a precursor to his act of judgment, Yahweh **will stretch out . . . the measuring line of chaos** [*tōhû*] **and the plumb line of *emptiness*** (*bōhû* [v 11]). Having measured and plumbed the nations against his own standards of "righteousness" (Oswalt 1986, 615), Yahweh has determined to return the earth to its condition prior to his act of placing humankind upon it, almost *tōhû* and *bōhû*, "formless and void" (Gen 1:2 NASB). But not quite, however, for earth is pictured as still inhabited by various kinds of fowl and **desert creatures** (v 14), both daytime and nocturnal (vv 11, 13, 14, 15). Glaringly absent will be humankind, as earth's **nobles**, ***kingdoms***, and **princes** will

come to an end (v 12). The ***palaces*** and ***fortresses*** that have represented the power brokers of humankind will be ***overgrown with*** thorns . . . , nettles and brambles (v 13).

■ **16-17** Appeal is made to undefined recipients to confirm the veracity of the prophet's message: ***search*** [*diršû* (impv.); *drš* is "to inquire," "to investigate"] ***within*** [*mēʾal* (Waltke and O'Connor 1990, §11.3.2)] **the scroll of *Yahweh*** (v 16). Commentators have given varying suggestions as to what this **scroll** might refer. Wildberger suggests that a later editor, at a time when at least some of Isaiah's prophecies are available in written form, viewing them as Holy Scripture, has inserted this into the Isaiah text (Wildberger 2002, 338), for reasons that we cannot now determine.

Seitz sees in the depiction of the destruction of Edom echoes of the world's condition immediately following the flood, "when all had been destroyed and only Noah and his animal collection remained." Thus **the scroll of *Yahweh*** would refer to the written account (Gen 6) of the Noah story (1993, 237). Motyer draws attention to Isa 8:16-20 and 29:11-12, suggesting that "Isaiah cultivated a 'book religion,'" and that searching such written sources was a way of nourishing one's "spiritual conviction" (1993, 272).

While Edom/the earth is depicted as empty of humankind, God is not absent from his creation. His **mouth** still ***commands***, **his Spirit** is active ***gathering*** the animal kingdom **together**, and **his hand** (v 17) is active ***measuring out for each its portion***. Thus God is guiding their habitations, habits, and lives. The animal kingdom, it is said, will **possess** [*yrš*] **it** (i.e., Edom/the earth) and **dwell** [*škn*] ***in it* forever** (*ʿad ʿôlām*).

FROM THE TEXT

"Forever" (v 17) certainly carries the implication of permanence: never, it seems, will Edom/the earth become any different from the uninhabited wasteland pictured in vv 9-17. But, just as the "forever" (*ʿad ʿôlām*) of 32:14 would be changed by God's ***until*** (*ʿad* [v 15]) (→ v 15), so here, Edom's/the earth's forever of "chaos" (34:11) and ***emptiness*** will be changed in God's time, a time in which "the wilderness will rejoice and blossom" (35:1). This is the time when God "will come to save" (v 4). Wildberger comments concerning the "hopelessly damaged" nations, that God's "vengeance" and "retribution," "in the sense that they have been used in this text, are necessary if order is to be reestablished once again" (2002, 339). This reestablished order is depicted in ch 35, where Zion/Judah is depicted in stark contrast to the Edoms of this world.

2. Judah Is Turned into a Garden (35:1-10)

BEHIND THE TEXT

In ch 35, the mention of Zion (v 10) indicates that the focus of the chapter is Judah, whose "desert"/"parched land"/"wilderness" (v 1) bursts into unprecedented "bloom," becoming like the preverbal luscious "Lebanon"/"Carmel"/"Sharon" (v 2). Here, then, is an eschatological reversal of wasted Edom/the earth, a re-creation. Judah, too, represents the nations of the world; so it is God's world that experiences this re-creation. Into this re-created world Yahweh pronounces his eschatological gathering of the "redeemed" (v 9), those of his people whom he "has rescued" (v 10) from the nations of the world. These, with much joy, stream up to "Zion" on a "highway" (v 8), which bears the name "the Way of *the Holy Ones*."

IN THE TEXT

■ **1-2** These opening two verses appear to fulfill the concluding promise of the new song of the vineyard of 27:6, that Jacob/Israel will someday "blossom and fill all the world with fruit" (Seitz 1993, 238). **The desert and the parched land will be glad [*of*] them** (v 1). The Hebrew verb translated **glad** has a third plural masculine pronominal suffix -*m*, **them**, which most commentators and translators, for various reasons, consider grammatically impossible; thus it is simply ignored, emended, or removed. Wildberger, for example, dismisses it on the basis that there is no antecedent to which "them" could refer (2002, 341). Motyer, however, suggests that this pronominal suffix points *forward*, anticipating the "they" of vv 2 and 8 ("those who"), and "the redeemed" of vv 9-10 (1993, 273). Thus the "desert"/"parched land"/"wilderness," through which "the Way of Holiness" (v 8) passes, "is actually shouting its welcome" (ibid.) to those journeying up to "Zion" (v 10).

Along the way, on their way to Zion, **they will see the glory [*kĕbôd*] of Yahweh, [*and*] the splendor [*hădar*] of our God.** This **glory/splendor** is reflected in the sudden beauty of the desert blanketed with the **blossoming** of the **crocus** (*ḥăbaṣṣāleh*; "rose" [KJV, ASV]; but the NIV "rose" in Song 2:1). Here, the poet anticipates the desert's response to the gush of water and flowing streams of Isa 35:6. **The glory [*kĕbôd*] of Lebanon/the splendor [*hădar*] of Carmel**, together, **will be given to it** (*nittan lāh* [Heb. 3rd fem. s.]), that is, to the **parched land/wilderness** (both fem.), enhancing its sudden beauty (v 1). Does this imply that these areas will go beyond the annual rainy season sprouting of flowers, to producing lush forests like **Carmel** and **Lebanon**, and the crops and vineyards of **Sharon**? (Goldingay 2001, 196).

Thus, in this once appearing dead and unproductive land, now in its new life, one sees reflected the God who comes to save (v 4). What a beautiful metaphorical depiction of Jacob/Israel/Judah, with her God in her midst, newly born to new life, filling the world with the fruit of God's salvation.

■ **3-4** The poet now shifts attention to the pilgrims traveling through the now enhanced landscape toward Zion. No longer need discouragement control their thoughts: **strengthen** [*your*] ***drooping*** **hands**, **steady** [*your*] ***staggering*** **knees** (v 3); no longer need **fear** (v 4) control their actions: **strengthen** [*your*] ***racing/hasty/impetuous*** **hearts**. How? Look up! ***Behold*** (NIV omits) your **God!** *He* [emph. pron.], [*with*] vengeance he *comes*, [*with*] divine retribution, *he* [emph.], **he will come**, *and he will* **save you** (pl. you).

■ **5-7** The healing benefits of God's salvation to those journeying toward Zion are both physical and spiritual: **eyes** (v 5), **ears**, bodies, and ***tongues*** (v 6), that were once nonfunctioning, now see, hear, **leap *about***, and **shout** (for a look back to previous references to the metaphor of blindness and deafness, compare 6:10; 28:7; 29:9-10, 18; 30:20-21; 32:3-4; for a look forward, compare 42:7, 16-19; 43:8). Why this leaping about and shouting? Because, in opposition to the chaotic reversal of creation depicted in ch 34 (the wasting of Edom/the nations; → 34:9-17), these redeemed ones on their way to Zion are passing through a veritable re-creation of a "majestic garden" (Wildberger 2002, 353). Wherever they look they see ***gushing*** water (35:6), flowing **streams**, and **bubbling springs** (v 7). **Jackals**, the desert animal often depicted inhabiting places deserted by humans (13:21-22; 34:13; Jer 9:11 [10 HB]; 10:22; 49:33; 51:37; compare Lam 4:3; Isa 43:20), are no longer present in their usual **haunts** (35:7). They have been displaced by a growth of **grass and reeds and papyrus**, nurtured by the abundance of water, not unlike the Nile Delta where such reeds and papyrus grow (Wildberger 2002, 353).

■ **8** Here the prophet speaks of **a highway** (*maslûl*; other references to a "highway" in Isaiah are 11:16; 19:23 [→]; 40:3; 43:19; 49:11; 62:10). He declares that it is to **be called the Way of the Holy Ones** (*derek haqqōdeš*; "way of the clean" [BDB 871]), the *holy* aspect being applied, not to the road itself, but to **those who walk the way** (Oswalt 1986, 620, 625). It is not for the **unclean** (*ṭāmē'*, here antonymous to *haqqōdeš*), which could refer to those ceremonially unclean, such as having touched something dead (Lev 11:24), having indulged in improper sexual relations (18:20), or having worshipped an idol (Hos 5:3). But, in the context of his life-changing vision of the holiness of **Yahweh Sebaoth**, Isaiah saw himself and his people as those with "unclean lips" (*ṭĕmē' śĕpātayim*). The removal of his uncleanness is expressed in terms of "guilt" removed and "sin atoned for" (6:3-7). Thus, this **Way** is for those no longer deemed guilty, for those whose sins have been forgiven.

The prophet adds one more disqualifier for walking on this **Way**: *no fools*. Goldingay defines these persons' character as "Stupidity . . . the moral obtuseness such as leaves God out of account" (2001, 198).

■ **9-10** Safety from **any ravenous beast** (v 9) is assured to **Yahweh's redeemed ones** (*gĕ'ûlîm*)/***ransomed ones*** (*pĕdûyîm*), those traveling on the highway to Zion. Even the **lion**, which inhabited Palestine/Israel in OT times, and was much feared (compare 1 Kgs 13:24-25; 2 Kgs 17:25), will be held at bay.

A number of times in the second half of Isaiah (compare 41:14; 43:14, etc.), the noun *gō'ēl* designates Yahweh as Israel's "Redeemer." In its normal usage the term refers to the nearest male relative of one who is in helpless need; it is he who assumes the right to do whatever is necessary to free his helpless relative from life-crippling obligations, such as financial debt, loss of land, or personal slavery (Lev 25:25, 48-49; Num 5:8). Thus these who stream into **Zion** have received their redemption at the hand of Yahweh their near relative. At Zion's entrance they will be waved through, for their entrance document will show the visa stamp: **redeemed/*ransomed*** (Goldingay 2001, 198).

In **Zion** (v 10), the sanctuary of ultimate safety, with Yahweh in its midst, where **joy** and **gladness** are **everlasting**, there will be no place for **sorrow and sighing**.

FROM THE TEXT

Commentators have noted the similarities of the imagery of ch 35 and that of chs 40—55. Childs, for example, notes "the desert blossoming, the joyful singing, the seeing of Yahweh's glory." He further points out that the exclamation in 35:4, "**Behold, your God!** He will come," is paralleled in 40:9-10; the admonition "do not fear" of 35:3 is paralleled in 43:1 and 51:7; and, the reversal of the blindness in 35:5 is effected in 40:5 and 42:7 (Childs 2001, 257-58).

A most significant linking of ch 35 and chs 40—55 is the similar wording of 35:10 and 51:11. The verb "return" is a focus of these parallel verses. Goldingay points out that "return" (*šûb*), when applied to Israel in the book of Isaiah, usually implies a spiritual returning to Yahweh. Thus, he suggests that ch 35 "presupposes the fulfillment of the vision of 1:27" (2001, 198), where it is promised that, "Zion will be ***ransomed*** [*pdh*] with justice [*mišpāṭ*], **and** her penitent ones [*šābêhā*] with righteousness [*ṣĕdāqâ*]." *Šābêhā* (*šûb*) is literally "her returners." Thus, if "return" implies primarily a spiritual returning, "returners" are those who turn away from their sins in repentance unto Yahweh.

Moreover, there is nothing in ch 35 that suggests that any particular historical event is being referenced (Wildberger 2002, 348), such as the forthcoming return from Babylonian exile. It simply leaves the future open. Thus "the redeemed"/"the ***ransomed***" are not limited only to those from among God's dispersed people. Those who ***walk the Way*** to Zion would well include those from all nations who have turned to Yahweh in the context of his salvation of Israel.

Chapter 51, however, is speaking of the return of the Jewish exiles from Babylonian exile to Zion, ***the ransomed ones of Yahweh***, and the rebuilding of Zion from its devastation prior to the exile (v 3). The prophet draws on imagery from the first exodus (51:10) to show that Yahweh's rescue action on behalf of his people in this "return" (51:11) is not unlike his rescue action on their behalf when he brought them out of Egypt long ago. Yet, in the larger context of ch 51, the effects of Yahweh's act of ***ransom*** are not for his "people" (51:4) alone; rather, declares Yahweh, "my instruction," "my justice," "my righteousness," and "my salvation," are for "the nations" and "the islands" (51:4-5).

Thus, both chs 35 and 51 point beyond the historical event of the return from Babylonian exile to an age of ultimate salvation. Chapter 51 speaks of the renewed Zion in terms of a new "Eden," "the garden of ***Yahweh***" (v 3). This is creation language, which leads Childs to suggest that chs 35 and 51 anticipate that final age, where salvation means "sharing in God's new creation," as pictured in 65:17-25 (2001, 258).

Chapter 35 brings to a close the section of this first "book" of Isaiah that began in ch 13. These chapters dealt with the question of Yahweh's relationship with and sovereignty over the nations of this world generally, and with Israel/Judah in particular. The specific question explored was, will Yahweh's people turn in repentance to Yahweh from their own arrogant, self-preserving ways? In so doing, will they believe that, in response to their faith, Yahweh can be trusted to preserve them, even within the context of arrogant, powerful nations that threaten to annihilate them? Is it possible that Isaiah's prophetic promise of a time when "sorrow and sighing will flee away" (35:10) can indeed be realized?

C. Hezekiah and the Assyrian Threat; Hezekiah and Babylon (36:1—39:8)

Oswalt suggests that the answer to the question posed above is, in part at least, given in chs 36—39 (1986, 627). These chapters give two illustrations of God's steadfast response to, in this case, personal faith.

Chapters 36—37 demonstrate God's response to Hezekiah's faith and prayer on behalf of Jerusalem, in delivering Jerusalem from Assyria. Yet the city was not spared for Hezekiah's sake only, but so that "the kingdoms of the earth" (the nations of chs 13—35) would recognize the absolute sovereignty of Yahweh (37:20). Moreover, the two chapters demonstrate the reliability of Prophet Isaiah's word that the future death of Sennacherib would not simply happen; his assassination would be because he had blasphemed Yahweh (37:6-7, 38) (Seitz 1993, 253).

Chapter 38 demonstrates God's response to Hezekiah's faith and prayer on behalf of himself, in restoring him from sickness to health. This demonstration of God's sparing of Hezekiah's life, too, is not for Hezekiah alone; rather, in the poem that Hezekiah wrote following his illness and recovery, he affirms that in such instances, parents must pass on to their children testimony of Yahweh's faithfulness (v 19).

I. Hezekiah and the Assyrian Threat (36:1—37:38)

BEHIND THE TEXT

Ahaz has passed off the scene; his son Hezekiah is now Judah's king, reigning from Jerusalem. These two chapters take up the account of the historical event of Assyrian Sennacherib's threat against Jerusalem during his "third campaign" to the west (also chronicled in 2 Kgs 18—20). Calling himself "king of the world," he invaded Judah and, at some point, destroyed many of Judah's towns. We learn of this, not from the biblical accounts but from Sennacherib's royal records (Pritchard 1969, 288-89). (However, → Isa 1:7-8, a passage that appears to depict Sennacherib's devastation of Judah.)

Sennacherib's southward journey included a defeat of Egyptian forces, "an army beyond counting," at Eltekeh, just north of Philistine territory along the main north-south route through Palestine. By Sennacherib's claim, these Egyptian forces had come north out of Egypt in response to a call from a coalition of smaller kingdoms, including Judah/Hezekiah, for help in stemming the Assyrian invasive tide (ibid., 288).

Bypassing Jerusalem on his southward journey, Sennacherib had come to the fortified (walled) southern Judean city of Lachish; this he sieged and captured, carrying away war booty and deporting its inhabitants to Assyria. This was such an important military event that Sennacherib depicted the whole process, from siege to receiving of booty, on a wall relief in a room of his palace in Nineveh (Ussishkin 1982).

From Lachish, Sennacherib sent a contingent of forces north to Jerusalem, demanding Hezekiah's surrender, of whom Sennacherib says, "I made a prisoner in Jerusalem, his royal residence, like a bird in a cage" (Pritchard 1969, 289).

There are seven subunits in chs 36—37: Sennacherib's first (verbal) surrender demand (36:1-20); Isaiah's response (36:21—37:7); Sennacherib's second (written) surrender demand (37:8-13); Hezekiah's response: a prayer to Yahweh (37:14-20); Yahweh's response: deliverance promised (37:21-35); Yahweh's mysterious intervention (37:36-37); and, Sennacherib's assassination (37:38).

IN THE TEXT
(PART 1, 36:1—37:7)

a. Sennacherib's First Surrender Demand: Verbal (36:1-20)

■ **1** From an analysis of Assyrian sources, scholars have determined that 701 BC is the year that **Sennacherib** [reigned 704-681 BC] **king of Assyria attacked all the fortified cities of Judah and captured them**. At that time King Hezekiah ruled in Jerusalem, having come to the throne, according to 2 Kgs 16:20 and 2 Chr 28:27, upon the death of his father Ahaz. Bright dates this transition at 715 BC (2000, 276). A chronological conundrum arises, however, when one notes that 2 Kgs 18:1 and 9 date Hezekiah's ascension year as coinciding with "the third year of Hoshea." Hoshea ascended the throne of northern Israel in 732 BC (ibid., 275). This would place Hezekiah's ascension in ca. 729 BC, and his **fourteenth year** at ca. 715 BC. Though several scholarly recalculations and emendations of the text have been advanced, the conundrum remains unresolved. If, however, Hezekiah's reign began in 715 BC, as Bright suggests, his **fourteenth year** would fall in 701 BC, coinciding with the year of Sennacherib's invasion of Judah. Additionally, 2 Chr 29:1 indicates that Hezekiah reigned for twenty-nine years; thus, if he came to the throne in 715 BC, he ruled until 687/86 BC.

■ **2** Sennacherib **sent his field commander** (*rab-šaqeh*, "chief cupbearer"), along with a **large army from Lachish**, to proposition **King Hezekiah at Jerusalem**. From this point in the narration, however, the military contingent is not again mentioned. The focus is upon the **commander**; he ***stands*** (*'md*) alone **at the aqueduct of the Upper Pool, on the road to the Launderer's Field**. This is the same spot, just south of the city in the Kidron Valley, where three decades earlier Prophet Isaiah, with his son Shear-Jashub, had challenged Hezekiah's father, King Ahaz, to "stand firm in your faith" in the face of an imminent Ephraim-Aramean threat. The question then was: would Ahaz trust in God or would he call on the world's great power broker, Assyria, for help? Regrettably, Ahaz had unwisely chosen to trust in Assyria's military strength, refusing to believe in God's ability to protect (Isa 7:3-12). The underlying question now being asked of Hezekiah by this textual juxtaposition of past and present is essentially the same: what will Hezekiah's response be to the present imminent Assyrian threat? Will he trust in God's ability to protect, or will he call on Assyria's rival power broker, Egypt (v 6), for military intervention?

■ **3** King Hezekiah does not personally go to meet King Sennacherib's messenger. Rather, **Eliakim**, **Shebna**, and **Joah**, three of his royal officials, **went out to him**, that is, outside the city walls to where the Assyrian was standing near the Launderer's Field. Thus, a king's representatives receive the message from a king's representative.

■ **4** Verses 4-10 present the first part of the message from the Assyrian field commander. **This is what the great king, the king of Assyria, says** (v 4), echoes Isaiah's words to Ahaz three decades before: "this is what ***Adonai Yahweh*** says" (7:7). **Great king** is a title appropriated by Hittite, Assyrian, Babylonian, and Persian kings (→ sidebar at 2:2, "The Boasts of Assyrian Kings" and "Behind the Text" for 2:6-22). The biblical view, however, is that there is no truly "great king" but Yahweh (Ps 95:3; Mal 1:14). So, in the Assyrian messenger's opening statement, the text anticipates the theme of the message: who is truly the **great king** on the world's scene, Sennacherib or Yahweh? The question actually asked, however, is literally, ***What is this trust*** [*bṭḥ*] ***that you are trusting*** [*bṭḥ*]? (The theme of trust [*bṭḥ*] occurs also in vv 5, 6, 7, 9, and 37:10.)

■ **5-6** The commander's words of derision continue: **You speak only *lip* words,** [*saying, "We have*] ***a plan*** [*'ēṣâ*] **and strength for war**"! (v 5). Indeed, Judah's leaders did have ***a plan*** (*'ēṣâ*), to "go down to Egypt," to seek "Pharaoh's protection," but they had not ***consulted*** Yahweh's ***mouth*** (30:1-5). According to this plan, Judah's reliance would be in the strength of Egypt's horses, chariots, and horsemen (31:1).

Words of mockery concerning **Pharaoh king of Egypt** follow: he is nothing but an untrustworthy **splintered reed of a staff**. If one **leans on it/*him***, one will be injured. The message is: you are ***trusting*** wrongly! In this, the Assyrian's message agrees with Isaiah's: do not trust in Egypt's military strength! (19:14-16; 30:1-5; 31:1-3).

■ **7** But, the focus of the Assyrian's message quickly shifts: ***trusting on Yahweh*** also is misplaced. After all, **is it not he** whose **high places and altars Hezekiah removed**? Your own king has denigrated and disdained Yahweh, the deity of your land. In this the Assyrian agrees with the Judean historian's succinct description of Hezekiah's religious reforms: "he removed the high places, smashed the sacred stones and cut down the Asherah" (2 Kgs 18:4). His words, ***when*** you say to me, "We are ***trusting*** [*bṭḥ*] **in Yahweh our God**," even echoes the historian's assessment of Hezekiah that, "in **Yahweh**, the God of Israel, **he trusted**" (*bṭḥ* [2 Kgs 18:5]).

Moreover, the Assyrian's reference to Hezekiah's requirement that all **must worship before this altar**, that is, that worship of Yahweh had been centralized at the temple in Jerusalem, is not mere mockery. What Hezekiah had done, in the Assyrian's eyes, truly is reprehensible. His words, on the one hand, reflect a complete misunderstanding of why Hezekiah has centralized the worship of Yahweh: to exclude the syncretistic worship of other deities at these outlying places of worship. We read of his father, King Ahaz, that, "In every town in Judah he built high places to burn sacrifices to other gods" (2 Chr 28:25). The Assyrian's words, on the other hand, do reveal an essential ancient Near Eastern theological concept: to deprive a deity of his places of worship throughout the land of his rule is cause to incur that deity's wrath. This concept is reflected in Persian Cyrus' reasoning as to why Babylon's chief deity, Marduk, became angry with King Nabonidus, selecting him, Cyrus, to replace Nabonidus as king of Babylon: Nabonidus had brought into Babylon all the gods from the towns throughout Sumer and Akkad, allowing their sanctuaries to fall into ruins. Thus Marduk chose Cyrus to reverse this despicable situation (Pritchard 1969, 315-17).

■ **8-9** Whether or not the Assyrian field commander is aware of it, there appears in v 8 an intertextual play in his reference to Sennacherib as **my master, the king** [*ădōnî hammelek*] **of Assyria**. Earlier, in ch 6 Isaiah bracketed his description of the One he encountered in the Jerusalem temple with, "I saw the **Sovereign/Master**" (*ădōnāy* [v 1]), and, "*the King* [*hammelek*], **Yahweh Sebaoth**, my eyes have seen" (v 5). Yahweh, the one whom Isaiah encountered, is "the Master, the King." So, the challenge remains: who is the sovereign king, Sennacherib or Yahweh?

The field commander's sarcasm revolves around Hezekiah's perceived inability to *mount* riders (36:8), even if Sennacherib generously should give him **two thousand horses**, or their *trust in* (v 9) Egypt's promised **chariots and horsemen** should be rewarded.

■ **10** The Assyrian field commander's claim that Sennacherib had **come to attack and destroy this land** at the command of *Yahweh* is another intertextual echo, though he no doubt was unaware of it. Earlier, Isaiah had certainly predicted that *the Sovereign* (*ădōnāy*) would send "the king of Assyria" against Judah (8:7-8; compare 10:5-6). So, again, Sennacherib and Isaiah are in agreement: it is Yahweh who has sent the Assyrians.

■ **11-12** The Assyrian field commander has been speaking in *Judahite* (Hebrew [v 11]), a dialect of the western group of Semitic languages and the common language of the Judeans. The commander's native language would have been Assyrian, a dialect of the eastern group of Semitic languages. The two dialects held many similarities in grammar and vocabulary, but one speaker would not have readily understood the other. Hezekiah's three representatives, of course, understood the field commander's *Judahite* well, but so would all **the people on the wall**, Jerusalemites who had gathered to see/hear what the hubbub was all about. Thus, so that the commander's words not discourage **the people** of the city, **Eliakim, Shebna and Joah** requested that he switch to **Aramaic**, the Semitic language of Aram/Syria, the diplomatic language (lingua franca) in use at that time. Being officials of the Judean government, they were trained in this language.

The commander, of course, rejected their request, saying that his **master** (v 12), Sennacherib, had not sent him to their **master**, Hezekiah, only, but also to **the people sitting on the wall**. Continuing in *Judahite*, and using the most vulgar of terms, he advised them that the time would come, when, obviously because of the threatened coming siege, they would have nothing to **eat** or **drink** but **their own excrement** and **their own urine**.

■ **13-15** The narrator emphasizes that the commander, now, so there would be doubt that the people on the wall could hear him, **called out** *in a loud voice* in *Judahite* (v 13). Again he makes sure the titles of his master are clear: **the great king, the king of Assyria**. In the face of such greatness, **trust** (v 15) in either **Hezekiah** or in *Yahweh* is misplaced. Both are powerless to **deliver you** (v 14).

■ **16-17** An alternative is offered: **make** *a blessing* **with me** (v 16), an idiom occurring only here, is perhaps equivalent to "an invitation to surrender" (Blenkinsopp 2000, 472). Thus, stop your resistance and **come out**. The alternative to the siege food and drink threatened in v 12 will be **fruit from your own vine and fig tree and . . . water from your own cistern**. This is the straight pitch. But then comes the curve ball: **your own** (land) will soon be replaced with **a land** not your own, but **like your own** (v 17). The inevitability of deportation, in "enthusiastic travel agent" rhetoric (ibid., 473), is beautified with the glossy picture of that land of exile: **grain, new wine, bread and vineyards**.

■ **18-20** This portion of the commander's speech questions, not the willingness, but the ability of *Yahweh* to deliver [*nṣl*] Jerusalem (v 20). After all, is Yahweh any different from **the gods of the nations** (v 18), each of whom has been powerless *to deliver its land* from the hand of the king of Assyria? The proof, the commander declares, is in the cases of already conquered northern cities (e.g., **Hamath, Arpad, Sepharvaim**, and **Samaria** [v 19]), whose **gods** were powerless **to save** (*nṣl* [v 20]). The conclusion seems logical: **How then can Yahweh** deliver [from the root *nṣl*] **Jerusalem from my** [i.e., Sennacherib's] **hand?** Surely, the mention of **Samaria** would evoke still fresh memories of that sister city's three-year siege and final capture a mere two decades earlier (722/1 BC).

Assyria's Attacks on Samaria, Hamath, Sepharvaim, and Arpad

After a three-year siege of Israel's capital Samaria, that Shalmaneser V started (but who died before the siege ended), Sargon II captured the city in 722/1 BC. He claims to have deported 27,290 of its inhabitants to Assyria (Pritchard 1969, 285). (→ 5:13 sidebar, "Assyrian Population Deportations.") Second Kings 17:1-6 gives a brief account of Samaria's siege and capture. After the fall of the city Samaria, Israel lost its status as an independent kingdom, was renamed Samaria, and was made a province of the Assyrian Empire.

In 720 BC Sargon II also devastated Hamath, located in central Syria on the Orontes river (ibid.). The location of Sepharvaim has not been identified. Second Kings 17:24, however, mentions both Sepharvaim and Hamath (along with Babylon, Kuthah, and Avva) as locations from which Sargon II deported inhabitants to repopulate the depopulated towns of Samaria. Tiglath-Pileser III had conquered Arpad/Arvad, located in northern Syria, in the mid 720s (ibid.).

b. Isaiah's Counsel: Do Not Fear! (36:21—37:7)

These verses give the responses of the inhabitants of Jerusalem, Hezekiah's three officials, King Hezekiah, and the prophet Isaiah to the Assyrian field commander's first surrender offer.

■ **21** This verse reads, *they* **remained silent and** *did not answer him a word*. It is obviously "the people sitting on the wall" (v 12) to whom the Assyrian addresses his words in vv 13-20, who make no **reply**. The reason is credited to Hezekiah, indicating that he is still in control of the city's internal life: **because** *the commandment of the king was this,* "Do not answer him." **The people** do not speak for their king.

■ **22** The three royal officials, **Eliakim**, **Hilkiah**, and **Joah**, leaving the Assyrian commander standing on the road to the Launderer's Field (36:2), (re)*entered* the city to report directly **to Hezekiah**. Coming before him with **their clothes torn**, a sign of mourning and distress, as loyal servants they **told him** *the words of* the field commander.

■ **37:1-2** The response of **King Hezekiah** (v 1) to the officials' report is twofold. (1) **He tore his clothes and put on sackcloth**, a coarse cloth made of either goat or camel hair, indicating grief, despair, or mourning. Dark in color, it might be worn as an entire garment covering the whole body or simply as a loincloth (*EDB*, §21173). Thus dressed, *he entered* the temple [*bêt*, **house**] *of Yahweh*. The reason for entry into the **temple** is not given, as it is in the case of his second entry in v 14. (2) Additionally, **he sent** a delegation **to the prophet Isaiah** (v 2) consisting of two of the three who had met the Assyrian commander outside the city walls, **Eliakim** and **Shebna** (Joah is not included). Accompanying them were the *elders of the* **priests**. Together they represented both the ruling and religious establishments. Taking their cue from their king, all these were now also **wearing sackcloth**. It is somewhat startling that, in view of Isaiah's longstanding public opposition to both of these establishments, the king would now turn to him, apparently with some measure of faith in what he might now counsel. Perhaps there would be a (good) word from God in this distressful situation. Where Isaiah was residing is not stated, but apparently he, too, was inside the city walls.

■ **3** The proverb with which the king's delegation opened their plea before Isaiah depicts perhaps a rather common occurrence: **children** *coming* **to the moment of birth**, but the mothers, from various causes, having **no strength to deliver**. Thus, it is with us, implies Hezekiah. Your earlier counsel, Isaiah, was right. All our plans for Egypt's assistance to deliver us have come to nothing. Neither in Egypt nor within ourselves do we find any **strength to deliver** this city. Jerusalem and her inhabitants have truly come to **a day of distress and rebuke and disgrace**.

■ **4** The two statements, **Perhaps Yahweh** your God *may* hear and **Yahweh your God has heard**, appear contradictory. This may be simply dialogic politeness, however, in which one's opening statement should not be too affirmative (*perhaps*), continuing on to a more affirmative conclusion. Of course Yahweh is listening! **He has heard the field commander's words of** ridicule **of the living God. Perhaps**, having heard, God **will rebuke him**. The request is not that Isaiah, as a prophet who has the ear of Yahweh, will attempt to induce Yahweh to rebuke Sennacherib, but rather to find out whether or not God is planning to do so.

The reference to **your God** has troubled commentators. Does Hezekiah not believe in Yahweh? Again, this too may be simply a dialogic nicety, rather than an issue of theological belief. In light of Hezekiah's advisers' earlier (failed) plan (*'ēṣâ*) in seeking Egyptian assistance without consulting (*š'l*) Yahweh (30:1-2), until one knows how the prophet may respond, caution should be used in presuming Yahweh's willingness to still be their God.

The living God distinguishes Yahweh from all other so-called gods; the OT views such deities as merely having the appearances of life, but which in fact, since they are humanly made, cannot speak, see, hear, smell, feel, or walk (Ps 115:4-7). Yahweh, as "Maker" (*'ōśēh*) of the universe (v 15), is active in the lives of those who fear and trust him, remembering and blessing them (vv 9-13). He is thus a living God. As such, he should receive praise from the living (vv 17-18), not mockery as the Assyrian commander has done (Isa 37:4).

Additional to Hezekiah's oblique request for information as to Yahweh's intention concerning the Assyrians, almost as a by-the-way addendum, Hezekiah has his delegation make a direct request: that Isaiah **pray for the remnant that is found**, that is, those found inside the walls of Jerusalem. This would include those already resident in the city and those who had escaped capture when Sennacherib devastated the surrounding Judean towns, fleeing to Jerusalem for refuge. In this time of desperate circumstances, the prophet's prayers are now seen possibly to be effective.

■ **5-7** Either there is an unrecorded time lapse here in which **Isaiah** consulted **Yahweh** on the delegation's behalf, or he had already done so, and had a ready reply (v 6). Isaiah's reply to Hezekiah, **your master**, is a ***thus says Yahweh*** message: **Do not be afraid** (*'al tîrā'*), the same counsel given to Hezekiah's father, Ahaz, three decades earlier (7:4) when facing the Ephraim-Aramean threat. Indeed, ***the* words with which the underlings of** [*na'ărê*] **the king of Assyria have blasphemed me**, they mean nothing to me (37:6). I, Yahweh, will have the last word. ***Behold! I will put a spirit within him*** (v 7), that is, Sennacherib (similar to the spirit that Yahweh sent to King Ahab's court prophets to deceive him into battle, and thus to his death [1 Kgs 22:20-23]). This ***spirit*** will manifest itself in the form of a ***rumor*** (*šěmû'â*), enticing him **to return to his own country, and I will *cause him to fall by a* sword.**

Thus, Hezekiah need not fear Sennacherib's boastful threats, because Yahweh's larger plan includes the preservation of Jerusalem, at least for some time yet.

FROM THE TEXT

The narrator of this account of Sennacherib's first demand for Jerusalem's surrender, and Hezekiah's response to it, leads us, the readers, from an initial point of potential panic to the calm acceptance that one need not be alarmed. At the beginning of the narrative, the Assyrian field commander has declared Israel's God, Yahweh, to be impotent. By the time the field commander has turned away, however, Yahweh, through his prophet Isaiah, has assured both Judah's king and his subjects that he, Yahweh, is in complete control of the situation. Thus, Hezekiah need not panic.

The theme of this passage is trust. Will Hezekiah choose to trust Yahweh, who has spoken through his prophet Isaiah? This, indeed, can be a difficult decision. Does the prophet truly speak a word from God? Is he truly God's mouthpiece? This is as much a difficult issue for us today as it was for Hezekiah. Isaiah did give a rather specific prediction concerning Sennacherib, that is, that he would hear a rumor that would cause him to flee Judah for his own home country. Yet, this prediction only pointed to Yahweh, who would be the cause of the rumor. It was Yahweh in whom Hezekiah must choose to trust.

We are faced with the same choice in situations of grave circumstances: will we trust God to perform his will, both for us and for all around us? One is reminded of the later Judahite king Jehoshaphat, when faced with the threat of "a vast army . . . from Edom" (2 Chr 20:2). He chose to pray to Yahweh in the midst of the assembly of Judah, reminding God that he (God) ruled over all kingdoms, and that "power and might are in your hand" (v 6). Concluding his prayer in total humility and trust, he admitted: "We have no power . . . We do not know what to do, but our eyes are on you" (v 12). From among the assembly, one named Jahaziel, a descendant of the singer Asaph, spoke a word of encouragement from Yahweh: "Do not be afraid or discouraged because of this vast army. For the battle is not yours, but God's" (v 15).

IN THE TEXT
(PART 2, 37:8-38)

c. Sennacherib's Second Demand: Written (37:8-13)

■ **8** The verse reads: ***And* the field commander *returned, and he* found the king *of Assyria* fighting against Libnah, *for he had* heard that *he had pulled out from* Lachish.** The reference to **Lachish** reconnects the account with its beginning at 36:2, for it was "from Lachish" that Sennacherib had sent his field commander to Jerusalem. But now, upon his return, having heard that his Assyrian master was no longer besieging **Lachish**, the field commander reports for duty at the nearby Judean walled city of **Libnah**, which Sennacherib was now besieging.

■ **9 Tirhakah, the king of Cush** is named as mounting a military campaign against Sennacherib. **Cush** refers to Nubia or Ethiopia, to the south of Egypt. At this time, the pharaohs of Egypt were from **Cush**. Nubian **Tirhakah**, however, did not become pharaoh until ca. 689 BC, more than a decade after Sennacherib's 701 BC campaign to Palestine. This is a chronological conundrum with no ready solution. One possibility may be that the later narrator uses "Tirhakah" to represent an Egyptian resurgent military advance that, if successful against Sennacherib, could have been the source of Jerusalem's deliverance after all. But in the context of Yahweh's assurance through Isaiah, that it would be Yahweh, not Egypt, who would force Sennacherib's exit from Judah (37:7), the efforts of "Tirhakah"/Egypt had failed.

So, a second time Sennacherib **sent** a message, this time written in a letter (v 14), **to Hezekiah**, by an unspecified number of **messengers**.

■ **10** In this message, Sennacherib accuses, not Hezekiah himself, but Yahweh of deception: **Do not let the god *in whom* you *trust*** [*bṭḥ*] **deceive you**. The alleged deception is Yahweh's claim that he can prevent **Jerusalem** from **being given into the *hand*** [*yad*, *power*] **of the king of Assyria**.

■ **11** Hezekiah becomes the butt of derision: **And will you be delivered, *when* surely you have heard *about* all the countries *that* the kings of Assyria *have already destroyed*?**

■ **12-13** Moreover, **the gods of the nations** are the butt of derision (v 12): these **gods** and the **king** of each conquered city listed were impotent to **deliver** from **my predecessors** (i.e., the Assyrian rulers preceding Sennacherib). By implication, Yahweh and Hezekiah would be just as impotent.

d. Hezekiah's Response: A Prayer to Yahweh (37:14-20)

■ **14-15** Sennacherib's message is identified here as a **letter** (pl. *hassĕpārîm*, perhaps referring to "leaves" or "pages" [Oswalt 1986, 652, citing Cheyne]). **Hezekiah received the letter** and **read it** (v 14). Nowhere else in the OT is recorded anyone doing what the king does next: **he went up to the *house*** [*bêt*] **of *Yahweh*** and **spread** this document **out before *Yahweh***. Then, **he prayed to *Yahweh*** (v 15).

■ **16** The prayer begins with an affirmation. Hezekiah's approach to God is not to declare that he, Hezekiah, as king of Judah, deserves to be heard. Rather, it is upon the very essence of who God is that he predicates his prayer: **you alone are God over all the kingdoms of the earth**, thus recognizing the unique universal kingship of ***Yahweh Sebaoth*, the God of Israel**. Hezekiah identifies

God as the one **enthroned between the cherubim** (lit. ***sitter of*** the cherubim [*yōšēb hakĕrubîm*]). Moreover, his universal kingship is derived from his being Creator: **you have made heaven and earth**.

The Cherubim

Cherubim (pl. of *kĕrûb*, "cherub") were ancient Near Eastern winged creatures (Akk. *kāribu*), viewed as guardians of the deities and religious centers. Some appear as winged bulls and other beasts at Assyrian and Babylonian temples and palaces. The OT cherubim first appear as guardians blocking humankind's reentry to the garden of Eden (Gen 3:24). Yahweh is depicted traversing the heavens riding on a cherub (2 Sam 22:11/Ps 18:10 [11 HB]). In his vision of God's glory, Ezekiel sees cherubim as "living creatures," having four faces and four wings (1:4-28; 10:1-22).

The cherubim referenced in Isa 37:16 were gold-covered, winged images, first placed by Moses in the tabernacle in the wilderness; these were in the holy of holies, on the cover of the ark of the covenant, facing each other from opposite sides of the mercy seat. From this mercy seat, Israel's invisible God would speak (Exod 25:18-20; 37:6-9; Num 7:89; 1 Sam 4:4). Later, as guardians of God's dwelling place in the midst of his people, Solomon placed two large gold-covered olive wood cherubim in the holy of holies in the Jerusalem temple (1 Kgs 6:23-28; 8:6-7).

■ **17** Hezekiah's first request follows his affirmation of Yahweh's kingship. Hezekiah's double request of **Yahweh** is not one of disrespect; rather, he is recognizing Yahweh's profound contrast with the "gods" of v 19: while they have only the appearance of life (eyes that cannot see, ears that cannot hear [Ps 115:5-6]), it is only **Yahweh** who has an **ear** that truly ***listens*** and **eyes** that truly ***see***. Thus, out of a heart of deep anguish, Hezekiah cries, **O *Yahweh*, take a look at this blasphemous document; listen to its words as I read them to you! Sennacherib is mocking you, the Living God!** (On **living God**, → 37:4.)

■ **18-19** Hezekiah's admission and denial follows his first request. Hezekiah admits to ***Yahweh*** that what the Assyrian messengers have said is true: **the people** and their lands (v 18) have known only devastation at the hands of **the Assyrian kings. Their gods** *have* been powerless when **thrown . . . into the fire** (v 19). This, however, was due to their falsity: after all, **they were not gods**, as claimed, **but only wood and stone, fashioned by human hands**.

■ **20** Hezekiah concludes the prayer with a second request. This time Hezekiah owns that ***Yahweh*** is **our God**, as opposed to his earlier "your God" when sending his request to Isaiah for a word from Yahweh (37:4). His request here is simply, and directly, stated: **deliver us from his** [i.e., Sennacherib's] **hand**. Yet, the motivation in Hezekiah's request is not that either Jerusalem or he, if delivered, might be forever famous as the city and king that stood against the great imperial world power. No, Hezekiah's motivation was much higher: that **all the kingdoms of the earth *might* know that *Yahweh* is God alone**.

Here, one hears an echo of Yahweh's long ago word to Egypt's pharaoh, giving motivation for sending plagues upon Egypt: "so you may know that there is no one like me in all the earth" (Exod 9:14). Or Yahweh's rationale for the calling and naming of Persian Cyrus to deliver Jacob/Israel from Babylonian captivity: "so that from the rising of the sun to the place of its setting, people may know there is none besides me. I am **Yahweh**, and there is no other" (Isa 45:6).

e. Yahweh's Response to Hezekiah's Prayer (37:21-35)

■ **21-22a** The editor/narrator's full designation, **Isaiah son of Amoz** (v 21) identifies the prophet who speaks here as the same one who was so identified in 1:1, 13:1, and 20:2. How does **Isaiah** know that Hezekiah has **prayed** in the temple, and the content of his prayer? It might appear from the brevity of the text that Hezekiah's temple visit was private, yet the narrator has come to know even the words of his prayer. Hezekiah certainly must have been observed and overheard. A king does not move about without attendants.

Isaiah makes clear that the words of his **message to Hezekiah** are not his; rather, they are the words of **Yahweh, the God of Israel**. Isaiah is but Yahweh's mouthpiece. The message from Yahweh is a taunt **against** Sennacherib (v 22a).

■ **22b Daughter Zion** is depicted as a **virgin** (*bĕtûlâ*) "helpless before a swaggering rapist" (Oswalt 1986, 660). *She* **despises** *you*, says Yahweh, *she* **mocks you**, [*and*] *behind you* [apparently as you depart the scene, having failed to ravish her] *she wags* her head in derision.

■ **23** On behalf of Yahweh, Isaiah accuses Sennacherib of *having* ridiculed and blasphemed . . . the Holy One of Israel. His **pride** has made him believe he could eyeball Israel's God as an equal (idiomatically, **raised your voice and lifted your eyes**).

■ **24a** Earlier, the narrator had granted Sennacherib's emissaries the status of "messengers" (*mal'ākîm* [v 14]). Here, however, in response to Sennacherib having **ridiculed the Sovereign One** (*'ădōnāy*), they are tauntingly demoted to the status of mere **servants** (*'ăbādîm*), or as Oswalt says, "mere lackeys" (1986, 661), effectively granting them no status at all.

■ **24b** Though Sennacherib does not mention in the records available to us his having harvested **cedars** and **junipers** of the **forests** found in **Lebanon**, other Assyrian kings do boast of such. The transporting of these prized timbers as war booty to Assyria for use in construction of palaces and temples was common. (→ sidebar at 14:4b-8, "The Trees of Lebanon and the Assyrian Kings")

■ **25** Sennacherib boasts of *having* **dried up all the streams of Egypt** [*yĕ'ōrê māṣôr*, a reference to the canals and tributaries of the Nile River] **with the soles of my feet**. He pictures himself as a giant with giant's feet, stomping across the Nile delta, blocking the flow of water. This is an empty boast, since he was a mere mortal. Moreover, Sennacherib, himself, never set foot in Egypt. Beyond the boasting, however, is the claim to a power that Isaiah previously has credited to Yahweh: it is Yahweh who has the power to dry up the "streams of Egypt" (*yĕ'ōrê māṣôr* [19:6]).

■ **26-27 Have you not heard?** is a question that Yahweh also asks of the Jewish exiles in 40:21. Both contexts assume that humans should know that Yahweh has a plan for the course of human history and that the actions of persons are guided by that plan. In the present case, it is Sennacherib who should know but has refused to acknowledge that, though it is indeed he (Sennacherib) who has **turned fortified cities into piles of stone**, it is Yahweh who ***determined it long ago*** (36:26). Thus, Sennacherib has been able to devastate these **cities**, and ***dismay and shame their inhabitants*** (v 27), only because Yahweh has **now** caused his plan ***to come to pass*** (v 26). It is Yahweh who controls rulers of empires, though they may think otherwise.

The imagery of **tender green shoots ... sprouting on the roof** (v 27), but soon **scorched**, serves to highlight the callousness with which Sennacherib treated the lives of the inhabitants of the **cities** he devastated (v 26).

■ **28-29** Not only has Yahweh planned the course of the grand sweep of history, but he knows even the minutest details of Sennacherib's movements: I know ***your sitting down, your going out, and your coming in***, **even your *raging*** against me (v 28).

It is Sennacherib's **rage against** Yahweh, and the **insolence** (v 29) with which he has dismissed Yahweh as powerless as the deities previously encountered, unable to defend their cities, that instigates Yahweh's reaction. The expression, **My hook in your nose and my bit in your *lips***, evokes the imagery of a farmer leading along an obstinate animal. In this way, Yahweh will **return** Sennacherib to his own land.

■ **30-32** Just as a **sign** (v 30) of God's ability to defend Judah/Jerusalem was offered to Ahaz at the time of the earlier Israelite-Aramaean threat (7:11), which he refused, a **sign** is now offered to **Hezekiah**. The sign is double-sided: the first side is agricultural. The sign does not signify that Sennacherib will leave Judah but that once gone he will not return. An occupying army will take all crops and grains to sustain its military personnel. When they depart, they leave the land's remaining inhabitants little for survival. The sign spans portions of three years, or planting/harvesting cycles. (1) **This year**, possibly only the latter portion of the agricultural cycle, too late for planting for the next year's growth and harvest; thus they **will eat what grows by itself**. (2) In **the second year** (or ***cycle***) they will similarly eat **what springs *up***, since there had been no planting in the previous cycle. (3) But, in **the third year** (or ***cycle***) the normal pattern begins to return: they will **sow and reap, plant vineyards and eat**. Thus, it is the promise of three planting and harvesting cycles, without interference, that constitutes the **sign** pointing to Sennacherib's permanent absence.

The second side of the **sign** concerns **a remnant/a band of survivors** (vv 31-32). The broad view is on **the *house* [*bêt*] of Judah**; the narrow focus is on **Jerusalem** and its sacred center, **Mount Zion**. The imagery here, too, is agricultural: it is from this sacred center that **Judah will take root below and bear fruit above**. The promise-sign is that **Judah** will survive and thrive, at least in Hezekiah's time and beyond. This can happen because of **the zeal of *Yahweh Sebaoth*.**

■ **33-35** The final assurance to Hezekiah is that *Yahweh*, himself, **will defend and save** this city (i.e., Jerusalem [v 35]). It is Yahweh, whom Sennacherib has ridiculed as impotent and powerless, who will be the shield around Jerusalem, preventing Sennacherib, **the king of Assyria**, from breaching the city (v 33). No Assyrian weapon of war (**arrow, shield**, or **siege ramp**) will be allowed to come **against it**. Sennacherib later boasts in his annals, "Himself [i.e., Hezekiah] I made a prisoner in Jerusalem, his royal residence, like a bird in a cage. I surrounded him with earthwork in order to molest those who were leaving his city's gate" (Pritchard 1969, 288). This is a boast, however, that hides defeat, as is shown in the memo appended in the next three verses.

f. Yahweh's Mysterious Intervention (37:36-37)

■ **36-37** The narrator is unconcerned with *how* **the angel of *Yahweh*** (v 36) wrought his **death**-blow to **a hundred and eighty-five thousand** soldiers of the **Assyrian** army while encamped (scholars assume roundabout Jerusalem, though the text does not indicate where Sennacherib's main army was at this time). His concern is to demonstrate that Yahweh, in a single night's miracle, validated his prophet Isaiah and fulfilled his promise unto Hezekiah. The sentence structure indicates the wonder of it all: *And they* [whether *they* means Judean inhabitants or Assyrian soldiers surviving the devastation is not clear] *arose early in the morning. And behold! All of them! Bodies! Dead ones!*

Again, the narrator puts it succinctly: **Sennacherib king of Assyria broke camp,** *went and returned. And he stayed in Nineveh* (v 37).

In the presence of the true great King (Mal 1:14), Sennacherib, whose field commander had earlier ascribed to him (Sennacherib) the title "great king" (Isa 36:4), in the eyes of the present narrator, is simply **king of Assyria**.

g. Sennacherib's Assassination (37:38)

■ **38** Just as the gods of conquered cities could not deliver them from Sennacherib's armies, so Sennacherib's own personal **god Nisrok** was powerless to protect him from the evil designs of **his sons Adrammelek and Sharezer**. Even while he was in the act of worship, they assassinated him **with the sword**. Another son, **Esarhaddon, succeeded** Sennacherib to the throne of Assyria. Though we have no extant Assyrian account of Sennacherib's assassination, historians have determined that Esarhaddon began to rule Assyria in 680 BC (Bright 2000, 311). Thus, Sennacherib continued to rule in Assyria for twenty-one more years after departing Judah with the remainder of his army (701-680 BC).

The narrator's purpose in adding this historical note concerning Sennacherib's assassination is theological (Seitz 1993, 253): Isaiah had earlier spoken Yahweh's word: that when Sennacherib "hears a certain report" he will "return to his own country." There, it would be Yahweh who "will have him cut down with the sword" (37:7). Thus, Isaiah's prophecy is fulfilled and Yahweh is vindicated.

The Angel of the Lord

The Angel of the Lord (*mal'ak yhwh*, "messenger of Yahweh") in most instances appears to be distinct from other divine angels/messengers and on occasion appears indistinguishable from Yahweh himself, as in Gideon's encounter (Judg 6:11, 14). The Angel of the Lord could provide deliverance and protection, as when he led the Israelites out of Egyptian slavery (Num 20:16), then moved to stand between the Egyptian army and the fleeing Israelites (Exod 14:19-20). At other times, the presence of the Angel of the Lord could bring disaster, as when he was about to destroy Jerusalem because King David had sinned in counting the number of Israel's fighting men (2 Sam 24:16-17).

FROM THE TEXT

As noted above, the narrator's ultimate purpose in relating the account of Assyrian king Sennacherib's invasion of Judah is theological. From the beginning of the account (36:1) to its conclusion (37:38), the two opposing figures are Assyrian Sennacherib and Judah's God, Yahweh. The predominant theological issue at stake is: is Yahweh no different from any of the other gods of the kingdoms that Sennacherib has conquered? Is he, in fact, impotent and powerless, but boastful? Or is it Sennacherib who is ultimately impotent and powerless, but boastful?

The other two main figures in the account are King Hezekiah and Prophet Isaiah. Lesser figures are Sennacherib's field commander (first confrontation) and his messengers (second confrontation). Hezekiah is essential to the outcome of the event to the extent that, as representative of all Judah, he is called upon, openly, in the sight of all Jerusalem, to trust Yahweh's promise and ability to deliver. It is to this commitment of trust that Yahweh will respond in an act of deliverance. Isaiah is in some sense ancillary to the whole operation, though not nonessential. It seems that it is through him that Yahweh speaks to Hezekiah, though not necessarily required for Hezekiah to speak to Yahweh, as demonstrated in Hezekiah's prayer to Yahweh in the temple.

Would Yahweh have intervened on behalf of Jerusalem if Hezekiah had not in faith requested Yahweh's help (v 20)? We cannot know. Isaiah, however, does convey to Hezekiah Yahweh's message: "Because you have prayed to me concerning Sennacherib king of Assyria" (v 21), and then predicates his promise of defense of the city (v 35) on that prayer. Even then, Yahweh does not defend Jerusalem for Hezekiah's sake or for the sake of its inhabitants; rather, it is "for my sake," that is, for the glory and acknowledgment of Yahweh alone. In fact, this is the very point Hezekiah makes in his prayer: "so that all the kingdoms of the earth may know that you **alone are Yahweh**" (v 20). Wildberger observes that most commentators find the Hebrew here to make no sense, in that "Who else beside the God of Israel could lay claim to being Yahweh?" Wildberger's response is that it makes good sense, in that the name Yahweh "is filled with all the ideas that Israel confessed about its God," especially, as Hezekiah notes in his prayer, Yahweh is Creator of heaven and earth, and supreme God of all kingdoms (v 16). Thus, the ultimate theological teaching of the account is that in seeing Yahweh's act of saving Jerusalem, the kingdoms might come to know Yahweh to the exclusion of all other gods (2002, 423; Seitz 1993, 253).

The application of this theological point to believers of the twenty-first century AD is that we, too, must never pray for God's help so we, in any way, might be elevated in the eyes of the world. Rather, our praying, for whatever reason, always must be that our Lord may be honored, glorified, and made known to the world.

2. Hezekiah's Sickness and Babylon (38:1—39:8)

BEHIND THE TEXT

It is the consensus of most commentators that chs 38 and 39 do not follow chronologically after chs 36 and 37. Rather, Hezekiah's sickness occurs sometime previous to Yahweh's deliverance of Jerusalem from the crisis of Sennacherib's demand for Jerusalem's surrender in 701 BC. This conclusion is based on Yahweh's promise to Hezekiah: "I will deliver you and this city from the hand of the king of Assyria" (38:6). That is, the deliverance is still in the future, whereas ch 37 concludes with the deliverance already an accomplished fact. Moreover, "Marduk-Baladan son of Baladan king of Babylon," mentioned in 39:1, was ruling Babylon (and in revolt against Assyria) during 703 BC, two years prior to Sennacherib's incursion into Judah. He was banished from Babylon that year (Bright 2000, 284-85). The narrator, himself, is rather imprecise as to the time of this event with the expressions "in those days" (38:1) and "at that time" (39:1).

The narrator's/editor's purpose in placing this event out of chronological order is theological: Yahweh is the God who delivers. Chapters 36 and 37 have highlighted Yahweh's act of deliverance of the city of Jerusalem from Assyria, and thus also of Judah, in response to Hezekiah's prayer/act of trust

(37:16-20). Chapter 38 highlights Yahweh's act of deliverance of Hezekiah from personal sickness, again, in response to Hezekiah's prayer/act of trust (vv 2-3). Additionally, this account of Yahweh's rescue of Hezekiah personally from death may have been placed following ch 37 so that it is juxtaposed "with the violent and untimely death of Sennacherib (37:38)" (Blenkinsopp 2000, 484). The contrast is stark: on the one hand, Nisrok, the personal god of Sennacherib the blasphemer, cannot deliver him from death by assassination; on the other hand, Yahweh, the God of Hezekiah the man of prayer, can and does deliver him from death by illness. Chapter 38, then, places Hezekiah's sickness still within the Assyrian context.

Chapter 39, however, links the event of Hezekiah's sickness and recovery with Babylon: Hezekiah receives "letters and a gift" from "Marduk-Baladan, king of Babylon" (v 1). This reintroduction of Babylon gives opportunity for Isaiah's prophecy of a future time when Judah's royal treasury, along with a later generation of Hezekiah's family, will be "carried off to Babylon"/"taken away" (vv 6-7). This prophecy says nothing of a general deportation and exile of Judah's general population, nor does it speak of a possible future restoration from Babylonian exile. It is, however, juxtaposed with the announcement with which ch 40 opens, that Yahweh is coming to rescue Jewish exiles from Babylon and bring them back home. Thus, the narrator of ch 39 assumes a link with the future of God's people who have gone into exile to Babylon.

IN THE TEXT

a. Sickness and Mortality (38:1-22)

(I) Hezekiah's Sickness and Promised Recovery (38:1-8)

■ **I** The time reference **in those days** is vague, apparently purposely so. The narrator is aware that this event, when **Hezekiah became ill and was at the point of death**, did not occur subsequent to Yahweh's deliverance of Jerusalem; but, according to the narrator's own words (v 6), was a prior event. (→ Behind the Text for 38:1—39:8, above, for comment on how the contents of ch 38 link with the contents of ch 39.)

Hezekiah's serious illness prompted **the prophet Isaiah son of Amoz** to give a preliminary prophecy: **you are *dying and* you will not recover**. Isaiah urges, therefore: **Put your house in order**. In v 21, however, contrary to his earlier prophecy, Isaiah predicts that Hezekiah "will *live*." Theologically, this change suggests that God is free to act as he chooses, even contrary to his earlier word (Blenkinsopp 2000, 484).

■ **2-3** Upon receiving the news of his impending death, **Hezekiah turned *away* his face . . . prayed to *Yahweh* . . . and . . . wept *a great weeping*** (vv 2-3). In his very brief prayer, Hezekiah asks for nothing; he only reminds Yahweh that he has been a good servant: **I have walked before you in *faithfulness* and with *a whole heart* (*bĕlēb šālēm*), and *I* have done what is good in your eyes** (v 3). Elsewhere, to receive the Judean historian's "A" rating, a king of Judah must have walked before God with a "whole heart" (*bĕlēb šālēm* [1 Kgs 8:61; 11:4; 15:3, 14]).

■ **4-6** Though Hezekiah has asked for nothing, **Yahweh** speaks to Hezekiah through Isaiah: **I have heard/*I have* seen**, affirming that he is God who actively listens for our **prayer** and watches for our **tears** (v 5; compare 37:17). This, the "gods" of the "lands" and the "idols" of the "nations" cannot do, as they are nothing but "wood and stone," and "silver and gold," unable to speak, see, or hear (37:14; Ps 115:2-6). The **word of Yahweh** is that **fifteen years** will be added to Hezekiah's life. Moreover, Yahweh promises that he **will defend** Jerusalem, preventing both king and **city** from being taken by **the king of Assyria**.

■ **7-8** To confirm his promise to Hezekiah, Yahweh gives him an immediate unrequested **sign** (v 7): the reversal of the sun's **shadow . . . on the stairway of Ahaz** (v 8). The **stairway**, or ***steps***, may have been a nearby normal stairway connecting two floor levels, or it may have been a stepped device constructed to measure time. The text does not indicate *how* this phenomenon occurred. Wildberger observes that

> A sign is all the more wonderful . . . [when] it goes against the natural order of things. It is to show that what is most unlikely is not impossible for God. . . . In any case, one cannot get around the fact that the sun did not just stand still, as was the case at Gibeon; it actually went backward. (2002, 449-50)

Second Chronicles 32:31 seems to imply that this sign/miracle had occurred only in Judah because a delegation from Babylon came to Hezekiah "to ask him about the miraculous sign that had occurred in the land" (Oswalt 1986, 678).

(2) The Writing on Mortality (38:9-22)

This psalm, containing elements of lament, thanksgiving, and praise, aptly expresses the inevitable mortality of humankind and the helplessness of even a king in the face of impending death: apart from the intervention of the **Sovereign One** (*'ădōnāy*), life cannot be extended (v 16). Thus, the psalm describes and celebrates a promise/a process toward full recovery from illness, culminating in a temple music fest celebrating the anticipation of the king's recovery (v 20).

■ **9** The superscription of this psalm is appropriately translated: **A writing of** [*lĕ*] Hezekiah **when he was ill** [*baḥălōtô*] **and *recovered*** [lit. ***lived***] ***from his illness***. Thus, it is not to be read as a psalm describing the king's circumstances **after** a full recovery, but in the process of, in the anticipation of full recovery.

■ **10-11** Illness prompts the king to lament the possible entering of **the gates of** *Sheol* in **the prime of my life**, when there should yet be a *remainder* of **my years** (v 10). Because he will no longer be **in the land of the living** (v 11), he mourns the impending loss of fellowship with **Yahweh** himself and fellow *mankind*, most likely implying a loss of "participation in temple worship" (Blenkinsopp 2000, 485).

■ **12-13** Three symbols of the abruptness of death are imagined here: (1) **like a shepherd's tent** (v 12), which, appearing so permanently in place, is suddenly **pulled down**, as the shepherd moves on to other grassy areas; (2) **like a weaver** who, having labored long on a project, suddenly completes the task, *cuts* the threads **from the loom**, rolls up the cloth, and moves on to another project; and, (3) **like a lion** (v 13), which, with a sudden pounce from hiding, *crushes* **all my bones**. Just so, cries Hezekiah, *from* [*min*] **day** *until* [*'ad*] **night**, that is, in the space of a single day, **you have** made an end of [or *completed*] me.

■ **14** The king's **eyes** become **weak from looking to the heavens** for help; in his weakened condition, his cries are nothing more than the *chirps* of the **swift or thrush**, or the *moaning* of **a mourning dove**. He can only gasp: **O** *Sovereign*, **come to my aid**.

■ **15-16** Hezekiah testifies that the *Sovereign* (v 16) heard and **has spoken to me** (v 15), and when he spoke, **my spirit** found **life; you restored me to health and let me live** (v 16). One is reminded here of the instances of Jesus' speaking to the sick and they were restored to wellness (e.g., John 5:1-9), or to the dead and life returned (e.g., John 11:43-44; esp. 5:19-29, when all dead will hear his voice and live).

■ **17** In the context of his restoration to wellness, Hezekiah notes a parallel aspect of God's grace: **you have** *cast* **all my sins behind your back**. Similarly, David asked of God, "Hide your face from my sins" (Ps 51:9 [11 HB]). Both actions imply that when God can no longer see one's sins, for him they no longer exist.

■ **18** Hezekiah expresses what may be the predominant view of his times: that those whom **death** has taken from this life, and are thus resident in *Sheol* [grave] **cannot hope for your** [i.e., Yahweh's] **faithfulness** (→ From the Text for chs 38—39, below). Yahweh, he implies, is unavailable to the dead; thus, they cannot **sing your praise**. So, what advantage is there in allowing me to die?

■ **19** Death and Sheol, however, will not control Hezekiah's immediate future, Isaiah assures him, because "*Yahweh*, the God or your father David" has spoken: a promise of an additional "fifteen years" of life has been extended (v 5). In response, Hezekiah bursts forth with his own praise: *A living one! A living one! [It is] he [who] praises* **you,** *[just]* **as I am doing today!** *A father must* **tell** *[his]* **sons about your faithfulness**. Wildberger suggests that this confession of personal experiences by a father to his children indicates "that praising

God is not limited to official worship services, but takes place in the private circle of the family home" (2002, 464).

■ **20** This conclusion to Hezekiah's psalm has moved from Hezekiah's being near death and about "to go through the gates of **Sheol**" (v 10), to **the house of Yahweh**. There, we now hear **singing** with stringed instruments, a rejoicing that Hezekiah anticipates continuing **all the days of our lives**. Thus, praising God for his **saving** me takes place both in the home (v 19) and in the public gathering of God's worshipping people.

■ **21-22** Isaiah had said (v 21) and **Hezekiah had asked** (v 22) is the NIV's interpretative attempt to (re)position these two actions immediately following Isaiah's prophetic word of v 7 that "*Yahweh* will do what he has promised," and thus before the psalm that hints at Hezekiah's recovery. Most commentators argue that somehow the narrator forgot to put them there, so, as an afterthought, added them in their present position. Seitz argues persuasively, however, that the two verses function correctly in their present position in the text, and for the translation, **Isaiah said**, and, **Hezekiah asked**. That is, in ch 38 both Hezekiah's recovery from illness (vv 5-6), and his return to the temple (v 20) still lie in the future. Thus, Isaiah prescribes the medical treatment for recovery, **a poultice of figs** (v 21), and Hezekiah asks concerning the **sign** (of his recovery) that will permit him to **go up to the *house of Yahweh*** (v 22). That is, he cannot enter the place of worship until cured from his illness (Lev 13—14) (1993, 260).

b. Hezekiah and the Babylonian Envoys (39:1-8)

■ **1** At that time Marduk-Baladan . . . king of Babylon (→ Behind the Text for 38:1—39:8, above). The reason that the **king of Babylon sent Hezekiah letters and a gift** is said to be the occasion of Hezekiah's **illness and recovery**. The narrator, thus, is linking the contents of ch 39 with the contents of ch 38. He has previously linked ch 38 with chs 36—37 with the time reference "In those days" (38:1). Chapters 36—39, then, form a four-chapter literary unit, displaying an opening and closing contrast: ch 36 opens with Assyrian "envoys bearing blasphemous speech," and a threat of destruction against Jerusalem, while ch 39 has Babylonian "envoys bearing gifts." Moreover, Judah is not "paying tribute to Egypt or Assyria," but "Babylon pays tribute to Jerusalem and its king" (Seitz 1993, 265). Even though the events are not chronological, this four-chapter literary unit intends to show Hezekiah's insight that Judah is promised a reprieve from superpower threat, at least during his own "lifetime" (v 8).

■ **2** It is in this context as recipient of tribute/honor that **Hezekiah received the envoys gladly**. The majority of commentators interpret Hezekiah's showing to the Babylonian envoys all that was in **his storehouses** and **his treasures** as an act of pride and boasting. This is conjecture, however, as the narrator gives no negative evaluation of Hezekiah's action. Seitz notes the Chronicler's evaluation that Hezekiah's treasures are signs of God's blessings (2 Chr 32:27-30), just as his recovery from illness is a sign of God's blessing (ibid.). Thus, Hezekiah is not boasting; rather, he is witnessing to the blessings of the God of Israel.

■ **3-4** **Isaiah the prophet** posed two questions to **King Hezekiah**: (1) **What did those men say?** (2) *From* **where did they come** *to you?* The king may have answered the first, but the narrator has recorded his reply to the second only: **From a distant land** *they came to me, from Babylon.*

■ **5-7** While many commentators view Hezekiah's (unwise/boastful) display of his wealth to the Babylonian envoys to have precipitated this prophetic judgment upon Judah, again, the narrator gives no such pejorative evaluation. Rather, it is the naming of Babylon that prompts the prophetic **word of Yahweh Sebaoth** that follows (v 5). The naming of "Babylon" literally both brings to a close this first great segment of the book of Isaiah, chs 1—39, and points forward to a time beyond Hezekiah's lifetime to a judgment upon Judah that will occur "according to a divine plan" (Childs 2001, 287). This judgment would be the carrying **off to Babylon** (v 6) all the treasures of Judah, along with **some of** Hezekiah's **descendants** to serve as **eunuchs in the palace of the king of Babylon** (v 7).

Eunuchs

Eunuchs were men who had undergone castration and served as officials in royal courts, both in ancient Israel and her neighboring kingdoms. They were deemed "safe" to serve the queen (2 Kgs 9:30-32; Esth 4:4-5; Acts 8:27) or the king's concubines/harem (Esth 2:14-15). Eunuchs, because of their damaged genitals, were prohibited from membership in the Israelite covenant community (Deut 23:1) or from the office of priesthood (Lev 21:17-21) (*EDB*, §8814).

■ **8** Many commentators interpret Hezekiah's reply as flippant and self-serving, implying something like, "*At least* **there will be peace and security in my lifetime**," a "why worry about the future" attitude. This, however, is not at all what the text implies. Rather, in stating that *good is the word of Yahweh* (**good** [*tôb*] is in emphatic first position), Hezekiah is simply acknowledging that God's larger plan goes way beyond his **lifetime**. This *good word* points to a future beyond anything he can know or understand (Seitz 1993, 266), yet it assures him of "divine blessing" during his own lifetime (Childs 2001, 287).

FROM THE TEXT

Further thoughts on 38:18. On the one hand, there are in the OT glimmers of understanding that God continues an awareness of those whom Sheol/death has claimed. Job cries out from the depths of his suffering, "If only you would hide me in **Sheol** . . . I will wait . . . You will call and I will answer" (Job 14:13-15). A psalmist declares, "If I make my bed in Sheol, you are there!"

(Ps 139:8 ESV). On the other hand, another psalmist cries out, "For in death there is no remembrance of you; in Sheol who can give you praise" (6:5 NRSV [6 HB]). Yet another psalmist laments to Yahweh in his troubles that his "life draws near to Sheol," that he is "like those forsaken among the dead, . . . like those whom you remember no more" (88:3, 5 NRSV [4, 6 HB]). So, this ambivalence must wait: a full understanding of life continuing beyond the grave and the resurrection would be more fully revealed in the death and resurrection of Jesus Christ in the NT Gospels. Later NT writers would explore a deeper understanding of what that would mean for humankind.

Further thoughts on 38:19. The OT text tells us that on one occasion Yahweh declared that he had chosen Abraham, "so that he will direct his children and his household after him to keep the way of the Lord by doing what is right and just" (Gen 18:19). Moses admonishes fathers to pass on to their children Yahweh's great act of deliverance of the Israelites from Egyptian slavery, lest they "forget the Lord." Fathers were to continuously teach their children the ways Yahweh had cared for them on the journey from Egypt to the verge of crossing into Canaan. They were to do this when sitting at home, walking along the road, lying down at night, or when arising in the morning. Thus, in knowing Yahweh of the past, the children would know to trust Yahweh of the future in the new land of Canaan (Deut 6; compare Josh 4:1-7; Ps 78:1-8).